Bieber's Dictionary of Legal Citations

Reference Guide For Attorneys,

Legal Secretaries, Paralegals

and Law Students

Third Edition
by

Mary Miles Prince

William S. Hein Company
Buffalo, New York
1988

LC 88-82511
ISBN 0-89941-664-0

Printed in the United States of America

TO

Raymond Prince,
Mary Whayne and Charles Miles, and
Doris M. Bieber

Preface
(Third Edition)

This work, like its first and second editions, is intended to assist the legal profession in citing legal authorities according to the rules given in *A Uniform System of Citation*.

While the first and second editions were based on the rules found in the 13th edition of *A Uniform System of Citation* (hereinafter referred to as the "Bluebook"), the third edition abbreviations and citation examples incorporate the abbreviations and rules provided in the 14th edition. The text has also been updated to reflect title changes and current edition information for the authorities listed. Footnoting information and general text arrangement remain the same as that of the second edition.

I wish to thank Professor Igor I. Kavass, Director of the Vanderbilt University Alyne Queener Massey Law Library, for his support on my behalf in updating this book, Annie Ling for her guidance on format and style and for the proficiency of her typing, Vivian Riesenman (Vanderbilt School of Law, Class of '88) for her assistance in updating the contents, and Richard Page (University of North Carolina School of Law Class of '86) for his assistance with the overall production of the third edition.

Mary Miles Prince
July 1988

Preface
(Second Edition)

The purpose of this edition is the same as that of its estimable predecessor, to assist in citing legal authorities according to the rules stated in *A Uniform System of Citation*, 13th edition (the "Bluebook).

Notable changes between this edition and the first include:

- Updates of abbreviations and examples for state codes
- Current information on state and regional reporters
- Numerous additional periodical titles, both foreign and domestic
- Additional looseleaf service abbreviations
- Incorporation of state bar association publications and updated information concerning American law Institute publications

Footnoting information has been added or changed as necessary to make this a companion to the Bluebook. Approximately one-third of the information in this edition is new.

The book is arranged with authorities listed in alphabetical order; abbreviations and examples are given beneath each title. The examples in this book are done according to citation forms used in briefs and legal memoranda. Where citation forms for law review footnotes vary from those for briefs and memoranda, the necessary information may be found in the footnotes at the bottom of each page in this volume.

I wish to thank Doris M. Bieber, whose genius created the original work, Professor Igor I. Kavass, Director of Vanderbilt University Alyne Queener Massey Law Library for affording me the opportunity to update this book Ellen Toplon for her guidance on format and style, Annie Ling for the proficiency of her typing, Carol Duncan for her assistance in gathering new information, Vivian Riesenman (Vanderbilt School of Law, Class of '88) for her keen-eyed proofreading, and my husband, Raymond Prince, for his patience and encouragement.

Mary Miles Prince
Associate Director
Alyne Queencr Massey Law Library
June 1986

Preface
(First Edition)

This work is intended to assist lawyers and law students in citing American legal authorities according to the rules stated in *A Uniform System of Citation* (13th ed. 1981, hereinafter the "Bluebook). It is designed as a companion to the Bluebook not a replacement. This work applies the Bluebook rules to various common United States authorities. The citations found herein are based either on the guidelines in the Bluebook, or on inferences and deductions from the guidelines. The bluebook, of course, should always be consulted in doubtful situations.

The predecessor of this work was entitled: *Dictionary of Current American Legal Citations*. The present work bears a different title to distinguish it from another work entitled: *Dictionary of Legal Abbreviations Used in American Law Books*. The main body of this work is derived from its predecessor.

The purpose of this work is (1) to give abbreviations for the legal publications of all United Stated jurisdictions, the international law publications directly affecting the United States, and privately published legal periodicals; and (2) to provide examples of the more commonly cited authorities. Included among the 2100 examples are American law reports, statutes, regulations, law reviews, treatises, looseleaf services, annotations, and publications of such important legal institutions as Congress, the American law Institute, and the American Bar Association. In addition, entries of generic terms such as "symposium," looseleaf services," and "law review" give examples of the citation forms for these types of publications.

The content is arranged in two columns. The left column lists alphabetically the full title entries of publications for which there are recognized citations. the right column contains the corresponding citation forms. The citation forms are accompanied by examples. Where the citation itself or an example requires elaboration, an explanation is preceded by four dashes (----). All citations included in this work conform with those of the Bluebook. Throughout this work, underlining is used in situations which customarily require itallcs: case names, signals, titles of periodicals, and as otherwise required by Bluebook Rules.

I express my indebtedness to Professor Igor I. Kavass, Director of Vanderbilt University Alyne Queener Massey Law Library, whose influence and encouragement pervade this work. I want to thank also Kevin C. Tyra (Vanderbilt School of Law, Class of '81) who gathered and devised many examples for the previous work, and Cornelia W. Shaw who typed the manuscript of the previous work. Also, I want to thank Robert P. Crowther (Vanderbilt School of Law, Class of '82) who gathered and devised many new examples for this work, and Mary Frances Lane who typed and made the manuscript of this work presentable.

Doris M. Bieber

A

ABA

    See   American Bar Association

ABF

    See   American Bar Foundation

ALI

    See   American Law Institute

ALI-ABA Course Materials Journal

    Abbreviation: ALI-ABA Course Mat. J.

    Examples: Martin, Recent Developments in Conflicts of Laws, ALI-ABA Course Mat. J., Dec. 1985, at 35. ——Article Cite.

              Martin, Recent Developments in Conflicts of Laws, ALI-ABA Course Mat. J., Dec. 1985, at 35, 41-44. ——Page Cite.

ALR (series)

    See   American Law Reports

ASILS International Law Journal

    Abbreviation: ASILS Int'l L.J.

    Examples: Starkman, Genocide and International Law: Is There a Cause of Action?, 8 ASILS Int'l L.J. 1 (1984). ——Article Cite.

              Starkman, Genocide and International Law: Is There A Cause of Action?, 8 ASILS Int'l L.J. 1, 46-48 (1984). ——Page Cite.

abridged

    Abbreviation: abr.

accord

    Abbreviation: accord

    Examples: Usery v. Kennecott Copper Corp., 577 F.2d 1113 (10th Cir. 1977); accord, Marshall v. Union Oil Co., 616 F.2d 1113 (9th Cir. 1980).

In law review footnotes, the following are in large and small capitals: periodicals, constitutions, codes, restatements, standards, authors of books, titles of books, and legislative materials except for bills and resolutions. Refer to Bluebook.

"Futhermore, conclusory allegations unsupported by any factual
assertions will not withstand a motion to dismiss. Briscoe v. LaHue,
663 F.2d 713, 723 (7th Cir. 1981). Accord Hiland Diary, Inc. v.
Kroger Co., 402 F.2d 968, 973 (8th Cir. 1968), cert denied., 395 U.S.
961, 89 S. Ct. 2096, 23 L. Ed. 2d 748 (1969) (In testing the legal
sufficiency of the complaint ...conclusions of law and unreasonable
inference or unwarranted deductions of fact are not admitted.)."
——Taken from 675 F.2d 881 (1982).

Accountancy Law Reporter (Commerce Clearing House)
    Abbreviation: Accountancy L. Rep. (CCH)

Accounting Standards, Generally Accepted
    Example: Accounting for the Costs of Computer Software to be Sold, Leased or
                Otherwise Marketed, Statement of Financial Accounting Standards No.
                86, § 16 (Fin. Accounting Standards Bd. 1985).

Acts and Joint Resolutions of the State of Iowa
    Abbreviation: year Acts

Acts and Joint Resolutions, South Carolina
    Abbreviation: year S.C. Acts

Acts and Resolves of Massachusetts
    Abbreviation: year Mass. Acts

Acts and Resolves of Rhode Island and Providence Plantations
    Abbreviation: year R.I. Acts & Resolves

Acts of Alabama
    Abbreviation: year Ala. Acts

Acts of Congress
    Abbreviation: Pub. L.

    Examples: Act of June 13, 1978, Pub. L. No. 95-292, 92 Stat. 307. ——Act Cite.

                Act of June 13, 1978, Pub. L. No. 95-292, § 4, 92 Stat. 307, 315.
                ——Section Cite.

Acts (of) Indiana
    Abbreviation: year Ind. Acts

Acts of the General Assembly of the Commonwealth of Virginia
    Abbreviation: year Va. Acts

In law review footnotes, the titles of books and the names of cases are not underlined.

Acts of the Legislature of West Virginia
    Abbreviation: year W. Va. Acts

Acts, Resolves and Constitutional Resolutions of the State of Maine
    Abbreviation: year Me. Acts

addenda
    ——Well explained and illustrated in Bluebook Rule 3.5.

Adelaide Law Review
    Abbreviations: Adel. L. Rev.
                    Adel. L.R. (publisher's abbreviation)

    Examples: Blackburn, Law School Curricula in Retrospect, 9 Adel. L. Rev. 43
                 (1983). ——Article Cite.

                 Blackburn, Law School Curricula in Retrospect, 9 Adel. L. Rev. 43,
                 46-49 (1983). ——Page Cite.

Administrative Decisions under Immigration and Nationality Laws
    Abbreviation: I. & N. Dec.

    Examples: The S.S. Favorit, 1 I. & N. Dec. 214 (Bd. Immigration App. 1942).

                 Silva, 16 I. & N. Dec. 26 (Bd. Immigration App. 1976).

                 Lin, Interim Decision No. 2900 (Bd. Immigration App. May 6, 1982).
                 ——Citation to current unbound material.

Administrative Digest (Arizona)
    Abbreviation: Ariz. Admin. Dig.

Administrative Law, by B. Schwartz
    ——Do not abbreviate the title.

    Examples: B. Schwartz, Administrative Law § 4.1 (2d ed. 1984).

                 B. Schwartz, Administrative Law § 4.1, at 143 (2d ed. 1984).

Administrative Law Judge
    Abbreviation: A.L.J.

Administrative Law Review
    Abbreviation: Admin. L. Rev.

    Examples: Saks, Holding the Independent Agencies Accountable: Legislative Veto
                 of Agency Rules, 36 Admin. L. Rev. 41 (1984). ——Article Cite.

                 Saks, Holding the Independent Agencies Accountable: Legislative Veto
                 of Agency Rules, 36 Admin. L. Rev. 41, 51-54 (1984). ——Page Cite.

In law review footnotes, the following are in large and small capitals: periodicals, constitutions, codes, restatements, standards, authors of books, titles of books, and legislative materials except for bills and resolutions. Refer to Bluebook.

Administrative Law Second (Pike and Fischer)
    Abbreviation: Admin. L. (P & F)

    Examples: Pratt v. Webster, [Current Materials] Admin. L. (P & F) (53 Ad. L.
    Rep. 2d) 101 (D.C. Cir. Jan. 22, 1982). ——Citation to looseleaf
    material.

    Eudey v. CIA, 46 Admin. L. (P & F) 1019 (D.D.C. 1979).
    ——Citation to bound material.

    Champion Home Builders Co., [Current Materials] Admin. L. (P & F)
    (53 Ad. L. Rep. 2d) 731 (F.T.C., March 9, 1982). ——Citation to
    looseleaf administrative material.

    American Medical Association, 41 Admin. L. (P & F) 194 (F.T.C.
    1977). ——Citation to bound administrative material.

——The above examples are proper if the case is not yet available in an official or West
reporter, or is not reported in an official or West reporter.

Administrative Law Review
    Abbreviation: Admin. L. Rev.

    Examples: Saks, Holding the Independent Agencies Accountable: Legislative Veto
    of Agency Rules, 36 Admin. L. Rev. 41 (1984). ——Article Cite.

    Saks, Holding the Independent Agencies Accountable: Legislative Veto
    of Agency Rules, 36 Admin. L. Rev. 41, 51-54 (1984). ——Page Cite.

Administrative Law Text, by Kenneth C. Davis (Single-volume edition)
    ——Do not abbreviate the title.

    Examples: K. Davis, Administrative Law Text § 7.13 (3d ed. 1972).

    K. Davis, Administrative Law Text § 7.13, at 183-84 (3d ed. 1972).

Administrative Law Treatise, by Kenneth C. Davis
    ——Do not abbreviate the title.

——Citation to first edition as follows:

    Examples: 4 K. Davis, Administrative Law Treatise § 30.07 (1958).

    4 K. Davis, Administrative Law Treatise § 30.07, at 230-32 (1958).

    3 K. Davis, Administrative Law Treatise § 22.10 (Supp. 1965).
    ——Cite to pocket part to volume 3.

    K. Davis, Administrative Law Treatise § 15.12 (Supp. 1970).
    ——1970 supplemental volume.

——Citation to second edition as follows:

    3 K. Davis, Administrative Law Treatise § 17.3 (2d ed. 1980).

    3 K. Davis, Administrative Law Treatise § 17.3, at 283 (2d ed. 1980).

    K. Davis, Administrative Law Treatise § 20.20 (2d ed. Supp. 1982).
    ——1982 Supplemented volume.

In law review footnotes, the titles of books and the names of cases are not underlined.

Administrative Rules of Montana
    Abbreviation: Mont. Admin. R. (year).

    Example: Mont. Admin. R. 2-21.1302 (1982).

Administrative Rules of South Dakota
    Abbreviation: S.D. Admin. R. (year).

    Example: S.D. Admin. R. 20:45:03:01 (1982).

Administrative Rules of the State of Utah
    Abbreviation: Utah Admin. R. (year).

    Example: Utah Admin. R. A10-001 (1982).

Admiralty [Court, Division]
    Abbreviation: Adm.

Advisory Opinions
    See Bluebook Rule 14.4.

affirmed
    Abbreviation: aff'd

    Examples: Cuppy v. Ward, 187 A.D. 625, 176 N.Y.S. 233, aff'd, 227 N.Y. 603, 125 N.E. 915 (1919).

                   68th St. Apts., Inc. v. Lauricella, 142 N.J. Super. 546, 362 A.2d 78 (Law Div. 1976), aff'd per curiam, 150 N.J. Super. 47, 374 A.2d 1222 (App. Div. 1977).

Agency, by W. Edward Sell
    ——Do not abbreviate the title.

    Examples: W. Sell, Agency § 84 (1975).

                   W. Sell, Agency § 84, at 69 (1975).

Agricultural Decisions (U.S.) (1942-date)
    Abbreviation: Agric. Dec.

    Examples: Berriman Live Poultry Corp., 1 Agric. Dec. 53 (1942).

                   Victor Fruit Growers, Inc., 1 Agric. Dec. 108 (1942).

                   George Blades, 40 Agric. Dec. 1725 (1981). ——Citation to current unbound material.

Agriculture
    Abbreviation: Agric.

In law review footnotes, the following are in large and small capitals: periodicals, constitutions, codes, restatements, standards, authors of books, titles of books, and legislative materials except for bills and resolutions. Refer to Bluebook.

Air Force Law Review
  Abbreviation: A.F. L. Rev.

  Examples: Swenson, <u>Pollution of the Extraterrestrial Environment</u>, 25 A.F. L.
                    Rev. 70 (1985). ——Article Cite.

                    Swenson, <u>Pollution of the Extraterrestrial Environment</u>, 25 A.F. L.
                    Rev. 70, 71-73 (1985). ——Page Cite.

Air Law
  Abbreviation: Air L.

  Examples: Barrett, <u>Australian Court Refuses to Follow Franklin Mint</u>, 10 Air L.
                    292 (1985). ——Article Cite.

                    Barrett, <u>Australian Court Refuses to Follow Franklin Mint</u>, 10 Air L.
                    292, 292 (1985). ——Page Cite.

Air and Space Lawyer
  Abbreviation: Air & Space Law.

Akron Law Review
  Abbreviation: Akron L. Rev.

  Examples: Nader, <u>The Legal Profession: A Time for Self-Analysis</u>, 13 Akron L.
                    Rev. 1 (1979). ——Article Cite.

                    Nader, <u>The Legal Profession: A Time for Self-Analysis</u>, 13 Akron L.
                    Rev. 1, 9-11 (1979). ——Page Cite.

Alabama Acts
  <u>See</u>   Acts of Alabama

Alabama Administrative Code
  Abbreviation: Ala. Admin. Code r.   (year).

Alabama Appellate Court Reports
  Abbreviation: Ala. App.

  ——Discontinued after 52 Ala. App. 702 (1974). Thereafter cite only to So. 2d.

  Examples:

  ——Before 45 Ala. App. 1 (1969) cite as follows:

                    <u>Rivers v. Johnston</u>, 44 Ala. App. 398, 210 So. 2d 707 (1968).
                    ——Case Cite.

                    <u>Rivers v. Johnston</u>, 44 Ala. App. 398, 400, 210 So. 2d 707, 709
                    (1968). ——Page Cite.

  After 45 Ala. App. 1 (1969) cite as follows:

                    <u>Holsombeck v. Pate</u>, 47 Ala. App. 39, 249 So.2d 861 (Civ. App. 1971).
                    ——Case Cite.

In law review footnotes, the titles of books and the names of cases are not underlined.

Holsombeck v. Pate, 47 Ala. App. 39, 42, 249 So.2d 861, 864 (Civ. App. 1971). ——Page Cite.

Hood v. State, 47 Ala. App. 192, 252, So. 2d 117 (Crim. App. 1971). ——Case Cite.

Hood v. State, 47 Ala. App. 192, 194, 252 So. 2d 117, 120 (Crim. App. 1971). ——Page Cite.

——After 52 Ala. App. 702 (1974), cite as follows:

Chonnell v. State, 477 So. 2d 522 (Ala. Crim. App. 1985). ——Case Cite.

Chonnell v. State, 477 So. 2d 522, 526 (Ala. Crim. App. 1985). ——Page Cite.

Shipe v. Shipe, 477 So. 2d 430 (Ala. Civ. App. 1985). ——Case Cite.

Shipe v. Shipe, 477 So. 2d 430, 433 (Ala. Civ. App. 1985). ——Page Cite.

Alabama Code
    See   Code of Alabama

Alabama Constitution
    Abbreviation: Ala. Const. art. , § .

    Examples: Ala. Const. art. XVI, § 279. ——Cite provisions without date unless the cited provisions have been repealed or amended (Bluebook Rule 11).

    Ala. Const. art. IV, § 74 (1901, amended 1939). ——Cite provisions which have been repealed or amended by giving the date of the adoption of the particular provision and the date of repeal or amendment (Bluebook Rule 11).

    Ala. Const. amend. 320. ——Amendments to the Alabama Constitution are not incorporated into the body of the constitution; they are numbered separately.

Alabama Law Review
    Abbreviation: Ala. L. Rev.

    Examples: Higginbotham, Bureaucracy—The Carcinoma of the Federal Judiciary, 31 Ala. L. Rev. 261 (1980). ——Article Cite.

    Higginbotham, Bureaucracy—The Carcinoma of the Federal Judiciary, 31 Ala. L. Rev. 261, 265-68 (1980). ——Page Cite.

Alabama Lawyer
    Abbreviation: Ala. Law.

    Examples: Stern, Avoiding Malpractice Claims, 42 Ala. Law. 632 (1981). ——Article Cite.

In law review footnotes, the following are in large and small capitals: periodicals, constitutions, codes, restatements, standards, authors of books, titles of books, and legislative materials except for bills and resolutions. Refer to Bluebook.

Stern, <u>Avoiding Malpractice Claims</u>, 42 Ala. Law. 632, 633 (1981).
——Page Cite.

Alabama Reports
Abbreviation: Ala.

——Discontinued after 295 Ala. 388 (1976). Thereafter cite only to So. 2d.

Examples: <u>Johnston v. Alabama Pub. Serv. Comm'n</u>, 287 Ala. 417, 252 So. 2d 75 (1971). ——Case Cite.

<u>Johnston v. Alabama Pub. Serv. Comm'n</u>, 287 Ala. 417, 423, 252 So. 2d 75, 79 (1971). ——Page Cite.

——After 295 Ala. 388 (1976), cite as follows:

<u>Guthrie v. Hartselle Medical Center, Inc.</u>, 477 So. 2d 377 (Ala. 1985).
——Case Cite.

<u>Guthrie v. Hartselle Medical Center, Inc.</u>, 477 So. 2d 377, 378 (Ala. 1985). ——Page Cite.

Alabama Session Laws
<u>See</u>   Acts of Alabama

Alaska Administrative Code
Abbreviation: Alaska Admin. Code tit. , § (month year).

Example: Alaska Admin. Code tit. 2, § 05.100 (Apr. 1984).

Alaska Constitution
Abbreviation: Alaska Const. art. , § .

Examples: Alaska Const. art. VIII, § 8. ——Cite provisions without date unless the cited provisions have been repealed or amended (Bluebook Rule 11).

Alaska Const. art. II, § 8 (1959, amended 1984). ——Cite provisions which have been repealed or amended by giving the date of the adoption of the particular provision and the date of repeal or amendment (Bluebook Rule 11).

Alaska Reports
Abbreviation: Alaska

——District Court of Alaska had local jurisdiction from 1884 to 1959. Cite to F. Supp., F. or F.2d if therein; otherwise cite to Alaska.

——Discontinued after 17 Alaska 779 (1959). Thereafter cite only to P.2d.

Examples: <u>Tapscott v. Page</u>, 17 Alaska 507 (D. Alaska 1958). ——Case Cite.

<u>Tapscott v. Page</u>, 17 Alaska 507, 510 (D. Alaska 1958). ——Page Cite.

——After 17 Alaska 779 (1959), cite as follows:

<u>State v. Jones</u>, 706 P.2d 317 (Alaska 1985). ——Case Cite.

In law review footnotes, the titles of books and the names of cases are not underlined.

State v. Jones, 706 P.2d 317, 319 (Alaska 1985). ——Page Cite.

Alaska Session Laws
  Abbreviation: year Alaska Sess. Laws

Alaska Statutes
  Abbreviation: Alaska Stat. §   (year).

  Examples: Alaska Stat. § 28.01.010 (1984).

                  Alaska Stat. § 34.35.120 (Supp. 1987).

Albany Law Review
  Abbreviation: Alb. L. Rev.

  Examples: Harvith, Exclusive Franchises for Hazardous Waste Disposal Plants:
                  The Commerce Clause and Related Considerations, 45 Alb. L. Rev. 553
                  (1981). ——Article Cite.

                  Harvith, Exclusive Franchises for Hazardous Waste Disposal Plants:
                  The Commerce Clause and Related Considerations, 45 Alb. L. Rev.
                  553, 600-04 (1981). ——Page Cite.

Alberta Law Review
  Abbreviation: Alta. L. Rev.

  Examples: Arnett, From Fira to Investment Canada, 24 Alta. L. Rev. 1 (1985).
                  ——Article Cite.

                  Arnett, From Fira To Investment Canada, 24 Alta. L. Rev. 1, 11-13
                  (1985). ——Page Cite.

All States Tax Guide (Prentice-Hall)
  Abbreviation: All States Tax Guide (P-H)

Am. Jur. 2d
  See   American Jurisprudence, Second Edition

amendment(s)
  Abbreviation: amend., amends.

American Bankruptcy Law Journal
  Abbreviation: Am. Bankr. L.J.

  Examples: Vihon, Classification of Unsecured Claims: Squaring in a Circle?, 55
                  Am. Bankr. L.J. 143 (1981). ——Article Cite.

                  Vihon, Classification of Unsecured Claims: Squaring in a Circle?, 55
                  Am. Bankr. L.J. 143, 145-49 (1981). ——Page Cite.

In law review footnotes, the following are in large and small capitals: periodicals, constitutions, codes, restatements, standards, authors of books, titles of books, and legislative materials except for bills and resolutions. Refer to Bluebook.

American Bar Association Code of Professional Responsibility
    <u>See</u>   American Bar Association Model Code of Professional Responsibility

American Bar Association Committee on Ethics and Professional Responsibility, Formal Opinion
    Abbreviation: ABA Comm. on Ethics and Professional Responsibility, Formal Op. (year).

    Examples: ABA Comm. on Ethics and Professional Responsibility, Formal Op. 352 (1985).

               ABA Comm. on Ethics and Professional Responsibility, Formal Op. 346 (1982) (tax law opinions in tax shelter investment offerings).
               ——Citation with a parenthetical reference to subject matter.

American Bar Association Committee on Ethics and Professional Responsibility, Informal Opinion
    Abbreviation: ABA Comm. on Ethics and Professional Responsibility, Informal Op. (year).

    Example: ABA Comm. on Ethics and Professional Responsibility, Informal Op. 1514 (1985).

American Bar Association Journal
    Abbreviation: A.B.A. J.

    Examples: Fossum, <u>Women in the Legal Profession: A Progress Report</u>, 67 A.B.A. J. 578 (1981). ——Article Cite.

               Fossum, <u>Women in the Legal Profession: A Progress Report</u>, 67 A.B.A. J. 578, 579-81 (1981). ——Page Cite.

American Bar Association Model Code of Professional Responsibility
    Abbreviation: Model Code of Professional Responsibility (provision) (year).

    Examples: Model Code of Professional Responsibility Canon 9 (1980).

               Model Code of Professional Responsibility DR 4-101 (1980).

               Model Code of Professional Responsibility EC 2-20 (1980).

American Bar Association Model Rules of Professional Conduct
    Abbreviation: Model Rules of Professional Conduct Rule (status if necessary, year).

    Example: Model Rules of Professional Conduct Rule 3.4 (1983).

American Bar Association Reports
    Abbreviation: A.B.A. Rep.

    Example: Report of the Commission on Standards of Judicial Administration, 97 A.B.A. Rep. 345 (1972).

In law review footnotes, the titles of books and the names of cases are not underlined.

American Bar Association Revised Model Business Corporation Act
    Abbreviation: Revised Model Business Corp. Act

    Examples: Revised Model Business Corp. Act § 3.02 (1984).

                  Revised Model Business Corp. Act § 3.02 comment (1984).

American Bar Foundation Code of Professional Responsibility, Annotated
    Abbreviation: Annot. Code of Professional Responsibility

    Example: Annot. Code of Professional Responsibility DR 4-101(c)(4) comment at
                  182 (Am. Bar Found. 1979).

American Bar Foundation Research Journal
    Abbreviation: Am. B. Found. Res. J.

    Examples: Hazard & Rice, <u>Judicial Management of the Pretrial Process in Massive
                  Litigation: Special Masters as Case Managers</u>, 1982 Am. B. Found.
                  Res. J. 377. ——Article Cite.

                  Hazard & Rice, <u>Judicial Management of the Pretrial Process in Massive
                  Litigation: Special Masters as Case Managers</u>, 1982 Am. B. Found.
                  Res. J. 377, 397-98. ——Page Cite.

American Business Law Journal
    Abbreviation: Am. Bus. L.J.

    Examples: Burgunder, <u>An Economic Approach to Trademark Genericism</u>, 23 Am.
                  Bus. L.J. 391 (1985). ——Article Cite.

                  Burgunder, <u>An Economic Approach to Trademark Genericism</u>, 23 Am.
                  Bus. L.J. 391, 408-10 (1985). ——Page Cite.

American Constitutional Law, by Laurence H. Tribe
    ——Do not abbreviate the title.

    Examples: L. Tribe, <u>American Constitutional Law</u> § 5-11 (1978).

                  L. Tribe, <u>American Constitutional Law</u> § 5-11, at 253 (1978).

American Criminal Law Review
    Abbreviation: Am. Crim. L. Rev.

    Examples: Panneton, <u>Federalizing Fires: The Evolving Federal Response to Arson
                  Related Crimes</u>, 23 Am. Crim. L. Rev. 151 (1985). ——Article Cite.

                  Panneton, <u>Federalizing Fires: The Evolving Federal Response to Arson
                  Related Crimes</u>, 23 Am. Crim. L. Rev. 151, 168-72 (1985). ——Page
                  Cite.

American Federal Tax Reports, second series (Prentice-Hall)
    Abbreviation: A.F.T.R.2d (P-H)

In law review footnotes, the following are in large and small capitals: periodicals, constitutions, codes, restatements, standards, authors of books, titles of books, and legislative materials except for bills and resolutions. Refer to Bluebook.

American Indian Law Review
  Abbreviation: Am. Indian L. Rev.

  Examples: Morgan, <u>Self-Government and the Constitution: A Comparative Look at Native Canadians and American Indians</u>, 12 Am. Indian L. Rev. 39 (1984). ——Article Cite.

       Morgan, <u>Self-Government and the Constitution: A Comparative Look at Native Canadians and American Indians</u>, 12 Am. Indian L. Rev. 39, 40-42 (1984). ——Page Cite.

American Institute for Certified Public Accountants—Professional Standards (Commerce Clearing House)
  Abbreviation: AICPA—Prof. Stand. (CCH)

American Journal of Comparative Law
  Abbreviation: Am. J. Comp. L.

  Examples: Fleming, <u>Drug Injury Compensation Plans</u>, 30 Am. J. Comp. L. 297 (1982). ——Article Cite.

       Fleming, <u>Drug Injury Compensation Plans</u>, 30 Am. J. Comp. L. 297, 312-13 (1982). ——Page Cite.

American Journal of Criminal Law
  Abbreviation: Am. J. Crim. L.

  Examples: Seman, <u>A Juvenile's Waiver of the Privilege Against Self-Incrimination: A Federal and State Comparison</u>, 10 Am. J. Crim. L. 27 (1982). ——Article Cite.

       Seman, <u>A Juvenile's Waiver of the Privilege Against Self-Incrimination: A Federal and State Comparison</u>, 10 Am. J. Crim. L. 27, 34-35 (1982). ——Page Cite.

American Journal of International Law
  Abbreviation: Am. J. Int'l L.

  Examples: Murphy, <u>The Grotian Vision of World Order</u>, 76 Am. J. Int'l L. 477 (1982). ——Article Cite.

       Murphy, <u>The Grotian Vision of World Order</u>, 76 Am. J. Int'l L. 477, 496-97 (1982). ——Page Cite.

American Journal of Jurisprudence
  Abbreviation: Am. J. Juris.

  Examples: Robbins, <u>Solipsism and Criminal Liability</u>, 25 Am. J. Juris. 75 (1980). ——Article Cite.

       Robbins, <u>Solipsism and Criminal Liability</u>, 25 Am. J. Juris. 75, 82-83 (1980). ——Page Cite.

In law review footnotes, the titles of books and the names of cases are not underlined.

American Journal of Law & Medicine
Abbreviation: Am. J.L. & Med.

Examples: Westfall, <u>Beyond Abortion: The Potential Reach of a Human Life Amendment</u>, 8 Am. J.L. & Med. 97 (1982). ——Article Cite.

Westfall, <u>Beyond Abortion: The Potential Reach of a Human Life Amendment</u>, 8 Am. J.L. & Med. 97, 98-99 (1982). ——Page Cite.

American Journal of Legal History
Abbreviation: Am. J. Legal Hist.

Examples: O'Keefe, <u>Sir George Jessel and the Union of Judicature</u>, 26 Am. J. Legal Hist. 227 (1982). ——Article Cite.

O'Keefe, <u>Sir George Jessel and the Union of Judicature</u>, 26 Am. J. Legal Hist. 227, 250-51 (1982). ——Page Cite.

American Journal of Tax Policy
Abbreviation: Am. J. Tax Pol'y

Examples: Lane, <u>A Theory of the Tax Base: The Exchange Model</u>, 3 Am. J. Tax Pol'y 1 (1984). ——Article Cite.

Lane, <u>A Theory of the Tax Base: The Exchange Model</u>, 3 Am. J. Tax Pol'y 1, 38-40 (1984). ——Page Cite.

American Journal of Trial Advocacy
Abbreviation: Am. J. Trial Advoc.

Examples: Allen, <u>Computers and the Litigator</u>, 7 Am. J. Trial Advoc. 493 (1984). ——Article Cite.

Allen, <u>Computers and the Litigator</u>, 7 Am. J. Trial Advoc. 493, 501-02 (1984). ——Page Cite.

American Jurisprudence, Second Edition
Abbreviation: Am. Jur. 2d §   (year).

Examples: 59 Am. Jur. 2d <u>Pardon and Parole</u> § 31 (1987). ——Cite to a section.

59 Am. Jur. 2d <u>Infants</u> § 55.5 (Supp. 1987). ——Cite to pocket part to volume 42.

59 Am. Jur. 2d <u>Pardon and Parole</u> § 81, at 73 n.40 (1971). ——Cite to footnote.

American Law Institute, Federal Estate and Gift Taxation
Abbreviation: ALI Federal Estate and Gift Taxation § (year).

Example: ALI Federal Estate and Gift Taxation § EX 10 (1968).

American Law Institute, Federal Income Tax Project
Abbreviation: ALI Fed. Income Tax Project at (status if necessary, year).

In law review footnotes, the following are in large and small capitals: periodicals, constitutions, codes, restatements, standards, authors of books, titles of books, and legislative materials except for bills and resolutions. Refer to Bluebook.

Example: ALI Fed. Income Tax Project at 20 (Tent. Draft No. 15, 1986).

American Law Institute, Federal Securities Code
Abbreviation: ALI Federal Securities Code § (year).

Example: ALI Federal Securities Code § 202 (1978).

American Law Institute Model Code of Evidence
Abbreviation: Model Code of Evidence Rule (year).

Example: Model Code of Evidence Rule 310 (1942).

American Law Institute Model Land Development Code
Abbreviation: Model Land Dev. Code § (status if necessary, year).

Example: Model Land Dev. Code § 4-101 (1975).

American Law Institute Model Penal Code
Abbreviation: Model Penal Code § (status if necessary, year).

Examples: Model Penal Code § 210.2 (Proposed Official Draft 1962).

                Model Penal Code § 210.2 note on status of section (Proposed Official
                Draft 1962). ——Citation to auxiliary material.

American Law Institute Principles of Corporate Governance: Analysis and
Recommendations
Abbreviation: ALI Principles of Corporate Governance: Analysis and
                Recommendations § (status if necessary, year).

Example: ALI Principles of Corporate Governance: Analysis and
                Recommendations § 5.04 (Tent. Draft No. 5, 1986).

American Law Institute Proceedings
Abbreviation: A.L.I. Proc.

Example: Lewis, Annual Report of the Director, 10 A.L.I. Proc. 38 (1932).

American Law Institute Restatements
See   Restatement...

American Law of Products Liability by R. Hursh & H. Bailey
——Do not abbreviate the title.

Examples: 4 American Law of Products Liability § 46:35 (T. Travers 3d ed.
                1987).

                4 American Law of Products Liability § 46:35, at 58 (T. Travers 3d ed.
                1987).

In law review footnotes, the titles of books and the names of cases are not underlined.

American Law of Property (Casner, ed.)
————Do not abbreviate the title.

Examples: 4 <u>American Law of Property</u> § 16.178 (A.J. Casner ed. 1952).

                4 <u>American Law of Property</u> § 16.178, at 429 (A.J. Casner ed. 1952).

American Law of Zoning, by H.R. Anderson
————Do not abbreviate the title.

Examples: 3 R. Anderson, <u>American Law of Zoning</u> § 18.03 (3d ed. 1986).

                3 R. Anderson, <u>American Law of Zoning</u> § 18.03, at 218 (3d ed. 1986).

American Law Reports
Abbreviation: A.L.R.

Example: Annotation, <u>Appreciation or Depreciation of Assets of Defendent's Estate Before Final Settlement, but After Partial Distribution or Setting Up of Trust</u>, 114 A.L.R. 458 (1938). ————Cite to annotation.

American Law Reports, second series
Abbreviation: A.L.R.2d

Example: Annotation, <u>Liability of Operator of Flight Training School for Injury or Death of Trainee</u>, 17 A.L.R.2d 557 (1951). ————Cite to annotation.

American Law Reports, third series
Abbreviation: A.L.R.3d

Example: Annotation, <u>Grant, Reservation, or Lease of Minerals and Mining Rights as Including, Without Expressly So Providing, the Right to Remove the Minerals by Surface Mining</u>, 70 A.L.R.3d 383 (1976). ————Cite to annotation.

American Law Reports, fourth series
Abbreviation: A.L.R.4th

Example: Annotation, <u>Applicability of Double Jeopardy to Juvenile Court Proceedings</u>, 5 A.L.R.4th 234 (1981). ————Cite to annotation.

American Law Reports, Federal
Abbreviation: A.L.R. Fed.

Example: Annotation, <u>Admissibility of Evidence Discovered in Search of Defendant's Property or Residence Authorized by Defendant's Relative</u>, 48 A.L.R. Fed. 131 (1980). ————Cite to annotation.

American Lawyer
Abbreviation: Am. Law.

In law review footnotes, the following are in large and small capitals: periodicals, constitutions, codes, restatements, standards, authors of books, titles of books, and legislative materials except for bills and resolutions. Refer to Bluebook.

Examples: Cramped Quarters in New York, Am. Law., September 1982, at 19, col. 4. ——news report.

——News reports may be cited without title or byline. Bluebook Rule 17.

Stewart, Counsel to a Conspiracy, Am. Law., September 1982, at 26, col. 1. ——signed article.

American Samoa Administrative Code
Abbreviation: Am. Samoa Admin. Code § (year)

Example: Am. Samoa Admin. Code § 4.1205 (1985).

American Samoa Code Annotated
Abbreviation: Am. Samoa Code Ann.

Example: Am. Samoa Code Ann. § 16.0101 (1981).

American Society of International Law Proceedings
Abbreviation: Am. Soc'y Int'l L. Proc.

Examples: Smit, The Foreign Sovereign Immunities Act of 1976: A Plea for Drastic Surgery, 1980 Am. Soc'y Int'l L. Proc. 49. ——Article Cite.

Smit, The Foreign Sovereign Immunities Act of 1976: A Plea for Drastic Surgery, 1980 Am. Soc'y Int'l L. Proc. 49, 54-55. ——Page Cite.

American State Papers
Abbreviations: Am. St. Papers

American Stock Exchange Guide (Commerce Clearing House)
Abbreviation: Am. Stock Ex. Guide (CCH)

American University Law Review
Abbreviation: Am. U.L. Rev.

Examples: Cabra, Rights and Duties Established by the American Convention on Human Rights, 30 Am. U.L. Rev. 21 (1980). ——Article Cite.

Cabra, Rights and Duties Established by the American Convention on Human Rights, 30 Am. U.L. Rev. 21, 30-35 (1980). ——Page Cite.

Anglo-American Law Review
Abbreviation: Anglo-Am. L. Rev.

Examples: Kahn, Medical Negligence: Some Recent Trends, 14 Anglo-Am. L. Rev. 155 (1985). ——Article Cite.

Kahn, Medical Negligence: Some Recent Trends, 14 Anglo-Am. L. Rev. 155, 159-61 (1985). ——Page Cite.

In law review footnotes, the titles of books and the names of cases are not underlined.

annotated
Abbreviation: annot.

——See Bluebook Rule 16.1.4 for exceptions.

Annotated Code of Maryland
Abbreviation: Md. subject Code Ann. §   (year).

——See Bluebook page 151 for abbreviation of each subject.

Examples: Md. Nat. Res. Code Ann. § 8-101 (1983).

Md. Corps. & Ass'ns Code Ann. § 5-504 (1985).

Annotated Code of Professional Responsibility (A.B.F.)
See   American Bar Foundation Code of Professional Responsibility, Annotated

Annotated Code of the Public General Laws of Maryland (1957)
Abbreviation: Md. Ann. Code art. , §   (year).

Examples: Md. Ann. Code art. 2, § 14 (1981).

Md. Ann. Code art. 2B, § 8 (Supp. 1987).

Annotated Laws of Massachusetts
Abbreviation: Mass. Ann. Laws ch.   , § (Law. Co-op.year).

Examples: Mass. Ann. Laws ch. 68, § 5 (Law. Co-op. 1978).

Mass. Ann. Laws ch. 66, § 18 (Law. Co-op. Supp. 1981).

Annotation
Examples: Annotation, Parking Facility Proprietor's Liability for Criminal Attack on Patron, 49 A.L.R. 4th 1257 (1986). ——Annotation Cite.

Annotation, Sex Discrimination in Employment Against Female Attorney in Violation of Federal Civil Rights Laws—Federal Cases, 81 L. Ed. 2d 894 (1986). ——Annotation Cite.

Annotation, Sex Discrimination in Employment Against Female Attorney in Violation of Federal Civil Rights Laws—Federal Cases, 81 L. Ed. 2d 894, 897 (1986). ——Page Cite.

anonymous
Abbreviation: anon.

Annual Report and Official Opinions of the Attorney General of Indiana
Abbreviation: Ind. Att'y Gen. Ann. Rep. & Official Op.

Example: 1980 Ind. Att'y Gen. Ann. Rep. & Official Op. No. 80-1.

Annual Report and Official Opinions of the Attorney General of Maryland
Abbreviation: Md. Att'y Gen. Ann. Rep. & Official Op.

In law review footnotes, the following are in large and small capitals: periodicals, constitutions, codes, restatements, standards, authors of books, titles of books, and legislative materials except for bills and resolutions. Refer to Bluebook.

Example: 65 Md. Att'y Gen. Ann. Rep. & Official Op. 58 (1980).

Annual Report of the Attorney General for the State of South Carolina to the General Assembly
Abbreviation: S.C. Att'y Gen. Ann. Rep.

Example: 1976-1977 S.C. Att'y Gen. Ann. Rep. 105.

Annual Report of the Attorney General, State of Florida
Abbreviation: Fla. Att'y Gen. Ann. Rep.

Example: 1977 Fla. Att'y Gen. Ann. Rep. No. 077-144.

Annual Survey of American Law
Abbreviation: Ann. Surv. Am. L.

Examples: Miller, <u>Right to Counsel; State Courts on the Front Line</u>, 1985 Ann. Surv. Am. L. 179. ——Article Cite.

Miller, <u>Right to Counsel; State Courts on the Front Line</u>, 1985 Ann. Surv. Am. L. 179, 181-82. ——Page Cite.

Antitrust Bulletin
Abbreviation: Antitrust Bull.

Examples: Bronsteen, <u>Product Market Definition in Commercial Bank Merger</u>, 30 Antitrust Bull. 677 (1985). ——Article Cite.

Bronsteen, <u>Product Market Definition in Commercial Bank Merger</u>, 30 Antitrust Bull. 677, 680-81 (1985). ——Page Cite.

Antitrust and Trade Regulation Report (Bureau of National Affairs)
Abbreviation: Antitrust & Trade Reg. Rep. (BNA)

Example: <u>Phototron Corp v. Eastman Kodak Co.</u>, [Jan.-June] Antitrust & Trade Reg. Rep. (BNA) No. 1355, at 374 (N.D. Tex. Feb. 22, 1988). ——Citation to looseleaf material.

——The above example is proper if the case is not yet available in an official or West reporter, or is not reported in an official or West reporter.

Antitrust Law, by Phillip Areeda & Donald F. Turner
——Do not abbreviate the title.

Examples: 2 P. Areeda & D. Turner, <u>Antitrust Law</u> § 311c (1978).

2 P. Areeda & D. Turner, <u>Antitrust Law</u> § 311c, at 35 (1978).

Antitrust Law Journal
Abbreviation: Antitrust L.J.

In law review footnotes, the titles of books and the names of cases are not underlined.

Examples: Calvani, <u>Private Sources of Market Share Data: A Comment on Their</u>
              <u>Utility to Antitrust Lawyers</u>, 47 Antitrust L.J. 1107 (1978).
              ——Article Cite.

              Calvani, <u>Private Sources of Market Share Data: A Comment on Their</u>
              <u>Utility to Antitrust Lawyers</u>, 47 Antitrust L.J. 1107, 1109-12 (1978).
              ——Page Cite.

Appeal Cases, District of Columbia (1893-1941)
Abbreviation: App. D.C.

Examples: <u>Army & Navy Club v. Dist. of Columbia</u>, 8 App. D.C. 544 (1896).
              ——Case Cite.

              <u>Army & Navy Club v. Dist. of Columbia</u>, 8 App. D.C. 544, 550
              (1896). ——Page Cite.

——Cite to App. D.C. only if the case is not reported in the Federal Reporter.

Appellate Court Administration Review
Abbreviation: App. Ct. Admin. Rev.

Appellate Department
Abbreviation: App. Dep't

Appellate Division
Abbreviation: App. Div.

appended materials
——Well explained and illustrated in Bluebook Rule 3.5.

appendix; appendices
Abbreviation: app., apps.

——Well explained and illustrated in Bluebook Rule 3.5.

Arbitration Journal
Abbreviation: Arb. J.

Examples: Delaume, <u>International Arbitration Under French Law: The Decree of</u>
              <u>May 12, 1981</u>, Arb. J., Mar. 1982, at 38. ——Article Cite.

              Delaume, <u>International Arbitration Under French Law: The Decree of</u>
              <u>May 12, 1981</u>, Arb. J., Mar. 1982, at 38, 40-41. ——Page Cite.

Areeda & Turner on Antitrust Law
<u>See</u>   Antitrust Law, by P. Areeda & D. Turner

Arizona Administrative Digest
See   Administrative Digest (Arizona)

In law review footnotes, the following are in large and small capitals: periodicals, constitutions,
codes, restatements, standards, authors of books, titles of books, and legislative materials except
for bills and resolutions. Refer to Bluebook.

Arizona Appeals Reports
Abbreviation: Ariz. App.

——Discontinued after 27 Ariz. App. 797 (1976). Thereafter cite to Arizona Reports and P.2d.

Examples: Committee for Neighborhood Preservation v. Graham, 14 Ariz. App. 457, 484 P.2d 226 (1971). ——Case Cite.

Committee for Neighborhood Preservation v. Graham, 14 Ariz. App. 457, 460, 484 P.2d 226, 229 (1971). ——Page Cite.

——After 27 Ariz. App. 797 (1976), cite as follows:

Manning v. Blackwelder, 146 Ariz. 411, 706 P.2d 737 (Ct. App. 1985). ——Case Cite.

Manning v. Blackwelder, 146 Ariz. 411, 415, 706 P.2d 737, 738 (Ct. App. 1985). ——Page Cite.

Arizona Bar Journal
Abbreviation: Ariz. B.J.

Examples: Whitney & Hienton, The Arizona Community Foundation, Inc.: An Easy Way to Create Your Own "Foundation," Ariz. B.J., Dec. 1979, at 36. ——Article Cite.

Whitney & Hienton, The Arizona Community Foundation, Inc.: An Easy Way to Create Your Own "Foundation," Ariz. B.J., Dec. 1979, at 36, 38-39. ——Page Cite.

Arizona Constitution
Abbreviation: Ariz. Const. art.   , pt.   , §   . ——Not all articles are subdivided into parts.

Examples: Ariz. Const. art. VIII, pt. 2, § 1. ——Cite provisions without date unless the cited provisions have been repealed or amended (Bluebook Rule 11).

Ariz. Const. art. II, § 4.

Ariz. Const. art. XV, § 2 (1912, amended 1974). ——Cite provisions which have been repealed or amended by giving the date of the adoption of the particular provision and the date of repeal or amendment (Bluebook Rule 11).

Arizona Law Review
Abbreviation: Ariz. L. Rev.

Examples: Stone, Equal Protection and the Search for Justice, 22 Ariz. L. Rev. 1 (1980). ——Article Cite.

Stone, Equal Protection and the Search for Justice, 22 Ariz. L. Rev. 1, 9-15 (1980). ——Page Cite.

In law review footnotes, the titles of books and the names of cases are not underlined.

Arizona Legislative Service (West)
    Abbreviation: year Ariz. Legis. Serv.   (West).

Arizona Official Compilation of Administrative Rules and Regulations
    Abbreviation: Ariz. Comp. Admin. R. & Regs.   (year).

    Example: Ariz. Comp. Admin. R. & Regs. 1-1-01 (1975).

Arizona Reports
    Abbreviation: Ariz.

    Examples: Malott v. Malott, 145 Ariz. 587, 703 P.2d 531 (1985). ——Case Cite.

                Malott v. Malott, 145 Ariz. 587, 590, 703 P.2d 531, 532 (1985).
                ——Page Cite.

Arizona Revised Statutes Annotated
    Abbreviation: Ariz. Rev. Stat. Ann. §   (year).

    Examples: Ariz. Rev. Stat. Ann. § 23-101 (1983).

                Ariz. Rev. Stat. Ann. § 23-901 (Supp. 1987).

Arizona Session Laws
    Abbreviation: year Ariz. Sess. Laws

Arizona State Law Journal
    Abbreviation: Ariz. St. L.J.

    Examples: Grossman, Statutes of Limitations and the Conflict of Laws: Modern
                Analysis, 1980 Ariz. St. L.J. 1. ——Article Cite.

                Grossman, Statutes of Limitations and the Conflict of Laws: Modern
                Analysis, 1980 Ariz. St. L.J. 1, 41-44. ——Page Cite.

Arkansas Appellate Reports
    Abbreviation: Ark. App.

    ——Beginning with volume 1 (1981), bound with Arkansas Reports, volume 272
        (1981).

    Examples: Harris v. Milloway, 9 Ark. App. 350, 660 S.W.2d 174 (1983).
                ——Case Cite.

                Harris v. Milloway, 9 Ark. App. 350, 356, 660 S.W.2d 174, 176
                (1983). ——Page Cite.

Arkansas Code of 1987 Annotated
    ——This code became effective on Dec. 31, 1987, after the 14th edition of the Bluebook
        was published.

    Abbreviation: Ark. Code Ann. §   (year).
                (no recommended cite by publisher)

In law review footnotes, the following are in large and small capitals: periodicals, constitutions, codes, restatements, standards, authors of books, titles of books, and legislative materials except for bills and resolutions. Refer to Bluebook.

Examples: Ark. Code Ann. § 27-67-316 (1987).

Ark. Code. Ann. § 27-50-308 (Supp. 1987).

Arkansas Constitution
Abbreviation: Ark. Const. art.   , §   .

Examples: Ark. Const. art. IX, § 3. ——Cite provisions without date unless the
cited provisions have been repealed or amended (Bluebook Rule 11).

Ark. Const. art. XIV, § 3 (1926, amended 1948). ——Cite provisions
which have been repealed or amended by giving the date of the adoption
of the particular provision and the date of repeal or amendment
(Bluebook Rule 11).

Ark. Const. of 1836, art. II. ——Cite constitutions that have been
totally superseded by year of adoption, giving parenthetically the year of
adoption of the specific provision cited if different (Bluebook Rule 11).

Ark. Const. amend. 18 (1929). ——Amendments to the Arkansas
Constitution are not incorporated into the body of the constitution; they
are numbered separately.

Arkansas Law Notes
Abbreviation: Ark. L. Notes

Examples: Flaccus, Farmers, Taxes, and Bankruptcy, 1986 Ark L. Notes 1.
——Article Cite.

Flaccus, Farmers, Taxes, and Bankruptcy, 1986 Ark L. Notes 1, 4-5.
——Page Cite.

Arkansas Law Review
Abbreviation: Ark. L. Rev.

Examples: Lancaster, Traps and Opportunities in the Generation-Skipping Transfer
Tax, 32 Ark. L. Rev. 611 (1979). ——Article Cite.

Lancaster, Traps and Opportunities in the Generation-Skipping Transfer
Tax, 32 Ark. L. Rev. 611, 615-18 (1979). ——Page Cite.

Arkansas Lawyer Quarterly
Abbreviation: Ark. Law. Q.

Examples: Barrier, Usury in Arkansas: Update and Countdown, 16 Ark. Law. Q.
168 (1982). ——Article Cite.

Barrier, Usury in Arkansas: Update and Countdown, 16 Ark. Law. Q.
168, 169 (1982). ——Page Cite.

Arkansas Register
Abbreviation: Ark. Reg.

In law review footnotes, the titles of books and the names of cases are not underlined.

Arkansas Reports
> Abbreviation: Ark.

> ——Beginning with volume 272 (1981), Arkansas Reports bound with Arkansas Appeals Reports, volume 1 (1981).

> Examples: Olson v. Riddle, 280 Ark. 535, 659 S.W.2d 759 (1983). ——Case Cite.

> Olson v. Riddle, 280 Ark. 535, 537-38, 659 S.W.2d 759, 760-61 (1983). ——Page Cite.

Arkansas Session Laws
> See   General Acts of Arkansas

Arkansas Statutes Annotated
> See   Arkansas Code of 1987 Annotated

Army Lawyer
> Abbreviation: Army Law.

> Examples: Allen, The Precedential Value of Decisions of the Courts of Military Review and the Need for En Banc Reconsiderations, Army Law., Mar. 1983, at 16. ——Article Cite.

> Allen, The Precedential Value of Decisions of the Courts of Military Review and the Need for En Banc Reconsiderations, Army Law., Mar. 1983, at 16, 20-21. ——Page Cite.

article(s)
> Abbreviation: art., arts.

Atkinson on Wills
> See   Handbook of the Law of Wills, by T. Atkinson

Atlantic Reporter
> Abbreviation: A.

> Examples: Zoglia v. T.W. Waterman Co., 39 R.I. 396, 98 A. 280 (1916). ——Case Cite.

> Zoglia v. T.W. Waterman Co., 39 R.I. 396, 401, 98 A. 280, 282 (1916). ——Page Cite.

Atlantic Reporter, Second Series
> Abbreviation: A.2d

> Examples: Bladensburg v. Berg, 216 Md. 292, 139 A.2d 703 (1958). ——Case Cite.

> Bladensburg v. Berg, 216 Md. 292, 295-96, 139 A.2d 703, 705 (1958). ——Page Cite.

In law review footnotes, the following are in large and small capitals: periodicals, constitutions, codes, restatements, standards, authors of books, titles of books, and legislative materials except for bills and resolutions. Refer to Bluebook.

——Cite only to A.2d for the following state reporters: Connecticut Circuit Court
Reports after 360 A.2d 909 (1974); Delaware Chancery Reports after 240 A.2d 757
(1968); Delaware Reports after 219 A.2d 374 (1966); District of Columbia Court
of Appeals; Maine Reports after 215 A.2d 83 (1965); Rhode Island Reports after
415 A.2d 744 (1980).

Delaware Chancery Reports:

——After 240 A.2d 757 (1968), cite as follows:

> Council of Unit Owners of Pilot Point Condominium v. Realty Growth
> Investers, 436 A.2d 1268 (Del. Ch. 1981). ——Case Cite.

> Council of Unit Owners of Pilot Point Condominium v. Realty Growth
> Investers, 436 A.2d 1268, 1269 (Del. Ch. 1981). ——Page Cite.

Delaware Reports:

——After 219 A.2d 374 (1966), cite as follows:

> Boyer v. State, 436 A.2d 1118 (Del. 1981). ——Case Cite.

> Boyer v. State, 436 A.2d 1118, 1119 (Del. 1981). ——Page Cite.

District of Columbia Court of Appeals:

——Cite as follows:

> Strand v. Frenkel, 500 A.2d 1368 (D.C. 1985). ——Case Cite.

> Strand v. Frenkel, 500 A.2d 1368, 1270 (D.C. 1985). ——Page Cite.

Maine Reports:

——After 215 A.2d 83 (1965), cite as follows:

> Matyskiela v. Emple Knitting Mills, 437 A.2d 611 (Me. 1981).
> ——Case Cite.

> Matyskiela v. Emple Knitting Mills, 437 A.2d 611, 613 (Me. 1981).
> ——Page Cite.

Rhode Island Reports:

——After 415 A.2d 744 (1980), cite as follows:

> Panciera v. Panciera, 500 A.2d 221 (R.I. 1985). ——Case Cite.

> Panciera v. Panciera, 500 A.2d 221, 223 (R.I. 1985). ——Page Cite.

Atomic Energy Commission Reports (U.S.) (1956-1975)
  Abbreviation: A.E.C.

  Examples: Southern California Edison Co., 7 A.E.C. 410 (1974).

              Tennessee Valley Auth. (Watts Bar Nuclear Plant, Units 1 and 2), 6
              A.E.C. 37 (1973).

Atomic Energy Law Journal
  Abbreviation: Atom. Energy L.J.

In law review footnotes, the titles of books and the names of cases are not underlined.

Examples: Frazier, <u>High-Level Radioactive Waste Management</u>, 18 Atom. Energy
              L.J. 255 (1977). ——Article Cite.

              Frazier, <u>High-Level Radioactive Waste Management</u>, 18 Atom. Energy
              L.J. 255, 258-60 (1977). ——Page Cite.

Attorney General
    Abbreviation: Att'y Gen.

Attorney General of the State of Wyoming Opinions
    Abbreviation: Op. Wyo. Att'y Gen.

    Example: 1975 Op. Wyo. Att'y Gen. 29.

Attorney General's Annual Report
    Abbreviation: Att'y Gen. Ann. Rep.

    Example: 1956 Att'y Gen. Ann. Rep. 118.

Attorney General Opinions, generally
    ——See Bluebook Rule 14.4.

Attorney General's Opinions, United States
    <u>See</u> Opinions of the Attorney General (U.S.) (1789-date)

Auckland University Law Review
    Abbreviation: Auckland U.L. Rev.

    Examples: Dench, <u>The Tort of Misfeasance in a Public Office</u>, 4 Auckland U.L.
                      Rev. 182 (1981). ——Article Cite.

                      Dench, <u>The Tort of Misfeasance in a Public Office</u>, 4 Auckland U.L.
                      Rev. 182, 183-85 (1981). ——Page Cite.

Auditing Standards, Generally Accepted
    Example: Reports on Audited Financial Statements, Statements on Auditing
                      Standards No. 2, § 509 (Am. Inst. of Certified Pub. Accountants 1974).

Australian Business Law Review
    Abbreviations: Austl. Bus. L. Rev.
                      A.B.L.R. (publisher's abbreviation)

    Examples: Tedeschi, <u>The Mareva Injunction—An Update</u>, 13 Austl. Bus. L. Rev.
                      236 (1985). ——Article Cite.

                      Tedeschi, <u>The Mareva Injunction—An Update</u>, 13 Austl. Bus. L. Rev.
                      236, 237-38 (1985). ——Page Cite.

In law review footnotes, the following are in large and small capitals: periodicals, constitutions,
codes, restatements, standards, authors of books, titles of books, and legislative materials except
for bills and resolutions. Refer to Bluebook.

Australian Law Journal
　　Abbreviations:　Austl. L.J.
　　　　　　　　　　A.L.J.R. (publisher's abbreviation)

　　Examples:　　　Finley, <u>Fault and Violence in the Family Court of Australia</u>, 59 Austl.
　　　　　　　　　　L.J. 559 (1985). ——Article Cite.

　　　　　　　　　　Finely, <u>Fault and Violence in the Family Court of Australia</u>, 59 Austl.
　　　　　　　　　　L.J. 559, 560-61 (1985). ——Page Cite.

Australian Yearbook of International Law
　　Abbreviation:　Austl. Y.B. Int'l L.

　　Examples:　　　Keith, <u>The Present State of International Humanitarian Law</u>, 9 Austl.
　　　　　　　　　　Y.B. Int'l L. 13 (1985). ——Article Cite.

　　　　　　　　　　Keith, <u>The Present State of International Humanitarian Law</u>, 9 Austl.
　　　　　　　　　　Y.B. Int'l L. 13, 14-15 (1985). ——Page Cite.

author
　　——See various title entries in this work. See also Bluebook Rule 15.1.

authorities, order of authorities within each signal
　　——See Bluebook Rule 2.4.

authors
　　——Use first initial for citing book authors, but not article or chapter authors. Give full
　　names of institutional authors.

　　Examples:　　　Kiss & Dominick, <u>The International Legal Significance of the Human
　　　　　　　　　　Rights Provisions of the Helsinki Final Act</u>, 13 Vand. J. Transnat'l L.
　　　　　　　　　　293 (1980). ——Article Cite.

　　　　　　　　　　M. Akehurst, <u>A Modern Introduction to International Law</u> 121 (5th ed.
　　　　　　　　　　1984). ——Book Cite.

　　　　　　　　　　Rogers, <u>Trade Relations in the Inter-American System</u>, in <u>The Future of
　　　　　　　　　　the Inter-American System</u> 54 (T. Farer ed. 1979). ——Article within
　　　　　　　　　　an edited book. See Bluebook Rule 15.5.1.

　　　　　　　　　　Federal Power Comm'n, <u>Annual Report, Fiscal Year 1967</u>, at 23
　　　　　　　　　　(1968). ——Institutional author.

　　　　　　　　　　Law Enforcement Assistance Administration, U.S. Dep't of Justice,
　　　　　　　　　　<u>Children in Custody: A Report on the Juvenile Detention and
　　　　　　　　　　Correctional Facility Census of 1975</u>, at 57 (1979). ——Subdivided
　　　　　　　　　　institutional author.

Automobile Law Reporter (Commerce Clearing House)
　　Abbreviation:　Auto. L. Rep. (CCH)

In law review footnotes, the titles of books and the names of cases are not underlined.

Aviation Law Reporter (Commerce Clearing House)
    Abbreviations: Av. L. Rep. (CCH)
                    Av. Cas. (CCH) ——When citing to cases.

In law review footnotes, the following are in large and small capitals: periodicals, constitutions, codes, restatements, standards, authors of books, titles of books, and legislative materials except for bills and resolutions. Refer to Bluebook.

In law review footnotes, the titles of books and the names of cases are not underlined.

B

Bail Court
    Abbreviation: Bail

Baldwin's Kentucky Revised Statutes Annotated
    Abbreviation: Ky. Rev. Stat. Ann. §   (Baldwin year).

    Examples: Ky. Rev. Stat. Ann. § 12.120 (Baldwin 1985).

                Ky. Rev. Stat. Ann. § 92.560 (Baldwin Supp. 1984).

Baldwin's Ohio Legislative Service. (Baldwin).
    Abbreviation: year Ohio Legis. Serv.   (Baldwin)

Baldwin's Ohio Revised Code Annotated
    Abbreviation: Ohio Rev. Code Ann. § (Baldwin year).

Ballentine's Law Dictionary
    Abbreviation: Ballentine's Law Dictionary page (ed. year).

    Example: Ballentine's Law Dictionary 98 (3d ed. 1969).

Banking Law Journal
    Abbreviation: Banking L.J.

    Examples: Todres, Tax Allocation of Premium Paid to Acquire a Bank, 102
                Banking L.J. 562 (1985). ——Article Cite.

                Todres, Tax Allocation of Premium Paid to Acquire a Bank, 102
                Banking L.J. 562, 563-65 (1985). ——Page Cite.

Bankruptcy Cases
    Examples: Ross v. Cunningham, 59 Bankr. 743 (Bankr. N.D. Ill. 1986).

——Cite both adversary and nonadversary names whenever both are listed at the
    beginning of opinions; otherwise, cite as follows:

                In re Bryson, 53 Bankr. 3 (Bankr. M.D. Tenn. 1985).

Bankruptcy Law Reports (Commerce Clearing House)
    (Formerly Reporter)

    Abbreviation: Bankr. L. Rep. (CCH)

In law review footnotes, the following are in large and small capitals: periodicals, constitutions, codes, restatements, standards, authors of books, titles of books, and legislative materials except for bills and resolutions. Refer to Bluebook.

Examples: In re Whitener, 3 Bankr. L. Rep. (CCH) ¶ 71,407 (Bankr. E.D. Pa. Aug. 15, 1986). ——Citation to looseleaf material.

In re Goodwin, [1985-1986 Transfer Binder] Bankr. L. Rep. (CCH) ¶ 71,025 (Bankr. D. Me. 1986). ——Citation to transfer binder material.

——The above examples are proper if the case is not yet available in an official or West reporter, or is not reported in an official or West reporter.

Bankruptcy Reporter
Abbreviation: Bankr.

Example: In re Bryson, 53 Bankr. 3 (Bankr. M.D. Tenn. 1985).

basic citation forms for briefs and legal memoranda.
——See various title entries of this work. See also excellent examples included on the inside cover of the Bluebook.

Basic Civil Procedure, by Milton D. Green
——Do not abbreviate the title.

Example: M. Green, Basic Civil Procedure 107 (2d ed. 1979).

Basic Text on Labor Law, by Robert A. Gorman
——Do not abbreviate the title.

Example: R. Gorman, Basic Text on Labor Law 407 (1976).

Baylor Law Review
Abbreviation: Baylor L. Rev.

Examples: Watkins, 1980 Amendments to the Federal Rules of Civil Procedure, 32 Baylor L. Rev. 533 (1980). ——Article Cite.

Watkins, 1980 Amendments to the Federal Rules of Civil Procedure, 32 Baylor L. Rev. 533, 537-39 (1980). ——Page Cite.

Bench and Bar of Minnesota
Abbreviation: Bench & B. Minn.

Bergin on Estates in Land and Future Interests
See   Preface to Estates in Land and Future Interests, by T. Bergin & P.Haskell

Beverly Hills Bar Association Journal
Abbreviation: Beverly Hills B.A.J.

Examples: Smolker, Guilty Until Proven Innocent, 16 Beverly Hills B.A.J. 259 (1982). ——Article Cite.

Smolker, Guilty Until Proven Innocent, 16 Beverly Hills B.A.J. 259, 260 (1982). ——Page Cite.

In law review footnotes, the titles of books and the names of cases are not underlined.

Biennial Report and Official Opinions of the Attorney General of the Stateof West Virginia
    Abbreviation: W. Va. Att'y Gen. Biennial Rep. & Official Op.

    Example: 1976-1978 W. Va. Att'y Gen. Biennial Rep. & Official Op. 34.

Biennial Report of the Attorney General of the State of Michigan
    Abbreviation: Mich. Att'y Gen. Biennial Rep.

    Example: 1980 Mich. Att'y Gen. Biennial Rep. 23.

Biennial Report of the Attorney General of the State of South Dakota
    Abbreviation: S.D. Att'y Gen. Biennial Rep.

    Example: 1973-1974 S.D. Att'y Gen. Biennial Rep. 52.

Biennial Report of the Attorney General of the State of Vermont
    Abbreviation: Vt. Att'y Gen. Biennial Rep.

    Example: 1972-1974 Vt. Att'y Gen. Biennial Rep. 33.

Biennial Report of the Attorney General, State of Iowa
    Abbreviation: Iowa Att'y Gen. Biennial Rep.

    Example: 1978 Iowa Att'y Gen. Biennial Rep. No. 77-11-10.

Bigham on Tennessee Practice
    See   Tennessee Practice, by W. Bigham & C. White

Bill of Rights Journal
    Abbreviation: Bill Rts. J.

Bills, Congressional
    See   Congressional Bills

Bittker and Eustice on Federal Income Taxation of Corporations and Shareholders
    See   Federal Income Taxation of Corporations and Shareholders, by B. Bittker & J. Eustice

Black (United States Reports)
    See   United States Reports

Black Law Journal
    Abbreviation: Black L.J.

    Examples: Kumando, <u>Judicial Review of Legislation in Ghana Since Independence</u>, 5 Black L.J. 208 (1976). ——Article Cite.

                  Kumando, <u>Judicial Review of Legislation in Ghana Since Independence</u>, 5 Black L.J. 208, 209-10 (1976). ——Page Cite.

In law review footnotes, the following are in large and small capitals: periodicals, constitutions, codes, restatements, standards, authors of books, titles of books, and legislative materials except for bills and resolutions. Refer to Bluebook.

Black's Law Dictionary
    Abbreviation: Black's Law Dictionary (ed.year).

    Example: Black's Law Dictionary 105 (5th ed. 1979).

Blue Sky Law Reports (Commerce Clearing House)
    Abbreviation: Blue Sky L. Rep. (CCH)

    Examples: Quick and Reilly, Inc. v. Perlin, 3 Blue Sky L. Rep. (CCH) ¶ 71,732
(Fla. Dist. Ct. App. Mar. 30, l982). ——Citation to looseleaf material.
Such a citation is proper if the case is not yet available in an official or
West reporter, or is not reported in an official or West reporter.

Canadian Pacific Enterprises v. Krouse, [1978-1981 Decisions Transfer
Binder] Blue Sky L. Rep. (CCH) ¶ 71,590 (S.D. Ohio 1981).
——Citation to transfer binder. Such a citation is proper only if the case
is not reported in an official or West reporter.

Board of Tax Appeals
    Abbreviation: B.T.A.

Board of Tax Appeals
    See   Reports of the United States Board of Tax Appeals

Bogert on Trusts and Trustees
    See   Handbook of the Law of Trusts, by George T. Bogert

Book Review
    Examples: Black, Book Review, 90 Yale L.J. 232 (1980).

Black, Book Review, 90 Yale L.J. 232 (1980) (reviewing D. Konig,
Law and Society in Puritan Massachusetts (1979)). ——Citation which
includes the title of the book reviewed.

Black, Community and Law in Seventeenth Century Massachusetts
(Book Review), 90 Yale L.J. 232 (1980). ——Alternative citation to a
book review with a title other than the title of the book reviewed.

Book Note, 32 N.Y.L. Sch. L. Rev. 199 (1987). ——Student-written
book review.

Boston Bar Journal
    Abbreviation: Boston B.J.

    Examples: Brown & McGuire, Damages for Pain and Suffering—What Are the
Courts Really Doing?, Boston B.J., Nov. 1979, at 5. ——Article Cite.

Brown & McGuire, Damages for Pain and Suffering—What Are the
Courts Really Doing?, Boston B.J., Nov. 1979, at 5, 6-7. ——Page
Cite.

In law review footnotes, the titles of books and the names of cases are not underlined.

Boston College Environmental Affairs Law Review
    Abbreviation: B.C. Envtl. Aff. L. Rev.

    Examples: Reitze, <u>Federal Compensation for Vaccination Induced Injuries</u>, 13 B.C.
            Envtl. Aff. L. Rev. 169 (1986). ——Article Cite.

            Reitze, <u>Federal Compensation for Vaccination Induced Injuries</u>, 13 B.C.
            Envtl. Aff. L. Rev. 169, 181 (1986). ——Page Cite.

Boston College Industrial and Commercial Law Review
    Abbreviation: B.C. Indus. & Com. L. Rev.

    Examples: Calvani, <u>Functional Discounts Under the Robinson—Patman Act</u>, 17
            B.C. Indus. & Com. L. Rev. 543 (1976). ——Article Cite.

            Calvani, <u>Functional Discounts Under the Robinson—Patman Act</u>, 17
            B.C. Indus. & Com. L. Rev. 543, 557 (1976). ——Page Cite.

Boston College International and Comparative Law Review
    Abbreviation: B.C. Int'l & Comp. L. Rev.

    Examples: Gordon, <u>Observations on the Nature of Joint Ventures in Mexico: Are</u>
            <u>They Involuntary and Transitory Institutions?</u>, 2 B.C. Int'l & Comp. L.
            Rev. 337 (1979). ——Article Cite.

            Gordon, <u>Observations on the Nature of Joint Ventures in Mexico: Are</u>
            <u>They Involuntary and Transitory Institutions?</u>, 2 B.C. Int'l & Comp. L.
            Rev. 337, 362-63 (1979). ——Page Cite.

Boston College Law Review
    Abbreviation: B.C.L. Rev.

    Examples: Gelfand, <u>The Burger Court and the New Federalism: Preliminary</u>
            <u>Reflections on the Roles of Local Government Actors in the Political</u>
            <u>Dramas of the 1980's</u>, 21 B.C.L. Rev. 763 (1980). ——Article Cite.

            Gelfand, <u>The Burger Court and the New Federalism: Preliminary</u>
            <u>Reflections on the Roles of Local Government Actors in the Political</u>
            <u>Dramas of the 1980's</u>, 21 B.C.L. Rev. 763, 768-73 (1980). ——Page
            Cite.

Boston College Third World Law Journal
    Abbreviation: B.C. Third World L.J.

Boston University International Law Journal
    Abbreviation: B.U. Int'l L.J.

    Examples: Short, <u>The Canadian Perspective</u>, 1 B.U. Int'l L.J. 71 (1982).
            ——Article Cite.

            Short, <u>The Canadian Perspective</u>, 1 B.U. Int'l L.J. 71, 72-74 (1982).
            ——Page Cite.

In law review footnotes, the following are in large and small capitals: periodicals, constitutions, codes, restatements, standards, authors of books, titles of books, and legislative materials except for bills and resolutions. Refer to Bluebook.

Boston University Law Review
    Abbreviation: B.U.L. Rev.

    Examples: Leubsdorf, Remedies for Uncertainty, 61 B.U.L. Rev. 132 (1981).
    ——Article Cite.

                  Leubsdorf, Remedies for Uncertainty, 61 B.U.L. Rev. 132, 150-53
                  (1981). ——Page Cite.

Bracton Law Journal
    Abbreviation: Bracton L.J.

brief, citation to
    ——Well explained and illustrated in Bluebook Rule 10.8.3.

briefs, basic citation forms
    ——See various title entries of this work. See also excellent examples included on the
    inside cover of the Bluebook.

briefs, typeface conventions for briefs
    ——See Bluebook Rules 1.1 and 7.

Brigham Young University Law Review
    Abbreviation: B.Y.U. L. Rev.

    Examples: Voros, Three Views of Equal Protection: A Backdrop to Bakke, 1979
                  B.Y.U. L. Rev. 25. ——Article Cite.

                  Voros, Three Views of Equal Protection: A Backdrop to Bakke, 1979
                  B.Y.U. L. Rev. 25, 32-48. ——Page Cite.

British Journal of Law and Society
    Abbreviation: Brit. J.L. & Soc'y

    Examples: Abel, A Critique of American Tort Law, 8 Brit. J.L. & Soc'y 199
                  (1981). ——Article Cite.

                  Abel, A Critique of American Tort Law, 8 Brit. J.L. & Soc'y 199, 210-
                  12 (1981). ——Page Cite.

British Tax Review
    Abbreviation: Brit. Tax Rev.

    Examples: Bartlett, The Constitutionality of the Ramsay Principle, 1985 Brit. Tax
                  Rev. 338. ——Article Cite.

                  Bartlett, The Constitutionality of the Ramsay Principle, 1985 Brit. Tax
                  Rev. 338, 339-40. ——Page Cite.

British Yearbook of International Law
    Abbreviation: Brit. Y.B. Int'l L.

In law review footnotes, the titles of books and the names of cases are not underlined.

Examples: Carter, <u>Rejection of Foreign Law: Some Private International Law Inhibitions</u>, 55 Brit. Y.B. Int'l L. 111 (1984). ——Article Cite.

Carter, <u>Rejection of Foreign Law: Some Private International Law Inhibitions</u>, 55 Brit. Y.B. Int'l L. 111, 119-20 (1984). ——Page Cite.

Broadcasts

Example: <u>ABC World News Tonight</u> (ABC television broadcast, Dec. 9, 1986) (transcript on file at Vanderbilt Law School Library).

Bromberg on Securities Law

<u>See</u>   Securities Fraud and Commodities Fraud, by A. Bromberg and L. Lowenfels

Brooklyn Journal of International Law

Abbreviation: Brooklyn J. Int'l L.

Examples: Macdonald, <u>Termination of the Strategic Trusteeship: Free Association, the United Nations and International Law</u>, 7 Brooklyn J. Int'l L. 235 (1981). ——Article Cite.

Macdonald, <u>Termination of the Strategic Trusteeship: Free Association, the United Nations and International Law</u>, 7 Brooklyn J. Int'l L. 235, 248-49 (1981). ——Page Cite.

Brooklyn Law Review

Abbreviation: Brooklyn L. Rev.

Examples: McLaughlin & Whisenand, <u>Jury Trial, Public Trial and Free Press in Juvenile Proceedings: An Analysis and Comparison of the IJA/ABA, Task Force and NAC Standards</u>, 46 Brooklyn L. Rev. 1 (1979). ——Article Cite.

McLaughlin & Whisenand, <u>Jury Trial, Public Trial and Free Press in Juvenile Proceedings: An Analysis and Comparison of the IJA/ABA, Task Force and NAC Standards</u>, 46 Brooklyn L. Rev. 1, 20-25 (1979). ——Page Cite.

Brown on Personal Property

<u>See</u>   Law of Personal Property, by Ray A. Brown

Buffalo Law Review

Abbreviation: Buffalo L. Rev.

Examples: Cappelletti & Garth, <u>Access to Justice: The Newest Wave in the Worldwide Movement to Make Rights Effective</u>, 27 Buffalo L. Rev. 181 (1978). ——Article Cite.

Cappelletti & Garth, <u>Access to Justice: The Newest Wave in the Worldwide Movement to Make Rights Effective</u>, 27 Buffalo L. Rev. 181, 186-96 (1978). ——Page Cite.

In law review footnotes, the following are in large and small capitals: periodicals, constitutions, codes, restatements, standards, authors of books, titles of books, and legislative materials except for bills and resolutions. Refer to Bluebook.

Bulletin of the Copyright Society of the U.S.A.
  Abbreviation: Bull. Copyright Soc'y

  Examples: DaSilva, <u>Droit Moral and the Amoral Copyright: A Comparison of Artists' Rights in France and the United States</u>, 28 Bull. Copyright Soc'y 7 (1980). ——Article Cite.

  DaSilva, <u>Droit Moral and the Amoral Copyright: A Comparison of Artists' Rights in France and the United States</u>, 28 Bull. Copyright Soc'y 7, 57-58 (1980). ——Page Cite.

Bulletin of the European Communities
  Abbreviation: Bull. Eur. Commmunities

  Examples: <u>The Community's Mediterranean Policy After Enlargement—Guidelines for Economic Cooperation</u>, Bull. Eur. Communities, Nov. 1985, at 18. ——Article Cite.

  <u>The Community's Mediterranean Policy After Enlargement—Guidelines for Economic Cooperation</u>, Bull. Eur. Communities, Nov. 1985, at 18, 18-19. ——Page Cite.

Burby on Real Property
  <u>See</u>   Handbook of the Law of Real Property, by W. Burby

Bureau of National Affairs, Inc.
  Abbreviation: BNA

Burns Indiana Statutes Annotated Code Edition
  Abbreviation: Ind. Code Ann. § (Burns year).

  Examples: Ind. Code Ann. § 15-1-1-7 (Burns 1983).

  Ind. Code Ann. § 15-1-1-2 (Burns Supp. 1987).

  ——A cite to Indiana Code would be preferable. See Bluebook Rule 12.3 and the tables in Part H.

Business Lawyer
  Abbreviation: Bus. Law.

  Examples: Knauss, <u>Disclosure Requirements—Changing Concepts of Liability</u>, 24 Bus. Law. 43 (1968). ——Article Cite.

  Knauss, <u>Disclosure Requirements—Changing Concepts of Liability</u>, 24 Bus. Law. 43, 48-53 (1968). ——Page Cite.

In law review footnotes, the titles of books and the names of cases are not underlined.

But cf.

    Examples: "This phenomenon, of course, lay at the root of the Supreme Court's application to the states of the protections of the federal Bill of Rights. See, e.g., Countryman, Why a State Bill of Rights?, 45 Wash. L. Rev. 454, 455-56 (1970). But cf. infra pp. 1396-97 & notes 190-92 (discussing potential for current use even of limited early state constitutional activity)." ——Taken from 95 Harv. L. Rev. 1324, 1393 n.176 (1982).

                 "See Epstein, Defenses and Subsequent Pleas in a System of Strict Liability, 3 J. Legal Stud. 165 (1974). But cf. Note, Assumption of Risk and Strict Products Liability, 95 Harv. L. Rev. 872, 881-82, 884-87 (1982) (criticizing the use of classical assumption of risk both as an independent defense and as a limitation on the use of a properly tailored contributory negligence defense." ——Taken from 95 Harv. L. Rev. 1717, 1741 n.79 (1982).

But see

    Examples: "In addition, unlike the resale price maintenance agreements in Albrecht and Kiefer-Stewart, which were arguably injurious to competition, see generally L.A. Sullivan, Antitrust 377-87 (1977); but see Easterbrook, Maximum Price Fixing, 48 U. Chi. L. Rev. 886 (1981) (prepaid drug insurance plans potentially promote competition and efficiency)." ——Taken from 675 F.2d 502, 506 (1982).

In law review footnotes, the following are in large and small capitals: periodicals, constitutions, codes, restatements, standards, authors of books, titles of books, and legislative materials except for bills and resolutions. Refer to Bluebook.

In law review footnotes, the titles of books and the names of cases are not underlined.

C

C.J.S.
See   Corpus Juris Secundum

COMM/ENT
Abbreviation: COMM-ENT

Les Cahiers de Droit
Abbreviation: C. de D.

Examples: Magnet, Les Ecoles et la Constitution, 24 Les Cahiers de Droit [C. de D.] 145 (1983).

Grandbois, Le Controle Juridique des Precipitations Acides, 26 C. de D. 591 (1985).

——When using foreign language titles, the first citation should indicate in brackets any abbreviation to be used subsequently. (See Bluebook Rule 20.6)

Calamari & Perillo on Contracts
See   Law of Contracts, by J. Calamari & J. Perillo

California Administrative Code
Abbreviations: Cal. Admin. Code tit. , § (year).

California Administrative Notice Register
Abbreviation: Cal. Admin. Notice Reg.

California Annotated Codes (Deering)
See   Deering's Annotated California Codes

California Appellate Reports
Abbreviation: Cal. App.

Examples: VanDerHoof v. Chambon, 121 Cal. App. 118, 8 P.2d 925 (1932). ——Case Cite.

VanDerHoof v. Chambon, 121 Cal. App. 118, 131, 8 P.2d 925, 930 (1932). ——Page Cite.

California Appellate Reports, second series
Abbreviation: Cal. App. 2d

In law review footnotes, the following are in large and small capitals: periodicals, constitutions, codes, restatements, standards, authors of books, titles of books, and legislative materials except for bills and resolutions. Refer to Bluebook.

Examples: People v. Kanan, 208 Cal. App. 2d 635, 25 Cal. Rptr. 427 (1962).
————Case Cite.

People v. Kanan, 208 Cal. App. 2d 635, 637, 25 Cal. Rptr. 427, 428
(1962). ————Page Cite.

California Appellate Reports, third series
Abbreviation: Cal. App. 3d

Examples: Mendibles v. Superior Court, 162 Cal. App. 3d 1191, 208 Cal. Rptr.
841 (1984). ————Case Cite.

Mendibles v. Superior Court, 162 Cal. App. 3d 1191, 1192, 208 Cal.
Rptr. 841, 842 (1984). ————Page Cite.

California Attorney General Opinions
See   Opinions of the Attorney General of California

California Code Annotated (West)
See   West's Annotated California Code

California Constitution
Abbreviation: Cal. Const. art.   , §   .

Examples: Cal. Const. art. I, § 6. ————Cite provisions without date unless the
cited provisions have been repealed or amended (Bluebook Rule 11).

Cal. Const. art. II, § 10 (1879, repealed 1910). ————Cite provisions
which have been repealed or amended by giving the date of the adoption
of the particular provision and the date of repeal or amendment
(Bluebook Rule 11).

Cal. Const. of 1849, art. I, § 1. ————Cite constitutions that have been
totally superseded by year of adoption, giving parenthetically the year of
adoption of the specific provision cited if different (Bluebook Rule 11).

California Jurisprudence, third edition
Abbreviation: Cal. Jur. 3d

Example: 58 Cal. Jur. 3d Specific Performance § 43 (1980).

California Law Review
Abbreviation: Calif. L. Rev.

Examples: Kamenshine, The First Amendment's Implied Political Establishment
Clause, 67 Calif. L. Rev. 1104 (1979). ————Article Cite.

Kamenshine, The First Amendment's Implied Political Establishment
Clause, 67 Calif. L. Rev. 1104, 1110-13 (1979). ————Page Cite.

California Lawyer
Abbreviation: Cal. Law.

In law review footnotes, the titles of books and the names of cases are not underlined.

Examples: Mosk, <u>Judges Have First Amendment Rights</u>, 2 Cal. Law. 30 (1982).
——Article Cite.

Mosk, <u>Judges Have First Amendment Rights</u>, 2 Cal. Law. 30, 76
(1982). ——Page Cite.

California Legislative Service (West)

Abbreviation: year Cal. Legis. Serv. (West)

Examples: Act of Sept. 23, 1981, ch. 647, 1981 Cal. Legis. Serv. 2135 (West).

Act of Feb. 17, 1982, ch. 46, § 5, 1982 Cal. Legis. Serv. 235, 238-39
(West). ——Citation to a section of a session law.

Confidentiality of Medical Information Act, ch. 782, 1981 Cal. Legis.
Serv. 2707 (West) (to be codified at Cal. Civ. Code ¶¶ 56-56.37).
——Citation to a session law with a popular name.

Act of March 1, 1982, ch. 85, 1982 Cal. Legis. Serv. 397 (West) (to be
codified at Cal. Health & Safety Code ¶¶ 190-194). ——Citation to a
session law when that law will be or is codified, and the code location is
known.

California Reporter, West's

<u>See</u>   West's California Reporter

California Reports

Abbreviation: Cal.

Examples: <u>Brougher v. Board of Pub. Works</u>, 205 Cal. 426, 271 P. 487 (1928).
——Case Cite.

<u>Brougher v. Board of Pub. Works</u>, 205 Cal. 426, 437-38, 271 P. 487,
492 (1928). ——Page Cite.

California Reports, second series

Abbreviation: Cal. 2d

Examples: <u>Russian Hill Improvement Ass'n v. Board of Permit Appeals</u>, 66 Cal.
2d 34, 423 P.2d 824, 56 Cal. Rptr. 672 (1967). ——Case Cite.

<u>Russian Hill Improvement Ass'n v. Board of Permit Appeals</u>, 66 Cal.
2d 34, 46, 423 P.2d 824, 833, 56 Cal. Rptr. 672, 681 (1967). ——Page
Cite.

California Reports, third series

Abbreviation: Cal. 3d

Examples: <u>Seaman's Direct Buying Serivce, Inc. v. Standard Oil Co.</u>, 36 Cal. 3d
752, 686 P.2d 1158, 206 Cal. Rptr. 354 (1984). ——Case Cite.

<u>Seaman's Direct Buying Serivce, Inc. v. Standard Oil Co.</u>, 36 Cal. 3d
752, 755, 686 P.2d 1158, 1160, 206 Cal. Rptr. 354, 356 (1984).
——Page Cite.

In law review footnotes, the following are in large and small capitals: periodicals, constitutions,
codes, restatements, standards, authors of books, titles of books, and legislative materials except
for bills and resolutions. Refer to Bluebook.

California Session Laws
See   Statutes and Amendments to the Code of California

California State Bar Journal
Abbreviation: Cal. St. B.J.

Examples: Miller, The Offer of Proof: A Trial Lawyer's Trial, 55 Cal. St. B.J. 498 (1980). ——Article Cite.

Miller, The Offer of Proof: A Trial Lawyer's Trial, 55 Cal. St. B.J. 498, 500 (1980). ——Page Cite.

California Unreported Cases
Abbreviation: Cal. Unrep.

Examples: Ganahl v. Soher, 2 Cal. Unrep. 415, 5 P. 80 (1884). ——Case Cite.

Ganahl v. Soher, 2 Cal. Unrep. 415, 416, 5 P. 80, 80-81 (1884). ——Page Cite.

California Western International Law Journal
Abbreviation: Cal. W. Int'l L.J.

Examples: Siqueiros, The Juridical Regulation of Transnational Enterprises, 8 Cal. W. Int'l L.J. 1 (1978). ——Article Cite.

Siqueiros, The Juridical Regulation of Transnational Enterprises, 8 Cal. W. Int'l L.J. 1, 7-10 (1978). ——Page Cite.

California Western Law Review
Abbreviation: Cal. W.L. Rev.

Examples: Lasky, Psychiatry and California Workers' Compensation Laws: A Threat and a Challenge, 17 Cal. W.L. Rev. 1 (1980). ——Article Cite.

Lasky, Psychiatry and California Workers' Compensation Laws: A Threat and a Challenge, 17 Cal. W.L. Rev. 1, 3-13 (1980). ——Page Cite.

Callaghan & Co.
Abbreviation: (Callaghan)

Cambrian Law Review
Abbreviation: Cambrian L. Rev.

Examples: Teeven, Problems of Proof and Early English Contract Law, 15 Cambrian L. Rev. 73 (1984). ——Article Cite.

Teeven, Problems of Proof and Early English Contract Law, 15 Cambrian L. Rev. 73, 80-81 (1984). ——Page Cite.

Cambridge Law Journal
Abbreviation: Cambridge L.J.

In law review footnotes, the titles of books and the names of cases are not underlined.

Campbell Law Review
      Abbreviation: Campbell L. Rev.

Canada-United States Law Journal
      Abbreviation: Can.-U.S. L.J.

      Examples: Baxter, <u>Settling Our Canadian-United States Differences: An American Perspective</u>, 1 Can.-U.S. L.J. 5 (1978). ——Article Cite.

                         Baxter, <u>Settling Our Canadian-United States Differences: An American Perspective</u>, 1 Can.-U.S. L.J. 5, 10-11 (1978). ——Page Cite.

Canadian American Law Journal
      Abbreviation: Can.-Am. L.J.

      Examples: Massey, <u>Tidal Power Development: Environmental Decisionmaking in the United States</u>, 3 Can.-Am. L.J. 49 (1984). ——Article Cite.

                         Massey, <u>Tidal Power Development: Environmental Decisionmaking in the United States</u>, 3 Can.-Am. L.J. 49, 52-54 (1984). ——Page Cite.

Canadian Bar Review
      Abbreviation: Can. B. Rev.

Canadian Commercial Law Guide (Commerce Clearing House)
      Abbreviation: Can. Com. L. Guide (CCH)

Canadian Sales Tax Reporter (Commerce Clearing House)
      Abbreviation: Can. Sales Tax Rep. (CCH)

Canadian Tax Journal
      Abbreviation: Can. Tax J.

Canadian Tax Reporter (Commerce Clearing House)
      Abbreviation: Can. Tax. Rep. (CCH)

Canadian Yearbook of International Law
      Abbreviation: Can. Y.B. Int'l L.

Canal Zone Code
      Abbreviation: C.Z. Code tit.   , §   (year).

      Examples: C.Z. Code tit. 7, § 902 (1963).

                         C.Z. Code tit. 7, § 1954 (Supp. 1976).

Capital University Law Review
      Abbreviation: Cap. U.L. Rev.

In law review footnotes, the following are in large and small capitals: periodicals, constitutions, codes, restatements, standards, authors of books, titles of books, and legislative materials except for bills and resolutions. Refer to Bluebook.

Examples: Browne, <u>Civil Rule 10(B) and the Three Basic Rules of Form</u>
                   <u>Applicable to the Drafting of Documents Used in Civil Litigation</u>, 8
                   Cap. U.L. Rev. 199 (1978). ——Article Cite.

                   Browne, <u>Civil Rule 10(B) and the Three Basic Rules of Form</u>
                   <u>Applicable to the Drafting of Documents Used in Civil Litigation</u>, 8
                   Cap. U.L. Rev. 199, 203-08 (1978). ——Page Cite.

Cardozo Law Review
Abbreviation: Cardozo L. Rev.

Examples: Lamm & Kirschenbaum, <u>Freedom and Constraint in the Jewish Judicial</u>
                   <u>Process</u>, 1 Cardozo L. Rev. 99 (1979). ——Article Cite.

                   Lamm & Kirschenbaum, <u>Freedom and Constraint in the Jewish Judicial</u>
                   <u>Process</u>, 1 Cardozo L. Rev. 99, 100-05 (1979). ——Page Cite.

Case and Comment
Abbreviation: Case & Com.

Examples: Purver & Taylor, <u>The Criminal Appeal: Writing to Win</u>, 87 Case &
                   Com. 3 (1982). ——Article Cite.

                   Purver & Taylor, <u>The Criminal Appeal: Writing to Win</u>, 87 Case &
                   Com. 3, 6 (1982). ——Page Cite.

Case citations
——See Bluebook Rule 10.1(a) for samples of case citations in law reviews, briefs, and
legal memoranda. Sample citations are provided for each stage in the course of
litigation and alternative citations are provided when the product of a litigation
stage could be available in alternative sources (i.e. a final decision by a federal
district court which may be available in the Federal Supplement, in a service, in a
newspaper, or as a slip opinion).

case names
——In text: Give the last name of an individual and the full name of an institution,
political entity, or corporation without abbreviation except as provided in Bluebook
Rule 10.2.1.

——In citations: In addition to the rules for a case name in text, abbreviate according to
Rule 10.2.2.

——basic citation forms: See various title entries in this work. See also Bluebook Rules
10.1, 10.2, 10.6, 10.7, and 10.8.

——in law review footnotes: See the guidelines and illustrations on pages 35-52 of the
Bluebook.

Case Western Reserve Journal of International Law
Abbreviation: Case W. Res. J. Int'l L.

Examples: Margain, <u>Respect in Friendship</u>, 12 Case W. Res. J. Int'l L. 455
                   (1980). ——Article Cite.

In law review footnotes, the titles of books and the names of cases are not underlined.

Margain, Respect in Friendship, 12 Case W. Res. J. Int'l L. 455, 460-64 (1980). ——Page Cite.

Case Western Reserve Law Review

Abbreviation: Case W. Res. L. Rev.

Examples: Samansky, Taxation of Nonqualifying Property Distributed in Reorganizations, 31 Case W. Res. L. Rev. 1 (1980). ——Article Cite.

Samansky, Taxation of Nonqualifying Property Distributed in Reorganizations, 31 Case W. Res. L. Rev. 1, 5-9 (1980). ——Page Cite.

cases, basic citation forms

——See various title entries in this work. See Bluebook Rule 10.

cases, subsequent citation to

See subsequent citations to cases, statutes, and prior citations.

Casner, American Law of Property

See American Law of Property, by A. Casner

Casner on Estate Planning

See Estate Planning, by A. Casner

Catholic Lawyer

Abbreviation: Cath. Law.

Examples: Kenyon, A Model for Ecclesial Mediation at the Local Level, 29 Cath. Law. 93 (1984). ——Article Cite.

Kenyon, A Model for Ecclesial Mediation at the Local Level, 29 Cath. Law. 93, 100 (1984). ——Page Cite.

Catholic University Law Review

Abbreviation: Cath. U.L. Rev.

Examples: Note, The Uniform Guidelines on Employee Selection Procedures: Compromises and Controversies, 28 Cath. U.L. Rev. 605 (1979). ——Article Cite.

Note, The Uniform Guidelines on Employee Selection Procedures: Compromises and Controversies, 28 Cath. U.L. Rev. 605, 612-19 (1979). ——Page Cite.

Mogel & Mapes, Assessment of Incremental Pricing Under the Natural Gas Policy Act, 29 Cath. U.L. Rev. 763 (1980). ——Article Cite.

Mogel & Mapes, Assessment of Incremental Pricing Under the Natural Gas Policy Act, 29 Cath. U.L. Rev. 763, 769-74 (1980). ——Page Cite.

In law review footnotes, the following are in large and small capitals: periodicals, constitutions, codes, restatements, standards, authors of books, titles of books, and legislative materials except for bills and resolutions. Refer to Bluebook.

certiorari denied
>   Abbreviations: cert. denied

cert. denied
>   Example: Bernhard v. Harrah's Club, 16 Cal. 3d 313, 546 P.2d 719, 128 Cal.
>   Rptr. 215, cert. denied, 429 U.S. 859 (1976).

certiorari granted
>   Abbreviations: cert. granted

>   Example: Walker v. Armco Steel Corp., 592 F.2d 1133 (10th Cir. 1979), cert.
>   granted, No. 78-1862, 48 U.S.L.W. 3186 (Oct. 1, 1979).

Cf.
>   Example: "Moreover, the evidence of the prior acts was germane to establish an
>   element of the offense, i.e. criminal intent. Cf. Commonwealth v.
>   Bond, 261 Pa. Super. 311, 318, 396 A.2d 414, 417 (1978) (evidence of
>   extortion attempt in a trial for robbery was inadmissible, since 'intent
>   was not at issue' and the two offenses were entirely 'dissimilar
>   actions')." ——Taken from 445 A.2d 1255, 1258 (1982).

Chancellor
>   Abbreviation: C.

Chancery
>   Abbreviation: Ch.

Chancery Court
>   Abbreviations: Ch.

Chancery Division
>   Abbreviations: Ch.

chapter(s)
>   Abbreviation: ch., chs.

Charter of the United Nations
>   Abbreviation: U.N. Charter

>   Example: U.N. Charter art. 33, para. 1.

Chicago Bar Record
>   Abbreviation: Chicago B. Rec.

>   Examples: Schuman, The Corporate Client and the Attorney-Client Privilege, 66
>   Chicago B. Rec. 84 (1984). ——Article Cite.

In law review footnotes, the titles of books and the names of cases are not underlined.

Schuman, <u>The Corporate Client and the Attorney-Client Privilege</u>, 66 Chicago B. Rec. 84, 91-92 (1984). ——Page Cite.

Chicago-Kent Law Review
> Abbreviation: Chi.-Kent L. Rev.

> Examples: Livingston, <u>Open Space Preservation and Acquisition Along Illinois Waterways</u>, 56 Chi.-Kent L. Rev. 753 (1980). ——Article Cite.

> Livingston, <u>Open Space Preservation and Acquisition Along Illinois Waterways</u>, 56 Chi.-Kent L. Rev. 753, 761-67 (1980). ——Page Cite.

Chicano Law Review
> Abbreviation: Chicano L. Rev.

Chief Baron
> Abbreviation: C.B.

Chief Judge
> Abbreviation: C.J.

Chief Justice
> Abbreviation: C.J.

Children's Court
> Abbreviation: Child. Ct.

Children's Legal Rights Journal
> Abbreviation: Child. Legal Rts. J.

China Law Reporter (ABA Section of International Law)
> Abbreviation: China L. Rep.

> Examples: Gholz, <u>China's New Trademark Law</u>, 2 China L. Rep. 103 (1982). ——Article Cite.

> Gholz, <u>China's New Trademark Law</u>, 2 China L. Rep. 103, 109-110 (1982). ——Page Cite.

Chitty's Law Journal
> Abbreviation: Chitty's L.J.

Chommie on Federal Income Taxation
> <u>See</u>   Law of Federal Income Taxation, by J. Chommie

Cincinnati Bar Association Journal
> Abbreviation: Cincinnati B.A.J.

In law review footnotes, the following are in large and small capitals: periodicals, constitutions, codes, restatements, standards, authors of books, titles of books, and legislative materials except for bills and resolutions. Refer to Bluebook.

Circuit Court (old federal)
　　　Abbreviation:　　C.C.

Circuit Court (state)
　　　Abbreviation:　　Cir. Ct.

Circuit Court of Appeal (state)
　　　Abbreviation:　　Cir. Ct. App.

Circuit Court of Appeals (federal)
　　　See　　U.S. Court of Appeals...

cited in
　　　Example:　　　Unif. Probate Code §§ 2-102, 2-103 (1969), <u>cited in</u> Wellman, <u>The</u>
　　　　　　　　　　<u>Uniform Probate Code: A Possible Answer to Probate Avoidance</u>, 44
　　　　　　　　　　Ind. L.J. 191, 200 (1969).

City Court
　　　Abbreviation:　　[name city] City Ct.

Civil Aeronautics Board Reports (U.S.) (1940-date) (Vol. 1 by C.A.A.)
　　　Abbreviation:　　C.A.B.

　　　Examples:　　　<u>Pandair Freight Ltd., Foreign Indirect Permit</u>, 60 C.A.B. 205 (1972).

　　　　　　　　　　<u>Braniff Airways</u>, 1 C.A.B. 291 (1939). ——Citation to the first volume
　　　　　　　　　　of the series, published by the Civil Aeronautics Authority.

Civil Appeals
　　　Abbreviation:　　Civ. App.

Civil Court of Record
　　　Abbreviation:　　Civ. Ct. Rec.

Civil Procedure, by Fleming James, Jr. & Geoffrey C. Hazard, Jr.
　　　——Do not abbreviate the title.

　　　Examples:　　　F. James & G. Hazard, <u>Civil Procedure</u> § 3.21 (3d ed. 1985).

　　　　　　　　　　F. James & G. Hazard, <u>Civil Procedure</u> § 3.21, at 178 (ed ed. 1985).

Civil Rights Digest
　　　Abbreviation:　　Civ. Rts. Dig.

Claims Court Reporter
　　　Abbreviation:　　Cl. Ct.

In law review footnotes, the titles of books and the names of cases are not underlined.

——Cite to Federal Supplement if therein, otherwise cite to the Claims Court Reporter
as follows:

Example: Mobley v. United States, 8 Cl. Ct. 767 (1985).

clause(s)
    Abbreviation: cl., cls.

Clearinghouse Review
    Abbreviation: Clearinghouse Rev.

    Examples: Bloch, Obtaining a Remand in District Court When Claimant Was
                  Unrepresented at a Social Security Disability Hearing, 15 Clearinghouse
                  Rev. 28 (1981). ——Article Cite.

                  Bloch, Obtaining a Remand in District Court When Claimant Was
                  Unrepresented at A Scoial Security Disability Hearing, 15
                  Clearinghouse Rev. 28, 30-31 (1981). ——Page Cite.

Cleveland-Marshall Law Review
    Abbreviation: Clev.-Mar. L. Rev.

    Examples: Summers, Industrial Democracy: America's Unfulfilled Promise, 28
                  Clev.-Mar. L. Rev. 29 (1979). ——Article Cite.

                  Summers, Industrial Democracy: America's Unfulfilled Promise, 28
                  Clev.-Mar. L. Rev. 29, 48-49 (1979). ——Page Cite.

Cleveland State Law Review
    Abbreviation: Clev. St. L. Rev.

    Examples: Gard & Endress, The Impact of Pacifica Foundation on Two Traditions
                  of Freedom of Expression, 27 Clev. St. L. Rev. 465 (1978).
                  ——Article Cite.

                  Gard & Endress, The Impact of Pacifica Foundation on Two Traditions
                  of Freedom of Expression, 27 Clev. St. L. Rev. 465, 469-75 (1978).
                  ——Page Cite.

Close Corporations, by F. O'Neal & R. Thompson
    See   O'Neal's Close Corporations, by F. O'Neal & R. Thompson

Code of Alabama
    Abbreviation: Ala. Code §   (year).

    Examples: Ala. Code § 25-5-11 (1986).

                  Ala. Code § 8-26-3 (Supp. 1987).

Code of Colorado Regulations
    Abbreviation: Colo. Code Regs. § (year).

In law review footnotes, the following are in large and small capitals: periodicals, constitutions,
codes, restatements, standards, authors of books, titles of books, and legislative materials except
for bills and resolutions. Refer to Bluebook.

Code of Federal Regulations
    Abbreviation: C.F.R.

    Examples: Regulation D, 12 C.F.R. § 204 (1981). ——Citation to a regulation with a popular name.

                  3 C.F.R. § 803 (1969). ——For citing Federal Register, see the entry under Federal Register.

Code of Georgia Annotated (Harrison Co.)
    Abbreviation: Ga. Code Ann. §   (Harrison year).

    Examples: Ga. Code Ann. § 110-104 (Harrison 1973).

                  Ga. Code Ann. § 67-2001 (Harrison Supp. 1984).

Code of Georgia Annotated, Official (Michie Co.)
    <u>See</u>   Official Code of Georgia Annotated

Code of Iowa
    Abbreviation: Iowa Code §   (year).

    Example: Iowa Code § 633.273 (1979).

Code of Laws of South Carolina Annotated
    Abbreviation: S.C. Code Ann. §   (Law. Co-op. year).

    Examples: S.C. Code Ann. § 5-23-190 (Law. Co-op. 1977).

                  S.C. Code Ann. § 6-23-300 (Law. Co-op. Supp. 1987).

Code of Laws of South Carolina 1976 Annotated (Law Co-op.), Code of Regulations
    Abbreviation: S.C. Code Regs. (year).

    Examples: S.C. Code Regs. 61-70 (1982).

                  S.C. Code Regs. 61-78 (Supp. 1985).

Code of Maryland Regulations
    Abbreviation: Md. Regs. Code tit. , § (year).

Code of Massachusetts Regulations
    Abbreviation: Mass. Regs. Code tit. , § (year).

Code of Professional Responsibility A.B.A.
    <u>See</u>   American Bar Association Model Code of Professional Responsibility

Code of Professional Responsibility Annotated (A.B.F.)
    <u>See</u>   American Bar Foundation Code of Professional Responsibility Annotated

---

In law review footnotes, the titles of books and the names of cases are not underlined.

Code of Virginia Annotated
  Abbreviation: Va. Code Ann. § (year).

  Examples: Va. Code Ann. § 9-16 (1985).

       Va. Code Ann. § 9-99.3 (Supp. 1987).

codified statutes
  Abbreviation: cod. st.

Collections of Decisions of the European Commission of Human Rights
  Abbreviation: Eur. Comm'n H.R.

  Example: <u>Unterpertinger v. Austria</u>, 33 Eur. Comm'n H.R. 80 (1983). ——Case
       Cite.

Collier Bankruptcy Cases, Second Series (Matthew Bender)
  Abbreviation: Collier Bankr. Cas. 2d (MB)

Collier on Bankruptcy
  ——Do not abbreviate the title.

  Examples: 5 <u>Collier on Bankruptcy</u> ¶ 1109.01 (L. King 15th ed. 1987).

       5 <u>Collier on Bankruptcy</u> ¶ 1109.01, at 1109-7 to 1109-9 (L. King 15th
       ed. 1987).

Colorado
  Abbreviation: Colo.

Colorado Bar Association
  Abbreviation: Colo. B.A.

Colorado Code of Regulations
  <u>See</u> Code of Colorado Regulations

Colorado Constitution
  Abbreviation: Colo. Const. art. , § .

  Examples: Colo. Const. art. II, § 7. ——Cite provisions without date unless the
       cited provisions have been repealed or amended (Bluebook Rule 11).

       Colo. Const. art. V, § 37 (1876, repealed 1974). ——Cite provisions
       which have been repealed or amended by giving the date of the adoption
       of the particular provision and the date of repeal or amendment
       (Bluebook Rule 11).

Colorado Court of Appeals Reports
  Abbreviation: Colo. App.

  ——Discontinued after 44 Colo. App. 561 (1980). Thereafter cite only to P.2d.

In law review footnotes, the following are in large and small capitals: periodicals, constitutions,
codes, restatements, standards, authors of books, titles of books, and legislative materials except
for bills and resolutions. Refer to Bluebook.

Examples: <u>Alley v. Kal</u>, 44 Colo. App. 561, 610 P.2d 191 (1980). ——Case Cite.

<u>Alley v. Kal</u>, 44 Colo. App. 561, 564, 610 P.2d 191, 193 (1980). ——Page Cite.

——After 44 Colo. App. 561 (1980), cite as follows:

<u>Zertuche v. Montgomery Ward & Co.</u>, 706 P.2d 424 (Colo. Ct. App. 1985). ——Case Cite.

<u>Zertuche v. Montgomery Ward & Co.</u>, 706 P.2d 424, 425-26 (Colo. Ct. App. 1985). ——Page Cite.

Colorado Lawyer
Abbreviation: Colo. Law.

Examples: Tomlinson, <u>The Labor Peace Act: Colorado Now Is a Modified Right-to-Work State</u>, 7 Colo. Law. 1124 (1978). ——Article Cite.

Tomlinson, <u>The Labor Peace Act: Colorado Now Is a Modified Right-to-Work State</u>, 7 Colo. Law. 1124, 1130 (1978). ——Page Cite.

Colorado Register
Abbreviation: Colo. Reg.

Colorado Reports
Abbreviation: Colo.

——Discontinued after 200 Colo. 549 (1980). Thereafter cite only to P.2d.

Examples: <u>Mishek v. Stanton</u>, 200 Colo. 514, 616 P.2d 135 (1980). ——Case Cite.

<u>Mishek v. Stanton</u>, 200 Colo. 514, 514-15, 616 P.2d 135, 135-36 (1980). ——Page Cite.

——After 200 Colo. 549 (1980), cite as follows:

<u>People v. Bertine</u>, 706 P.2d 411 (Colo. 1985). ——Case Cite.

<u>People v. Bertine</u>, 706 P.2d 411, 412-13 (Colo. 1985). ——Page Cite.

Colorado Revised Statutes
Abbreviation: Colo. Rev. Stat. §   (year).

Examples: Colo. Rev. Stat. § 37-26-117 (1974).

Colo. Rev. Stat. § 37-45-122 (Supp. 1985).

Colorado Session Laws
<u>See</u> Session Laws of Colorado

Columbia Business Law Review
Abbreviation: Colum. Bus. Law Rev.

In law review footnotes, the titles of books and the names of cases are not underlined.

Examples: Preston, <u>Extrinsic Evidence in Federal Trade Commission Deceptiveness Cases</u>, 1987 Colum. Bus. Law Rev. 633. ——Article Cite.

Preston, <u>Extrinsic Evidence in Federal Trade Commission Deceptiveness Cases</u>, 1987 Colum. Bus. Law Rev. 633, 635. ——Page Cite.

Columbia Human Rights Law Review
Abbreviation: Colum. Hum. Rts. L. Rev.

Examples: Leaf, <u>Legalizing the Illegals: A Case for Amnesty</u>, 12 Colum. Hum. Rts. L. Rev. 65 (1980). ——Article Cite.

Leaf, <u>Legalizing the Illegals: A Case for Amnesty</u>, 12 Colum. Hum. Rts. L. Rev. 65, 75-76 (1980). ——Page Cite.

Columbia Journal of Environmental Law
Abbreviation: Colum. J. Envtl. L.

Examples: Ostrov, <u>Interboundary Stationary Source Pollution—Clean Air Act Section 126 and Beyond</u>, 8 Colum. J. Envtl. L. 37 (1982). ——Article Cite.

Ostrov, <u>Interboundary Stationary Source Pollution—Clean Air Act Section 126 and Beyond</u>, 8 Colum. J. Envtl. L. 37, 64-65 (1982). ——Page Cite.

Columbia Journal of International Affairs
Abbreviation: Colum. J. Int'l Aff.

Columbia Journal of Law and Social Problems
Abbreviation: Colum. J.L. & Soc. Probs.

Examples: Adler, <u>The Impact of FOIA on Scientific Research Grantees</u>, 17 Colum. J.L. & Soc. Probs. 1 (1981). ——Article Cite.

Adler, <u>The Impact of FOIA on Scientific Research Grantees</u>, 17 Colum. J.L. & Soc. Probs. 1, 33-35 (1981). ——Page Cite.

Columbia Journal of Law and the Arts
Abbreviation: Colum. J.L. & Arts

Columbia Journal of Transnational Law
Abbreviation: Colum. J. Transnat'l L.

Examples: Hellawell, <u>CHOOSE: A Computer Program for Legal Planning and Analysis</u>, 19 Colum. J. Transnat'l L. 339 (1981). ——Article Cite.

Hellawell, <u>CHOOSE: A Computer Program for Legal Planning and Analysis</u>, 19 Colum. J. Transnat'l L. 339, 340-45 (1981). ——Page Cite.

In law review footnotes, the following are in large and small capitals: periodicals, constitutions, codes, restatements, standards, authors of books, titles of books, and legislative materials except for bills and resolutions. Refer to Bluebook.

Columbia Law Review
>   Abbreviation: Colum. L. Rev.
>
>   Examples: Sive, <u>Some Thoughts of an Environmental Lawyer in the Wilderness of</u>
>   <u>Administrative Law</u>, 70 Colum. L. Rev. 612 (1970). ——Article Cite.
>
>   Sive, <u>Some Thoughts of an Environmental Lawyer in the Wilderness of</u>
>   <u>Administrative Law</u>, 70 Colum. L. Rev. 612, 614-19 (1970). ——Page
>   Cite.

Columbia Survey of Human Rights Law
>   Abbreviation: Colum. Surv. Hum. Rts. L.
>
>   Examples: Silard, <u>Invalid Disruption Rules for CO Alternative Service</u>, 3 Colum.
>   Surv. Hum. Rts. L. 136 (1971). ——Article Cite.
>
>   Silard, <u>Invalid Disruption rules for CO Alternative Service</u>, 3 Colum.
>   Suv. Hum. Rts. L. 136, 141 (1971). ——Page Cite.

Columbia-VLA Journal of Law and the Arts
>   Abbreviation: Colum.-VLA J.L. & Arts
>
>   Examples: Feldman, <u>Commodities and Art: A Delicate Relationship</u>, 10 Colum.-
>   VLA J.L. & Arts 197 (1986). ——Article Cite.
>
>   Feldman, <u>Commodities and Art: A Delicate Relationship</u>, 10 Colum.-
>   VLA J.L. & Arts 197, 198 (1986). ——Page Cite.

Commentaries, by W. Blackstone
>   Example: W. Blackstone, <u>Commentaries</u> *35. ——The asterisk denotes the page
>   number in the original edition.

Commerce Clearing House, Inc.
>   Abbreviation: CCH

Commerce Court
>   Abbreviation: Comm. Ct.

Commercial Law Journal
>   Abbreviation: Com. L.J.
>
>   Examples: Levit & Mason, <u>Where Do We Go from Here? Bankruptcy</u>
>   <u>Administration Post-Marathon</u>, 87 Com. L.J. 353 (1982). ——Article
>   Cite.
>
>   Levit & Mason, <u>Where Do We Go from Here? Bankruptcy</u>
>   <u>Administration Post-Marathon</u>, 87 Com. L.J. 353, 356-57 (1982).
>   ——Page Cite.

Commissioner's Decisions, U.S. Patent Office
>   <u>See</u>   Patents, Decisions of the Commissioner and of U.S. Courts (1869-date)

In law review footnotes, the titles of books and the names of cases are not underlined.

Committee prints, Congressional
    See   Congressional Committee prints

Commodity Futures Law Reporter (Commerce Clearing House)
    Abbreviation: Comm. Fut. L. Rep. (CCH)

    Examples: First Commodity Corp. v. Commodity Futures Trading Comm'n, 2 Comm. Fut. L. Rep. (CCH) ¶ 21,368 (lst Cir. Mar. 25, 1982). ——Citation to looseleaf material.

    Ames v. Merrill Lynch, Pierce, Fenner & Smith, Inc., [1975-1977 Decisions Transfer Binder] Comm. Fut. L. Rep. (CCH) ¶ 20,283 (S.D.N.Y. 1977). ——Citation to transfer binder.

    Stephen D. Flaxman, 2 Comm. Fut. L. Rep. (CCH) ¶ 21,364 (Comm. Fut. Trading Comm'n Feb. 22, 1982). ——Citation to looseleaf administrative material.

    Hohenberg Bros. [1975-1977 Decisions Transfer Binder] Comm. Fut. L. Rep. (CCH) ¶ 20,271 (Comm. Fut. Trading Comm'n 1977). ——Citation to transfer binder.

——The above examples are proper if the case is not yet available in an official or West reporter, or is not reported in an official or West reporter.

Common Market Law Review
    Abbreviation: Common Mkt. L. Rev.

    Examples: Louis, Free Movement of Capital in the Community: The Casati Judgment, 19 Common Mkt. L. Rev. 443 (1982). ——Article Cite.

    Louis, Free Movement of Capital in the Community: The Casati Judgment, 19 Common Mkt. L. Rev. 443, 448-49 (1982). ——Page Cite.

Common Market Reports (Commerce Clearing House)
    (Formerly Reporter)

    Abbreviation: Common Mkt. Rep. (CCH)

    Examples: Pharmon BV v. Hoeschst AG, 4 Common Mkt. Rep. (CCH) ¶ 14,206 (Jul. 9, 1985). ——Citation to looseleaf materials.

    Regina v. Kirk, [1983-1985 Transfer Binder] Common Mkt. Rep. (CCH) ¶ 14,070 (1984). ——Citation to transfer binder.

Common Pleas
    Abbreviation: C.P.

Common Pleas Division, English Law Reports
    Abbreviation: C.P.D.

In law review footnotes, the following are in large and small capitals: periodicals, constitutions, codes, restatements, standards, authors of books, titles of books, and legislative materials except for bills and resolutions. Refer to Bluebook.

Commonwealth
    Abbreviation: Commw.

Commonwealth Court
    Abbreviation: Commw. Ct.

Communication[s]
    Abbreviation: Comm.

Comparative Juridical Review
    Abbreviation: Comp. Jurid. Rev.

Comparative Labor Law
    Abbreviation: Comp. Lab. L.

    Examples: Jakhelln, <u>New Form of Atypical Employment Relationships in Norway</u>,
                       7 Comp. Lab. L. 343 (1986). ——Article Cite.

                       Jakhelln, <u>New Forms of Atypical Employment Relationships in
                       Norway</u>, 7 Comp. Lab. L. 343, 346 (1986). ——Page Cite.

compare
    Abbreviation: cf.

    Example: "[N]itrofurantoin, is not generally recognized among qualified experts
                       as safe and effective and is therefore a 'new drug.' <u>Compare</u> <u>Generix</u>,
                       654 F.2d at 1115-20 (the term 'new drug' as used in 21 U.S.C. § 321(p)
                       applies only to the active ingredients of a drug product), <u>with</u> <u>Premo I</u>,
                       629 F.2d at 80l (a drug product is a 'new drug' unless generally
                       recognized among qualified experts as safe and effective)... ."
                       ——Taken from 675 F.2d 994, 1002 (1982).

compilation
    Abbreviation: comp.

compiled
    Abbreviation: comp.

compiled statutes
    Abbreviations: comp. stat.
                       c.s.

Complete Manual of Criminal Forms, by F. Bailey & H. Rothblatt
    ——Do not abbreviate the title.

    Examples: 2 F. Bailey & H. Rothblatt, <u>Complete Manual of Criminal Forms Form</u>
                       47:31 (2d ed. 1974).

In law review footnotes, the titles of books and the names of cases are not underlined.

2 F. Bailey & H. Rothblatt, <u>Complete Manual of Criminal Forms Form</u> 47:31, at 268 (2d ed. 1974).

Comptroller General
Abbreviation: Comp. Gen.

Comptroller General's Opinion (U.S. Treasury Department)
Abbreviations: Comp. Gen. Op.

Comptroller Treasury Decisions (U.S.)
Abbreviation: Comp. Treas. Dec.

Computer/Law Journal
Abbreviation: Computer L.J.

Examples: Davidson, <u>Project Controls in Computer Contracting</u>, 4 Computer L.J. 133 (1983). ——Article Cite.

Davidson, <u>Project Controls in Computer Contracting</u>, 4 Computer L.J. 133, 141 (1983). ——Page Cite.

Computers and Law
Abbreviation: Computers & L.

Conditional Sale—Chattel Mortgage Reporter (Commerce Clearing House)
Abbreviation: Condit. Sale—Chat. Mort. Rep. (CCH)

Conference on Charitable Foundations Proceedings, New York University
Abbreviation: N.Y.U. Conf. on Char. Found. Proc.

Examples: Kennedy, <u>Financial Problems of Foundations Today</u>, 12 N.Y.U. Conf. on Char. Found. Proc. 15 (1975). ——Article Cite.

Kennedy, <u>Financial Problems of Foundations Today</u>, 12 N.Y.U. Conf. on Char. Found. Proc. 15, 22-23 (1975). ——Page Cite.

Congress
Abbreviation: Cong.

Congressional
Abbreviations: Cong.
                  Cong'l

Congressional Bills
——pre-enactment and post enactment when used to document legislative history

Senate:

Abbreviation: S.

In law review footnotes, the following are in large and small capitals: periodicals, constitutions, codes, restatements, standards, authors of books, titles of books, and legislative materials except for bills and resolutions. Refer to Bluebook.

Examples: S. 70, 95th Cong., 1st Sess. (1977).

                 S. 70, 95th Cong., 1st Sess. § 101 (1977). ——Citation to a section of
                 a bill.

                 S. 70, 95th Cong., 1st Sess., 123 Cong. Rec. 611-16 (1977).
                 ——Citation if the bill is printed in the Congressional Record.

House of Representatives:

Abbreviation: H.R.

Examples: H.R. 6168, 93d Cong., 1st Sess. (1973).

                 H.R. 6168, 93d Cong., 1st Sess. § 2 (1973).

                 H.R. 6168, 93d Cong., 1st Sess., 119 Cong. Rec. 12535-36 (1973).
                 ——Citation if the bill is printed in the Congressional Record.

Congressional Committee Prints
Abbreviation: Comm. Print

Examples: Subcommittee on Constitutional Rights of the Senate Judiciary Comm.,
                 98th Cong., 2d Sess., Federal Civil Rights Laws: A Sourcebook 25
                 (Comm. Print 1984).

                 Staff of the Securities Exchange Comm'n Div. of Corporate Finance,
                 96th Cong., 2d Sess., Report of Corporate Accountability B12 (Comm.
                 Print 1980).

Congressional Debates
Examples: 126 Cong. Rec. H2061 (daily ed. Mar. 24, 1980) (remark of Rep.
                 Duncan). ——Unbound.

                 122 Cong. Rec. 5447-48 (1976). ——Bound.

Congressional Documents
House Document

Abbreviation: H.R. Doc.

Examples: H.R. Doc. No. 182, 99th Cong., 2d Sess. 1 (1986).

                 National Commission on Water Quality, Final Report of the National
                 Commission on Water Quality, H.R. Doc. No. 418, 94th Cong., 2d
                 Sess. 5 (1976). ——Citation if the title and author are to be given.

——Give parallel citation to the permanent edition of United States Code and
   Administrative News. See Bluebook Rule 13.4(a).

Senate Document

Abbreviation: S. Doc.

Examples: S. Doc. No. 22, 99th Cong., 2d Sess. 1 (1986).

In law review footnotes, the titles of books and the names of cases are not underlined.

Congressional Research Service, Library of Congress, <u>United States and Soviet City Defense—Considerations for Congress</u>, S. Doc. No. 268, 94th Cong., 2d Sess. 1 (1976). ——Citation if the title and author are to be given.

——Give parallel citation to the permanent edition of United States Code and Administrative News. See Bluebook Rule 13.4(a).

Congressional Hearings
    ——Use full title.

Examples: <u>Insider Trading Sanctions and SEC Enforcement Legislation: Hearing on H.R. 559 Before the Subcomm. on Telecommunications, Consumer Protection, and Finance of the House Comm. on Energy and Commerce</u>, 98th Cong., 1st Sess. 13 (1983) (statement of John S. R. Shad, Chairman, SEC).

    <u>Elderly Catastrophic Health Care Insurance Proposals: Hearing Before the Subcomm. on Economic Goals and Intergovernmental Policy of the Joint Economic Comm.</u>, 98th Cong., 2d Sess. 9 (1984) (statement of Karen Davis, Johns Hopkins University).

Congressional Index (Commerce Clearing House)
    Abbreviation: Cong. Index (CCH)

Congressional Record (U.S.)
    Abbreviation: Cong. Rec.

Examples: 95 Cong. Rec. 7441 (1949).

    Debate:130 Cong. Rec. H7758 (daily ed. July 25, 1984) (statement of Rep. Dingell)

    Statement:130 Cong. Rec. S8955 (daily ed. June 29, 1984) (statement of Sen. Cranston)

Congressional Reports
    House of Representatives Reports:

    Abbreviation: H.R. Rep.

    Examples: H.R. Rep. No. 355, 98th Cong., 1st Sess. 6 (1983).

    H.R. Rep. No. 355, 98th Cong., 1st Sess. 6, <u>reprinted in</u> 1984 U.S. Code Cong. & Ad. News 2274, 2279. ——Citation when a parallel citation to the permanent edition of United States Code Congressional and Administrative News exists.

    Senate Reports:

    Abbreviation: S. Rep.

    Examples: S. Rep. No. 368, 96th Cong., 1st Sess. 4-5 (1980).

In law review footnotes, the following are in large and small capitals: periodicals, constitutions, codes, restatements, standards, authors of books, titles of books, and legislative materials except for bills and resolutions. Refer to Bluebook.

S. Rep. No. 368, 96th Cong., 1st Sess. 4-5, <u>reprinted in</u> 1980 U.S. Code Cong. & Ad. News 236, 239-41. ——Citation when a parallel citation to United States Code Congressional and Administrative News exists.

Congressional Resolutions
House of Representatives:

Abbreviation: H.R. Res.

Examples: H.R. Res. 419, 99th Cong., 2d Sess., (1986). ——Unenacted.

H.R. Res. 269, 94th Cong., 1st Sess., 121 Cong. Rec. 4878 (1975). ——When this unenacted resolution is printed in the Congressional Record.

H.R. Res. 1121, 92d Cong., 2d Sess., 118 Cong. Rec. 32,133 (1972). ——When the resolution has been enacted.

House of Representatives Concurrent:

Abbreviation: H.R. Con. Res.

Examples: H.R. Con. Res. 147, 94th Cong., 1st Sess. (1975). ——Unenacted.

H.R. Con. Res. 388, 95th Cong., 1st Sess., 123 Cong. Rec. 35,965 (1977). ——When this unenacted resolution is printed in the Congressional Record.

H.R. Con. Res. 182, 91 Stat. 1690 (1977). ——When the resolution has been enacted and appears in Statutes at Large (if it has yet to appear, cite to the Congressional Record).

House of Representatives Joint Resolutions:

Abbreviation: H.R.J. Res.

Examples: H.R.J. Res. 234, 99th Cong., 2d Sess. (1986). ——Unenacted.

H.R.J. Res. 863, 94th Cong., 1st Sess., 121 Cong. Rec. 36,277 (1975). ——When a printing of the unenacted resolution can be found in the Congressional Record.

——Cite enacted Joint Resolutions as statutes except when used to document legislative history or when the enacted resolution did not become a statute when enacted. To document legislative history, use the format for unenacted joint resolutions. For joint resolutions which did not become statutes when enacted, cite to Statutes at Large if it has appeared in the Statutes at Large, or to the Congressional Record if it has not. ——See Bluebook Rule 13.2.

H.R.J. Res. 208, 92d Cong., 2d Sess., 86 Stat. 1523 (1972). ——Citation for a joint resolution that did not become a statute when enacted.

Senate Resolutions:

Abbreviation: S. Res.

Examples: S. Res. 89, 95th Cong., 1st Sess. (1977). ——Unenacted.

In law review footnotes, the titles of books and the names of cases are not underlined.

S. Res. 258, 95th Cong., 1st Sess., 123 Cong. Rec. 28,286-88 (1977).
——When a printing of the unenacted resolution can be found in the
Congressional Record.

S. Res. 372, 92d Cong., 2d Sess., 118 Cong. Rec. 33,996 (1972).
——When the resolution has been enacted.

Senate Concurrent Resolutions:

Abbreviation: S. Con. Res.

Examples: S. Con. Res. 11, 95th Cong., 1st Sess. (1977). ——Unenacted.

S. Con. Res. 47, 95th Cong., 1st Sess., 123 Cong. Rec. 31,900 (1977).
——When a printing of the unenacted resolution can be found in the
Congressional Record and has yet to appear in Statutes at Large.

S. Con. Res. 12, 91 Stat. 1667 (1977). ——When the resolution has
been enacted and appears in Statutes at Large.

Senate Joint Resolutions:

Abbreviation: S.J. Res.

Examples: S.J. Res. 252, 93d Cong., 2d Sess. (1974). ——Unenacted.

S.J. Res. 41, 93d Cong., 2d Sess., 120 Cong. Rec. 39,987 (1971).
——When a printing of the unenacted resolution can be found in the
Congressional Record.

——Cite enacted Joint Resolutions as statutes except when used to document legislative
history or when the enacted resolution did not become a statute when enacted. To
document legislative history, use the format for unenacted joint resolutions. For
joint resolutions which did not become statutes when enacted, cite to Statutes at
Large if it has appeared in the Statutes at Large, or to the Congressional Record if it
has not. ——See Bluebook Rule 13.2.

S.J. Res. 7, 92d Cong., 1st Sess., 85 Stat. 823 (1971). ——Citation for
a joint resolution that did not become a statute when enacted.

Connecticut
Abbreviation: Conn.

Connecticut Appellate Reports
Abbreviation: Conn. App.

Examples: Zuch v. Connecticut Bank & Trust Co., 5 Conn. App. 457, 500 A.2d
565 (1985). ——Case Cite.

Zuch v. Connecticut Bank & Trust Co., 5 Conn. App. 457, 461, 500
A.2d 565, 567 (1985). ——Page Cite.

Connecticut Bar Journal
Abbreviation: Conn. B.J.

Examples: Barrante, State Protection of Freedom of Speech: Cologne v. Westfarms
Associates, 56 Conn. B.J. 305 (1982). ——Article Cite.

In law review footnotes, the following are in large and small capitals: periodicals, constitutions,
codes, restatements, standards, authors of books, titles of books, and legislative materials except
for bills and resolutions. Refer to Bluebook.

Barrante, <u>State Protection of Freedom of Speech: Cologne v. Westfarms</u>
<u>Associates</u>, 56 Conn. B.J. 305, 312-13 (1982). ——Page Cite.

Connecticut Circuit Court Reports
Abbreviation: Conn. Cir. Ct.

——Discontinued after 6 Conn. Cir. Ct. 751 (1974). Thereafter cite only to A.2d.

Examples: <u>LeClair v. Woodward</u>, 6 Conn. Cir. Ct. 727, 316 A.2d 791 (1970).
——Case Cite.

<u>LeClair v. Woodward</u>, 6 Conn. Cir. Ct. 727, 729, 316 A.2d 791, 792
(1970). ——Page Cite.

Connecticut Constitution
Abbreviation: Conn. Const. art.   , §   .

Examples: Conn. Const. art. IV, § 15. ——Cite provisions without date unless the
cited provisions have been repealed or amended (Bluebook Rule 11).

Conn. Const. art. XIII, § 9 (1965, repealed 1980). ——Cite provisions
which have been repealed or amended by giving the date of the adoption
of the particular provision and the date of repeal or amendment
(Bluebook Rule 11).

Conn. Const. of 1818, art. VI, § 8. ——Cite constitutions that have
been totally superseded by year of adoption, giving parenthetically the
year of adoption of the specific provision cited if different (Bluebook
Rule 11).

Connecticut General Statutes
<u>See</u>   General Statutes of Connecticut, The

Connecticut General Statutes Annotated
Abbreviation: Conn. Gen. Stat. Ann. §   (West year).

Examples: Conn. Gen. Stat. Ann. § 17-2-101 (West 1986).

Conn. Gen. Stat. Ann. § 42a-9-317 (West Supp. 1988).

Connecticut Law Journal
Abbreviation: Conn. L.J.

Connecticut Law Review
Abbreviation: Conn. L. Rev.

Examples: Satter, <u>Changing Roles of Courts and Legislatures</u>, 11 Conn. L. Rev.
230 (1979). ——Article Cite.

Satter, <u>Changing Roles of Courts and Legislatures</u>, 11 Conn. L. Rev.
230, 243-44 (1979). ——Page Cite.

In law review footnotes, the titles of books and the names of cases are not underlined.

Connecticut Legislative Service
  Abbreviation: year Conn. Legis. Serv.   (West).

Connecticut Public Acts
  Abbreviation: year Conn. Pub. Acts

Connecticut Public and Special Acts
  Abbreviation: year Conn. Acts   (Reg. [Spec.] Sess.)

Connecticut Regulations of State Agencies
  See   Regulations of Connecticut State Agencies

Connecticut Reports
  Abbreviation: Conn.

  Examples: Pellegrino v. O'Neill, 193 Conn. 670, 480 A.2d 476 (1984). ——Case
  Cite.

  Pellegrino v. O'Neill, 193 Conn. 670, 673, 480 A.2d 476, 478 (1984).
  ——Page Cite.

Connecticut Special Acts
  Abbreviation: year Conn. Spec. Acts

Connecticut Supplement
  Abbreviation: Conn. Supp.

  Examples: DeForest Indus., Inc. v. Gaetano, 38 Conn. Supp. 703, 461 A.2d 452
  (Super. Ct. 1983). ——Case Cite.

  DeForest Indus., Inc. v. Gaetano, 38 Conn. Supp. 703, 706-07, 461
  A.2d 452, 454-55 (Super. Ct. 1983). ——Page Cite.

Consolidated Treaty Series (a.k.a. Parry's Consolidated Treaty Series)
  Abbreviation: Parry's T.S.

  Examples: Exchange of Declarations for the Provisional Regulation of Commercial
  Relations, Nov. 5, 1876, France—Roumania, 151 Parry's T.S. 121.

constitution
  Abbreviation: const.

Constitution of the United States
  See   United States Constitution

constitutional
  Abbreviation: const.

In law review footnotes, the following are in large and small capitals: periodicals, constitutions, codes, restatements, standards, authors of books, titles of books, and legislative materials except for bills and resolutions. Refer to Bluebook.

Constitutional Commentary

Abbreviation: Const. Commentary

Examples: Jacobsohn, E.T.: The Extra-Textual in Constitutional Interpretation,
                  1984 Const. Commentary 21. ——Article Cite.

                  Jacobsohn, E.T.: The Extra-Textual in Constitutional Interpretation,
                  1984 Const. Commentary 21, 30-32. ——Page Cite.

construed in

Example: Congressional Budget and Impoundment Control Act § 402, 31 U.S.C.
                  § 1352 (1974), construed in Muskie, Sunset Legislation: Restoring
                  Public Confidence in Government, 4 J. Legis. 11, 13 (1977).

Consumer Credit Guide (Commerce Clearing House)

Abbreviation: Consumer Cred. Guide (CCH)

Examples: Department of Fin. Insts. v. Beneficial Fin. Co., 5 Consumer Cred.
                  Guide (CCH) ¶ 97,022 (Ind. Ct. App. Oct. 14, 1981). ——Citation to
                  looseleaf material.

                  Equifax Services, Inc. v. Cohen, [1974-1980 Decisions Transfer Binder]
                  Consumer Cred. Guide (CCH) ¶ 97,369 (Me. 1980). ——Citation to
                  transfer binder.

——The above examples are proper if the case is not yet available in an official or West
   reporter, or is not reported in an official or West reporter.

Consumer Product Safety Guide (Commerce Clearing House)

Abbreviation: Consumer Prod. Safety Guide (CCH)

Examples: Center for Auto Safety v. Lewis, 3 Consumer Prod. Safety Guide
                  (CCH) ¶ 75,280 (D.D.C. Oct. 21, 1981). ——Citation to looseleaf
                  material.

                  United States v. Salem Carpet Mills, Inc., [1977-1979 Developments
                  Transfer Binder] Consumer Prod. Safety Guide (CCH) ¶ 75,212 (N.D.
                  Ga. 1978). ——Citation to transfer binder.

——The above examples are proper if the case is not yet available in an official or West
   reporter, or is not reported in an official or West reporter.

contra

Examples: "State v. Duplechain, 52 La. Ann. 448, 26 So. 1000 (1899) (that the
                  conviction had been set aside, and the case nolle prossed, allowed); and
                  see the intimations in cases cited supra § 980. Contra: Commonwealth
                  v. Hayes, 253 Mass. 541, 149 N.E. 417 (1925) (after cross-
                  examination to an arrest, the witness on reexamination was not allowed
                  to tell that the judge had discharged him; a singular ruling." ——Taken
                  from 4 Wigmore on Evidence, § 1117, at 250 n.6 (rev. ed. 1972).

——The above examples are used mainly in footnotes of treatises or law reviews.

In law review footnotes, the titles of books and the names of cases are not underlined.

Contracts and Conveyances of Real Property, by M. Freidman
——Do not abbreviate the title.

Examples: M. Freidman, Contracts and Conveyances of Real Property § 1.2(j) (4th ed. 1984).

Conveyancer and Property Lawyer
Abbreviation: Conv. & Prop. Law. (n.s.)
Conv. (publisher's abbreviation)

Examples: Aughterson, Enforcement of Positive Burdens, 1985 Conv. & Prop. Law. (n.s.) 12. ——Article Cite.

Aughterson, Enforcement of Positive Burdens, 1985 Conv. & Prop. Law. (n.s.) 12, 15-16. ——Page Cite.

Cooley Law Review
Abbreviation: Cooley L. Rev.

Examples: McGee, Financial Accounting for Computer Software, 3 Cooley L. Rev. 97 (1985). ——Article Cite.

McGee, Financial Accounting for Computer Software, 3 Cooley L. Rev. 97, 108-10 (1985). ——Page Cite.

Cooper's Tennessee Chancery Reports
Abbreviation: Coop. Tenn. Ch.

Copyright Decisions (1909-date) (U.S.)
Abbreviation: Copy. Dec.

Example: Jackson v. Stone and Simon Advertising, Inc., 40 Copy. Dec. 693 (E.D. Mich. 1974)

Copyright Law Reporter (Commerce Clearing House)
Abbreviation: Copyright L. Rep. (CCH)

Examples: Grosset and Dunlap, Inc. v. Gulf and Western Corp., 2 Copyright L. Rep. (CCH) (Copyright L. Dec.) ¶ 25,374 (S.D.N.Y. Mar. 17, 1982). ——Citation to looseleaf material.

Pillsbury Co. v. Milky Way Productions, 1978-1981 Copyright L. Dec. (CCH) ¶ 25,l39 (N.D. Ga. 1978). ——Citation to bound material.

——The above examples are proper if the case is not yet available in an official or West reporter, or is not reported in an official or West reporter.

Copyright Law Symposium (ASCAP)
Abbreviation: Copyright L. Symp. (ASCAP)

Examples: Pierce, Copyright Protection for Computer Programs, 30 Copyright L. Symp. (ASCAP) 1 (1983). ——Article Cite.

In law review footnotes, the following are in large and small capitals: periodicals, constitutions, codes, restatements, standards, authors of books, titles of books, and legislative materials except for bills and resolutions. Refer to Bluebook.

Pierce, <u>Copyright Protection for Computer Programs</u>, 30 Copyright L. Symp. (ASCAP) 1, 23-25 (1983). ——Page Cite.

Corbin on Contracts
>——Do not abbreviate the title.

Examples: 5A A. Corbin, <u>Corbin on Contracts</u> § 1157 (1964).

5A A. Corbin, <u>Corbin on Contracts</u> § 1157, at 181 (1964).

5 A. Corbin, <u>Corbin on Contracts</u> § 1113 (1964 & Supp. 1984). ——Cite for pocket part to volume 4.

Cornell International Law Journal
Abbreviation: Cornell Int'l L.J.

Examples: Georges, <u>The Foreign Corrupt Practices Act Review Procedure: A Quest for Clarity</u>, 14 Cornell Int'l L.J. 57 (1981). ——Article Cite.

Georges, <u>The Foreign Corrupt Practices Act Review Procedure: A Quest for Clarity</u>, 14 Cornell Int'l L.J. 57, 59-64 (1981). ——Page Cite.

Cornell Law Review
Abbreviation: Cornell L. Rev.

Examples: Clermont, <u>Restating Territorial Jurisdiction and Venue for State and Federal Courts</u>, 66 Cornell L. Rev. 411 (1981). ——Article Cite.

Clermont, <u>Restating Territorial Jurisdiction and Venue for State and Federal Courts</u>, 66 Cornell L. Rev. 411, 420-25 (1981). ——Page Cite.

Corporate Practice Commentator
Abbreviations: Corp. Prac. Commentator
                  Corp. Prac. Comm. (publisher's abbreviation)

Corporate Practice Series (Bureau of National Affairs)
Abbreviation: Corp. Prac. Ser. (BNA)

Corporation Forms (Prentice-Hall)
Abbreviation: Corp. Forms (P-H)

Corporation Guide (Prentice-Hall)
Abbreviation: Corp. Guide (P-H)

Corporation Law Guide (Commerce Clearing House)
Abbreviation: Corp. L. Guide (CCH)

In law review footnotes, the titles of books and the names of cases are not underlined.

Example: How to Find Contract Opportunities: Government Procurement
                  Agencies, 2 Corp. L. Guide (CCH) ¶ 3004 (Oct. 1984). ——Citation to
                  current or non-current looseleaf material; this citation is to an editorial
                  comment written by the publisher's staff. Cite to looseleaf services only
                  until the case is available in the official or West reporter.

Corporation Law Review
    Abbreviation: Corp. L. Rev.

    Examples: Dranginis, Tax Planning: The "No Fault" Penalty for Substantial
                  Understatement of Tax Liability, 9 Corp. L. Rev. 186 (1986).
                  ——Article Cite.

                  Dranginis, Tax Planning: The "No Fault" Penalty for Substantial
                  Understatement of Tax Liability, 9 Corp. L. Rev. 186, 188 (1986).
                  ——Page Cite.

Corpus Juris Secundum
    Abbreviation: C.J.S.

    Example: 95 C.J.S. Wills § 306 (1957).

County Court
    Abbreviation: [name County] County Ct.

County Judge's Court
    Abbreviation: County J. Ct.

Court-Martial Reports
    Abbreviation: C.M.R.

    Example: United States v. Scott, 16 C.M.A. 478, 37 C.M.R. 98 (1967).

Court of Appeal (English)
    Abbreviation: C.A.

Court of Appeal [s] (state)
    Abbreviation: Ct. App.

Court of Appeals (federal)
    Abbreviation: Cir.

Court of Claims
    Abbreviation: Ct. Cl.

Court of Claims Reports
    Abbreviation: Ct. Cl.

In law review footnotes, the following are in large and small capitals: periodicals, constitutions,
codes, restatements, standards, authors of books, titles of books, and legislative materials except
for bills and resolutions. Refer to Bluebook.

——Cite to Federal Reporter series or Federal Supplement series if therein; otherwise, cite to the Reports as follows:

Example: Kay Mfg. Co. v. United States, 230 Ct. Cl. 83 (1982).

——After 231 Ct. Cl 105 (1982) see Claims Court Reporter.

Court of Claims Rules (Rules of the Court of Claims of the United States)
Abbreviation: Ct. Cl. R.

Example: Ct. Cl. R. 176.

Court of Criminal Appeals
Abbreviation: Crim. App.

Court of Customs and Patent Appeals Reports
Abbreviation: C.C.P.A.

——Cite to F.2d or F. Supp. if therein; otherwise, cite as follows:

Example: Krupp Int'l Inc. v. United States Int'l Trade Comm'n, 67 C.C.P.A. 166 (1980).

Court of Customs Appeals
Abbreviation: Ct. Cust. App.

Court of Customs Appeals Reports
Abbreviation: Ct. Cust. App.

——Cite to F. or F.2d if therein; otherwise, cite as follows:

Example: Wells Fargo & Co. v. United States, 7 Ct. Cust. App. 346 (1916).

——Becomes C.C.P.A after volume 16.

Court of Errors and Appeals
Abbreviation: Ct. Err. & App.

Court of International Trade
Abbreviation: Ct. Int'l Trade

Court of Justice of the European Communities
(Common Market cases)

Abbreviation: E. Comm. Ct. J. Rep.

Example: Firma A. Racke v. Hauptzollamt Mainz, 1984 E. Comm. Ct. J. Rep. 3791, [1983-1985] Common Mkt. Rep. (CCH) ¶ 14,153 (1984).
                ——See Bluebook Rule 19.3 (b).

Court of Military Appeals
Abbreviation: C.M.A.

In law review footnotes, the titles of books and the names of cases are not underlined.

Court of Military Review
Abbreviation: C.M.R.

Court of [General, Special] Sessions
Abbreviations: Ct. Gen. Sess.
                  Ct. Spec. Sess.

Court Management Journal
Abbreviation: Ct. Mgmt. J.

Examples: Schwartz, <u>Monitoring Delay Reduction Efforts</u>, 1985 Ct. Mgmt. J. 4.
                  ——Article Cite.

                  Schwartz, <u>Monitoring Delay Reduction Efforts</u>, 1985 Ct. Mgmt. J. 4, 6-
                  7. ——Page Cite.

Courts-Martial Appeal Court
Abbreviation: C.-M. A.C.

Cranch (United States Reports)
<u>See</u>   United States Reports

Crane and Bromberg on Partnership, by Alan R. Bromberg
——Do not abbreviate the title.

Examples: A. Bromberg, <u>Crane and Bromberg on Partnership</u> § 68 (1968).

                  A. Bromberg, <u>Crane and Bromberg on Partnership</u> § 68, at 391 (1968).

Creighton Law Review
Abbreviation: Creighton L. Rev.

Examples: Weber, <u>Building on Sand: Supreme Court Construction and Educational
                  Tax Credits</u>, 12 Creighton L. Rev. 531 (1978). ——Article Cite.

                  Weber, <u>Building on Sand: Supreme Court Construction and Educational
                  Tax Credits</u>, 12 Creighton L. Rev. 531, 558-60 (1978). ——Page Cite.

Crime and Delinquency
Abbreviation: Crime & Delinq.

Examples: Conrad, <u>Criminal Justice Research Is About People</u>, 28 Crime &
                  Delinq. 618 (1982). ——Article Cite.

                  Conrad, <u>Criminal Justice Research Is About People</u>, 28 Crime &
                  Delinq. 618, 623 (1982). ——Page Cite.

Crime and Justice
Abbreviation: Crime & Just.

In law review footnotes, the following are in large and small capitals: periodicals, constitutions, codes, restatements, standards, authors of books, titles of books, and legislative materials except for bills and resolutions. Refer to Bluebook.

Criminal Appeals
    Abbreviation: Crim. App.

Criminal Law, by W. LaFave & A. Scott
    ——Do not abbreviate the title.

    Examples: W. LaFave & A. Scott, Jr., <u>Criminal Law</u> § 6.8 (2d ed. 1986).

                 W. LaFave & A. Scott, Jr., <u>Criminal Law</u> § 6.8, at 590 (2d ed. 1986).

Criminal Law Bulletin
    Abbreviation: Crim. L. Bull.

Criminal Law Reporter (Bureau of National Affairs)
    Abbreviation: Crim. L. Rep. (BNA)

Criminal Law Review
    Abbreviation: Crim. L. Rev.
                    Crim. L.R. (publisher's abbreviation)

    Examples: Corre, <u>Bail or Custody: A Contemporary Problem and an Ancient Solution</u>, 1986 Crim. L. Rev. 162. ——Case Cite.

                 Corre, <u>Bail or Custody: A Contemporary Problem and an Ancient Solution</u>, 1986 Crim. L. Rev. 162, 162. ——Page Cite.

Cumberland Law Review
    Abbreviation: Cumb. L. Rev.

    Examples: Cole, <u>Public Employee Strikes—The Law and Possible Alternatives</u>, 11 Cumb. L. Rev. 315 (1980-1981). ——Article Cite.

                 Cole, <u>Public Employee Strikes—The Law and Possible Alternatives</u>, 11 Cumb. L. Rev. 315, 318-19 (1980-1981). ——Page Cite.

Cumulative Bulletin (U.S.)
    Abbreviation: C.B.

    Examples:

    (1919-1921)   T.B.R. 39, 1 C.B. 45 (1919). ——Citation to volumes of the Cumulative Bulletin from 1919-1921 are by volume number.

    (1921-1936)   I.T. 2258, 5-1 C.B. 10 (1926). ——Citation to volumes of the Cumulative Bulletin from 1921-1936 are by volume and part numbers.

    (1937-date)   Rev. Rul. 81-1, 1981-1 C.B. 18. ——Citation to volumes of the Cumulative Bulletin from 1937 to date are by year and part numbers.

                 Rev. Rul. 82-4, 1982-1 I.R.B. 14. ——Citation to the material found in the Cumulative Bulletin before a bound volume is issued is to the Internal Revenue Bulletin.

In law review footnotes, the titles of books and the names of cases are not underlined.

Current Legal Forms with Tax Analysis, by Jacob Rabkin & Mark H. Johnson
——Do not abbreviate the title.

Examples: 7A J. Rabkin & M. Johnson, Current Legal Forms with Tax Analysis 19-115, 19-116 (1982). ——Cite to material on pages 19-115 and 19-116 of volume 7A.

7A J. Rabkin & M. Johnson, Current Legal Forms with Tax Analysis, Form 19-88 (1987). ——Cite to legal form.

7A J. Rabkin & M. Johnson, Current Legal Forms With Tax Analysis 19-123 (Supp. Feb. 1988). ——Cite to the Supplement in the front of volume 7A.

Current Legal Problems
Abbreviation: Current Legal Probs.

Current Medicine for Attorneys
Abbreviation: Current Med. for Att'ys

Customs Bulletin and Decisions (U.S.) (1967-date)
Abbreviation: Cust. B. & Dec.

Examples: T.D. 67-1, 1 Cust. B. & Dec. 1 (1967).

C.S.D. 79-4, 13 Cust. B. & Dec. 998 (1978).

T.D. 82-89, 16 Cust. B. & Dec. No. 21, at 1 (May 11, 1982). ——Citation to current, unbound material.

Customs Court Reports (1938-1980)
Abbreviation: Cust. Ct.

——Cite to Federal Reporter series or Federal Supplement series if therein, otherwise cite to the Reports as follows:

Examples: T.D. Downing Co. v. United States, 60 Cust. Ct. 345 (1968). ——Case Cite.

T.D. Downing Co. v. United States, 60 Cust. Ct. 345, 347 (1968). ——Page Cite.

Customs Court Rules (Rules of the United States Customs Court)
Abbreviation: Cust. Ct. R.

Example: Cust. Ct. R. 11.1.

In law review footnotes, the following are in large and small capitals: periodicals, constitutions, codes, restatements, standards, authors of books, titles of books, and legislative materials except for bills and resolutions. Refer to Bluebook.

In law review footnotes, the titles of books and the names of cases are not underlined.

D

Dalhousie Law Journal
Abbreviation: Dalhousie L.J.

Examples: McEvoy, Atlantic Canada: The Constitutional Offshore Regime, 8
Dalhousie L.J. 284 (1984). ——Article Cite.

McEvoy, Atlantic Canada: The Constitutional Offshore Regime, 8
Dalhousie L.J. 284, 321-22 (1984). ——Page Cite.

Dallas (United States Reports)
See   United States Reports

Davis on Administrative Law
See   Administrative Law Text, by Kenneth C. Davis

Debates, Congressional
See   Congressional Debates

Decisiones de Puerto Rico
Abbreviation: P.R. Dec.

Decisions and Orders of the National Labor Relations Board (U.S.) (1935-date)
Abbreviation: N.L.R.B.

Examples: Checker Cab Co., 260 N.L.R.B. 955 (1982). ——Citation to official
reporter.

Inland Container Corp., 275 N.L.R.B. No. 60 (May 7, 1985). ——Slip
opinion.

Inland Container Corp., 275 N.L.R.B. No 60, [5 Labor Relations] Lab.
L. Rep. (CCH) (1985-1986 NLRB Dec.) ¶ 17,343 (May 7, 1985).
——Slip opinion when reported in looseleaf unofficial case service.

Inland Container Corp., 275 N.L.R.B. No. 60, 1985-1986 NLRB Dec.
(CCH) ¶ 17,343 (May 7, 1985). ——Slip opinion when reported in
bound unofficial case service.

Decisions of the Commissioner of Patents
Abbreviation: Dec. Comm'r Pat.

——See examples under Patents, Decisions of the Commissioner.

In law review footnotes, the following are in large and small capitals: periodicals, constitutions,
codes, restatements, standards, authors of books, titles of books, and legislative materials except
for bills and resolutions. Refer to Bluebook.

Decisions of the Comptroller General (1921-date) (U.S.)
 Abbreviation: Comp. Gen.

 Examples: Trans Country Van Lines, Inc., 53 Comp. Gen. 603 (1974).

    Decision of the Comptroller General B-196480 (Jan. 30, 1980).
    ——Citation to unpublished decisions.

Decisions of the Department of the Interior (U.S.) (1881-date)
 Abbreviations: Pub. Lands. Dec. ——Citation for vols. 1-52.
      Interior Dec. ——Citation for vol. 53 onward.

 Examples: Union Pacific Ry. Co., 25 Pub. Lands Dec. 540 (1897).

    Washington University, 87 Interior Dec. 88 (1980).

Decisions of the Employees' Compensation Appeals Board (U.S.) (1947-date)
 Abbreviation: Empl. Comp. App. Bd.

 Examples: Fred Foster, 1 Empl. Comp. App. Bd. 21 (1947).

    Jack G. Clemings, 31 Empl. Comp. App. Bd. 1092 (1980).

Decisions of the Federal Labor Relations Authority
 Abbreviation: F.L.R.A.

 Examples: Norfolk Naval Shipyard, 14 F.L.R.A. 82 (1984). ——Case Cite.

    Norfolk Naval Shipyard, 14 F.L.R.A. 82, 83 (1984). ——Page Cite.

Decisions of the Federal Maritime Commission (U.S.) (1947-date)
 Abbreviation: F.M.C.

 Examples: American President Lines, 4 F.M.C. 555 (1955).

    Universal Nolin UMC Industries, 19 F.M.C. 780 (1977).

Decisions of the United States Maritime Commission (U.S.) (1919-1947)
 Abbreviation: Dec. U.S. Mar. Comm'n

 Examples: Acme Novelty Co., 2 Dec. U.S. Mar. Comm'n 412 (1940).

    East-Bound Intercoastal Brandy and Champagne Rates, 2 Dec. U.S. Mar. Comm'n 178 (1939).

Deering's Annotated California Codes
 Abbreviation: Cal. subject Code § (Deering year).

 ——See page 180 of the Bluebook for an abbreviation of each subject.

 Example: Cal. Corp. Code § 317 (Deering Supp. 1979)

In law review footnotes, the titles of books and the names of cases are not underlined.

Defense of Drunk Driving Cases, by R. Erwin, M. Minzer, L. Greenberg, H. Goldstein & A. Bergh
——Do not abbreviate the title.

Example: 3 R. Erwin, M. Minzer, L. Greenberg, H. Goldstein & A. Bergh, Defense of Drunk Driving Cases § 40.02[2] (3d ed. 1985).

Defense Law Journal
Abbreviation: Def. L.J.

Examples: Knepper, Review of Recent Tort Trends, 30 Def. L.J. 1 (1981). ——Article Cite.

Knepper, Review of Recent Tort Trends, 30 Def. L.J. 1, 24-25 (1981). ——Page Cite.

Delaware Chancery Reports
Abbreviation: Del. Ch.

——Discontinued after 43 Del. Ch. 534 (1968). Thereafter cite only to A.2d.

Examples: Mayer v. Mayer, 36 Del. Ch. 457, 132 A.2d 617 (1957). ——Case Cite.

Mayer v. Mayer, 36 Del. Ch. 457, 461, 132 A.2d 617, 619 (1957). ——Page Cite.

——After 43 Del. Ch. 534 (1968), cite as follows:

Shields v. Shields, 498 A.2d 161 (Del. Ch. 1985). ——Case Cite.

Shields v. Shields, 498 A.2d 161, 163 (Del. Ch. 1985). ——Page Cite.

Delaware Code Annotated
Abbreviation: Del. Code Ann. tit.   , §   (year).

Examples: Del. Code Ann. tit. 10, § 541 (1975).

Del. Code Ann. tit. 10, § 8707 (Supp. 1986).

Delaware Constitution
Abbreviation: Del. Const. art.   , §   .

Examples: Del. Const. art. II, § 6. ——Cite provisions without date unless the cited provisions have been repealed or amended (Bluebook Rule 11).

Del. Const. art. II, § 15 (1897, amended 1975). ——Cite provisions which have been repealed or amended by giving the date of the adoption of the particular provision and the date of repeal or amendment (Bluebook Rule 11).

Del. Const. of 1792, art. I, § 19. ——Cite constitutions that have been totally superseded by year of adoption, giving parenthetically the year of adoption of the specific provision cited if different (Bluebook Rule 11).

In law review footnotes, the following are in large and small capitals: periodicals, constitutions, codes, restatements, standards, authors of books, titles of books, and legislative materials except for bills and resolutions. Refer to Bluebook.

Delaware Journal of Corporate Law
    Abbreviation: Del. J. Corp. L.

    Examples: Terrell, Indemnification of Employees, 5 Del. J. Corp. L. 251 (1980).
    ——Article Cite.

                Terrell, Indemnification of Employees, 5 Del. J. Corp. L. 251, 256-58
    (1980). ——Page Cite.

Delaware Lawyer
    Abbreviation: Del. Law.

    Examples: Alldridge, The American Abortion Debate: An English Perspective,
    Del. Law., Fall 1985, at 16. ——Article Cite.

                Alldridge, The American Abortion Debate: An English Perspective,
    Del. Law., Fall 1985, at 16, 16. ——Page Cite.

Delaware Register of Regulations
    Abbreviation: Del. Reg. of Regs.

Delaware Reports (1920-1966):
    Abbreviations: Del.

    ——Discontinued after 59 Del. 302 (1966). Thereafter cite only to A.2d.

    Examples: Carey v. Bryan & Rollins, 48 Del. 395, 105 A.2d 201 (1954).
    ——Case Cite.

                Carey v. Bryan & Rollins, 48 Del. 395, 396, 105 A.2d 201, 202 (1954).
    ——Page Cite.

    ——For reports dated prior to 1920, the editor's name is used. See Bluebook page 182.

    ——After 59 Del. 302 (1966), cite as follows:

                In re Frabizzio, 498 A.2d 1076 (Del. 1985). ——Case Cite.

                In re Frabizzio, 498 A.2d 1076, 1078-79 (Del. 1985). ——Page Cite.

Delaware Session Laws
    See   Laws of Delaware

Denver Journal of International Law and Policy
    Abbreviation: Denver J. Int'l L. & Pol'y

    Examples: Kassim, The Palestine Liberation Organization's Claim to Status: A
    Juridical Analysis Under International Law, 9 Denver J. Int'l L. &
    Pol'y 1 (1980). ——Article Cite.

                Kassim, The Palestine Liberation Organization's Claim to Status: A
    Juridical Analysis Under International Law, 9 Denver J. Int'l L. &
    Pol'y 1, 20-25 (1980). ——Page Cite.

In law review footnotes, the titles of books and the names of cases are not underlined.

Denver Law Journal
    Abbreviations: Denver. L.J. (v. 1-61)
                       Den. U.L. Rev. (v. 61-present)

    Examples: Martin & Prescott, The Problem of Delay in the Colorado Court of Appeals, 58 Denver L.J. 1 (1980). ——Article Cite.

                      Martin & Prescott, The Problem of Delay in the Colorado Court of Appeals, 58 Denver L.J. 1, 2-6 (1980). ——Page Cite.

Denver University Law Review
    Abbreviation: Den. U.L. Rev.

Department of State Bulletin (U.S.)
    Abbreviation: Dep't St. Bull.

    Example: Young Human Rights, 79 Dep't State Bull. No. 2023, at 59 (1979). ——The word "at" is used here to differentiate between two kinds of numbers.

DePaul Law Review
    Abbreviation: De Paul L. Rev.

    Examples: Krause, Securities Litigation: The Unsolved Problem of Predispute Arbitration Agreements for Pendent Claims, 29 De Paul L. Rev. 693 (1980). ——Article Cite.

                      Krause, Securities Litigation: The Unsolved Problem of Predispute Arbitration Agreements for Pendent Claims, 29 De Paul L. Rev. 693, 700-05 (1980). ——Page Cite.

Detroit College of Law Review
    Abbreviation: Det. C.L. Rev.

    Examples: Higgins, Section 18 of the Exchange Act: A New Defense Weapon in Securities Litigation, 1980 Det. C.L. Rev. 761. ——Article Cite.

                      Higgins, Section 18 of the Exchange Act: A New Defense Weapon in Securities Litigation, 1980 Det. C.L. Rev. 761, 780-84. ——Page Cite.

Dickinson International Law Annual
    Abbreviation: Dick. Int'l L. Ann.

Dickinson Law Review
    Abbreviation: Dick. L. Rev.

    Examples: Murphy, Suggested Standard Jury Instructions on Criminal Homicide, 85 Dick. L. Rev. 1 (1980). ——Article Cite.

                      Murphy, Suggested Standard Jury Instructions on Criminal Homicide, 85 Dick. L. Rev. 1, 15-17 (1980). ——Page Cite.

In law review footnotes, the following are in large and small capitals: periodicals, constitutions, codes, restatements, standards, authors of books, titles of books, and legislative materials except for bills and resolutions. Refer to Bluebook.

Digest of International Law, by J. Moore
——Do not abbreviate the title.

Examples: 4 J. Moore, A Digest of International Law § 590 (1906).

                       4 J. Moore, A Digest of International Law § 590, at 272 (1906).

Digest of Opinions of the Attorney General of Texas
Abbreviation: Dig. Op. Tex. Att'y Gen.

Example: 1980 Dig. Op. Tex. Att'y Gen. 89. ——See Bluebook Rule 14.4.

dissenting opinion
Example: Roe v. Wade, 410 U.S. 113, 171 (1973) (Rehnquist, J., dissenting).

District Court (federal)
Abbreviation: D.

District Court (state)
Abbreviation: Dist. Ct.

District Court of Appeal
Abbreviation: Dist. Ct. App.

District Lawyer
Abbreviation: District Law.

District of Columbia Appeals Cases (1893-1941)
See   Appeal Cases, District of Columbia (1893-1941)

District of Columbia Code Annotated
Abbreviation: D.C. Code Ann. §   (year).

Examples: D.C. Code Ann. § 22-104 (1981).

                       D.C. Code Ann. § 2-504 (Supp. 1987).

District of Columbia Code Encyclopedia
Abbreviation: D.C. Code Encycl. §   (West year).

District of Columbia Court of Appeals
Abbreviation: D.C.

Examples: Strand v. Frenkel, 500 A.2d 1368 (D.C. 1985). ——Article Cite.

                       Strand v. Frenkel, 500 A.2d 1368, 1370 (D.C. 1985). ——Page Cite.

——1943-date, cite to A.2d. See Bluebook page 143

In law review footnotes, the titles of books and the names of cases are not underlined.

District of Columbia, laws in Statutes at Large relating to
  Abbreviation: volume Stat. (year).

District of Columbia Register
  Abbreviation: D.C. Reg.

Divisional Court
  Abbreviation: Div. Ct.

Dobbs on Remedies
  <u>See</u> Handbook on the Law of Remedies, by D. Dobbs

Documents, Congressional
  <u>See</u> Congressional Documents

Domestic Relations Court
  Abbreviation: Dom. Rel. Ct.

Drake Law Review
  Abbreviation: Drake L. Rev.

  Examples: Schlesinger & Malloy, <u>Plea Bargaining and the Judiciary: An Argument for Reform</u>, 30 Drake L. Rev. 581 (1980-1981). ——Article Cite.

      Schlesinger & Malloy, <u>Plea Bargaining and the Judiciary: An Argument for Reform</u>, 30 Drake L. Rev. 581, 590-93 (1980-1981). ——Page Cite.

Duke Law Journal
  Abbreviation: Duke L.J.

  Examples: Soderquist & Vecchio, <u>Reconciling Shareholders' Rights and Corporate Responsibility: New Guidelines for Management</u>, 1978 Duke L.J. 819. ——Article Cite.

      Soderquist & Vecchio, <u>Reconciling Shareholders' Rights and Corporate Responsibility: New Guidelines for Management</u>, 1978 Duke L.J. 819, 830-34. ——Page Cite.

Duquesne Law Review
  Abbreviation: Duq. L. Rev.

  Examples: Connolly & Connolly, <u>Employers' Rights Relative to Sympathy Strikes</u>, 14 Duq. L. Rev. 121 (1976). ——Article Cite.

      Connolly & Connolly, <u>Employers' Rights Relative to Sympathy Strikes</u>, 14 Duq. L. Rev. 121, 126-43 (1976). ——Page Cite.

In law review footnotes, the following are in large and small capitals: periodicals, constitutions, codes, restatements, standards, authors of books, titles of books, and legislative materials except for bills and resolutions. Refer to Bluebook.

In law review footnotes, the titles of books and the names of cases are not underlined.

E

Ecclesiastical
    Abbreviation: Eccl.

Ecclesiastical Court
    Abbreviation: Eccl. Ct.

Ecology Law Quarterly
    Abbreviation: Ecology L.Q.

    Examples: Horberry, The Accountability of Development Assistance Agencies: The Case of Environmental Policy, 12 Ecology L.Q. 817 (1985). ——Article Cite.

        Horberry, The Accountability of Development Assistance Agencies: The Case of Environmental Policy, 12 Ecology L.Q. 817, 851-53 (1985). ——Page Cite.

editor, edition
    Abbreviation: ed.

Emergency Court of Appeals
    Abbreviation: Emer. Ct. App.

E.g.
    Example: "A determination of likelihood of confusion, mistake, or deception is a matter of fact that we may overturn only if clearly erroneous. E.g., Sun Banks of Florida v. Sun Fed. Sav. & Loan, 651 F.2d 311, 314 (5th Cir. 1981); Exxon Corp. v. Texas Motor Exchange Corp., 628 F.2d 500, 504 (5th Cir. 1981)." ——Taken from 675 F.2d 1160, 1163 (1982).

Emory Law Journal
    Abbreviation: Emory L.J.

    Examples: Marshall, The Applicability of the Uniform Commercial Code to Construction Contracts, 28 Emory L.J. 335 (1979). ——Article Cite.

        Marshall, The Applicability of the Uniform Commercial Code to Construction Contracts, 28 Emory L.J. 335, 336-50 (1979). ——Page Cite.

Employee Relations Law Journal
    Abbreviation: Employee Rel. L.J.

In law review footnotes, the following are in large and small capitals: periodicals, constitutions, codes, restatements, standards, authors of books, titles of books, and legislative materials except for bills and resolutions. Refer to Bluebook.

Examples: Brown, <u>Hard Bargaining: The Board Says No, the Courts Say Yes</u>, 8
                Employee Rel. L.J. 37 (1982). ——Article Cite.

                Brown, <u>Hard Bargaining: The Board Says No, the Courts Say Yes</u>, 8
                Employee Rel. L.J. 37, 50-51 (1982). ——Page Cite.

Employment Practices Guide (Commerce Clearing House)
        Abbreviation: Empl. Prac. Guide (CCH)

        Examples: <u>Horn v. Eltra Corp.</u>, 4 Empl. Prac. Guide (CCH) (30 Empl. Prac. Dec.)
                        ¶ 33,023 (6th Cir. Aug. 26, 1982). ——Citation to looseleaf material.

                        <u>Guertin v. Hackman</u>, 25 Empl. Prac. Dec. ¶ 31,604 (S.D. Tex. 1981).
                        ——Citation to bound material.

——The above examples are proper if the case is not yet available in an official or West
        reporter, or is not reported in an official or West reporter.

                        Decision of the EEOC No. 82-2, 2 Empl. Prac. Guide (CCH) ¶ 6818
                        (Jan. 18, 1982). ——Citation to looseleaf administrative material. Such
                        a citation is proper if the material is not yet available or is not reported
                        in an official reporter.

                        Decision of EEOC No. 71-779, l973 EEOC Decisions (CCH) ¶ 6180
                        (1970). ——Citation to bound administrative material. Such a citation
                        is proper only if the material is not currently available in an official
                        reporter.

Encyclopedia of European Community Law
        Abbreviation: E.E.C.L.

Encyclopedia of Public International Law
        ——Do not abbreviate the title

        Example: 8 <u>Encyclopedia of Public International Law</u> 53 (1985).

Energy Law Journal
        Abbreviation: Energy L.J.

        Examples: Chartoff, Mayo & Smith, <u>The Case Against the Use of the Capital Asset</u>
                        <u>Principle Model in Public Ratemaking</u>, 3 Energy L.J. 67 (1982).
                        ——Article Cite.

                        Chartoff, Mayo & Smith, <u>The Case Against the Use of the Capital Asset</u>
                        <u>Principle Model in Public Ratemaking</u>, 3 Energy L.J. 67, 82-83 (1982).
                        ——Page Cite.

Energy Users Report (Bureau of National Affairs)
        Abbreviation: Energy Users Rep. (BNA)

English Law Reports and other materials
        ——Well explained and illustrated in Bluebook at pages 152-57.

In law review footnotes, the titles of books and the names of cases are not underlined.

English Reports—Full Reprint
    Abbreviation: Eng. Rep.

Entertainment and Sports Lawyer
    Abbreviation: Ent. & Sports Law.

    Examples: Feller, Let Me Count the Ways—Dispute Resolution in the
                 Entertainment Industry, Ent. & Sports Law., Fall 1985, at 1.
                 ——Article Cite.

                 Feller, Let Me Count the Ways—Dispute Resolution in the
                 Entertainment Industry, Ent. & Sports Law., Fall 1985, at 1, 1.
                 ——Page Cite.

Environment Reporter (Bureau of National Affairs)
    Abbreviation: Env't Rep. (BNA)

    Examples: Appalachian Power Co. v. EPA, [Decisions] Env't Rep. (BNA) (17
                 Env't Rep. Cas.) 1105 (4th Cir. Feb. 8, 1982). ——Citation to looseleaf
                 material.

                 Shawnee Coal Co. v. Andrus, 15 Env't Rep. Cas. (BNA) 1266 (S.D.
                 Ohio 1979). ——Citation to bound material.

——The above examples are proper if the case is not yet available in an official or West
    reporter, or is not reported in an official or West reporter.

                 Doyle, Phosphates—An Unresolved Water Quality Problem,
                 [Monographs] Env't Rep. (BNA) No. 9 (Aug. 20, 1971). ——Citation
                 to looseleaf material; this citation is to a monograph written by the
                 named contributor.

Environmental Law
    Abbreviation: Envtl. L.

Environmental Law Reporter (Environmental Law Institute)
    Abbreviation: Envtl. L. Rep. (Envtl. L. Inst.)

    Examples: Alabama Power Co. v. Gorsuch, 12 Envtl. L. Rep. (Envtl. L. Inst.)
                 20218 (D.C. Cir. Feb. 5, 1982). ——Citation to looseleaf material.

                 Committee for Charter Protection for Parks v. Brown, 10 Envtl. L.
                 Rep. (Envtl. L. Inst.) 20,246 (S.D. Cal. 1980). ——Citation to non-
                 current looseleaf material.

——The above examples are proper if the case is not yet available in an official or West
    reporter, or is not reported in an official or West reporter.

                 Trauberman, Dunwoody & Horne, Compensation for Toxic Substances
                 Pollution: Michigan Case Study, 10 Envtl. L. Rep. (Envtl. L. Inst.)
                 50,021 (Sept. 1980). ——Citation to current or non-current looseleaf
                 material. The citation is to an article or monograph written by the
                 named contributors.

In law review footnotes, the following are in large and small capitals: periodicals, constitutions,
codes, restatements, standards, authors of books, titles of books, and legislative materials except
for bills and resolutions. Refer to Bluebook.

Nuclear Weapons and "Secret" Impact Statements: High Court Applies FOIA Exemptions to EIS Disclosure Rules, 12 Envtl. L. Rep. (Envtl. L. Inst.) 10,007 (Feb. 1982). ——Citation to current or non-current looseleaf material; this citation is to an editorial comment written by the publisher's staff.

equity

    Abbreviation: eq.

Equity Court or Division

    Abbreviation: Eq.

Estate Planning, by A. James Casner

    ——Do not abbreviate the title.

    Example: 2 A. Casner, Estate Planning § 16.12.1 (5th ed. 1985).

European Court of Human Rights, Series A or B

    Abbreviation: Eur. Ct. H.R. (ser.)

    Example: Dudgeon Case, 40 Eur. Ct. H.R. (ser. B) (1980).

European Law Review

    Abbreviations: Eur. L. Rev.
                E.L. Rev. (publisher's abbreviation)

    Examples: Everling, The Member States of the European Community Before Their Court of Justice, 9 Eur. L. Rev. 215 (1984). ——Article Cite.

              Everling, The Member States of the European Community Before Their Court of Justice, 9 Eur. L. Rev. 215, 219-20 (1984). ——Page Cite.

European Treaty Series

    Abbreviation: Europ. T.S. No.

Evidence in Trials at Common Law, by John H. Wigmore

    ——Do not abbreviate the title.

    Examples: 9 J. Wigmore, Evidence in Trials at Common Law § 2421 (rev. 1981).

              9 J. Wigmore, Evidence in Trials at Common Law § 2421, at 71 (rev. 1981).

              3 J. Wigmore, Evidence in Trials at Common Law § 748 (rev. 1970).

              3 J. Wigmore, Evidence in Trials at Common Law § 748, at 101 (rev. 1970).

              9 J. Wigmore, Evidence in Trials at Common Law § 2493K (rev. 1981 & Supp. 1988).

In law review footnotes, the titles of books and the names of cases are not underlined.

Executive Agreement Series (U.S. Dep't State) (1922-1945)
    Abbreviation: E.A.S. No.

    Example: Agreement Respecting a Committee of Inquiry into the Position of Jews in Europe and Palestine, Dec. 10, 1945, United States—United Kingdom, 59 Stat. 1729, E.A.S. No. 491.

Executive Document
    Abbreviation: Exec. Doc.

Executive Order
    Abbreviation: Exec. Order

    Examples: Exec. Order No. 12,289, 46 Fed. Reg. 12,693 (1981).

                  Exec. Order No. 12,173, 35 C.F.R. 6 (1980).

——Parallel citation to U.S.C. (or, if that is not possible, U.S.C.A. or U.S.C.S.) whenever possible. Bluebook Rule 14.7(a)

——Cite to the Federal Register only if the executive order is not in C.F.R. Bluebook Rule 14.7(a).

In law review footnotes, the following are in large and small capitals: periodicals, constitutions, codes, restatements, standards, authors of books, titles of books, and legislative materials except for bills and resolutions. Refer to Bluebook.

In law review footnotes, the titles of books and the names of cases are not underlined.

F

Fair Employment Practice Cases (Bureau of National Affairs)
    Abbreviation: Fair Empl. Prac. Cas. (BNA)

Family Court
    Abbreviation: Fam. Ct.

Family Division
    Abbreviation: Fam. Div.

Family Law Quarterly
    Abbreviation: Fam. L.Q.

Family Law Reporter (Bureau of National Affairs)
    Abbreviation: Fam. L. Rep. (BNA)

    Examples: Paul W. v. Margaret W., [Current Developments] Fam. L. Rep. (BNA) 3013 (Pa. C.P. Allegheny County Dec. 1, 1981). ——Citation to looseleaf material.

                Lynn v. Lynn, 7 Fam. L. Rep. (BNA) 3001 (N.J. Super. Ct. Ch. Div. 1980). ——Citation to bound material.

——The above examples are proper if the case is not yet available in an official or West reporter, or is not reported in an official or West reporter.

                Dwoskin, The Representation of Foster Parents, [Current Developments] Fam. L. Rep. (BNA) 4009 (Feb. 2, 1982). ——Citation to looseleaf material. The citation is to an article or monograph written by the named contributors.

                Foster and Freed, Marvin v. Marvin: New Wine in Old Bottles, 5 Fam. L. Rep. (BNA) 4001 (1979). ——Citation to bound material. The citation is to an article or monograph written by the named contributors.

Federal Banking Law Reports (Commerce Clearing House)
    Abbreviation: Fed. Banking L. Rep. (CCH)

    Example: Bank of Am. Nat'l Trust & Sav. Ass'n v. Cory, [Current] Fed. Banking L. Rep. (CCH) ¶ 98,744 (Cal. Super. Ct. May 4, 1981). ——Cite to looseleaf services only until the case is available in official or West reporter.

In law review footnotes, the following are in large and small capitals: periodicals, constitutions, codes, restatements, standards, authors of books, titles of books, and legislative materials except for bills and resolutions. Refer to Bluebook.

Federal Bar Journal
    Abbreviation: Fed. B.J.

    Examples: Cooper, <u>Patent Protection for New Forms of Life</u>, 38 Fed. B.J. 34
           (1979). ——Article Cite.

           Cooper, <u>Patent Protection for New Forms of Life</u>, 38 Fed. B.J. 34, 44-
           45 (1979). ——Page Cite.

Federal Carriers Reports (Commerce Clearing House)
    (formerly Reporter)

    Abbreviation: Fed. Carr. Rep. (CCH)

Federal Cases
    Abbreviation: F. Cas.

    Examples: <u>Corfield v. Coryell</u>, 6 F. Cas. 546 (C.C.E.D Pa. 1825) (No. 3230).

           <u>DeLovio v. Boit</u>, 7 F. Cas. 418 (C.C.D. Mass. 1815) (No. 3776).

Federal Civil Rights Acts: Civil Practice, by C. Antieau
    ——Do not abbreviate the title.

    Examples: 2 C. Antieau, <u>Federal Civil Rights Acts: Civil Practice</u> § 443 (2d ed.
           1980).

           2 C. Antieau, <u>Federal Civil Rights Acts: Civil Practice</u> § 443, at 93 (2d
           ed. 1980).

Federal Communications Commission Record
    Abbreviation: FCC Rcd. (publisher's abbreviation)

    Example: <u>Review of Technical Assignment Criteria for the AM Broadcast Service</u>,
           3 FCC Rcd. 268 (1987).

Federal Communications Commission Reports (1934-1986)
    Abbreviation: F.C.C.
                     F.C.C.2d

    Examples: <u>Deregulation of Radio</u>, 73 F.C.C.2d 457 (1979).

           <u>A.T. & T. Co.</u>, 88 F.C.C.2d 1656 (1982).

Federal Communications Law Journal
    Abbreviations: Fed. Comm. L.J.

    Examples: Geller, <u>Communications Law—A Half Century Later</u>, 37 Fed. Comm.
           L.J. 73 (1985). ——Article Cite.

           Geller, <u>Communications Law—A Half Century Later</u>, 37 Fed. Comm.
           L.J. 73, 80-81 (1985). ——Page Cite.

In law review footnotes, the titles of books and the names of cases are not underlined.

Federal Contracts Report (Bureau of National Affairs)
Abbreviation: Fed. Cont. Rep. (BNA)

Federal Estate and Gift Tax Reports (Commerce Clearing House)
Abbreviation: Fed. Est. & Gift Tax Rep. (CCH)

Examples: United States v. Vohland, 3 Fed. Est. & Gift Tax Rep. (CCH) (82-1
                U.S. Tax Cas.) ¶ 13,468 (9th Cir. Apr. 29, 1982). ——Citation to
                looseleaf material.

                Estate of Moran v. United States, 79-1 U.S. Tax Cas. (CCH) ¶ 13,273
                (E.D. Wis. 1978). ——Citation to bound material.

——The above examples are proper if the case is not yet available in an official or West
reporter, or is not reported in an official or West reporter.

                Priv. Ltr. Rul. 81-90-011 (June 29, 1981), reprinted in 3 Fed. Est. &
                Gift Tax Rep. (CCH) ¶ 12,446 E. ——Proper citation to an IRS private
                letter ruling found in this service.

Federal Excise Tax Reports (Commerce Clearing House)
Abbreviation: Fed. Ex. Tax Rep. (CCH)

Examples: Morgan Drive Away, Inc. v. United States, Fed. Ex. Tax Rep. (CCH)
                (82-1 U.S. Tax Cas.) ¶ 16,380 (Ct. Cl. Apr. 16, 1982). ——Citation to
                looseleaf material.

                United States v. Miller, 79-2 U.S. Tax Cas. (CCH) ¶ 16,318 (N.D.
                Tex. 1979). ——Citation to bound material.

——The above examples are proper if the case is not yet available in an official or West
reporter, or is not reported in an official or West reporter.

Federal Home Loan Bank Board Journal
Abbreviation: Fed. Home Loan Bank Board J.

Federal Income Taxation, by B. Bittker, L. Stone & W. Klein
——Do not abbreviate the title.

Example: B. Bittker, L. Stone & W. Klein, Federal Income Taxation 126-27 (6th
               ed. 1984).

Federal Income Taxation of Corporations and Shareholders, by B. Bittker and J. Eustice
——Do not abbreviate the title.

Examples: B. Bittker & J. Eustice, Federal Income Taxation of Corporations and
                Shareholders ¶ 5.06 (5th ed. 1987).

                B. Bittker & J. Eustice, Federal Income Taxation of Corporations and
                Shareholders ¶ 5.06, at 5-33 (5th ed. 1987).

Federal Income Taxation of Individuals, by D. Posin
——Do not abbreviate the title.

In law review footnotes, the following are in large and small capitals: periodicals, constitutions,
codes, restatements, standards, authors of books, titles of books, and legislative materials except
for bills and resolutions. Refer to Bluebook.

Example: D. Posin, Federal Income Taxation of Individuals 74 (1983).

Federal Law Review
Abbreviations: Fed. L. Rev.
                 F.L. Rev. (publisher's abbreviation)

Examples: Curtis, Freedom of Information in Australia, 14 Fed. L. Rev. 5 (1983).
                ——Article Cite.

                Curtis, Freedom of Information in Australia, 14 Fed. L. Rev. 5, 18-19
                (1983). ——Page Cite.

Federal Mine Safety and Health Review Commission Decisions
Abbreviation: F.M.S.H.R.C.

Examples: Local 2274, United Mine Workers, 8 F.M.S.H.R.C. 1310 (1986).
                ——Case Cite.

                Local 2274, United Mine Workers, 8 F.M.S.H.R.C. 1310, 1313
                (1986). ——Page Cite.

Federal Power Commission Reports (U.S.) (1931-1977)
Abbreviation: F.P.C.

Examples: Northern Natural Gas Co., 58 F.P.C. 1744 (1977).

                Arkansas Louisiana Gas Co., 58 F.P.C. 1617 (1977).

Federal Practice and Procedure, by Charles A. Wright & Arthur R. Miller
——Do not abbreviate the title.

Examples: 11 C. Wright & A. Miller, Federal Practice and Procedure § 2858
                (1973).

                11 C. Wright & A. Miller, Federal Practice and Procedure § 2858, at
                164-69 (1973).

                6 C. Wright, A. Miller & M. Kane, Federal Practice and Procedure
                § 1530 (Supp. 1987).

Federal Probation
Abbreviation: Fed. Probation

Federal Register
Abbreviation: Fed. Reg.

Examples: 45 Fed. Reg. 81,252 (1980).

                51 Fed. Reg. 12,700 (1986) (to be codified at 24 C.F.R. pt. 511).
                ——Where Fed. Reg. so indicates.

                Objection, 51 Fed. Reg. 12,734 (1986). ——When material is not of a
                permanent nature.

In law review footnotes, the titles of books and the names of cases are not underlined.

51 Fed. Reg. 12,711 (1986) (to be codified at C.F.R. pt. 226) (proposed April 10, 1986). ——Proposed Rule.

Federal Reporter
Abbreviation: F.

Examples: Pan-Am. Petroleum Transp. Co. v. Robins Dry Dock & Repair Co., 281 F. 97 (2d Cir. 1922). ——Case Cite.

Pan-Am. Petroleum Transp. Co. v. Robins Dry Dock & Repair Co., 281 F. 97, 98 (2d Cir. 1922). ——Page Cite.

Federal Reporter, Second Series
Abbreviation: F.2d

Examples: Darrow v. Gunn, 551 F.2d 312 (9th Cir. 1977). ——Case Cite.

Darrow v. Gunn, 551 F.2d 312, 314 (9th Cir. 1977). ——Page Cite.

Federal Reserve Bulletin (1915-date)
Abbreviation: Fed. Res. Bull.

Examples: Fikins, An Approach to Regulatory Simplification, 67 Fed. Res. Bull. 535 (1981).

Statement by Paul A. Volcker Before the Subcommittee on Domestic Monetary Policy of the Committee on Banking, Finance and Urban Affairs, U.S. House of Representatives, June 25, 1981, 67 Fed. Res. Bull. 548 (1981).

First National Boston Corp., 67 Fed. Res. Bull. 576 (1981).

Federal Revenue Forms (Prentice-Hall)
Abbreviation: Fed. Revenue Forms (P-H)

Federal Rules Decisions
Abbreviation: F.R.D.

Example: Gouldman v. Seligman & Latz of Houston, Inc., 82 F.R.D. 727 (S.D. Tex. 1979).

Federal Rules of Appellate Procedure
Abbreviation: Fed. R. App. P.

Example: Fed. R. App. P. 34.

Federal Rules of Civil Procedure
Abbreviation: Fed. R. Civ. P.

Example: Fed. R. Civ. P. 23.

In law review footnotes, the following are in large and small capitals: periodicals, constitutions, codes, restatements, standards, authors of books, titles of books, and legislative materials except for bills and resolutions. Refer to Bluebook.

Federal Rules of Criminal Procedure
    Abbreviation: Fed. R. Crim. P.

    Example: Fed. R. Crim. P. 18.

Federal Rules of Evidence
    Abbreviation: Fed. R. Evid.

    Example: Fed. R. Evid. 804(b)(4).

Federal Rules Service, Second Series
    Abbreviation: Fed. R. Serv. 2d (Callaghan)

    Examples: Financial Gen. Bankshares v. Metzer, [Current Volume] Fed. R. Serv.
                2d (Callaghan) (34 Fed. R. Serv. 2d) 17 (D.C. Cir. May 18, 1982).
                ——Citation to looseleaf material.

                Morse v. Gerity, 32 Fed. R. Serv. 2d (Callaghan) 1538 (D. Conn.
                1981). ——Citation to bound material.

  ——The above examples are proper if the case is not yet available in an official or West
  reporter, or is not reported in an official or West reporter.

Federal Securities Code (A.L.I.)
    See   American Law Institute Federal Securities Code

Federal Securities Law Reports (Commerce Clearing House)
    Abbreviation: Fed. Sec. L. Rep. (CCH)

    Examples: Portnoy v. Texas Int'l Airlines, [Current] Fed. Sec. L. Rep. (CCH)
                ¶ 98,687 (7th Cir. May 14, 1982). ——Citation to looseleaf material.

                SEC v. Weil, [1980 Decisions Transfer Binder] Fed. Sec. L. Rep.
                (CCH) ¶ 97,541 (M.D. Fla. 1980). ——Citation to transfer binder.

  ——The above examples are proper if the case is not yet available in an official or West
  reporter, or is not reported in an official or West reporter.

                Telex Corp., Exchange Act Release No. 18,694, [Current] Fed. Sec. L.
                Rep. (CCH) ¶ 83,209 (Apr. 29, 1982). ——Citation to looseleaf
                administrative material.

Federal Supplement
    Abbreviation: F. Supp.

    Examples: Marchwinski v. Oliver Tyrone Corp., 461 F. Supp. 160 (W.D. Pa.
                1978). ——Case Cite.

                Marchwinski v. Oliver Tyrone Corp., 461 F. Supp. 160, 162 (W.D.
                Pa. 1978). ——Page Cite.

Federal Tax Coordinator Second (Tax Research Institute of America)
    Abbreviation: Fed. Tax Coordinator 2d (Res. Inst. Am.)

In law review footnotes, the titles of books and the names of cases are not underlined.

Federal Tax Forms (Commerce Clearing House)
Abbreviation: Fed. Tax Forms (CCH)

Federal Taxation of Income, Estates and Gifts, by B. Bittker
——Do not abbreviate the title.

Examples: 5 B. Bittker, <u>Federal Taxation of Income, Estates and Gifts</u> § 123.6
(1984).

5 B. Bittker, <u>Federal Taxation of Income, Estates and Gifts</u> § 123.6, at
123-27 (1984).

Federal Taxes (Prentice-Hall)
Abbreviation: Fed. Taxes (P-H)

Examples: <u>Cousino v. Commissioner</u>, [Advance Sheets] Fed. Taxes (P-H) (50
A.F.T.R.2d) ¶ 82-5009 (6th Cir. May 26, 1982). ——Citation to
looseleaf material.

<u>Marshall Foods, Inc. v. United States</u>, 40 A.F.T.R.2d (P-H) ¶ 77-5244
(D. Minn. 1977). ——Citation to bound material.

<u>St. Louis County Bank v. United States</u>, [Estate and Gift Taxes II] Fed.
Taxes (P-H) (49 A.F.T.R.2d) ¶ 148,515 (8th Cir. Apr. 5, 1982).
——Citation to looseleaf material.

<u>Davis v. United States</u>, 40 A.F.T.R.2d (P-H) ¶ 148,163 (N.D. Tex.
1977). ——Citation to bound material.

<u>Morgan Drive Away, Inc. v. United States</u>, [Excise Taxes] Fed. Taxes
(P-H) (50 A.F.T.R.2d) ¶ 198,601 (Ct. Cl. Apr. 16, 1982). ——Citation
to looseleaf material.

<u>F & D Trading Corp. v. United States</u>, 40 A.F.T.R.2d (P-H) ¶ 199,307
(Ct. Cl. 1977). ——Citation to bound material.

——The above examples are proper if the case is not yet available in an official or West
reporter, or is not reported in an official or West reporter.

Federal Trade Commission Decisions (U.S.) (1915-date)
Abbreviation: F.T.C.

Example: <u>Hastings Mfg. Co.</u>, 95 F.T.C. 345 (1980).

Federalist, The
Abbreviation: The Federalist No. (author).

Examples: <u>The Federalist</u> No. 15 (A. Hamilton).

<u>The Federalist</u> No. 41, at 248 (J. Madison) (H. Lodge ed. 1888).

Films
Example: <u>To Catch a Thief</u> (Paramount 1955).

In law review footnotes, the following are in large and small capitals: periodicals, constitutions,
codes, restatements, standards, authors of books, titles of books, and legislative materials except
for bills and resolutions. Refer to Bluebook.

Fleming and Hazard on Civil Procedure
> See   Civil Procedure, by J. Fleming, Jr. & G. Hazard, Jr.

Fletcher Forum
> Abbreviation: Fletcher F.

Fletcher's Cyclopedia of the Law of Private Corporations
> ——Do not abbreviate the title.
>
> Examples: 3 W. Fletcher, Cyclopedia of the Law of Private Corporations § 840 (rev. perm. ed. 1986).
>
> 3 W. Fletcher, Cyclopedia of the Law of Private Corporations § 840, at 205 (rev. perm. ed. 1986).

Florida Administrative Code Annotated
> Abbreviations: Fla. Admin. Code Ann. r.   (year).

Florida Administrative Weekly
> Abbreviation: Fla. Admin. Weekly

Florida, Annual Report of the Attorney General
> See   Annual Report of the Attorney General, State of Florida

Florida Bar Journal
> Abbreviation: Fla. B.J.
>
> Examples: Miller, Compulsory Examinations Re-examined, 56 Fla. B.J. 700 (1982). ——Article Cite.
>
> Miller, Compulsory Examinations Re-examined, 56 Fla. B.J. 700, 703 (1982). ——Page Cite.

Florida Constitution
> Abbreviation: Fla. Const. art.   , §   .
>
> Examples: Fla. Const. art. 3, § 5. ——Cite provisions without date unless the cited provisions have been repealed or amended (Bluebook Rule 11).
>
> Fla. Const. art. 3, § 7 (1968, amended 1980). ——Cite provisions which have been repealed or amended by giving the date of the adoption of the particular provision and the date of repeal or amendment (Bluebook Rule 11).
>
> Fla. Const. of 1868, art. 7, § 10. ——Cite constitutions that have been totally superseded by year of adoption, giving parenthetically the year of adoption of the specific provision cited if different (Bluebook Rule 11).

Florida Reports
> Abbreviation: Fla.

In law review footnotes, the titles of books and the names of cases are not underlined.

——Discontinued after 160 Fla. 974 (1948). Thereafter cite only to So. and So. 2d.

Examples: Winfield v. Truitt, 71 Fla. 38, 70 So. 775 (1916). ——Case Cite.

Winfield v. Truitt, 71 Fla. 38, 48, 70 So. 775, 778-79 (1916).
——Page Cite.

——After 160 Fla. 974 (1948), cite as follows:

Florida Bar v. Quittner, 478 So. 2d 818 (Fla. 1985). ——Case Cite.

Florida Bar v. Quittner, 478 So. 2d 818, 820 (Fla. 1985). ——Page
Cite.

Florida Session Laws
See   Florida Session Law Service and Laws of Florida

Florida Session Law Service
year Fla. Sess. Law Serv.   (West).

Florida State University Law Review
Abbreviation: Fla. St. U.L. Rev.

Examples: Levinson, Interpreting State Constitutions by Resort to the Record, 6
Fla. St. U.L. Rev. 567 (1978). ——Article Cite.

Levinson, Interpreting State Constitutions by Resort to the Record, 6
Fla. St. U.L. Rev. 567, 568-70 (1978). ——Page Cite.

Florida Statutes
Abbreviation: Fla. Stat. §   (year).

Example: Fla. Stat. § 236.012(1) (1977).

Florida Statutes Annotated
Abbreviation: Fla. Stat. Ann. § (West year).

Examples: Fla. Stat. Ann. § 60.04 (West 1969).

Fla. Stat. Ann. § 95.11 (West Supp. 1988).

Florida Supplement
Abbreviation: Fla. Supp.

Examples: State v. Rinehart, 49 Fla. Supp. 64 (Cir. Ct. 1978). ——Case Cite.

State v. Rinehart, 49 Fla. Supp. 64, 66 (Cir. Ct. 1978). ——Page Cite.

Florida Supplement, 2nd Series
Abbreviation: Fla. Supp. 2d

Examples: Forrest v. Van Wezel, 9 Fla. Supp. 2d 173 (Cir. Ct. 1984). ——Case
Cite.

In law review footnotes, the following are in large and small capitals: periodicals, constitutions, codes, restatements, standards, authors of books, titles of books, and legislative materials except for bills and resolutions. Refer to Bluebook.

Forrest v. Van Wezel, 9 Fla. Supp. 2d 173, 174-75 (Cir. Ct. 1984).
——Page Cite.

Food Drug Cosmetic Law Journal
    Abbreviation: Food Drug Cosm. L.J.

    Examples: Mahinka, The Setting of Standards: Concerns for Medical Device
                    Regulation, 35 Food Drug Cosm. L.J. 244 (1980). ——Article Cite.

                    Mahinka, The Setting of Standards: Concerns for Medical Device
                    Regulation, 35 Food Drug Cosm. L.J. 244, 245-47 (1980). ——Page
                    Cite.

footnote(s)
    Abbreviations: note, notes
                     n., nn.

    Examples: supra note 211.

                     Futrell, The Hidden Crisis in Georgia Land Use, 10 Ga. L. Rev. 53, 88
                     n.124 (1975).

                     Futrell, The Hidden Crisis in Georgia Land Use, 10 Ga. L. Rev. 53, 89
                     nn.133-34 (1975).

Fordham International Law Forum
    Abbreviation: Fordham Int'l L.F.

Fordham International Law Journal
    Abbreviation: Fordham Int'l L.J.

    Examples: Sweeney, Judicial Review of Arbitral Proceedings, 5 Fordham Int'l L.J.
                     253 (1981-1982). ——Article Cite.

                     Sweeney, Judicial Review of Arbitral Proceedings, 5 Fordham Int'l L.J.
                     253, 268-69 (1981-1982). ——Page Cite.

Fordham Law Review
    Abbreviation: Fordham L. Rev.

    Examples: Jacobs, What is a Misleading Statement or Omission Under Rule 10b-
                     5?, 42 Fordham L. Rev. 243 (1973). ——Article Cite.

                     Jacobs, What is a Misleading Statement or Omission Under Rule 10b-
                     5?, 42 Fordham L. Rev. 243, 246-60 (1973). ——Page Cite.

Fordham Urban Law Journal
    Abbreviation: Fordham Urb. L.J.

    Examples: McDougall, Gentrification: The Class Conflict over Urban Space
                     Moves into the Courts, 10 Fordham Urb. L.J. 177 (1981-1982).
                     ——Article Cite.

In law review footnotes, the titles of books and the names of cases are not underlined.

McDougall, <u>Gentrification: The Class Conflict over Urban Space Moves into the Courts</u>, 10 Fordham Urb. L.J. 177, 195-96 (1981-1982). ——Page Cite.

forewords (to books)
<u>See</u> prefaces and forewords (to books)

Forum (ABA)
Abbreviation: Forum

Examples: Clore, <u>Suits Against Financial Institutions: Coverage and Considerations</u>, 20 Forum 84 (1984). ——Article Cite.

Clore, <u>Suits Against Financial Institutions: Coverage and Considerations</u>, 20 Forum 84, 91-92 (1984). ——Page Cite.

Franchise Law Journal
Abbreviation: Franchise L.J.

Examples: Madson, <u>Guidelines for Analyzing Franchise Arbitration Provisions</u>, Franchise L.J., Winter 1985, at 1. ——Article Cite.

Madson, <u>Guidelines for Analyzing Franchise Arbitration Provisions</u>, Franchise L.J., Winter 1985, at 1, 16. ——Page Cite.

Fundamentals of Securities Regulation, by L. Loss
——Do not abbreviate the title.

Example: L. Loss, <u>Fundamentals of Securities Regulation</u> 216 (1988).

In law review footnotes, the following are in large and small capitals: periodicals, constitutions, codes, restatements, standards, authors of books, titles of books, and legislative materials except for bills and resolutions. Refer to Bluebook.

In law review footnotes, the titles of books and the names of cases are not underlined.

G

General Acts of Arkansas
    Abbreviation: year Ark. Acts

General and Special Laws of the State of Texas
    Abbreviations: year Tex. Gen. Laws

General Laws of Mississippi
    Abbreviation: year Miss. Laws

General Laws of Rhode Island
    Abbreviation: R.I. Gen. Laws. §   (year).

    Examples: R.I. Gen. Laws § 23-27.1-2 (1985).

                   R.I. Gen. Laws § 19-2.1-1 (Supp. 1987).

General Laws of the Commonwealth of Massachusetts
    Abbreviation: Mass. Gen. L. ch.   , §   (year).

General Statutes of Connecticut, The
    Abbreviation: Conn. Gen. Stat. §   (year).

    Examples: Conn. Gen. Stat. § 31-22 (1987).

                   Conn. Gen. Stat. § 12-110 (Supp. 1988).

General Statutes of North Carolina, The
    Abbreviation: N.C. Gen. Stat. §   (year).

    Examples: N.C. Gen. Stat. § 54-109.1 (1982).

                   N.C. Gen. Stat. § 55A-15 (Supp. 1987).

George Mason University Law Review
    Abbreviation: Geo. Mason U.L. Rev.

    Examples: McDermid, Merger Directions in the United States and EEC: An Ominous Picture for United States Multinationals, 3 Geo. Mason U.L. Rev. 1 (1980). ——Article Cite.

                   McDermid, Merger Directions in the United States and EEC: An Ominous Picture for United States Multinationals, 3 Geo. Mason U.L. Rev. 1, 5-7 (1980). ——Page Cite.

In law review footnotes, the following are in large and small capitals: periodicals, constitutions, codes, restatements, standards, authors of books, titles of books, and legislative materials except for bills and resolutions. Refer to Bluebook.

George Washington Journal of International Law and Economics
    Abbreviation: Geo. Wash. J. Int'l L. & Econ.

    Examples: Grippando, <u>Warsaw Convention—Federal Jurisdiction and Air Carrier Liability for Mental Injury: A Matter of Limits</u>, 19 Geo. Wash. J. Int'l L. & Econ. 59 (1985). ——Article Cite.

                  Grippando, <u>Warsaw Convention—Federal Jurisdiction and Air Carrier Liability for Mental Injury: A Matter of Limits</u>, 19 Geo. Wash. J. Int'l L. & Econ. 59, 98-99 (1985). ——Page Cite.

George Washington Law Review
    Abbreviation: Geo. Wash. L. Rev.

    Examples: Smith, <u>Constitutional Privacy in Psychotherapy</u>, 49 Geo. Wash. L. Rev. 1 (1980). ——Article Cite.

                  Smith, <u>Constitutional Privacy in Psychotherapy</u>, 49 Geo. Wash. L. Rev. 1, 45-50 (1980). ——Page Cite.

Georgetown Law Journal
    Abbreviation: Geo. L.J.

    Examples: Bruce, <u>Mortgage Law Reform Under the Uniform Land Transactions Act</u>, 64 Geo. L.J. 1245 (1976). ——Article Cite.

                  Bruce, <u>Mortgage Reform Law Under the Uniform Land Transactions Act</u>, 64 Geo. L.J. 1245, 1262-69 (1976). ——Page Cite.

Georgia Appeals Reports
    Abbreviation: Ga. App.

    Examples: <u>Rider v. Albea</u>, 175 Ga. App. 53, 332 S.E.2d 168 (1985). ——Case Cite.

                  <u>Rider v. Albea</u>, 175 Ga. App. 53, 56-57, 332 S.E.2d 168, 170-71 (1985). ——Page Cite.

Georgia Code
    <u>See</u>   Official Code of Georgia Annotated (Michie).

Georgia Code Annotated
    <u>See</u>   Code of Georgia Annotated

Georgia Constitution
    Abbreviation: Ga. Const. art. , § , ¶ .

    Examples: Ga. Const. art. II, § III, ¶ V. ——Cite provisions without date unless the cited provisions have been repealed or amended (Bluebook Rule 11).

In law review footnotes, the titles of books and the names of cases are not underlined.

Ga. Const. art. III, § VIII, ¶ XII (1976, amended 1979). ——Cite provisions which have been repealed or amended by giving the date of the adoption of the particular provision and the date of repeal or amendment (Bluebook Rule 11).

Ga. Const. of 1943, art. I, § I. ——Cite constitutions that have been totally superseded by year of adoption, giving parenthetically the year of adoption of the specific provision cited if different (Bluebook Rule 11).

Georgia Journal of International and Comparative Law
Abbreviation: Ga. J. Int'l & Comp. L.

Examples: Rusk & Ball, Sea Changes and the American Republic, 9 Ga. J. Int'l & Comp. L. 1 (1979). ——Article Cite.

Rusk & Ball, Sea Changes and the American Republic, 9 Ga. J. Int'l & Comp. L. 1, 3-10 (1979). ——Page Cite.

Georgia Law Review
Abbreviation: Ga. L. Rev.

Examples: Chaffin, A Reappraisal of the Wealth Transmission Process: The Surviving Spouse, Year's Support and Intestate Succession, 10 Ga. L. Rev. 447 (1979). ——Article Cite.

Chaffin, A Reappraisal of the Wealth Transmission Process: The Surviving Spouse, Year's Support and Intestate Succession, 10 Ga. L. Rev. 447, 448-49 (1979). ——Page Cite.

Georgia Laws
Abbreviation: year Ga. Laws

Georgia Official Code
See   Official Code of Georgia Annotated

Georgia, Opinions of the Attorney General
See   Opinions of the Attorney General, State of Georgia

Georgia Reports
Abbreviation: Ga.

Examples: In re White, 254 Ga. 678, 333 S.E.2d 588 (1985). ——Case Cite.

In re White, 254 Ga. 678, 681, 333 S.E.2d 588, 590 (1985). ——Page Cite.

Georgia Rules and Regulations
See   Official Compilation of the Rules and Regulations of the State of Georgia

Georgia Session Laws
See   Georgia Laws

In law review footnotes, the following are in large and small capitals: periodicals, constitutions, codes, restatements, standards, authors of books, titles of books, and legislative materials except for bills and resolutions. Refer to Bluebook.

Georgia State Bar Journal
Abbreviation: Ga. St. B.J.

Examples: Thrash & Blank, <u>Latent Injuries and the Statute of Limitations</u>, 19 Ga. St. B.J. 12 (1982). ——Article Cite.

Thrash & Blank, <u>Latent Injuries and the Statute of Limitations</u>, 19 Ga. St. B.J. 12, 14-15 (1982). ——Page Cite.

German Yearbook of International Law
Abbreviations: German Y.B. Int'l L.
GYIL (publisher's abbreviation)

Glendale Law Review
Abbreviation: Glendale L. Rev.

Golden Gate University Law Review
Abbreviation: Golden Gate U.L. Rev.

Examples: Mitchell, <u>Misappropriation and the New Copyright Act: An Overview</u>, 10 Golden Gate U.L. Rev. 587 (1980). ——Article Cite.

Mitchell, <u>Misappropriation and the New Copyright Act: An Overview</u>, 10 Golden Gate U.L. Rev. 587, 591-93 (1980). ——Page Cite.

Goldstein Trial Technique, by I. Goldstein & F. Lane
——Do not abbreviate the title.

Examples: 3 F. Lane, <u>Goldstein Trial Techniques</u> § 19.08 (3d ed. 1986).

3 F. Lane, <u>Goldstein Trial Techniques</u> § 19.08, at 11 (3d ed. 1986).

Gonzaga Law Review
Abbreviation: Gonz. L. Rev.

Examples: Becker, <u>Washington State's New Juvenile Code: An Introduction</u>, 14 Gonz. L. Rev. 289 (1979). ——Article Cite.

Becker, <u>Washington State's New Juvenile Code: An Introduction</u>, 14 Gonz. L. Rev. 289, 297-307 (1979). ——Page Cite.

Gordon & Rosenfield on Immigration Law and Procedure
——Do not abbreviate the title.

Examples: 2 C. Gordon & H. Rosenfield, <u>Immigration Law and Procedure</u> § 7.12a (rev. ed. 1987).

2 C. Gordon & H. Rosenfield, <u>Immigration Law and Procedure</u> § 7.12a, at 9-49 (rev. ed. 1987).

Gorman on Labor Law
<u>See</u>   Basic Text on Labor Law, by R. Gorman

In law review footnotes, the titles of books and the names of cases are not underlined.

Government Contracts Reports (Commerce Clearing House)
     Abbreviation: Gov't Cont. Rep. (CCH)

     Examples: Massman Constr. Co. v. Tennessee Valley Auth., 8 Gov't Cont. Rep.
                (CCH) (33 Cont. Cas. Fed.) ¶ 73,773 (6th Cir. Aug. 13, 1985).
                ——Citation to looseleaf material.

                Owen of Georgia, Inc. v. Shelby County, 29 Cont. Cas. Fed. (CCH)
                ¶ 81,750 (6th Cir. 1981). ——Citation to transfer binder.

——The above examples are proper if the case is not yet available in an official or West
reporter, or is not reported in an official or West reporter.

Government Employee Relations Report (Bureau of National Affairs)
     Abbreviation: Gov't Empl. Rel. Rep. (BNA)

     Examples: Freeman v. Lewis, [Current Reports Jan.-June] Gov't Empl. Rel. Rep.
                (BNA) 960:65 (D.C. Cir. Apr. 13, 1982). ——Citation to looseleaf
                material.

                EEOC v. Wyoming, [Jan.-June 1981] Gov't Empl. Rel. Rep. (BNA)
                916:37 (D. Wyo. 1981). ——Citation to bound material.

                United States Dep't of Justice Immigration and Naturalization Serv.,
                Western Regional Office v. American Fed'n of Government
                Employees, Local 2805, [Current Reports Jan.-June] Gov't Empl. Rel.
                Rep. (BNA) 958:30 (Feb. 15, 1982) (Rule, Arb.). ——Citation to
                looseleaf administrative material.

                United States Dep't of Agriculture, Meat Grading Branch Livestock
                Div. v. American Fed'n of Government Employees, [July-Dec. 1978]
                Gov't Empl. Rel. Rep. (BNA) 780:45 (1978) (Doyle, Arb.).
                ——Citation to bound administrative material.

——The above examples are proper if the case is not yet available in an official or West
reporter, or is not reported in an official or West reporter.

Green on Civil Procedure
     See   Basic Civil Procedure, by M. Green

In law review footnotes, the following are in large and small capitals: periodicals, constitutions,
codes, restatements, standards, authors of books, titles of books, and legislative materials except
for bills and resolutions. Refer to Bluebook.

In law review footnotes, the titles of books and the names of cases are not underlined.

H

Hamline Law Review
    Abbreviation: Hamline L. Rev.

    Examples: Wahl, Equal Justice Under Law: Dream or Reality?, 1979 Hamline L. Rev. 1. ——Article Cite.

        Wahl, Equal Justice Under Law: Dream or Reality?, 1979 Hamline L. Rev. 1, 10-12. ——Page Cite.

Handbook of the Law of Antitrust, by Lawrence A. Sullivan
    ——Do not abbreviate the title.

    Examples: L. Sullivan, Handbook of the Law of Antitrust § 184 (1977).

        L. Sullivan, Handbook of the Law of Antitrust § 184, at 529 (1977).

Handbook of the Law of Corporations, by Harry G. Henn
    ——Do not abbreviate the title

    Examples: H. Henn, Handbook of the Law of Corporations § 156 (3d ed. 1983).

        H. Henn, Handbook of the Law of Corporations § 156, at 387 (3d ed. 1983).

Handbook of the Law of Wills, by Thomas E. Atkinson
    ——Do not abbreviate the title.

    Examples: T. Atkinson, Handbook of the Law of Wills § 86 (2d ed. 1953).

        T. Atkinson, Handbook of the Law of Wills § 86, at 442 (2d ed. 1953).

Handbook of the Law Under the Uniform Commercial Code, by James J. White & Robert S. Summers
    ——Do not abbreviate the title.

    Examples: J. White & R. Summers, Handbook of the Law Under the Uniform Commercial Code § 13-10 (2d ed. 1980).

        J. White & R. Summers, Handbook of the Law Under the Uniform Commercial Code § 13-10, at 505-06 (2d ed. 1980).

Handbook of the Principles of Equity, by Henry L. McClintock
    ——Do not abbreviate the title.

    Examples: H. McClintock, Handbook of the Principles of Equity § 196 (2d ed. 1948).

In law review footnotes, the following are in large and small capitals: periodicals, constitutions, codes, restatements, standards, authors of books, titles of books, and legislative materials except for bills and resolutions. Refer to Bluebook.

H. McClintock, <u>Handbook of the Principles of Equity</u> § 196, at 529 (2d ed. 1948).

Handbook on the Law of Remedies, by Dan B. Dobbs
——Do not abbreviate the title.

Examples: D. Dobbs, <u>Handbook on the Law of Remedies</u> § 12.13 (1973).

D. Dobbs, <u>Handbook on the Law of Remedies</u> § 12.13, at 861 (1973).

Harvard Civil Rights—Civil Liberties Law Review
Abbreviation: Harv. C.R.-C.L. L. Rev.

Examples: Delgado, <u>Words That Wound: A Tort Action for Racial Insults, Epithets, and Name-Calling</u>, 17 Harv. C.R.-C.L. L. Rev. 133 (1982). ——Article Cite.

Delgado, <u>Words That Wound: A Tort Action for Racial Insults, Epithets, and Name-Calling</u>, 17 Harv. C.R.-C.L. L. Rev. 133, 157-58 (1982). ——Page Cite.

Harvard Environmental Law Review
Abbreviation: Harv. Envtl. L. Rev.

Examples: Stewart, <u>Interstate Resource Conflicts: The Role of the Federal Courts</u>, 6 Harv. Envtl. L. Rev. 241 (1982). ——Article Cite.

Stewart, <u>Interstate Resource Conflicts: The Role of the Federal Courts</u>, 6 Harv. Envtl. L. Rev. 241, 256-57 (1982). ——Page Cite.

Harvard International Law Journal
Abbreviation: Harv. Int'l L.J.

Examples: Charney, <u>The International Regime for the Deep Seabed: Past Conflicts and Proposals for Progress</u>, 17 Harv. Int'l L.J. 1 (1976). ——Article Cite.

Charney, <u>The International Regime for the Deep Seabed: Past Conflicts and Proposals for Progress</u>, 17 Harv. Int'l L.J. 1, 13-21 (1976). ——Page Cite.

Harvard Journal of Law and Public Policy
Abbreviation: Harv. J.L. & Pub. Pol'y

Examples: Schifrin, <u>Lessons From the Drug Lag: A Retrospective Analysis of the 1962 Drug Regulations</u>, 5 Harv. J.L. & Pub. Pol'y 91 (1982). ——Article Cite.

Schifrin, <u>Lessons From the Drug Lag: A Retrospective Analysis of the 1962 Drug Regulations</u>, 5 Harv. J.L. & Pub. Pol'y 91, 111-12 (1982). ——Page Cite.

In law review footnotes, the titles of books and the names of cases are not underlined.

Harvard Journal on Legislation
    Abbreviation: Harv. J. on Legis.

    Examples: Jones, <u>Educational Rights of Handicapped Children</u>, 19 Harv. J. on Legis. 287 (1982). ——Article Cite.

                Jones, <u>Educational Rights of Handicapped Children</u>, 19 Harv. J. on Legis. 287, 297-98 (1982). ——Page Cite.

Harvard Law Review
    Abbreviation: Harv. L. Rev.

    Examples: Landes & Posner, <u>Market Power in Antitrust Cases</u>, 94 Harv. L. Rev. 937 (1981). ——Article Cite.

                Landes & Posner, <u>Market Power in Antitrust Cases</u>, 94 Harv. L. Rev. 937, 946-52 (1981). ——Page Cite.

Harvard Women's Law Journal
    Abbreviation: Harv. Women's L.J.

Harvard World Tax Series
    Abbreviation: Harv. W. Tax Ser.

Hastings Constitutlonal Law Quarterly
    Abbreviation: Hastings Const. L.Q.

    Examples: Wilson, <u>Shifting Burdens in Criminal Law: A Burden on Due Process</u>, 8 Hastings Const. L.Q. 731 (1981). ——Article Clte.

                Wilson, <u>Shifting Burdens in Criminal Law: A Burden on Due Process</u>, 8 Hastings Const. L.Q. 731, 732-33 (1981). ——Page Cite.

Hastings International and Comparative Law Review
    Abbreviation: Hastings Int'l & Comp. L. Rev.

    Examples: Meador, <u>Appellate Subject Matter Organization: The German Design from an American Perspective</u>, 5 Hastings Int'l & Comp. L. Rev. 27 (1981). ——Article Cite.

                Meador, <u>Appellate Subject Matter Organization: The German Design from an American Perspective</u>, 5 Hastings Int'l & Comp. L. Rev. 27, 28-31 (1981). ——Page Cite.

Hastings Law Journal
    Abbreviation: Hastings L.J.

    Examples: DuBoff, <u>Controlling the Artful Con: Authentication and Regulation</u>, 27 Hastings L.J. 973 (1976). ——Article Cite.

                DuBoff, <u>Controlling the Artful Con: Authentication and Regulation</u>, 27 Hastings L.J. 973, 974-80 (1976). ——Page Cite.

In law review footnotes, the following are in large and small capitals: periodicals, constitutions, codes, restatements, standards, authors of books, titles of books, and legislative materials except for bills and resolutions. Refer to Bluebook.

Hawaii Appellate Reports
Abbreviation: Haw. App.

Examples: Hong v. Kong, 5 Haw. App. 174, 683 P.2d 833 (1984). ——Case Cite.

Hong v. Kong, 5 Haw. App. 174, 177, 683 P.2d 833, 835 (1984).
——Page Cite.

Hawaii Attorney General Report
Abbreviation: Haw. Att'y Gen. Rep.

Example: 1978 Haw. Att'y Gen. Rep. No. 78-1. ——The name of the opinion
may be included. See Bluebook Rule 14.4.

Hawaii Bar Journal
Abbreviation: Haw. B.J.

Examples: Peckron, Tax Consequences of Land Trusts, 16 Haw. B.J. 3 (1981).
——Article Cite.

Peckron, Tax Consequences of Land Trusts, 16 Haw. B.J. 3, 10-11
(1981). ——Page Cite.

Hawaii Constitution
Abbreviation: Haw. Const. art.   , §   .

Examples: Haw. Const. art. 1, § 1. ——Cite provisions without date unless the
cited provisions have been repealed or amended (Bluebook Rule 11).

Haw. Const. art 1, § 1 (1968, amended 1978). ——Cite provisions
which have been repealed or amended by giving the date of the adoption
of the particular provision and the date of repeal or amendment
(Bluebook Rule 11).

Haw. Const. of 1949, art. 1, § 1. ——Cite constitutions that have been
totally superseded by year of adoption, giving parenthetically the year of
adoption of the specific provision cited if different (Bluebook Rule 11).

Hawaii Reports
Abbreviation: Haw.

Examples: Beamer v. Nishiki, 66 Haw. 572, 670 P.2d 1264 (1983). ——Case
Cite.

Beamer v. Nishiki, 66 Haw. 572, 573, 670 P.2d 1264, 1265 (1983).
——Page Cite.

Hawaii Revised Statutes
Abbreviation: Haw. Rev. Stat. §   (year).

Examples: Haw. Rev. Stat. § 576-31 (1985).

Haw. Rev. Stat. § 201E-200 (Supp. 1987).

In law review footnotes, the titles of books and the names of cases are not underlined.

Hawaii Rules and Regulations
>   Abbreviation: Hawaii Rules & Reg.

Hawaii Session Laws
>   See   Session Laws of Hawaii

Hearings, Congressional
>   See   Congressional hearings

Henn on Corporations
>   See   Handbook of the Law of Corporations, by H. Henn

hereinafter
>   ——Should not be used in referring to cases, statutes, or similar material except in extraordinary circumstances (Bluebook Rule 4.2(b)).

Hofstra Labor Law Journal
>   Abbreviation: Hofstra Lab. L.J.

Hofstra Law Review
>   Abbreviation: Hofstra L. Rev.
>
>   Examples: Posner, The Ethical and Political Basis of the Efficiency Norm in Common Law Adjudication, 8 Hofstra L. Rev. 487 (1980). ——Article Cite.
>
>   Posner, The Ethical and Political Basis of the Efficiency Norm in Common Law Adjudication, 8 Hofstra L. Rev. 487, 501-03 (1980). ——Page Cite.

House bills (U.S. Congress)
>   See   Congressional Bills

House Concurrent Resolution
>   See   Congressional Resolutions

House Conference Report
>   Example: H.R. Conf. Rep. No. 962, 99th Cong., 2d Sess. 7 (1986).

House Joint Resolution
>   See   Congressional Resolutions

House Resolution
>   See   Congressional Resolutions

In law review footnotes, the following are in large and small capitals: periodicals, constitutions, codes, restatements, standards, authors of books, titles of books, and legislative materials except for bills and resolutions. Refer to Bluebook.

Housing and Development Reporter (Bureau of National Affairs)
  Abbreviation: Hous. & Dev. Rep. (BNA)

Houston Journal of International Law
  Abbreviation: Hous. J. Int'l L.

  Examples: Pitts, <u>American Investment in Mexico</u>, 2 Hous. J. Int'l L. 261 (1980).
     ——Article Cite.

     Pitts, <u>American Investment in Mexico</u>, 2 Hous. J. Int'l L. 261, 286-87
     (1980). ——Page Cite.

Houston Law Review
  Abbreviation: Hous. L. Rev.

  Examples: Allison, <u>Ambiguous Price Fixing and the Sherman Act: Simplistic</u>
     <u>Labels or Unavoidable Analysis?</u>, 16 Hous. L. Rev. 761 (1979).
     ——Article Cite.

     Allison, <u>Ambiguous Price Fixing and the Sherman Act: Simplistic</u>
     <u>Labels or Unavoidable Analysis?</u>, 16 Hous. L. Rev. 761, 763-70
     (1979). ——Page Cite.

Howard (United States Reports)
  See United States Reports

Howard Law Journal
  Abbreviation: How. L.J.

  Examples: Washington, <u>Comment: History and Role of Black Law Schools</u>, 18
     How. L.J. 385 (1974). ——Article Cite.

     Washington, <u>Comment: History and Role of Black Law Schools</u>, 18
     How. L.J. 385, 388-97 (1974). ——Page Cite.

Human Rights
  Abbreviation: Hum. Rts.

Human Rights Quarterly
  Abbreviation: Hum. Rts. Q.

Hursh & Bailey on American Law of Products Liability
  See American Law of Products Liability, by R. Hursh & H. Bailey

---

In law review footnotes, the titles of books and the names of cases are not underlined.

I

ICC Practitioner's Journal
> Abbreviation: ICC Prac. J.

Id.; id.
> text:

> Example: "And in <u>Faretta v. California</u>, 422 U.S. 806, 95 S. Ct. 2525, 45 L. Ed.
> 2d 562 (1975), the Supreme Court listed a defendant's right to testify in
> his own behalf as one of several constitutional rights 'essential to due
> process of law in a fair adversary process,' <u>id.</u>, at 819 n.15, 95 S. Ct.
> 2533 no.15..." ——Taken from 675 F.2d 913, 921 (1982).

> footnotes:

> Examples: 397 U.S. 254 (1970).
> <u>See id.</u>, Tatum v. Mathews, 541 F.2d 161 (6th Cir. 1976); Johnson v.
> Matthews, 539 F.2d 1111 (8th Cir. 1976). ——Taken from 95 Harv. L.
> Rev. 1195, 1266 nn.302-303 (1982).

> 595 F.2d, at 1291-92.
> <u>Id.</u> at 1292.
> <u>Id.</u> at 1299 (Adams, J., concurring). ——Taken from 95 Harv. L. Rev.
> 1976, 1981 nn.28-30 (1982).

Idaho Code (Containing The General Laws of Idaho Annotated)
> Abbreviation: Idaho Code §   (year).

> Examples: Idaho Code § 49-409 (1980).

> Idaho Code § 18-6401 (Supp. 1987).

Idaho Constitution
> Abbreviation: Idaho Const. art.   , §   .

> Examples: Idaho Const. art. I, § 13. ——Cite provisions without date unless the
> cited provisions have been repealed or amended (Bluebook Rule 11).

> Idaho Const. art. XVIII, § 5 (1890, amended 1898). ——Cite
> provisions which have been repealed or amended by giving the date of
> the adoption of the particular provision and the date of repeal or
> amendment (Bluebook Rule 11).

Idaho Law Review
> Abbreviation: Idaho L. Rev.

In law review footnotes, the following are in large and small capitals: periodicals, constitutions,
codes, restatements, standards, authors of books, titles of books, and legislative materials except
for bills and resolutions. Refer to Bluebook.

Examples: Grant, <u>Registration of Constitutional Method Water Rights</u>, 17 Idaho L. Rev. 7 (1980). ——Article Cite.

Grant, <u>Registration of Constitutional Method Water Rights</u>, 17 Idaho L. Rev. 7, 40-45 (1980). ——Page Cite.

Idaho Reports
Abbreviation: Idaho

Examples: <u>Hansen v. Sweet</u>, 108 Idaho 785, 702 P.2d 823 (1985). ——Case Cite.

<u>Hansen v. Sweet</u>, 108 Idaho 785, 786-87, 702 P.2d 823, 824-25 (1985). ——Page Cite.

Idaho Session Laws
<u>See</u> Session Laws (of) Idaho

Idea
Abbreviation: Idea

Illinois Administrative Code
Abbreviation: Ill. Admin. Code tit. , § (year).

Illinois Annotated Statutes, Smith-Hurd
<u>See</u> Smith-Hurd Illinois Annotated Statutes

Illinois Appellate Court Reports
Abbreviation: Ill. App.

Examples: <u>People v. Potter</u>, 319 Ill. App. 409, 49 N.E.2d 307 (1943). ——Case Cite.

<u>People v. Potter</u>, 319 Ill. App. 409, 410-11, 49 N.E.2d 307, 308 (1943). ——Page Cite.

Illinois Appellate Court Reports, second series
Abbreviation: Ill. App. 2d

Examples: <u>People v. Hartfield</u>, 94 Ill. App. 2d 421, 237 N.E.2d 193 (1968). ——Case Cite.

<u>People v. Hartfield</u>, 94 Ill. App. 2d 421, 430-31, 237 N.E.2d 193, 197-98 (1968). ——Page Cite.

Illinois Appellate Court Reports, third series
Abbreviation: Ill. App. 3d

Examples: <u>Brucato v. Edgar</u>, 128 Ill. App. 3d 260, 470 N.E.2d 615 (1984). ——Case Cite.

<u>Brucato v. Edgar</u>, 128 Ill. App. 3d 260, 263-64, 470 N.E.2d 615, 617-18 (1984). ——Page Cite.

In law review footnotes, the titles of books and the names of cases are not underlined.

Illinois Attorney General's Opinion
    Abbreviation: Op. Ill. Att'y Gen.

    Example: 1980 Op. Ill. Att'y Gen. 90. ——The name of the opinion may be
    included. See Bluebook Rule 14.4.

Illinois Bar Journal
    Abbreviation: Ill. B.J.

    Examples: Ladden, Irrationally Held Truths: A Mildly Iconoclastic Look at the
    Illinois Marriage and Dissolution of Marriage Act, 70 Ill. B.J. 628
    (1982). ——Article Cite.

    Ladden, Irrationally Held Truths: A Mildly Iconoclastic Look at the
    Illinois Marriage and Dissolution of Marriage Act, 70 Ill. B.J. 628,
    630-31 (1982). ——Page Cite.

Illinois Constitution
    Abbreviation: Ill. Const. art.   , §   .

    Examples: Ill. Const. art. VIII, § 1. ——Cite provisions without date unless the
    cited provisions have been repealed or amended (Bluebook Rule 11).

    Ill. Const. art.   , §   (year, amended year). ——No amended
    provisions have yet appeared (Ed.). Cite provisions which have been
    repealed or amended by giving the date of the adoption of the particular
    provision and the date of repeal or amendment (Bluebook Rule 11).

    Ill. Const. of 1870, art. XI, § 3. ——Cite constitutions that have been
    totally superseded by year of adoption, giving parenthetically the year of
    adoption of the specific provision cited if different (Bluebook Rule 11).

Illinois Court of Claims Reports
    Abbreviation: Ill. Ct. Cl.

    Examples: Maier v. State, 32 Ill. Ct. Cl. 924 (1979). ——Case Cite.

    Maier v. State, 32 Ill. Ct. Cl. 924, 926-27 (1979). ——Page Cite.

Illinois Law Review
    See   Northwestern University Law Review

Illinois Legislative Service (West)
    Abbreviation: year Ill. Legis. Serv.   (West).

Illinois Register
    Abbreviation: Ill. Reg.

    Example: 6 Ill. Reg. 12.367 (1982).

Illinois Reports
    Abbreviation: Ill.

In law review footnotes, the following are in large and small capitals: periodicals, constitutions,
codes, restatements, standards, authors of books, titles of books, and legislative materials except
for bills and resolutions. Refer to Bluebook.

Examples: <u>Nye v. Nye</u>, 411 Ill. 408, 105 N.E.2d 300 (1952). ——Case Cite.

               <u>Nye v. Nye</u>, 411 Ill. 408, 416, 105 N.E.2d 300, 304 (1952). ——Page Cite.

Illinois Reports, second series
Abbreviation: Ill. 2d

Examples: <u>Cockrum v. Baumgartner</u>, 95 Ill. 2d 193, 447 N.E.2d 385 (1983). ——Case Cite.

               <u>Cockrum v. Baumgartner</u>, 95 Ill. 2d 193, 196, 447 N.E.2d 385, 387 (1983). ——Page Cite.

Illinois Revised Statutes
Abbreviation: Ill. Rev. Stat. ch.   , para.   (year).

Example: Ill. Rev. Stat. ch. 77, para. 1 (1977).

Illinois Session Laws
<u>See</u>   Laws of Illinois and Illinois Legislative Service

Immigration Journal
Abbreviation: Immigr. J.

Examples: Myers, <u>Do Immigration Lawyers Know Their Place?</u>, Immigr. J., Oct.-Nov. 1979, at 7. ——Article Cite.

               Myers, <u>Do Immigration Lawyers Know Their Place?</u>, Immigr. J., Oct.-Nov. 1979, at 7, 7. ——Page Cite.

Indiana Administrative Code
Abbreviation: Ind. Admin. Code tit.   , r.   (year).

Indiana, Annual Report and Official Opinions of the Attorney General
<u>See</u>   Annual Report and Official Opinions of the Attorney General of Indiana

Indiana Appellate Court Reports (1890-1971) (continued as Indiana Court of Appeals Reports)
Abbreviation: Ind. App.

Examples: <u>Evans v. Enoco Colleries, Inc.</u>, 137 Ind. App. 11, 202 N.E.2d 595 (App. 1964). ——Case Cite.

               <u>Evans v. Enoco Colleries, Inc.</u>, 137 Ind. App. 11, 13, 202 N.E.2d 595, 596 (App. 1964). ——Page Cite.

Indiana Code
Abbreviation: Ind. Code §   (year).

Examples: Ind. Code § 8-1-282 (1977).

In law review footnotes, the titles of books and the names of cases are not underlined.

Ind. Code § 35-3.1-1-9 (Supp. 1979).

Indiana Code Annotated
    See   West's Annotated Indiana Code

Indiana Constitution
    Abbreviation: Ind. Const. art.   , §   .

    Examples: Ind. Const. art. I, § 1. ——Cite provisions without date unless the cited provisions have been repealed or amended (Bluebook Rule 11).

                Ind. Const. art. II, § 5 (1851, repealed 1881). ——Cite provisions which have been repealed or amended by giving the date of the adoption of the particular provision and the date of repeal or amendment (Bluebook Rule 11).

                Ind. Const. of 1816, art. XII, § 4. ——Cite constitutions that have been totally superseded by year of adoption, giving parenthetically the year of adoption of the specific provision cited if different (Bluebook Rule 11).

Indiana Court of Appeals Reports
    Abbreviation: Ind. App.

——Discontinued after 182 Ind. App. 697 (1979). Thereafter cite only to N.E.2d

    Examples: Keck v. Kerbs, 182 Ind. App. 530, 395 N.E.2d 845 (Ct. App. 1979). ——Case Cite.

                Keck v. Kerbs, 192 Ind. App. 530, 530, 395 N.E.2d 845, 845 (Ct. App. 1979). ——Page Cite.

——After 182 Ind. App. 697 (1979) cite as follows:

                Smith v. Beasley, 504 N.E.2d 1028 (Ind. Ct. App. 1987). ——Case Cite.

                Smith v. Beasley, 504 N.E.2d 1028, 1029 (Ind. Ct. App. 1987). ——Page Cite.

Indiana Law Journal
    Abbreviation: Ind. L.J.

    Examples: Trautman, The Income Taxation of Estate Distributions—A Need for Reform, 44 Ind. L.J. 397 (1968). ——Article Cite.

                Trautman, The Income Taxation of Estate Distributions—A Need for Reform, 44 Ind. L.J. 397, 403-10 (1968). ——Page Cite.

Indiana Law Review
    Abbreviation: Ind. L. Rev.

    Examples: Trant, Prospective Labor Injunctions: Do They Have a Future?, 14 Ind. L. Rev. 581 (1981). ——Article Cite.

In law review footnotes, the following are in large and small capitals: periodicals, constitutions, codes, restatements, standards, authors of books, titles of books, and legislative materials except for bills and resolutions. Refer to Bluebook.

Trant, <u>Prospective Labor Injunctions: Do They Have a Future?</u>, 14 Ind. L. Rev. 581, 585-92 (1981). ——Page Cite.

Indiana Register
     Abbreviation: Ind. Reg.

Indiana Reports
     Abbreviation: Ind.

——Discontinued after 275 Ind. 699 (1981). Thereafter cite only to N.E.2d.

Examples: <u>Moon v. State</u>, 275 Ind. 651, 419 N.E.2d 740 (1981). ——Case Cite.

                    <u>Moon v. State</u>, 275 Ind. 651, 655, 419 N.E.2d 740, 743 (1981). ——Page Cite.

——After 275 Ind. 699 (1981) cite as follows:

                    <u>Kroslack v. Estate of Kroslack</u>, 504 N.E.2d 1024 (Ind. 1987). ——Case Cite.

                    <u>Kroslack v. Estate of Kroslack</u>, 504 N.E.2d 1024, 1027 (Ind. 1987). ——Page Cite.

Indiana Session Laws
     <u>See</u>   Acts (of) Indiana

Indiana Statutes Annotated Code Edition, Burns
     <u>See</u>   Burns Indiana Statutes Annotated Code Edition

Industrial and Labor Relations Review
     Abbreviation: Indus. & Lab. Rel. Rev.
                             ILR Rev. (publisher's abbreviation)

Industrial Law Journal
     Abbreviation: Indus. L.J.

Examples: Lewis, <u>The Privatisation of Sickness Benefit</u>, 11 Indus. L.J. 245 (1982). ——Article Cite.

                    Lewis, <u>The Privatisation of Sickness Benefit</u>, 11 Indus. L.J. 245, 250-51 (1982). ——Page Cite.

Industrial Relations
     Abbreviation: Indus. Rel.

Industrial Relations Guide (Prentice-Hall)
     Abbreviation: Indus. Rel. Guide (P-H)

Inheritance, Estate & Gift Tax Reports (Commerce Clearing House)
     Abbreviation: Inher. Est. & Gift Tax Rep. (CCH)

In law review footnotes, the titles of books and the names of cases are not underlined.

Institute on Estate Planning (University of Miami Law Center)
Abbreviation: Inst. on Est. Plan.

Examples: Schoenblum, <u>Working With the Unified Credit</u>, 1 Inst. on Est. Plan.
¶ 1400 (1981). ——Article Cite.

Schoenblum, <u>Working With the Unified Credit</u>, 1 Inst. on Est.
Plan. ¶ 1400, ¶ 1404.2 (1981). ——Paragraph Cite.

Institute on Federal Taxation (New York University)
Abbreviation: Inst. on Fed. Tax'n

Examples: Hardee, <u>Income and Deductions of Estates</u>, 40 Inst. on Fed. Tax'n
§ 8.00 (1982). ——Article Cite.

Hardee, <u>Income and Deductions of Estates</u>, 40 Inst. on Fed. Tax'n
§ 8.00, § 8.09 (1982). ——Section Cite.

Institute on Mineral Law (Louisiana State University)
Abbreviation: Inst. on Min. L.

Examples: Willey, <u>The Lessee's Implied Obligations Under the Mineral Code</u>,
1976 Inst. on Min. L. 155. ——Article Cite.

Willey, <u>The Lessee's Implied Obligations Under the Mineral Code</u>,
1976 Inst. on Min. L. 155, 164-65. ——Page Cite.

Institute on Oil and Gas Law and Taxation (Southwestern Legal Foundation)
Abbreviation: Inst. on Oil & Gas L. & Tax'n

Examples: Bell & Mackenzie, <u>Windfall Profit Tax and DOE Regulation: Problems
in Property Definition</u>, 32 Inst. on Oil & Gas L. & Tax'n 301 (1981).
——Article Cite.

Bell & Mackenzie, <u>Windfall Profit Tax and DOE Regulation: Problems
in Property Definition</u>, 32 Inst. on Oil & Gas L. & Tax'n 301, 312-13
(1981). ——Page Cite.

**Institute on Planning, Zoning and Eminent Domain Proceedings (Southwestern Legal
Foundation)**
Abbreviation: Inst. on Plan. Zoning & Eminent Domain

Examples: Hicks, <u>New and Significant Decisions: the Interest Groups Involved in
the Planning and Zoning Process</u>, 1978 Inst. on Plan. Zoning &
Eminent Domain 1. ——Article Cite.

Hicks, <u>New and Significant Decisions: the Interest Groups Involved in
the Planning and Zoning Process</u>, 1978 Inst. on Plan. Zoning &
Eminent Domain 1, 33-34. ——Page Cite.

Institute on Private Investments and Investors Abroad Proceedings
Abbreviation: Inst. on Priv. Inv. & Inv. Abroad

In law review footnotes, the following are in large and small capitals: periodicals, constitutions,
codes, restatements, standards, authors of books, titles of books, and legislative materials except
for bills and resolutions. Refer to Bluebook.

Institute on Securities Regulation
      Abbreviation: Inst. on Sec. Reg.

      Examples: Messmer & Borden, Guidelines for Going Private, 11 Inst. on Sec. Reg.
                        197 (1980). ——Article Cite.

                        Messmer & Borden, Guidelines for Going Private, 11 Inst. on Sec. Reg.
                        197, 244-45 (1980). ——Page Cite.

institutional authors
      See   authors

Insurance Counsel Journal
      Abbreviation: Ins. Couns. J.
                        Insc. Counsel J. (publisher's abbreviation)

      Examples: Gilman, Dishonesty Alone Does Not Deck a Fidelity Insurer, 51 Ins.
                        Couns. J. 529 (1984). ——Article Cite.

                        Gilman, Dishonesty Alone Does Not Deck a Fidelity Insurer, 51 Ins.
                        Couns. J. 529, 530-31 (1984). ——Page Cite.

Insurance Law Reports (Commerce Clearing House)
      (formerly Reporter)

      Abbreviation: Ins. L. Rep. (CCH)

Intellectual Property Law Review
      Abbreviations: Intell. Prop. L. Rev.

      Examples: Goodman, The Policy Implications of Granting Patent Protection to
                        Computer Software: An Economic Analysis, 17 Intell. Prop. L. Rev. 3
                        (1985). ——Article Cite.

                        Goodman, The Policy Implications of Granting Patent Protection of
                        Computer Software: An Economic Analysis, 17 Intell. Prop. L. Rev. 3,
                        10-11 (1985). ——Page Cite.

Inter-Alia
      Abbreviation: Inter-Alia

      Examples: Orenschall & Pereos, A Primer in Nevada Water Law, Inter-Alia, April
                        1978, at 7. ——Article Cite.

                        Orenschall & Pereos, A Primer in Nevada Water Law, Inter-Alia, April
                        1978, at 7, 9-10. ——Page Cite.

Internal Revenue Code
      Abbreviations: I.R.C. §   (year)

      Example: Revenue Act of 1938, ch. 289, § 112(i), 52 Stat. 447, 489 (1938)
                        (current version at I.R.C. § 367 (West Supp. 1988)).

In law review footnotes, the titles of books and the names of cases are not underlined.

——Citation to a provision no longer in force. See Bluebook Rule 12.6.2. Parenthetical citation to current amended version in U.S.C.A. See Bluebook Rules 12.6.2, 12.8.1.

Internal Revenue Regulations
See   Treasury Regulations

Internal Revenue Rulings
See   Revenue Rulings

International and Comparative Law Quarterly
Abbreviation: Int'l & Comp. L.Q.

Examples: Cheang, The Intoxicated Offender Under Singapore Law, 35 Int'l & Comp. L.Q. 106 (1986). ——Article Cite.

Cheang, The Intoxicated Offender Under Singapore Law, 35 Int'l & Comp. L.Q. 106, 111-12 (1986). ——Page Cite.

International Arbitrations
Example: Argentine-Chile Frontier Case (Argentine v. Chile), 16 R. Int'l Arb. Awards 109 (1969).

——See Bluebook Rule 19.3(h).

International Business Lawyer
Abbreviation: Int'l Bus. Law.

International Court of Justice Reports of Judgments, Advisory Opinions, and Orders
Abbreviation: I.C.J.

Example: South West Africa Cases (Ethiopia v. South Africa; Liberia v. South Africa), 1966 I.C.J. 4.

International Court of Justice, Statute of
See   Statute of the International Court of Justice

International Court of Justice Yearbook
Abbreviation: I.C.J.Y.B.

Example: 1954-1955 I.C.J.Y.B. 80 (1955).

International Financial Law Review
Abbreviations: Int'l Fin. L. Rev.
                 IFL Rev. (publisher's abbreviation)

International Journal of Law and Psychiatry
Abbreviation: Int'l J.L. & Psychiatry

In law review footnotes, the following are in large and small capitals: periodicals, constitutions, codes, restatements, standards, authors of books, titles of books, and legislative materials except for bills and resolutions. Refer to Bluebook.

Examples: Brown, Psychiatric Treatment Refusal, Patient Competence, and
                 Informed Consent, 8 Int'l J.L. & Psychiatry 83 (1986). ——Article
                 Cite.

                 Brown, Psychiatric Treatment Refusal, Patient Competence, and
                 Informed Consent, 8 Int'l J.L. & Psychiatry 83, 83-84 (1986).
                 ——Page Cite.

International Journal of Law Libraries
Abbreviation: Int'l J.L. Libr.

Examples: Parry, Where to Look for Your Treaties, 8 Int'l J.L. Libr. 8 (1980).
                 ——Article Cite.

                 Parry, Where to Look for Your Treaties, 8 Int'l J.L. Libr. 8, 10-12
                 (1980). ——Page Cite.

International Journal of Legal Information
Abbreviation: Int'l J. Legal Info.

Examples: McDorman, Researching Law of the Sea, 10 Int'l J. Legal Info. 147
                 (1982). ——Article Cite.

                 McDorman, Researching Law of the Sea, 10 Int'l J. Legal Info. 147,
                 150-51 (1982). ——Page Cite.

International Law, by L. Oppenheim
——Do not abbreviate the title.

Examples: 1 L. Oppenheim, International Law § 53 (H. Lauterpacht 8th ed. 1955).

                 1 L. Oppenheim, International Law § 53, at 92 (H. Lauterpacht 8th ed.
                 1955).

International Law Commission
Abbreviation: Int'l L. Comm'n

International Law Commission Yearbook
Abbreviation: Y.B. Int'l L. Comm'n

Example: Summary Records of the 1814th Meeting, [1984] 1 Y.B. Int'l L.
                 Comm'n 2, U.N. Doc. A/CN.4/SER.A/1984.

International Law Reports
Abbreviations: I.L.R.
                 Int'l L. Rep.

International Lawyer
Abbreviation: Int'l Law.

In law review footnotes, the titles of books and the names of cases are not underlined.

International Legal Materials
    Abbreviation: Int'l Legal Mat.

International Organization
    Abbreviation: Int'l Org.

    Examples: McKeown, The Limitations of "Structural" Theories of Commerical Policy, 40 Int'l Org. 43 (1986). ——Article Cite.

        McKeown, The Limitations of "Structural" Theories of Commercial Policy, 40 Int'l Org. 43, 51-52 (1986). ——Page Cite.

International Symposium on Comparative Law
    Abbreviation: Int'l Symp. on Comp. L.

International Tax Journal
    Abbreviation: Int'l Tax J.

    Examples: Anton, The Impact of the Spanish Corporation Tax on Foreign Companies Doing Business in Spain, 12 Int'l Tax J. 49 (1986). ——Article Cite.

        Anton, The Impact of the Spanish Corporation Tax on Foreign Companies Doing Business in Spain, 12 Int'l Tax J. 49, 50 (1986). ——Page Cite.

International Tax & Business Lawyer
    Abbreviation: Int'l Tax & Bus. Law.

International Trade Law Journal
    Abbreviation: Int'l Trade L.J.

    Examples: Dickey, Antidumping: Currency Fluctuations as a Cause of Dumping Margins, 7 Int'l Trade L.J. 67 (1981-1982). ——Article Cite.

        Dickey, Antidumping: Currency Fluctuations as a Cause of Dumping Margins, 7 Int'l Trade L.J. 67, 68-69 (1981-1982). ——Page Cite.

Interstate Commerce Commission Reports (U.S.)
    Abbreviation: I.C.C.

    Examples: New York Cent. Unification, 154 I.C.C. 489 (1929).

        Winnebago Farmers Elevator Co., 354 I.C.C. 859 (1978).

Interstate Commerce Commission Reports (U.S.), Motor Carrier Cases
    Abbreviation: M.C.C.

    Example: Floyd & Beasley Transfer Co., 130 M.C.C. 72 (1977).

Interstate Commerce Commission (U.S.), Valuation Reports
    Abbreviation: I.C.C. Valuation Rep.

In law review footnotes, the following are in large and small capitals: periodicals, constitutions, codes, restatements, standards, authors of books, titles of books, and legislative materials except for bills and resolutions. Refer to Bluebook.

Example: <u>New England Steamship Co.</u>, 36 I.C.C. Valuation Rep. 741 (1931).

Iowa Administrative Bulletin
    Abbreviation: Iowa Admin. Bull.

Iowa Administrative Code
    Abbreviations: Iowa Admin. Code r.   (year).

Iowa, Biennial Report of the Attorney General
    <u>See</u>   Biennial Report of the Attorney General, State of Iowa

Iowa Code
    <u>See</u>   Code of Iowa

Iowa Code Annotated
    Abbreviation: Iowa Code Ann. §   (West year).

    Examples: Iowa Code Ann. § 17.25 (West 1978).

                           Iowa Code Ann. § 713.1 (West Supp. 1987).

Iowa Constitution
    Abbreviation: Iowa Const. art.   , §   .

    Examples: Iowa Const. art. I, § 5. ——Cite provisions without date unless the
                           cited provisions have been repealed or amended (Bluebook Rule 11).

                           Iowa. Const. art. V, § 11 (1857, repealed 1962). ——Cite provisions
                           which have been repealed or amended by giving the date of the adoption
                           of the particular provision and the date of repeal or amendment
                           (Bluebook Rule 11).

                           Iowa. Const. of 1846, art. V, § 4. ——Cite constitutions that have been
                           totally superseded by year of adoption, giving parenthetically the year of
                           adoption of the specific provision cited if different (Bluebook Rule 11).

Iowa Law Review
    Abbreviation: Iowa L. Rev.

    Examples: Adamski, <u>Contribution and Settlement in Multiparty Actions Under</u>
                           <u>Rule 10b-5</u>, 66 Iowa L. Rev. 533 (1981). ——Article Cite.

                           Adamski, <u>Contribution and Settlement in Multiparty Actions Under</u>
                           <u>Rule 10b-5</u>, 66 Iowa L. Rev. 533, 540-45 (1981). ——Page Cite.

Iowa Legislative Service (West)
    Abbreviation: year Iowa Legis. Serv. (West).

Iowa Reports
    Abbreviation: Iowa

In law review footnotes, the titles of books and the names of cases are not underlined.

——Discontinued after 261 Iowa 1395 (1968). Thereafter cite only to N.W.2d.

Examples: <u>Burlington & Summit Apartments v. Manolato</u>, 233 Iowa 15, 7 N.W.2d 26 (1943). ——Case Cite.

    <u>Burlington & Summit Apartments v. Manolato</u>, 233 Iowa 15, 18, 7 N.W.2d 26, 28 (1943). ——Page Cite.

——After 261 Iowa 1395 (1968), cite as follows:

    <u>Klaes v. Scholl</u>, 375 N.W.2d 671 (Iowa 1985). ——Case Cite.

    <u>Klaes v. Scholl</u>, 375 N.W.2d 671, 673 (Iowa 1985). ——Page Cite.

Iowa Session Laws
 <u>See</u> Acts and Joint Resolutions of the State of Iowa and Iowa Legislative Service

---

In law review footnotes, the following are in large and small capitals: periodicals, constitutions, codes, restatements, standards, authors of books, titles of books, and legislative materials except for bills and resolutions. Refer to Bluebook.

J

JAG Journal
Abbreviation: JAG J.

Examples: Fidell, The Specification of Appellate Issues by the United States Court of Military Appeals, 31 JAG J. 99 (1980). ——Article Cite.

Fidell, The Specification of Appellate Issues by the United States Court of Military Appeals, 31 JAG J. 99, 112-13 (1980). ——Page Cite.

John Marshall Journal of Practice and Procedure
Abbreviation: J. Marshall J. Prac. & Proc.

Examples: Polelle, The Unconstitutionality of Qualified Truth Defense to Libel Actions, 11 J. Marshall J. Prac. & Proc. 259 (1977-1978). ——Article Cite.

Polelle, The Unconstitutionality of Qualified Truth Defense to Libel Actions, 11 J. Marshall J. Prac. & Proc. 259, 260-61 (1977-1978). ——Page Cite.

John Marshall Law Review
Abbreviation: J. Marshall L. Rev.

Examples: Gardner & Ebers, Federal Protections of Individual Rights in Local Elections, 13 J. Marshall L. Rev. 503 (1980). ——Article Cite.

Gardner & Ebers, Federal Protections of Individual Rights in Local Elections, 13 J. Marshall L. Rev. 503, 509-12 (1980). ——Page Cite.

Journal of Accountancy
Abbreviation: J. Acct.

Examples: Grace, Wielding the Gramm-Rudman Ax, J. Acct., April 1986, at 66. ——Article Cite.

Grace, Wielding the Gramm-Rudman Ax, J. Acct., April 1986, at 66, 68. ——Page Cite.

Journal of African Law
Abbreviation: J. Afr. L.

Examples: Schapera, Tswana Concept of Custom and Law, 27 J. Afr. L. 141 (1983). ——Article Cite.

Schapera, Tswana Concepts of Custom and Law, 27 J. Afr. L. 141, 148-49 (1983). ——Page Cite.

In law review footnotes, the following are in large and small capitals: periodicals, constitutions, codes, restatements, standards, authors of books, titles of books, and legislative materials except for bills and resolutions. Refer to Bluebook.

Journal of Air Law and Commerce
     Abbreviation: J. Air L. & Com.

     Examples: Allen, <u>The Federal Income Tax Consequences of Commercial Conveyance of Rights in Airspace</u>, 47 J. Air L. & Com. 91 (1981). ——Article Cite.

                      Allen, <u>The Federal Income Tax Consequences of Commercial Conveyances of Rights in Airspace</u>, 47 J. Air L. & Com. 91, 101-02 (1981). ——Page Cite.

Journal of Arts Management and Law
     Abbreviation: J. Arts Mgmt. & L.

Journal of Bar Association of the District of Columbia
     Abbreviation: J.B.A.D.C.

     Examples: Schwartz, <u>Litigating the Right to Treatment: Wyatt v. Stickney</u>, 41 J.B.A.D.C. 15 (1974). ——Article Cite.

                      Schwartz, <u>Litigating the Right to Treatment: Wyatt v. Stickney</u>, 41 J.B.A.D.C. 15, 16-17 (1974). ——Page Cite.

Journal of Broadcasting
     Abbreviation: J. Broadcasting

     Examples: Miller, <u>The President's Advocate: OTP and Broadcast Issues</u>, 26 J. Broadcasting 625 (1982). ——Article Cite.

                      Miller, <u>The President's Advocate: OTP and Broadcast Issues</u>, 26 J. Broadcasting 625, 629 (1982). ——Page Cite.

Journal of Business Law
     Abbreviation: J. Bus. L.

Journal of Church and State
     Abbreviation: J. Church & St.

     Examples: Devins, <u>Religious Symbols and the Establishment Clause</u>, 27 J. Church & St. 19 (1985). ——Article Cite.

                      Devins, <u>Religious Symbols and the Establishment Clause</u>, 27 J. Church & St. 19, 29-30 (1985). ——Page Cite.

Journal of College and University Law
     Abbreviation: J.C. & U.L.

     Examples: Hunter, <u>Collecting Defaulted Student Loans: How Much Diligence Is Due?</u>, 9 J.C. & U.L. 149 (1982-1983). ——Article Cite.

                      Hunter, <u>Collecting Defaulted Student Loans: How Much Diligence Is Due?</u>, 9 J.C. & U.L. 149, 160-61 (1982-1983). ——Page Cite.

In law review footnotes, the titles of books and the names of cases are not underlined.

Journal of Common Market Studies

  Abbreviation: J. Common Market Stud.

  Examples: Allen, <u>Fishing for a Common Policy</u>, 19 J. Common Market Stud. 123 (1980). ——Article Cite.

       Allen, <u>Fishing for a Common Policy</u>, 19 J. Common Market Stud. 123, 128-29 (1980). ——Page Cite.

Journal of Copyright, Entertainment and Sports Law

  Abbreviation: J. Copyright Ent. & Sports L.

  Examples: Kaler, <u>Software v. Hardware: The Battle for Cable Television Copyright Liability</u>, 1 J. Copyright Ent. & Sports L. 1 (1982). ——Article Cite.

       Kaler, <u>Software v. Hardware: The Battle for Cable Television Copyright Liability</u>, 1 J. Copyright Ent. & Sports L. 1, 9-10 (1982). ——Page Cite.

Journal of Corporate Taxation

  Abbreviation: J. Corp. Tax'n

  Examples: Krieger, <u>Tax Accounting: TRA '84 and Vacation Pay</u>, 12 J. Corp. Tax'n 88 (1985). ——Article Cite.

       Krieger, <u>Tax Accounting: TRA '84 and Vacation Pay</u>, 12 J. Corp. Tax'n 88, 89-90 (1985). ——Page Cite.

Journal of Corporation Law

  Abbreviation: J. Corp. L.

  Examples: Milich, <u>Securities Fraud Under Section 10(b) and Rule 10b-5: Scienter, Recklessness, and the Good Faith Defense</u>, 11 J. Corp. L. 179 (1986). ——Article Cite.

       Milich, <u>Securities Fraud Under Section 10(b) and Rule 10b-5: Scienter, Recklessness, and the Good Faith Defense</u>, 11 J. Corp. L. 179, 199-200 (1986). ——Page Cite.

Journal of Criminal Law

  Abbreviation: J. Crim. L.

Journal of Criminal Law and Criminology

  Abbreviation: J. Crim. L. & Criminology

  Examples: Lytton, <u>Grand Jury Secrecy—Time for a Reevaluation</u>, 75 J. Crim. L. & Criminology 1100 (1984). ——Article Cite.

       Lytton, <u>Grand Jury Secrecy—Time for a Reevaluation</u>, 75 J. Crim. L. & Criminology 1100, 1119-20 (1984). ——Page Cite.

In law review footnotes, the following are in large and small capitals: periodicals, constitutions, codes, restatements, standards, authors of books, titles of books, and legislative materials except for bills and resolutions. Refer to Bluebook.

Journal of Energy Law and Policy
     Abbreviation: J. Energy L. & Pol'y

     Examples: McNamara, <u>Mineral Resources in Lands Owned by Australian Aborigines</u>, 7 J. Energy L. & Pol'y 1 (1986). ——Article Cite.

                     McNamara, <u>Mineral Resources in Lands Owned by Australian Aborigines</u>, 7 J. Energy L. & Pol'y 1, 19-20 (1986). ——Page Cite.

Journal of Family Law
     Abbreviation: J. Fam. L.

     Examples: Kirshner, <u>Child Custody Determination—A Better Way!</u>, 17 J. Fam. L. 275 (1978-1979). ——Article Cite.

                     Kirshner, <u>Child Custody Determination—A Better Way!</u>, 17 J. Fam. L. 275, 280-86 (1978-1979). ——Page Cite.

Journal of Forensic Sciences
     Abbreviation: J. Forensic Sci.

Journal of Health, Politics, Policy and Law
     Abbreviation: J. Health Pol. Pol'y & L.

     Examples: Blumstein, <u>Certificate-of-Need in an Antitrust Context</u>, 8 J. Health Pol. Pol'y & L. 314 (1983). ——Article Cite.

                     Blumstein, <u>Certificate-of-Need in an Antitrust Context</u>, 8 J. Health Pol. Pol'y & L. 314, 319 (1983). ——Page Cite.

Journal of International and Comparative Law
     Abbreviation: J. Int'l & Comp. L.

Journal of International Law and Economics
     Abbreviation: J. Int'l L. & Econ.

     Examples: Weiss, <u>A Critical Evaluation of Reciprocity in Foreign Bank Acquisitions</u>, 15 J. Int'l L. & Econ. 371 (1981). ——Article Cite.

                     Weiss, <u>A Critical Evaluation of Reciprocity in Foreign Bank Acquisitions</u>, 15 J. Int'l L. & Econ. 371, 379-80 (1981). ——Page Cite.

Journal of Juvenile Law
     Abbreviation: J. Juv. L.

Journal of Law and Commerce
     Abbreviation: J.L. & Com.

     Examples: Merges & Reynolds, <u>Toward a Computerized System for Negotiating Ocean Bills of Lading</u>, 6 J.L. & Com. 23 (1986). ——Article Cite.

In law review footnotes, the titles of books and the names of cases are not underlined.

Merges & Reynolds, <u>Toward a Computerized System for Negotiating Ocean Bills of Lading</u>, 6 J.L. & Com. 23, 29-30 (1986). ——Page Cite.

Journal of Law and Economic Development
 Abbreviation: J.L. & Econ. Dev.

 Examples: Maier, <u>International Patent Conventions and Access to Foreign Technology</u>, 4 J.L. & Econ. Dev. 207 (1969). ——Article Cite.

 Maier, <u>International Patent Conventions and Access to Foreign Technology</u>, 4 J.L. & Econ. Dev. 207, 210-17 (1969). ——Page Cite.

Journal of Law & Economics
 Abbreviation: J.L. & Econ.

 Examples: Beales, Craswell & Salop, <u>The Efficient Regulation of Consumer Information</u>, 24 J.L. & Econ. 491 (1981). ——Article Cite.

 Beales, Craswell & Salop, <u>The Efficient Regulation of Consumer Information</u>, 24 J.L. & Econ. 491, 498-99 (1981). ——Page Cite.

Journal of Law and Education
 Abbreviation: J.L. & Educ.

 Examples: Shaw & Clark, <u>Public Sector Strikes: An Empirical Analysis</u>, 2 J.L. & Educ. 217 (1973). ——Article Cite.

 Shaw & Clark, <u>Public Sector Strikes: An Empirical Analysis</u>, 2 J.L. & Educ. 217, 219-26 (1973). ——Page Cite.

Journal of Law and Politics
 Abbreviation: J.L. & Pol.

Journal of Law and Religion
 Abbreviation: J.L. & Religion

Journal of Law, Economics, and Organization
 Abbreviation: J. L. Econ. & Org

 Examples: Priest, <u>Measuring Legal Change</u>, 3 J.L. Econ. & Org. 193 (1987). ——Article Cite.

 Priest, <u>Measuring Legal Change</u>, 3 J.L. Econ. & Org. 193, 199 (1987). ——Page Cite.

Journal of Legal Education
 Abbreviation: J. Legal Educ.

 Examples: Barnhizer, <u>The Clinical Method of Legal Instruction: Its Theory and Implementation</u>, 30 J. Legal Educ. 67 (1979). ——Article Cite.

 Barnhizer, <u>The Clinical Method of Legal Instruction: Its Theory and Implementation</u>, 30 J. Legal Educ. 67, 69-71 (1979). ——Page Cite.

In law review footnotes, the following are in large and small capitals: periodicals, constitutions, codes, restatements, standards, authors of books, titles of books, and legislative materials except for bills and resolutions. Refer to Bluebook.

Journal of Legal History
Abbreviation: J. Legal Hist.

Examples: Meekings, A King's Bench Bill Formulary, 6 J. Legal Hist. 86 (1985).
——Article Cite.

Meekings, A King's Bench Bill Formulary, 6 J. Legal Hist. 86, 89-90 (1985). ——Page Cite.

Journal of Legal Medicine
Abbreviation: J. Legal Med.

Examples: Henderson, The Admissibility of Hypnotically Enhanced Testimony: Have the Courts Been Mesmerized?, 6 J. Legal Med. 293 (1985). ——Article Cite.

Henderson, The Admissibility of Hypnotically Enhanced Testimony: Have the Courts Been Mesmerized?, 6 J. Legal Med. 293, 294-295 (1985). ——Page Cite.

Journal of Legal Studies
Abbreviation: J. Legal Stud.

Examples: Baird, The Uneasy Case for Corporate Reorganization, 15 J. Legal Stud. 127 (1986). ——Article Cite.

Baird, The Uneasy Case for Corporate Reorganization, 15 J. Legal Stud. 127, 131-32 (1986). ——Page Cite.

Journal of Legislation
Abbreviation: J. Legis.

Examples: Nevin, Enforcing the Antidumping Laws: The Television Dumping Case, 6 J. Legis. 24 (1979). ——Article Cite.

Nevin, Enforcing the Antidumping Laws: The Television Dumping Case, 6 J. Legis. 24, 30-35 (1975). ——Page Cite.

Journal of Maritime Law and Commerce
Abbreviation: J. Mar. L. & Com.

Examples: Healy, An Introduction to the Federal Arbitration Act, 13 J. Mar. L. & Com. 223 (1982). ——Article Cite.

Healy, An Introduction to the Federal Arbitration Act, 13 J. Mar. L. & Com. 223, 233-34 (1982). ——Page Cite.

Journal of National Association of Referees in Bankruptcy (Referees' Journal)
Abbreviation: Ref. J.

Journal of Pension Planning & Compliance
Abbreviation: J. Pension Plan. & Compliance

In law review footnotes, the titles of books and the names of cases are not underlined.

Examples: Emering, <u>The New Benefit Limitations</u>, 8 J. Pension Plan. &
                 Compliance 367 (1982). ——Article Cite.

                 Emering, <u>The New Benefit Limitations</u>, 8 J. Pension Plan. &
                 Compliance 367, 367-68 (1982). ——Page Cite.

Journal of Planning and Environmental Law
Abbreviation: J. Plan. & Envtl. L.

Examples: Newsom, <u>Restrictive Covenants: Costs in the Lands Tribunal</u>, 1982 J.
                 Plan. & Envtl. L. 552. ——Article Cite.

                 Newsom, <u>Restrictive Covenants: Costs in the Lands Tribunal</u>, 1982 J.
                 Plan. & Envtl. L. 552, 553-54. ——Page Cite.

Journal of Police Science and Administration
Abbreviation: J. Police Sci. & Admin.

Journal of Products Law
Abbreviation: J. Prod. L.

Examples: Hollenshead, <u>Historical Perspective on Product Liability Reform</u>, 1982
                 J. Prod. L. 75. ——Article Cite.

                 Hollenshead, <u>Historical Perspective on Product Liability Reform</u>, 1982
                 J. Prod. L. 75, 124-25. ——Page Cite.

Journal of Products Liability
Abbreviation: J. Prod. Liab.

Journal of Psychiatry and Law
Abbreviation: J. Psychiatry & L.

Examples: Weinberg, <u>The Mental Illness Dispute: The Critical Faith Assumptions</u>,
                 9 J. Psychiatry & L. 305 (1981). ——Article Cite.

                 Weinberg, <u>The Mental Illness Dispute: The Critical Faith Assumptions</u>,
                 9 J. Psychiatry & L. 305, 306-07 (1981). ——Page Cite.

Journal of Public Law
Abbreviation: J. Pub. L.

Examples: Hall, <u>Judicial Removal for Off-Bench Behavior: Why?</u>, 21 J. Pub. L.
                 127 (1972). ——Article Cite.

                 Hall, <u>Judicial Removal for Off-Bench Behavior: Why?</u>, 21 J. Pub. L.
                 127, 129-32 (1972). ——Page Cite.

Journal of Real Estate Taxation
Abbreviation: J. Real Est. Tax'n

In law review footnotes, the following are in large and small capitals: periodicals, constitutions,
codes, restatements, standards, authors of books, titles of books, and legislative materials except
for bills and resolutions. Refer to Bluebook.

Journal of Space Law
Abbreviation: J. Space L.

Examples: Brado, <u>The European Space Agency: Example of a Successful Regional Cooperation</u>, 13 J. Space L. 169 (1985). ——Article Cite.

Brado, <u>The European Space Agency: Example of a Successful Regional Cooperation</u>, 13 J. Space L. 169, 170 (1985). ——Page Cite.

Journal of State Taxation
Abbreviation: J. St. Tax'n

Examples: Lambert, <u>Planning for Transfers of California Real Property: Avoiding the Adverse Aspects of Proposition 13</u>, 1 J. St. Tax'n 119 (1982). ——Article Cite.

Lambert, <u>Planning for Transfers of California Real Property: Avoiding the Adverse Aspects of Proposition 13</u>, 1 J. St. Tax'n 119, 125-26 (1982). ——Page Cite.

Journal of Taxation
Abbreviation: J. Tax'n

Examples: O'Hare, <u>Application of Tax Benefit Rule in New Case Threatens Certain Liquidations</u>, 44 J. Tax'n 200 (1976). ——Article Cite.

O'Hare, <u>Application of Tax Benefit Rule in New Case Threatens Certain Liquidations</u>, 44 J. Tax'n 200, 202-04 (1976). ——Page Cite.

Journal of the American Society of CLU
Abbreviation: J. Am. Soc'y CLU

Journal of the Copyright Society of the U.S.A.
Abbreviations: J. Copyright Soc'y U.S.A.
                    J. Copr. Soc'y (publisher's abbreviation)

Journal of the Kansas Bar Association
Abbreviation: J. Kan. B.A.

Examples: Snyder, <u>Researching Legislative Intent</u>, 51 J. Kan. B.A. 93 (1982). ——Article Cite.

Snyder, <u>Researching Legislative Intent</u>, 51 J. Kan. B.A. 93, 94-95 (1982). ——Page Cite.

Journal of the Legal Profession
Abbreviation: J. Legal Prof.

Examples: Brown, <u>A Memorandum on Nonadversarial Law Practice and Preventive Law</u>, 6 J. Legal Prof. 39 (1981). ——Article Cite.

Brown, <u>A Memorandum on Nonadversarial Law Practice and Preventive Law</u>, 6 J. Legal Prof. 39, 53-54 (1981). ——Page Cite.

In law review footnotes, the titles of books and the names of cases are not underlined.

Journal of the Missouri Bar
       Abbreviation: J. Mo. B.

       Examples: Agatstein, <u>The Contempt Remedy in Dissolution of Marriage Decrees</u>,
                          38 J. Mo. B. 347 (1982). ——Article Cite.

                          Agatstein, <u>The Contempt Remedy in Dissolution of Marriage Decrees</u>,
                          38 J. Mo. B. 347, 352-53 (1982). ——Page Cite.

Journal of World Trade Law
       Abbreviations: J. World Trade L.
                          J.W.T.L. (publisher's abbreviation)

       Examples: Stubbs, <u>The International Natural Rubber Agreement</u>, 18 J. World
                          Trade L. 16 (1984). ——Article Cite.

                          Stubbs, <u>The International Natural Rubber Agreement</u>, 18 J. World
                          Trade L. 16, 23-24 (1984). ——Page Cite.

Judge
       Abbreviation: J.

Judges
       Abbreviation: JJ.

Judicial Panel on Multi-District Litigation
       Abbreviation: J.P.M.D.L.

Juridical Review
       Abbreviation: Jurid. Rev.

       Examples: MacCormack, <u>Standards of Liability in Early Law</u>, 1985 Jurid. Rev.
                          166. ——Article Cite.

                          MacCormack, <u>Standards of Liability in Early Law</u>, 1985 Jurid. Rev.
                          166, 170. ——Page Cite.

Jurimetrics: Journal of Law, Science and Technology
       Abbreviation: Jurimetrics J.

       Examples: Reynolds & Merges, <u>The Role of Commercial Development in
                          Preventing War in Outer Space</u>, 25 Jurimetrics J. 130 (1985).
                          ——Article Cite.

                          Reynolds & Merges, <u>The Role of Commercial Development in
                          Preventing War in Outer Space</u>, 25 Jurimetrics J. 130, 135 (1985).
                          ——Page Cite.

Justice
       Abbreviation: J.

In law review footnotes, the following are in large and small capitals: periodicals, constitutions,
codes, restatements, standards, authors of books, titles of books, and legislative materials except
for bills and resolutions. Refer to Bluebook.

Justice of the Peace's Court
    Abbreviation: J.P. Ct.

Juvenile and Family Court Journal
    Abbreviation: Juv. & Fam. Ct. J.

    Examples: Levi, <u>Relative Redemption: Labeling in Juvenile Restitution</u>, 33 Juv. & Fam. Ct. J. 3 (1982). ——Article Cite.

                  Levi, <u>Relative Redemption: Labeling in Juvenile Restitution</u>, 33 Juv. & Fam. Ct. J. 3, 7 (1982). ——Page Cite.

Juvenile Court
    Abbreviation: Juv. Ct.

In law review footnotes, the titles of books and the names of cases are not underlined.

K

Kansas Administrative Regulations
Abbreviation: Kan. Admin. Regs. (year).

Kansas Bar Association Journal
Abbreviation: Kan. B.A.J.

Kansas City Law Review
See   UMKC Law Review

Kansas Constitution
Abbreviation: Kan. Const. art , § .

Examples: Kan. Const. art. 11, § 2. ——Cite provisions without date unless the cited provisions have been repealed or amended (Bluebook Rule 11).

Kan. Const. art. 10, § 3 (1861, repealed 1972). ——Cite provisions which have been repealed or amended by giving the date of the adoption of the particular provision and the date of repeal or amendment (Bluebook Rule 11).

Kan. Const. Bill of Rights, § 1. ——The Bill of Rights is listed separately from the body of the constitution.

Kansas Court of Appeals Reports
Abbreviation: Kan. App.

Examples: Zimmerman v. Gither, 10 Kan. App. 331, 63 P. 657 (1901). ——Case Cite.

Zimmerman v. Gither, 10 Kan. App. 331, 332, 63 P. 657, 658 (1901). ——Page Cite.

Kansas Court of Appeals Reports 2d
Abbreviation: Kan. App. 2d

Examples: Carey v. Carey, 9 Kan. App. 2d 779, 689 P.2d 917 (1984). ——Case Cite.

Carey v. Carey, 9 Kan. App. 2d 779, 783, 689 P.2d 917, 920 (1984). ——Page Cite.

Kansas Law Review
See   University of Kansas Law Review

In law review footnotes, the following are in large and small capitals: periodicals, constitutions, codes, restatements, standards, authors of books, titles of books, and legislative materials except for bills and resolutions. Refer to Bluebook.

Kansas, Opinions of the Attorney General
See   Opinions of the Attorney General, State of Kansas

Kansas Register
Abbreviation: Kan. Reg.

Kansas Reports
Abbreviation: Kan.

Examples: Roe v. Diefendorf, 236 Kan. 218, 689 P.2d 855 (1984). ——Case Cite.

Roe v. Diefendorf, 236 Kan. 218, 220, 689 P.2d 855, 857 (1984).
——Page Cite.

Kansas Session Laws
See   Session Laws of Kansas

Kansas Statutes Annotated
Abbreviation: Kan. Stat. Ann. §   (year).

Examples: Kan. Stat. Ann. § 71-402 (1985).

Kan. Stat. Ann. § 65-4015 (Supp. 1987).

Kansas Statutes Annotated, Vernon's
See   Vernon's Kansas Statutes Annotated

Kentucky Acts
Abbreviation: (year) Ky. Acts

Kentucky Administrative Register.
Abbreviation: Ky. Admin. Reg.

Example: 2 Ky. Admin. Reg. 318.

Kentucky Administrative Regulations Service
Abbreviation: Ky. Admin. Regs. : (year).

Example: 806 Ky. Admin. Regs. 50:155 (1982).

Kentucky Bench and Bar
Abbreviation: Ky. Bench & B.

Examples: Pennington, Regionalization of Kentucky's Trial Courts, 1982 Ky.
Bench & B. 19. ——Article Cite.

Pennington, Regionalization of Kentucky's Trial Courts, 1982 Ky.
Bench & B. 19, 20-21. ——Page Cite.

In law review footnotes, the titles of books and the names of cases are not underlined.

Kentucky Constitution

Abbreviation: Ky. Const. § .

Examples: Ky. Const. § 6. ——Cite provisions without date unless the cited provisions have been repealed or amended (Bluebook Rule 11).

Ky. Const. § 170 (1891, amended 1975). ——Cite provisions which have been repealed or amended by giving the date of the adoption of the particular provision and the date of repeal or amendment (Bluebook Rule 11).

Ky. Const. of 1792, art. I, § 1. ——Cite constitutions that have been totally superseded by year of adoption, giving parenthetically the year of adoption of the specific provision cited if different (Bluebook Rule 11).

Kentucky Law Journal

Abbreviation: Ky. L.J.

Examples: Nichol, Causation as a Standing Requirement: The Unprincipled Use of Judicial Restraint, 69 Ky. L.J. 185 (1980-1981). ——Article Cite.

Nichol, Causation as a Standing Requirement: The Unprincipled Use of Judicial Restraint, 69 Ky. L.J. 185, 190-95 (1980-1981). ——Page Cite.

Kentucky Opinion of Attorney General

Abbreviation: Op. Ky. Att'y Gen.

Example: 1980-1981 Op. Ky. Att'y Gen. No. 81-381 (November 2, 1981). ——See Bluebook Rule 14.4.

Kentucky Reports

Abbreviation: Ky.

——Discontinued after 314 Ky. 885 (1951). Thereafter cite only to S.W.2d.

Examples: Wagner v. Wagner's Adm'x, 188 Ky. 692, 223 S.W. 1011 (1920). ——Case Cite.

Wagner v. Wagner's Adm'x, 188 Ky. 692, 693, 223 S.W. 1011, 1011-12 (1920). ——Page Cite.

——After 314 Ky. 885 (1951), cite as follows:

Bishir v. Bishir, 698 S.W.2d 823 (Ky. 1985). ——Case Cite.

Bishir v. Bishir, 698 S.W.2d 823, 825 (Ky. 1985). ——Page Cite.

Kentucky Revised Statutes Annotated, Official Edition (Michie/Bobbs Merrill)

Abbreviation: Ky. Rev. Stat. Ann. § (Michie/Bobs-Merrill year).

Examples: Ky. Rev. Stat. Ann. § 189.080 (Michie/Bobbs-Merrill 1980).

Ky. Rev. Stat. Ann. § 247.994 (Michie/Bobbs-Merrill Supp. 1986).

In law review footnotes, the following are in large and small capitals: periodicals, constitutions, codes, restatements, standards, authors of books, titles of books, and legislative materials except for bills and resolutions. Refer to Bluebook.

Kentucky Revised Statutes Annotated (Baldwin)
    <u>See</u>   Baldwin's Kentucky Revised Statutes Annotated

Kingston Law Review
    Abbreviation: Kingston L. Rev.

    Examples: Dewar, <u>Transsexualism and Marriage</u>, 15 Kingston L. Rev. 58 (1985).
               ——Article Cite.

               Dewar, <u>Transsexualism and Marriage</u>, 15 Kingston L. Rev. 58, 60-61
               (1985). ——Page Cite.

In law review footnotes, the titles of books and the names of cases are not underlined.

L

Labor Arbitration and Dispute Settlements (Bureau of National Affairs)
See   Labor Relations Reporter (Bureau of National Affairs)

Labor Arbitration Awards (Commerce Clearing House)
Abbreviation: Lab. Arb. Awards (CCH)

Examples: San Bernadino City Unified School Dist. v. San Bernadino Teachers'
Ass'n., Lab. Arb. Awards (CCH) (82-2 Lab. Arb. Awards) ¶ 8491
(June 26, 1982) (Jones, Arb.). ——Citation to looseleaf administrative
material.

Greyhound Lines v. International Ass'n of Machinists, 73-2 Lab. Arb.
Awards ¶ 8519 (1973) (Rimer, Arb.). ——Citation to bound
administrative material.

——The above examples are proper if the case is not yet available in an official or West
reporter, or is not reported in an official or West reporter.

Labor Arbitration Service (Prentice-Hall)
Abbreviation: Lab. Arb. Serv. (P-H)

Labor Law Journal
Abbreviation: Lab. L.J.

Labor Law Reporter (Commerce Clearing House)
Abbreviation: Lab. L. Rep. (CCH)

Examples: Donovan v. Janitorial Servs., Inc., [2 Wages—Hours] Lab. L. Rep.
(CCH) (93 Lab. Cas.) ¶ 34,165 (5th Cir. Apr. 8, 1982). ——Citation
to looseleaf material.

Parker v. Laundry, Dry Cleaning & Dye House Workers Union Local
218, 77 Lab. Cas. (CCH) ¶ 10,998 (N.D. Ala. 1974). ——Citation to
bound material.

Opinion Letter of the Wage—Hour Administrator. No. 1566
(WH—513), [2 Wages—Hours] Lab. L. Rep. (CCH) ¶ 31,376 (Feb.
24, 1982). ——Citation to looseleaf administrative material.

Opinion Letter of the Wage—Hour Administrator No. 1546 (WH 493)
[Sept. 1978 - Jan. 1981 Transfer Binder, Wages—Hours Administrative
Rulings] Lab. L. Rep. (CCH) ¶ 31,281 (1979). ——Citation to transfer
binder.

In law review footnotes, the following are in large and small capitals: periodicals, constitutions,
codes, restatements, standards, authors of books, titles of books, and legislative materials except
for bills and resolutions. Refer to Bluebook.

Office Cleaners, Inc., [2 Wages-Hours] Lab. L. Rep. (CCH) ¶ 31,374 (Dec. 23, 1980). ——Citation to looseleaf administrative material.

Batchelor's Building Maintenance Service, [Sept. 1978 -Jan. 1981 Transfer Binder, Wages—Hours Administrative Rulings] Lab. L. Rep. (CCH) ¶ 31,266 (1979). ——Citation to transfer binder.

Retail and Professional Employees Union, Local 1015 v. Lof, [3 State Laws] Lab. L. Rep. (CCH) (93 Lab. Cas.) ¶ 55,315 (Dist. Ct. of Douglas County, Neb., Aug. 31, 1981). ——Citation to looseleaf material.

Checker Cab Co., 1981-1982 NLRB Dec. (CCH) ¶ 18,827 (1982). ——Citation to bound material.

——The above examples are proper if the case is not yet available in an official or West reporter, or is not reported in an official or West reporter.

Labor Relations Guide (Prentice-Hall)
    Abbreviation: Lab. Rel. Guide (P-H)

Labor Relations Reference Manual (Bureau of National Affairs)
    Abbreviation: L.R.R.M. (BNA)

Labor Relations Reporter (Bureau of National Affairs)
    Abbreviation: Lab. Rel. Rep. (BNA)

    Examples: Sears v. Automobile Carriers, Inc., 2 Lab. Rel. Rep. (BNA) (111 L.R.R.M.) 2292 (E.D. Mich. Nov. 23, 1981). ——Citation to looseleaf material.

Singleton v. Cory, 100 L.R.R.M. (BNA) 2605 (S.D.N.Y. 1978). ——Citation to bound material.

Globe Refractories, Inc. v. United Brick & Clay Workers, Local 647, 3 Lab. Rel. Rep. (BNA) (78 Lab. Arb.) 320 (Jan. 29, 1982) (Bolte, Arb.). ——Citation to looseleaf administrative material.

Materials Fabrication Corp. v. Carpenters Local 1489, 70 Lab. Arb. (BNA) 440 (1978) (Stark Arb.). ——Citation to bound administrative material.

Kahal v. Wilson & Assocs., 5 Lab. Rel. Rep. (BNA) (25 Wage & Hour Cas.) 477 (D.C. Cir. Mar. 23, 1982). ——Citation to looseleaf material.

Hodgson v. Sears, Roebuck & Co., 20 Wage & Hour Cas. (BNA) 611 (W.D. Ky. 1972). ——Citation to bound material.

EEOC v. Westinghouse Elec. Corp., 7 Lab. Rel. Rep. (BNA) (28 Fair Empl. Prac. Cas.) 815 (8th Cir. Apr. 2, 1982). ——Citation to looseleaf material.

EEOC v. Spector Freight Sys., Inc., 20 Fair Empl. Prac. Cas. (BNA) 1627 (N.D. Miss. 1977). ——Citation to bound material.

In law review footnotes, the titles of books and the names of cases are not underlined.

———The above examples are proper if the case is not yet available in an official or West reporter, or is not reported in an official or West reporter.

LaFave & Scott on Criminal Law
See   Criminal Law, by W. LaFave & A. Scott

Land and Water Law Review
Abbreviation: Land & Water L. Rev.

Examples: Huffman & Plantico, Toward a Theory of Land Use Planning: Lessons from Oregon, 14 Land & Water L. Rev. 1 (1979). ———Article Cite.

Huffman & Plantico, Toward a Theory of Land Use Planning: Lessons from Oregon, 14 Land & Water L. Rev. 1, 17-24 (1979). ———Page Cite.

Land Use and Environment Law Review
Abbreviation: Land Use & Env't L. Rev.
Land Use & Environment L. Rev. (publisher's abbrevition)

Examples: Stensvaag, State Regulation of Nuclear Generating Plants Under the Clean Air Act Amendments of 1977, 14 Land Use & Env't L. Rev. 575 (1983). ———Article Cite.

Stensvaag, State Regulation of Nuclear Generating Plants Under the Clean Air Act Amendments of 1977, 14 Land Use & Env't L. Rev. 575, 601-02 (1983). ———Page Cite.

Larson on Workmen's Compensation
See   Law of Workmen's Compensation, by A. Larson

Law and Computer Technology
Abbreviation: Law & Computer Tech.

Examples: Katzenberger, Copyright and Reprography: Law in Force and Reform Endeavors in the Federal Republic of Germany, 11 Law & Computer Tech. 30 (1978). ———Article Cite.

Katzenberger, Copyright and Reprography: Law in Force and Reform Endeavors in the Federal Republic of Germany, 11 Law & Computer Tech. 30, 34-35 (1978). ———Page Cite.

Law and Contemporary Problems
Abbreviation: Law & Contemp. Probs.

Examples: Blumstein, A Prolegomenon to Growth Management and Exclusionary Zoning Issues, 43 Law & Contemp. Probs. Spring 1979, at 5.
———Article Cite.

Blumstein, A Prolegomenon to Growth Management and Exclusionary Zoning Issues, 43 Law & Contemp. Probs. Spring 1979, at 5, 49-58.
———Page Cite.

In law review footnotes, the following are in large and small capitals: periodicals, constitutions, codes, restatements, standards, authors of books, titles of books, and legislative materials except for bills and resolutions. Refer to Bluebook.

Law and History Review
    Abbreviation: Law & Hist. Rev.

    Examples: Clark, <u>The Custody of Children in English Manor Courts</u>, 3 Law &
                       Hist. Rev. 333 (1985). ——Article Cite.

                       Clark, <u>The Custody of Children in English Manor Courts</u>, 3 Law &
                       Hist. Rev. 333, 340-42 (1985). ——Page Cite.

Law and Policy in International Business
    Abbreviation: Law & Pol'y Int'l Bus.

    Examples: Geisen, <u>Upstream Subsidies: Policy and Enforcement Questions After</u>
                       <u>the Trade Tariff Act of 1984</u>, 17 Law & Pol'y Int'l Bus. 241 (1985).
                       ——Article Cite.

                       Geisen, <u>Upstream Subsidies: Policy and Enforcement Questions After</u>
                       <u>the Trade Tariff Act of 1984</u>, 17 Law & Pol'y Int'l Bus. 241, 311-12
                       (1985). ——Page Cite.

Law and Policy Quarterly
    Abbreviation: Law & Pol'y Q.

Law and Psychology Review
    Abbreviation: Law & Psychology Rev.
                       L. & Psychology Rev. (publisher's abbreviation)

    Examples: Clements, <u>Towards an Objective Approach to Offender Classification</u>, 9
                       Law & Psychology Rev. 45 (1985). ——Article Cite.

                       Clements, <u>Towards an Objective Approach to Offender Classification</u>, 9
                       Law & Psychology Rev. 45, 55-56 (1985). ——Page Cite.

Law and Social Problems
    Abbreviation: Law & Soc. Probs.

    Examples: Benford, <u>Tennessee Prisons: Implementation of Judicial Decrees</u>
                       <u>Mandating Institutional Reform</u>, 1 Law & Soc. Prob. 99 (1980).
                       ——Article Cite.

                       Benford, <u>Tennessee Prisons: Implementation of Judicial Decrees</u>
                       <u>Mandating Institutional Reform</u>, 1 Law & Soc. Prob. 99, 108 (1980).
                       ——Page Cite.

Law Library Journal
    Abbreviation: Law Libr. J.

    Examples: Smith, <u>The Freedom of Information Act of 1966: A Legislative History</u>
                       <u>Analysis</u>, 74 Law Libr. J. 231 (1981). ——Article Cite.

                       Smith, <u>The Freedom of Information Act of 1966: A Legislative History</u>
                       <u>Analysis</u>, 74 Law Libr. J. 231, 238-39 (1981). ——Page Cite.

In law review footnotes, the titles of books and the names of cases are not underlined.

Law of Contracts, by John D. Calamari & Joseph M. Perillo
    ——Do not abbreviate the title.

 Examples: J. Calamari & J. Perillo, The Law of Contracts § 2-5 (3d ed. 1987).

       J. Calamari & J. Perillo, The Law of Contracts § 2-5, at 32 (3d ed. 1987).

Law of Federal Courts, The, by Charles A. Wright
    ——Do not abbreviate the title.

 Examples: C. Wright, The Law of Federal Courts § 46 (4th ed. 1983).

       C. Wright, The Law of Federal Courts § 46, at 278 (4th ed. 1983).

Law of Federal Income Taxation, Second Edition, by John C. Chommie
    ——Do not abbreviate the title.

 Examples: J. Chommie, Law of Federal Income Taxation § 139 (2d ed. 1973).

       J. Chommie, Law of Federal Income Taxation § 139, at 431 (2d ed. 1973).

Law of Personal Property, by Ray A. Brown
    ——Do not abbreviate the title.

 Examples: R. Brown, The Law of Personal Property § 7.10 (3d ed. 1975).

       R. Brown, The Law of Personal Property § 7.10, at 108 (3d ed. 1975).

Law of Property, The
    ——Do not abbreviate the title.

 Examples: R. Cunningham, W. Stoebuck, & D. Whitman, The Law of Property § 2.14 (1984).

       R. Cunningham, W. Stoebuck, & D. Whitman, The Law of Property § 2.14, at 81 (1984).

Law of Real Property, by R. Powell and P. Rohan
    ——Do not abbreviate the title.

 Examples: 7 R. Powell & P. Rohan, The Law of Real Property ¶ 971.4 (1981). ——Paragraph Cite.

       7 R. Powell & P. Rohan, The Law of Real Property ¶ 971.4, at 558.59-558.60 (1981). ——A specific page in a paragraph.

       7 R. Powell & P. Rohan, The Law of Real Property ¶ 990 (Supp. 1982). ——Supplement in the front of volume 7.

Law of Restitution, The, by G. Palmer
    ——Do not abbreviate the title.

 Examples: 3 G. Palmer, The Law of Restitution § 13.16 (1978).

In law review footnotes, the following are in large and small capitals: periodicals, constitutions, codes, restatements, standards, authors of books, titles of books, and legislative materials except for bills and resolutions. Refer to Bluebook.

3 G. Palmer, <u>The Law of Restitution</u> § 13.16, at 121 (1978).

Law of Trusts, by Austin W. Scott
——Do not abbreviate the title.

Examples: 2 A. Scott and W.F. Franklin, <u>The Law of Trusts</u> § 99.2 (4th ed. 1987).

2 A. Scott and W.F. Franklin, <u>The Law of Trusts</u> § 99.2, at 52 (4th ed. 1987).

Law of Trusts and Trustees, The, by George T. Bogert
——Do not abbreviate the title.

Examples: 6 G. Bogert, <u>The Law of Trusts and Trustees</u> § 273.45 (rev. 2d ed. 1977).

6 G. Bogert, <u>The Law of Trusts and Trustees</u> § 273.45, at 156-159 (rev. 2d ed. 1977).

Law of Workmen's Compensation, by A. Larson
——Do not abbreviate the title.

Examples: 1A A. Larson, <u>The Law of Workmen's Compensation</u> § 24.21 (1985).

1A A. Larson, <u>The Law of Workmen's Compensation</u> § 24.21, at 5-217 (1985).

4 A. Larson, <u>The Law of Workmen's Compensation</u> § 92.31 (Supp. Dec. 1987).

Law Quarterly Review
Abbreviation: Law Q. Rev.

Law Reports Probate, Divorce & Admiralty Division
Abbreviations: P.
P.D.

law review
<u>See</u>   periodicals

law review footnotes, typeface conventions for law review footnotes
——See Bluebook Rules 1.2.2 and 7. See also the excellent examples on facing page next to the inside cover of the Bluebook.

law review texts, typeface conventions for law review texts
——See Bluebook Rules 1.2.1 and 7.

Laws of Delaware
Abbreviation: volume Del. Laws   (year)

In law review footnotes, the titles of books and the names of cases are not underlined.

Laws of Florida
    Abbreviation: year Fla. Laws

Laws of Illinois
    Abbreviations: year Ill. Laws

Laws of Maryland
    Abbreviation: year Md. Laws

Laws of Minnesota
    Abbreviation: year Minn. Laws

Laws of Missouri
    Abbreviation: year Mo. Laws

Laws of Montana
    Abbreviation: year Mont. Laws

Laws of Nebraska
    Abbreviation: year Neb. Laws

Laws of New Jersey
    Abbreviation: year N.J. Laws

Laws of New Mexico
    Abbreviation: year N.M. Laws

Laws of New York
    Abbreviation: year N.Y. Laws

    Examples: Act of June 4, 1980, ch. 195, 1980 N.Y. Laws 1126.

    Act of June 9, 1980, ch. 211, § 6, 1980 N.Y. Laws 1140, 1141.
    ——Citation to a section of a session law.

    Insanity Defense Reform Act of 1980, ch. 548, 1980 N.Y. Laws 1616.
    ——Citation to a session law with a popular name.

    Act of June 26, 1980, ch. 552, § 3, 1980 N.Y. Laws 1636, 1637-39
    (codified at N.Y. Envtl. Conserv. Law ¶ 27-0101, 27-0103, and 27-0401 (Supp. 1981-1982)). ——Citation to a session law when that law will be or is codified, and the code location is known.

Laws of North Dakota
    Abbreviation: year N.D. Sess. Laws

Laws of Pennsylvania
    Abbreviation: year Pa. Laws

In law review footnotes, the following are in large and small capitals: periodicals, constitutions, codes, restatements, standards, authors of books, titles of books, and legislative materials except for bills and resolutions. Refer to Bluebook.

Laws of Puerto Rico
     Abbreviation: year P.R. Laws

Laws of South Dakota
     Abbreviation: year S.D. Sess. Laws

Laws of the State of New Hampshire
     Abbreviation: year N.H. Laws

Laws of the State of Maine
     Abbreviation: year Me. Laws

Laws of Utah
     Abbreviation: year Utah Laws

Laws of Vermont
     Abbreviation: year Vt. Acts

Laws of Washington
     Abbreviation: year Wash. Laws

Laws of Wisconsin
     Abbreviation: year Wis. Laws

Law Teacher
     Abbreviation: Law Tchr.

     Examples: Kenny, <u>Teaching Land Law—A Novel Approach</u>, 16 Law Tchr. 23 (1982). ——Article Cite.

                  Kenny, <u>Teaching Land Law—A Novel Approach</u>, 16 Law Tchr. 23, 30-31 (1982). ——Page Cite.

Lawyer's Edition, United States Supreme Court Reports
     <u>See</u>   United States Supreme Court Reports, Lawyer's Edition.

Lawyer's Reports Annotated
     Abbreviation: L.R.A.

League of Nations Treaty Series
     Abbreviation: L.N.T.S.

     Example: International Convention for the Unification of Certain Rules Relating to the Immunity of State-owned Vessels, April 10, 1926, 176 L.N.T.S. 199.

In law review footnotes, the titles of books and the names of cases are not underlined.

Legal Administrator
Abbreviation: Legal Admin.

Examples: Turnbow, <u>Why ALA Sponsors An Economic Survey</u>, Legal Admin.,
               Winter 1986, at 34. ——Article Cite.

               Turnbow, <u>Why ALA Sponsors An Economic Survey</u>, Legal Admin.,
               Winter 1986, at 34, 34. ——Page Cite.

Legal Aspects of Medical Practice
Abbreviation: Legal Aspects Med. Prac.

Legal Economics
Abbreviation: Legal Econ.

Examples: Shrager, <u>The Human Problems in Practicing Law</u>, Legal Econ., Jan.-
               Feb. 1984, at 20. ——Article Cite.

               Shrager, <u>The Human Problems in Practicing Law</u>, Legal Econ., Jan.-
               Feb. 1984, at 20, 22-23. ——Page Cite.

Legal Medicine
Abbreviation: Legal Med.

Legal Medicine Annual
Abbreviation: Legal Med. Ann.

legal memoranda, basic citation forms
       ——See various title entries of this work. See also excellent examples included on the
          inside cover of the Bluebook.

legal memoranda, typeface conventions for legal memoranda
       ——See Bluebook Rules 1.1 and 7.

Legal Research Journal
Abbreviation: Legal Res. J.

Legal Studies
Abbreviation: Legal Stud.

Examples: Smith, <u>Liability for Ommissions in the Criminal Law</u>, 4 Legal Stud. 88
               (1984). ——Article Cite.

               Smith, <u>Liability for Ommissions in the Criminal Law</u>, 4 Legal Stud. 88,
               90-91 (1984). ——Page Cite.

Legal Times
Abbreviation: Legal Times

In law review footnotes, the following are in large and small capitals: periodicals, constitutions,
codes, restatements, standards, authors of books, titles of books, and legislative materials except
for bills and resolutions. Refer to Bluebook.

Examples: <u>TECH Upholds Energy's Tertiary Incentive Program</u>, Legal Times,
                 Sept. 6, 1982, at 4, col. 1. ——news report.

                 Masters, <u>Pension Plan Termination Challenged</u>, Legal Times, Sept. 6,
                 1982, at 1, col. 1. ——signed article.

Legislative History
Example: H.R. Rep. No. 901, 91st Cong., 2d Sess. 3 (1970), <u>reprinted in</u> 4
                 <u>Railway Labor Act of 1926: A Legislative History</u> § 5 (M. Campbell &
                 E. Brewer eds. 1988).

Lex et Scientia
Abbreviation: Lex et Scientia

See Bluebook Rule 20.6.

LEXIS
<u>See</u>   pending and unreported cases.

Licensing Law and Business Report
Abbreviation: Licensing L. & Bus. Rep.

Lincoln Law Reveiw
Abbreviation: Lincoln L. Rev.

Examples: Swan, <u>Article III, § 2/14th Amendment, § 5 Roe Responses: Roe from
                 Lincoln's Dred Scott Viewpoint</u>, 15 Lincoln L. Rev. 23 (1984).
                 ——Case Cite.

                 Swan, <u>Article III, § 2/14th Amendment, § 5 Roe Responses: Roe from
                 Lincoln's Dred Scott Viewpoint</u>, 15 Lincoln L. Rev. 23 (1984).
                 ——Page Cite.

Lindey on Entertainment, Publishing and the Arts, by A. Lindey
——Do not abbreviate the title.

Example: 2A A. Lindey, <u>Lindey on Entertainment, Publishing and the Arts</u>
                 1508.124 (1987).

Litigation
Abbreviation: Litigation

Liverpool Law Review
Abbreviation: Liverpool L. Rev.

Lloyds Maritime and Commercial Law Quarterly
Abbreviation: Lloyd's Mar. & Com. L.Q.
                 LMCLQ (publisher's abbreviation)

In law review footnotes, the titles of books and the names of cases are not underlined.

Examples: Luksic, <u>Tort Liability of the Shipowner or Operator for Physical Injuries to Persons in the Sea</u>, 1984 Lloyd's Mar. & Com. L.Q. 44. ——Article Cite.

Luksic, <u>Tort Liability of the Shipowner or Operator for Physical Injuries to Persons in the Sea</u>, 1984 Lloyd's Mar. & Com. L.Q. 44, 51-52. ——Page Cite.

looseleaf services
Examples:

current unbound:

<u>Standard Metals Corp. v. Tomlin</u>, [Current] Fed. Sec. L. Rep. (CCH) ¶ 98,004 (S.D.N.Y. May 20, 1981). ——Citation for a case.

<u>Sea-Land Service, Inc. v. Federal Maritime Comm'n</u>, [Current Materials] Admin. L.2d (P & F) (50 Admin. L. 2d) 927 (D.C. Cir. April 14, 1981). ——Citation for a case for which the bound volume number is known.

transfer binder:

<u>SEC v. Wencke</u>, [1980 Transfer Binder] Fed. Sec. L. Rep. (CCH) ¶ 97,533 (9th Cir. June 9, 1980). ——Citation to transfer binder when case is less than a year old.

<u>SEC v. Wencke</u>, [1980 Transfer Binder] Fed. Sec. L. Rep. (CCH) ¶ 97,533 (9th Cir.). ——Citation to transfer binder when case is more than a year old and year of case is the same as volume number.

bound:

<u>Bartell v. Cohen</u>, 29 Admin. L. 2d (P & F) 342 (7th Cir. 1971).

——Cite to looseleaf services only until case is available in official or West reporters.

Loss on Securities Regulation
<u>See</u>   Securities Regulations, by L. Loss

Louisiana Administrative Code
Abbreviation: La. Admin. Code tit.   , §   (year).

Louisiana Annual Reports
Abbreviation: La. Ann.

Examples: <u>State v. Edwards</u>, 34 La. Ann. 1012 (1882). ——Case Cite.

<u>State v. Edwards</u>, 34 La. Ann. 1012, 1013 (1882). ——Page Cite.

Louisiana Appeals Reports
<u>See</u>   Louisiana Courts of Appeal Reports

In law review footnotes, the following are in large and small capitals: periodicals, constitutions, codes, restatements, standards, authors of books, titles of books, and legislative materials except for bills and resolutions. Refer to Bluebook.

Louisiana Bar Journal
Abbreviation: La. B.J.

Example: Hardin, <u>Workers' Compensation—An Underview</u>, 27 La. B.J. 145
(1979). ——Article Cite.

Hardin, <u>Workers' Compensation—An Underview</u>, 27 La. B.J. 145, 147
(1979). ——Page Cite.

Louisiana Civil Code Annotated
<u>See</u>   West's Louisiana Civil Code Annotated

Louisiana Code of Civil Procedure Annotated
<u>See</u>   West's Louisiana Code of Civil Procedure Annotated

Louisiana Code of Criminal Procedure Annotated
<u>See</u>   West's Louisiana Code of Criminal Procedure Annotated

Louisiana Code of Juvenile Procedure Annotated
<u>See</u>   West's Louisiana Code of Juvenile Procedure Annotated

Louisiana Constitution
Abbreviation: La. Const. art. , pt. , § .

——Not all articles are subdivided into parts.

Examples: La. Const. art. XIV, pt. 1, § 1. ——Cite provisions without date
unless the cited provisions have been repealed or amended (Bluebook
Rule 11).

La. Const. art. I, § 5.

La. Const. art. V, § 5(d) (1975, amended 1980). ——Cite provisions
which have been repealed or amended by giving the date of the adoption
of the particular provision and the date of repeal or amendment
(Bluebook Rule 11).

La. Const. of 1921, art. IV, § 18. ——Cite constitutions that have been
totally superseded by year of adoption, giving parenthetically the year of
adoption of the specific provision cited if different (Bluebook Rule 11).

Louisiana Courts of Appeal Reports
Abbreviation: La. App.

——Discontinued after 19 La. App. 881 (1932). Thereafter cite only to So. and So. 2d.

Examples: <u>Perry v. W.K. Henderson Iron Works & Supply Co.</u>, 16 La. App. 271,
133 So. 805 (1931). ——Case Cite.

<u>Perry v. W.K. Henderson Iron Works & Supply Co.</u>, 16 La. App. 271,
272, 133 So. 805, 806 (1931). ——Page Cite.

——After 19 La. App. 881 (1932), cite as follows:

In law review footnotes, the titles of books and the names of cases are not underlined.

Matt v. Cox, 478 So. 2d 918 (La. Ct. App. 1985). ——Case Cite.

Matt v. Cox, 478 So. 2d 918, 919 (La. Ct. App. 1985). ——Page Cite.

Louisiana Law Review
Abbreviation: La. L. Rev.

Examples: Tunc, A Codified Law of Tort—The French Experience, 39 La. L.
Rev. 1051 (1979). ——Article Cite.

Tunc, A Codified Law of Tort—The French Experience, 39 La. L.
Rev. 1051, 1059-64 (1979). ——Page Cite.

Louisiana, Opinions of the Attorney General
See   Opinions of the Attorney General of the State of Louisiana

Louisiana Register
Abbreviation: La. Reg.

Louisiana Reports
Abbreviation: La.

——Discontinued after 263 La. 1111 (1972). Thereafter cite only to So. 2d.

Examples: Schmidt v. City of New Orleans, 164 La. 1006, 115 So. 63 (1927).
——Case Cite.

Schmidt v. City of New Orleans, 164 La. 1006, 1008-09, 115 So. 63,
64 (1927). ——Page Cite.

——After 263 La. 1111 (1972), cite as follows:

In re Milkovich, 478 So. 2d 895 (La. 1985). ——Case Cite.

In re Milkovich, 478 So. 2d 895, 896 (La. 1985). ——Page Cite.

Louisiana Revised Statutes Annotated
See   West's Louisiana Revised Statutes Annotated

Louisiana Session Laws
See   State of Louisiana: Acts of the Legislature and Louisiana Session Law Service

Louisiana Session Law Service. (West).
Abbreviation: year La. Sess. Law Serv. (West)

Loyola Law Review
Abbreviation: Loy. L. Rev.

Examples: Swaim, Requiem for Moragne: The New Uniformity, 25 Loy. L. Rev.
1 (1979). ——Article Cite.

Swaim, Requiem for Moragne: The New Uniformity, 25 Loy. L. Rev.
1, 4-18 (1979). ——Page Cite.

In law review footnotes, the following are in large and small capitals: periodicals, constitutions,
codes, restatements, standards, authors of books, titles of books, and legislative materials except
for bills and resolutions. Refer to Bluebook.

Loyola of Los Angeles International and Comparative Law Annual
    Abbreviation: Loy. L.A. Int'l & Comp. L. Ann.

    Examples: Higgins, <u>Japanese Fair Trade Commission Review of International
                     Agreements,</u> 3 Loy. L.A. Int'l & Comp. L. Ann. 43 (1980).
                     ——Article Cite.

                     Higgins, <u>Japanese Fair Trade Commission Review of International
                     Agreements,</u> 3 Loy. L.A. Int'l & Comp. L. Ann. 43, 54-55 (1980).
                     ——Page Cite.

Loyola of Los Angeles International and Comparative Law Journal
    Abbreviation: Loy. L.A. Int'l & Comp. L.J.

Loyola of Los Angeles Law Review
    Abbreviation: Loy. L.A.L. Rev.

    Examples: <u>Developments in Criminal Law and Procedure in the Ninth Circuit,
                     1976: A Survey,</u> 10 Loy. L.A.L. Rev. 855 (1977). ——Article Cite.

                     <u>Developments in Criminal Law and Procedure in the Ninth Circuit,
                     1976: A Survey,</u> 10 Loy. L.A.L. Rev. 855, 863-67 (1977). ——Page
                     Cite.

Loyola University of Chicago Law Journal
    Abbreviation: Loy. U. Chi. L.J.

    Examples: LeBlang, <u>Epilepsy, Motor Vehicle Licensure and the Law: The
                     Physician's Rights and Responsibilities in Illinois,</u> 19 Loy. U. Chi. L.J.
                     203 (1979). ——Article Cite.

                     LeBlang, <u>Epilepsy, Motor Vehicle Licensure and the Law: The
                     Physician's Rights and Responsibilities in Illinois,</u> 19 Loy. U. Chi. L.J.
                     203, 220-23 (1979). ——Page Cite.

In law review footnotes, the titles of books and the names of cases are not underlined.

M

Magistrate
> Abbreviation: Mag.

Magistrate's Court
> Abbreviation: Magis. Ct.

Maine Constitution
> Abbreviation: Me. Const. art.   , pt.   , §   .

——Not all articles are subdivided into parts.

> Examples: Me. Const. art. IV, pt. 3, § 5. ——Cite provisions without date unless
> the cited provisions have been repealed or amended (Bluebook Rule 11).

> Me. Const. art. IV, pt. 3, § 10 (1820, amended 1975). ——Cite
> provisions which have been repealed or amended by giving the date of
> the adoption of the particular provision and the date of repeal or
> amendment (Bluebook Rule 11).

Maine Law Review
> Abbreviation: Me. L. Rev.

> Examples: Rogoff, The International Legal Obligations of Signatories to an
> Unratified Treaty, 32 Me. L. Rev. 263 (1980). ——Article Cite.

> Rogoff, The International Legal Obligations of Signatories to an
> Unratified Treaty, 32 Me. L. Rev. 263, 270-75 (1980). ——Page Cite.

Maine Legislative Service
> Abbreviation: year Me. Legis. Serv.

Maine Reports
> Abbreviation: Me.

——Discontinued after 161 Me. 541 (1965). Thereafter cite only to A.2d.

> Examples: Porter v. Porter, 138 Me. 1, 20 A.2d 465 (1941). ——Case Cite.

> Porter v. Porter, 138 Me. 1, 8, 20 A.2d 465, 468 (1941). ——Page
> Cite.

——After 161 Me. 541 (1965), cite as follows:

> State v. Friel, 500 A.2d 631 (Me. 1985). ——Case Cite.

> State v. Friel, 500 A.2d 631, 633 (Me. 1985). ——Page Cite.

In law review footnotes, the following are in large and small capitals: periodicals, constitutions,
codes, restatements, standards, authors of books, titles of books, and legislative materials except
for bills and resolutions. Refer to Bluebook.

Maine Revised Statutes Annotated
        Abbreviation: Me. Rev. Stat. Ann. tit.   ,§   (year).

        Examples: Me. Rev. Stat. Ann. tit. 14, § 163 (1980).

                           Me. Rev. Stat. Ann. tit. 14, § 153 (Supp. 1987).

Maine Session Laws
        See   Acts, Resolves and Constitutional Resolutions of the State of Maine and Laws of
               the State of Maine and Maine Legislative Service

Manitoba Law Journal
        Abbreviation: Man. L.J.

        Examples: Magnet, Validity of Manitoba Laws After Forest: What Is to Be Done,
                           10 Man. L.J. 241 (1980). ——Article Cite.

                           Magnet, Validity of Manitoba Laws After Forest: What Is to Be Done,
                           10 Man. L. J. 241, 255-56 (1980). ——Page Cite.

Manual for Complex Litigation Second
        Abbreviation: Manual for Complex Litigation 2d §   (ed. year).

        Examples: Manual for Complex Litigation 2d § 1.10 (1985).

manuscript
        Abbreviation: ms.

Maritime Lawyer
        Abbreviation: Mar. Law.

Marquette Law Review
        Abbreviation: Marq. L. Rev.

        Examples: Anderson, Life Insurance, Conditional Receipts and Judicial
                           Intervention, 63 Marq. L. Rev. 593 (1980). ——Article Cite.

                           Anderson, Life Insurance, Conditional Receipts and Judicial
                           Intervention, 63 Marq. L. Rev. 593, 595-99 (1980). ——Page Cite.

Maryland, Annotated Code of the Public General Laws
        See   Annotated Code of the Public General Laws of Maryland and Annotated Code of
               Maryland

Maryland, Annual Report and Official Opinions of the Attorney General
        See   Annual Report and Official Opinions of the Attorney General of Maryland

Maryland Appellate Reports
        Abbreviation: Md. App.

        Examples: Smith v. State, 55 Md. App. 728, 466 A.2d 526 (1983). ——Case Cite.

In law review footnotes, the titles of books and the names of cases are not underlined.

Smith v. State, 55 Md. App. 728, 730, 466 A.2d 526, 527 (1983).
——Page Cite.

Maryland Bar Journal
Abbreviation: Md. B.J.

Examples: Douglas, Buying Time, Md. B.J., April 1986, at 5. ——Article Cite.

Douglas, Buying Time, Md. B.J., April 1986, at 5, 8-9. ——Page Cite.

Maryland Code of Regulations
See   Code of Maryland Regulations

Maryland Constitution
Abbreviation: Md. Const. art.   , §   .

Examples: Md. Const. art. II, § 18. ——Cite provisions without date unless the
cited provisions have been repealed or amended (Bluebook Rule 11).

Md. Const. art. II, § 21 (1954, amended 1976). ——Cite provisions
which have been repealed or amended by giving the date of the adoption
of the particular provision and the date of repeal or amendment
(Bluebook Rule 11).

Md. Declaration of Rights art. 8. ——The Declaration of Rights is
listed separately from the body of the constitution. The form for the
citation is that used by Maryland Law Review.

Maryland Journal of International Law & Trade
Abbreviation: Md. J. Int'l L. & Trade

Examples: Chen, Legal Aspects of Offshore Banking in Taiwan, 8 Md. J. Int'l L.
& Trade 237 (1984). ——Article Cite.

Chen, Legal Aspects of Offshore Banking in Taiwan, 8 Md. J. Int'l L.
& Trade 237, 241-42 (1984). ——Page Cite.

Maryland Law Forum
Abbreviation: Md. L.F.

Examples: Smith, The Coming Renaissance in Law and Literature, 7 Md. L.F. 84
(1977). ——Article Cite.

Smith, The Coming Renaissance in Law and Literature, 7 Md. L.F. 84,
87-89 (1977). ——Page Cite.

Maryland Law Review
Abbreviation: Md. L. Rev.

Examples: Brown, The Law/Equity Dichotomy in Maryland, 39 Md. L. Rev. 427
(1980). ——Article Cite.

Brown, The Law/Equity Dichotomy in Maryland, 39 Md. L. Rev. 427,
460-65 (1980). ——Page Clte.

In law review footnotes, the following are in large and small capitals: periodicals, constitutions,
codes, restatements, standards, authors of books, titles of books, and legislative materials except
for bills and resolutions. Refer to Bluebook.

Maryland Register
   Abbreviation: Md. Reg.

Maryland Reports
   Abbreviation: Md.

   Examples: Harris v. State, 303 Md. 685, 496 A.2d 1074 (1985). ——Case Cite.

                Harris v. State, 303 Md. 685, 686, 496 A.2d 1074, 1075 (1985).
                ——Page Cite.

Maryland Session Laws
   See   Laws of Maryland

Massachusetts Advance Legislative Service (Lawyers' Co-op)
   Abbreviation: year Mass. Adv. Legis. Serv. (Law. Co-op).

Massachusetts Annotated Laws
   See   Annotated Laws of Massachusetts

Massachusetts Appeals Court Reports
   Abbreviation: Mass. App. Ct.

   Examples: Hickey v. Green, 14 Mass. App. Ct. 671, 442 N.E.2d 37 (1982).
                ——Case Cite.

                Hickey v. Green, 14 Mass. App. Ct. 671, 673-74, 442 N.E.2d 37, 39-
                40 (1982). ——Page Cite.

Massachusetts Appellate Decisions (1941-1976)
   Abbreviation: Mass. App. Dec.

   Examples: Cutler-Hammer, Inc. v. Progulske & Shoppe, 59 Mass. App. Dec. 194
                (Dist. Ct. 1976). ——Case Cite.

                Cutler-Hammer, Inc. v. Progulske & Shoppe, 59 Mass. App. Dec. 194,
                196 (Dist. Ct. 1976). ——Page Cite.

Massachusetts Appellate Division Reports
   Abbreviation: Mass. App. Div.

   Examples: Ryan v. Vera, 1984 Mass. App. Div. 216. ——Case Cite.

                Ryan v. Vera, 1984 Mass. App. Div. 216, 219. ——Page Cite.

Massachusetts Appellate Division, Advance Sheets
   Abbreviation: year Mass. App. Div. Adv. Sh.

Massachusetts Code of Regulations
   See   Code of Massachusetts Regulations

In law review footnotes, the titles of books and the names of cases are not underlined.

Massachusetts Constitution

  Abbreviations: Mass. Const. pt. , ch. , sec. , art. .

  Mass. Const. amend. art. . ——Citing to amendments.

  Examples: Mass. Const. pt. II, ch. 2, sec. 3, art. 1. ——Cite provisions without date unless the cited provisions have been repealed or amended (Bluebook Rule 11).

  Mass. Const. amend. art. XLIV.

Massachusetts General Laws

  See   General Laws of the Commonwealth of Massachusetts.

Massachusetts General Laws Annotated

  Abbreviation: Mass. Gen. Laws Ann. ch. ,§ (West year).

  Examples: Mass. Gen. Laws Ann. ch. 260, § 2 (West 1959).

  Mass. Gen. Laws Ann. ch. 272, § 35A (West Supp. 1985).

Massachusetts Law Review

  Abbreviation: Mass. L. Rev.

  Examples: Glannon, Governmental Tort Liability Under the Massachusetts Tort Claims Act of 1978, 66 Mass. L. Rev. 7 (1981). ——Article Cite.

  Glannon, Governmental Tort Liability Under the Massachusetts Tort Claims Act of 1978, 66 Mass. L. Rev. 7, 12-14 (1981). ——Page Cite.

Massachusetts, Report of the Attorney General

  See   Report of the Attorney General, State of Massachusetts

Massachusetts Register

  Abbreviation: Mass. Reg.

Massachusetts Reports

  Abbreviation: Mass.

  Examples: Freeman v. Chaplics, 388 Mass. 398, 446 N.E.2d 1369 (1983). ——Case Cite.

  Freeman v. Chaplics, 388 Mass. 398, 400, 446 N.E.2d 1369, 1370 (1983). ——Page Cite.

Massachusetts Session Laws

  See   Acts and Resolves of Massachusetts

Massachusetts Supplement

  Abbreviation: Mass. Supp.

In law review footnotes, the following are in large and small capitals: periodicals, constitutions, codes, restatements, standards, authors of books, titles of books, and legislative materials except for bills and resolutions. Refer to Bluebook.

Master of the Rolls
    Abbreviation: M.R.

Matthew Bender
    Abbreviation: (MB)

McClintock on Equity
    See   Handbook of the Principles of Equity, by H. McClintock

McCormick on Evidence, by Edward W. Cleary
    ——Do not abbreviate the title.

    Examples: E. Cleary, <u>McCormick on Evidence</u> § 93 (3d ed. 1984).

                   E. Cleary, <u>McCormick on Evidence</u> § 93, at 225 (3d ed. 1984).

McGill Law Journal
    Abbreviation: McGill L.J.

    Examples: Deutch, <u>Controlling Standard Contracts—The Israeli Version</u>, 30
                   McGill L.J. 458 (1984-1985). ——Article Cite.

                   Deutch, <u>Controlling Standard Contracts—The Israeli Version</u>, 30
                   McGill L.J. 458, 460-61 (1984-1985). ——Page Cite.

McKinney's Consolidated Laws of New York Annotated
    Abbreviation: N.Y. subject Law §   (McKinney year).

    ——See Bluebook pages 200-02 for the abbreviation of each subject.

    Examples: N.Y. Crim. Proc. Law § 300.50(1) (McKinney 1982).

                   N.Y. Crim. Proc. Law § 230.20(2)(a) (McKinney Supp. 1986).

Media Law Reporter (Bureau of National Affairs)
    Abbreviation: Media L. Rep. (BNA)

Medicare and Medicaid Guide (Commerce Clearing House)
    Abbreviation: Medicare & Medicaid Guide (CCH)

    Examples: <u>Winter v. Miller</u>, 4 Medicare & Medicaid Guide (CCH) ¶ 31,925 (7th
                   Cir. Apr. 20, l982). ——Citation to looseleaf material.

                   <u>Westchester General Hospital v. HEW</u>, [l979-1 Transfer Binder]
                   Medicare & Medicaid Guide (CCH) ¶ 29,526 (M.D. Fla. 1979).
                   ——Citation to transfer binder.

    ——The above examples are proper if the case is not yet available in an official or West
    reporter, or is not reported in an official or West reporter.

Medicine, Science, and the Law
    Abbreviation: Med. Sci. & L.

In law review footnotes, the titles of books and the names of cases are not underlined.

Melanesian Law Journal
Abbreviation: Melanesian L.J.

Examples: Jessep, <u>Land Demarcation in New Ireland</u>, 8 Melanesian L.J. 112 (1980). ——Article Cite.

Jessep, <u>Land Demarcation in New Ireland</u>, 8 Melanesian L.J. 112, 120-22 (1980). ——Page Cite.

Melbourne University Law Review
Abbreviation: Melb. U.L. Rev.
M.U.L.R. (publisher's abbreviation)

Examples: Cameron, <u>Majority Rule; the Development of General Principles in Cases on Chartered Corporations</u>, 15 Melb. U.L. Rev. 116 (1985). ——Article Cite.

Cameron, <u>Majority Rule; the Development of General Principles in Cases on Chartered Corporations</u>, 15 Melb. U.L. Rev. 116, 123-24 (1985). ——Page Cite.

memoranda, basic citation forms
——See various title entries of this work. See also excellent examples included on the inside cover of the Bluebook.

memoranda, typeface conventions for legal memoranda
——See Bluebook Rules 1.1 and 7.

Memphis State University Law Review
Abbreviation: Mem. St. U.L. Rev.

Examples: Conway, <u>The Per Se Rule and Gypsum: Presuming the Element of Intent</u>, 10 Mem. St. U.L. Rev. 485 (1980). ——Article Cite.

Conway, <u>The Per Se Rule and Gypsum: Presuming the Element of Intent</u>, 10 Mem. St. U.L. Rev. 485, 486-90 (1980). ——Page Cite.

Mental & Physical Disability Law Reporter
Abbreviation: Mental & Physical Disab. L. Rep.

Examples: Brown, <u>Public Policy and the Rights of Mental Patients</u>, 6 Mental & Physical Disab. L. Rep. 55 (1982). ——Article Cite.

Brown, <u>Public Policy and the Rights of Mental Patients</u>, 6 Mental & Physical Disab. L. Rep. 55, 56 (1982). ——Page Cite.

Mercer Law Review
Abbreviation: Mercer L. Rev.

Examples: Wade, <u>Products Liability and Plaintiff's Fault—The Uniform Comparative Fault Act</u>, 29 Mercer L. Rev. 373 (1978). ——Article Cite.

In law review footnotes, the following are in large and small capitals: periodicals, constitutions, codes, restatements, standards, authors of books, titles of books, and legislative materials except for bills and resolutions. Refer to Bluebook.

Wade, <u>Products Liability and Plaintiff's Fault—The Uniform Comparative Fault Act</u>, 29 Mercer L. Rev. 373, 376-81 (1978). ——Page Cite.

Metropolitan
    Abbreviation: Metro.

Michigan Administrative Code
    Abbreviation: Mich. Admin. Code r.   (year).

Michigan Appeals Reports
    Abbreviation: Mich. App.

    Examples: <u>Morgan v. Kamil</u>, 144 Mich. App. 171, 375 N.W.2d 378 (1985). ——Case Cite.

                    <u>Morgan v. Kamil</u>, 144 Mich. App. 171, 174, 375 N.W.2d 378, 380 (1985). ——Page Cite.

Michigan Bar Journal
    Abbreviation: Mich. B.J.

    Examples: Peck & Schriemer, <u>Law Office Business Problems—A Business Approach</u>, 61 Mich. B.J. 742 (1982). ——Article Cite.

                    Peck & Schriemer, <u>Law Office Business Problems—A Business Approach</u>, 61 Mich. B.J. 742, 744-45 (1982). ——Page Cite.

Michigan, Biennial Report of the Attorney General
    <u>See</u>   Biennial Report of the Attorney General of the State of Michigan

Michigan Compiled Laws
    Abbreviation: Mich. Comp. Laws §   (year).

Michigan Compiled Laws Annotated
    Abbreviation: Mich. Comp. Laws Ann. §   (West year).

    Examples: Mich. Comp. Laws Ann. § 125.214 (West 1986).

                    Mich. Comp. Laws Ann. § 333.7411 (West Supp. 1987).

Michigan Constitution
    Abbreviation: Mich. Const. art. , §   .

    Examples: Mich. Const. art. I, § 23. ——Cite provisions without date unless the cited provisions have been repealed or amended (Bluebook Rule 11).

                    Mich. Const. art. I, § 15 (1963, amended 1978). ——Cite provisions which have been repealed or amended by giving the date of the adoption of the particular provision and the date of repeal or amendment (Bluebook Rule 11).

In law review footnotes, the titles of books and the names of cases are not underlined.

Mich. Const of 1850, art. 4, § 1. ——Cite constitutions that have been totally superseded by year of adoption, giving parenthetically the year of adoption of the specific provision cited if different (Bluebook Rule 11).

Michigan Corporate Finance and Business Law Journal
Abbreviation: Mich. Corp. Fin. & Bus. L.J.

Michigan Court of Claims Reports (1938-1942)
Abbreviation: Mich. Ct. Cl.

Michigan Law Review
Abbreviation: Mich. L. Rev.

Examples: Blakey & Goldsmith, <u>Criminal Redistribution of Stolen Property: The Need for Law Reform</u>, 74 Mich. L. Rev. 1511 (1976). ——Article Cite.

Blakey & Goldsmith, <u>Criminal Redistribution of Stolen Property: The Need for Law Reform</u>, 74 Mich. L. Rev. 1511, 1540-45 (1976). ——Page Cite.

Michigan Legislative Service. (West)
Abbreviation: year Mich. Legis. Serv. (West).

Michigan Register
Abbreviation: Mich. Reg. (month year).

Michigan Reports
Abbreviation: Mich.

Examples: <u>People v. Boscaglia</u>, 419 Mich. 556, 357 N.W.2d 648 (1984). ——Case Cite.

<u>People v. Boscaglia</u>, 419 Mich. 556, 559-60, 357 N.W.2d 648, 650-51 (1984). ——Page Cite.

Michigan Session Laws
<u>See</u>   Public and Local Acts of the Legislature of the State of Michigan and Michigan Legislative Service

Michigan Statutes Annotated
Abbreviation: Mich. Stat. Ann. §   (Callaghan year).

Examples: Mich. Stat. Ann. § 28.1072 (Callaghan 1978).

Mich. Stat. Ann. § 28.1058 (Callaghan Supp. 1980).

Michigan Yearbook of International Legal Studies
Abbreviation: Mich. Y.B. Int'l Legal Stud.

In law review footnotes, the following are in large and small capitals: periodicals, constitutions, codes, restatements, standards, authors of books, titles of books, and legislative materials except for bills and resolutions. Refer to Bluebook.

Examples: Chelberg, <u>The Contours of Extraterritorial Jurisdiction in Drug
                 Smuggling Cases</u>, 1983 Mich. Y.B. Int'l Legal Stud. 43. ——Article
                 Cite.

                 Chelberg, <u>The Contours of Extraterritorial Jurisdiction in Drug
                 Smuggling Cases</u>, 1983 Mich Y.B. Int'l Legal Stud. 43, 58-59.
                 ——Page Cite.

Military Justice Reporter
    Abbreviation: M.J.

    Example: <u>United States v. Parkes</u>, 5 M.J. 489 (C.M.A. 1978).

Military Law Reporter
    Abbreviation: Mil. L. Rep. (Pub. L. Educ. Inst.)

Military Law Review
    Abbreviation: Mil. L. Rev.

Milwaukee Lawyer
    Abbreviation: Milwaukee Law.

Minnesota Constitution
    Abbreviation: Minn. Const. art.   , §   .

    Examples: Minn. Const. art. 1, § 2. ——Cite provisions without date unless the
                     cited provisions have been repealed or amended (Bluebook Rule 11).

                     Minn. Const. art. 10, § 9 (1857, amended 1980). ——Cite provisions
                     which have been repealed or amended by giving the date of the adoption
                     of the particular provision and the date of repeal or amendment
                     (Bluebook Rule 11).

Minnesota, Opinions of the Attorney General
    <u>See</u>   Opinions of the Attorney General, State of Minnesota

Minnesota Law Review
    Abbreviation: Minn. L. Rev.

    Examples: Winick, <u>Legal Limitation on Correctional Therapy and Research</u>, 65
                     Minn. L. Rev. 331 (1981). ——Article Cite.

                     Winick, <u>Legal Limitation on Correctional Therapy and Research</u>, 65
                     Minn. L. Rev. 331, 336-40 (1981). ——Page Cite.

Minnesota Reports
    Abbreviation: Minn.

    ——Discontinued after 312 Minn. 602 (1977). Thereafter cite only to N.W.2d.

    Examples: <u>Tyra v. Cheney</u>, 129 Minn. 428, 152 N.W. 835 (1915). ——Case Cite.

In law review footnotes, the titles of books and the names of cases are not underlined.

<u>Tyra v. Cheney</u>, 129 Minn. 428, 430, 152 N.W. 835, 835 (1915).
——Page Cite.

——After 312 Minn. 602 (1977), cite as follows:

<u>Cargill, Inc. v. Hedge</u>, 375 N.W.2d 477 (Minn. 1985). ——Case Cite.

<u>Cargill, Inc. v. Hedge</u>, 375 N.W.2d 477, 478 (Minn. 1985). ——Page Cite.

Minnesota Rules
(Formerly Minnesota Code of Agency Rules)

Abbreviation: Minn. R. (year).

Minnesota Session Laws
<u>See</u>   Minnesota Session Law Service

Minnesota Session Law Service (West)
Abbreviation: year Minn. Sess. Law Serv.   (West).

Minnesota State Register
Abbreviation: Minn. Reg.

Minnesota Statutes
Abbreviation: Minn. Stat. §   (year).

Examples: Minn. Stat. § 611.07 (1978).

Minn. Stat. § 363.01 (Supp. 1979).

Minnesota Statutes Annotated
Abbreviation: Minn. Stat. Ann. §   (West year).

Examples: Minn. Stat. Ann. § 609.185 (West 1987).

Minn. Stat. Ann. § 609.346 (West Supp. 1988).

Mississippi Code Annotated
Abbreviation: Miss. Code Ann. §   (year).

Examples: Miss. Code Ann. § 55-7-27 (1973).

Miss. Code Ann. § 77-1-29 (Supp. 1987).

Mississippi College Law Review
Abbreviation: Miss. C.L. Rev.

Mississippi Constitution
Abbreviation: Miss. Const. art.   , §   .

In law review footnotes, the following are in large and small capitals: periodicals, constitutions, codes, restatements, standards, authors of books, titles of books, and legislative materials except for bills and resolutions. Refer to Bluebook.

Examples: Miss. Const. art. 3, § 23. ——Cite provisions without date unless the
                 cited provisions have been repealed or amended (Bluebook Rule 11).

                 Miss. Const. art. 4, § 505 (1890, repealed 1978). ——Cite provisions
                 which have been repealed or amended by giving the date of the adoption
                 of the particular provision and the date of repeal or amendment
                 (Bluebook Rule 11).

Mississippi Law Journal
Abbreviation: Miss. L.J.

Examples: Gerhart, These Unloved Men, 50 Miss. L.J. 513 (1979). ——Article
                 Cite.

                 Gerhart, These Unloved Men, 50 Miss. L.J. 513, 519-24 (1979).
                 ——Page Cite.

Mississippi Lawyer
Abbreviation: Miss. Law.

Example: American Bar Starts First National Lawyer Placement Service, Miss.
                 Law., Jan. 1962, at 6.

Mississippi Reports
Abbreviation: Miss.

——Discontinued after 254 Miss. 944 (1966). Thereafter cite only to So. 2d.

Examples: Carter v. Witherspoon, 156 Miss. 597, 126 So. 388 (1930). ——Case
                 Cite.

                 Carter v. Witherspoon, 156 Miss. 597, 603, 126 So. 388, 389 (1930).
                 ——Page Cite.

——After 254 Miss. 944 (1966), cite as follows:

                 White v. Hancock Bank, 477 So. 2d 265 (Miss. 1985). ——Case Cite.

                 White v. Hancock Bank, 477 So. 2d 265, 267 (Miss. 1985). ——Page
                 Cite.

Mississippi Session Laws
See   General Laws of Mississippi

Missouri Annotated Statutes, Vernon's
See   Vernon's Missouri Annotated Statutes

Missouri Appeals Reports
Abbreviation: Mo. App.

——Discontinued after 241 Mo. App. 1244 (1952). Thereafter cite only to S.W.2d.

Examples: Williams v. Williams, 240 Mo. App. 336, 205 S.W.2d 949 (1947).
                 ——Case Cite.

In law review footnotes, the titles of books and the names of cases are not underlined.

Williams v. Williams, 240 Mo. App. 336, 342-43, 205 S.W.2d 949, 953-54 (1947). ——Page Cite.

——After 241 Mo. App. 1244 (1952), cite as follows:

Forinash v. Daugherty, 697 S.W.2d 294 (Mo. Ct. App. 1985). ——Case Cite.

Forinash v. Daugherty, 697 S.W.2d 294, 295 (Mo. Ct. App. 1985). ——Page Cite.

Missouri Bar Journal
    Abbreviation: Mo. B.J.

    Examples: Agatstein, The Contempt Remedy in Dissolution of Marriage Decrees, 38 Mo. B.J. 347 (1982). ——Article Cite.

        Agatstein, The Contempt Remedy in Dissolution of Marriage Decrees, 38 Mo. B.J. 347, 348-49 (1982). ——Page Cite.

Missouri Code of State Regulations
    Abbreviation: Mo. Code Regs. tit. , § (year)

Missouri Constitution
    Abbreviation: Mo. Const. art. , § .

    Examples: Mo. Const. art. 1, § 6. ——Cite provisions without date unless the cited provisions have been repealed or amended (Bluebook Rule 11).

        Mo. Const. art. 4, § 35 (1945, amended 1972). ——Cite provisions which have been repealed or amended by giving the date of the adoption of the particular provision and the date of repeal or amendment (Bluebook Rule 11).

        Mo. Const. of 1875, art. 2, § 16. ——Cite constitutions that have been totally superseded by year of adoption, giving parenthetically the year of adoption of the specific provision cited if different (Bluebook Rule 11).

Missouri Law Review
    Abbreviation: Mo. L. Rev.

    Examples: Brant, Last Rights: An Analysis of Refusal and Withholding of Treatment Cases, 46 Mo. L. Rev. 337 (1981). ——Article Cite.

        Brant, Last Rights: An Analysis of Refusal and Withholding of Treatment Cases, 46 Mo. L. Rev. 337, 350-55 (1981). ——Page Cite.

Missouri Legislative Service (Vernon)
    Abbreviation: year Mo. Legis. Serv. (Vernon).

Missouri Register
    Abbreviation: Mo. Reg.

In law review footnotes, the following are in large and small capitals: periodicals, constitutions, codes, restatements, standards, authors of books, titles of books, and legislative materials except for bills and resolutions. Refer to Bluebook.

Missouri Reports
>   Abbreviation: Mo.

——Discontinued after 365 Mo. 1238 (1956). Thereafter cite only to S.W.2d.

>   Examples: State v. Anderson, 252 Mo. 83, 158 S.W. 817 (1913). ——Case Cite.
>
>   State v. Anderson, 252 Mo. 83, 97, 158 S.W. 817, 821 (1913).
>   ——Page Cite.

——After 365 Mo. 1238 (1956), cite as follows:

>   State v. Gilmore, 697 S.W.2d 172 (Mo. 1985). ——Case Cite.
>
>   State v. Gilmore, 697 S.W.2d 172, 174 (Mo. 1985). ——Page Cite.

Missouri Revised Statutes
>   Abbreviation: Mo. Rev. Stat. §   (year).
>
>   Example: Mo. Rev. Stat. § 506.500 (1978).

Missouri Session Laws
>   See   Laws of Missouri and Missouri Legislative Service

Model Business Corporation Act Annotated (A.B.A.)
>   See   American Bar Association Model Business Corporation Act Annotated 2d

Model Code of Evidence
>   See   American Law Institute, Model Code of Evidence

Model Code of Professional Responsibility (A.B.A.)
>   See   American Bar Association Model Code of Professional Responsibility

Model Land Development Code
>   See   American Law Institute, Model Land Development Code

Model Penal Code (A.L.I.)
>   See   American Law Institute Model Penal Code

Model Rules of Professional Conduct
>   See   American Law Institute, Model Rules of Professional Conduct

Modern Law Review
>   Abbreviation: Mod. L. Rev.
>
>   Examples: Drury, Nullity of Companies in English Law, 48 Mod. L. Rev. 644
>   (1985). ——Article Cite.
>
>   Drury, Nullity of Companies in English Law, 48 Mod. L. Rev. 644,
>   654-55 (1985). ——Page Cite.

In law review footnotes, the titles of books and the names of cases are not underlined.

modified

    Abbreviation: modified

    Example: Bonner v. Coughlin, 517 F.2d 1311 (7th Cir. 1975), modified en banc, 545 F.2d 565 (7th Cir. 1976).

Monash University Law Review

    Abbreviation: Monash U.L. Rev.

Montana Administrative Register

    Abbreviation: Mont. Admin. Reg.

Montana Administrative Rules

    See   Administrative Rules of Montana

Montana Code Annotated

    Abbreviation: Mont. Code Ann. §   (year).

    Example: Mont. Code Ann. § 31-2-324 (1985).

Montana Constitution

    Abbreviation: Mont. Const. art. , § .

    Examples: Mont. Const. art. II, § 12. ——Cite provisions without date unless the cited provisions have been repealed or amended (Bluebook Rule 11).

                  Mont. Const. art. XI, § 5 (1972, amended 1978). ——Cite provisions which have been repealed or amended by giving the date of the adoption of the particular provision and the date of repeal or amendment (Bluebook Rule 11).

Montana Law Review

    Abbreviation: Mont. L. Rev.

    Examples: Clarke, Montana Rules of Evidence: A General Survey, 39 Mont. L. Rev. 79 (1978). ——Article Cite.

                  Clarke, Montana Rules of Evidence: A General Survey, 39 Mont. L. Rev. 79, 84-89 (1978). ——Page Cite.

Montana Lawyer

    Abbreviation: Mont. Law.

    Example: Professional Liability Insurance Company Update, Mont. Law., Mar. 1986, at 9.

Montana Reports

    Abbreviation: Mont.

    Examples: Turley v. Turley, 199 Mont. 265, 649 P.2d 434 (1982). ——Case Cite.

In law review footnotes, the following are in large and small capitals: periodicals, constitutions, codes, restatements, standards, authors of books, titles of books, and legislative materials except for bills and resolutions. Refer to Bluebook.

Turley v. Turley, 199 Mont. 265, 267, 649 P.2d 434, 435 (1982).
——Page Cite.

Montana Session Laws
See   Laws of Montana

Monthly Labor Review
Abbreviation: Monthly Lab. Rev.

Moore on International Law
See   Digest of International Law, by J. Moore

Moore's Federal Practice
——Do not abbreviate the title.

Examples: 8A J. Moore, Moore's Federal Practice ¶ 24.05 (2d ed. 1988).

8A J. Moore, Moore's Federal Practice ¶ 24.05, at 24-59 (2d ed. (1988).

8A J. Moore, Moore's Federal Practice ¶ 24.05 (2d ed. Supp. 1982).

motion, citation to
——Well explained in Bluebook Rule 10.8.3.

Motor Carrier Cases (U.S.) (1936-date)
See   Interstate Commerce Commission (U.S.), Motor Carrier Cases

Municipal Court
Abbreviation: [city] Mun. Ct.

Murray on Contracts, by John E. Murray, Jr.
——Do not abbreviate the title.

Examples: J. Murray, Murray on Contracts § 128 (1974).

J. Murray, Murray on Contracts § 128, at 265 (1974).

Mutual Funds Guide (Commerce Clearing House)
Abbreviation: Mut. Funds Guide (CCH)

In law review footnotes, the titles of books and the names of cases are not underlined.

N

National Labor Relations Board Annual Report
    Abbreviation: NLRB Ann. Rep. (year).

    Example: 45 NLRB Ann. Rep. 20 (1980).

National Labor Relations Board, Decisions and Orders of the (U.S.) (1935-date)
    Abbreviation: N.L.R.B.

    Examples: General Motors Corp., 14 N.L.R.B. 113 (1939).

        Bethlehem Steel Corp., 252 N.L.R.B. 982 (1980).

National Law Journal, The
    Abbreviation: Nat'l L.J.

    Examples: Seller of Handgun Can Be Held Liable for Buyer's Crime, Nat'l L.J., Aug. 16, 1982, at 16, col. 1. ——news report.

        Berreby, Turning Away from Law, Nat'l L.J., Aug. 16, 1982, at 1, col. 1. ——signed article.

National Railroad Adjustment Board 1st-4th Div. (U.S.) (1934-date)
    Abbreviation: N.R.A.B. (x Div.)

    Example: Order of Ry. Conductors, 15 N.R.A.B. (1st Div.) 198 (1938).

National Tax Journal
    Abbreviation: Nat'l Tax J.

    Examples: Rose, Inflation, Tax Rules, and the Price of Land Relative to Capital, 39 Nat'l Tax. J. 59 (1986). ——Article Cite.

        Rose, Inflation, Tax Rules, and the Price of Land Relative to Capital, 39 Nat'l Tax. J. 59, 60-61 (1986). ——Page Cite.

National Transportation Safety Board Decisions (U.S.) (1967-date)
    Abbreviation: N.T.S.B.

    Example: Metro Air Sys., 2 N.T.S.B. 285 (1973).

Natural Resources Journal
    Abbreviation: Nat. Resources J.

In law review footnotes, the following are in large and small capitals: periodicals, constitutions, codes, restatements, standards, authors of books, titles of books, and legislative materials except for bills and resolutions. Refer to Bluebook.

Nebraska Administrative Rules & Regulations
    Abbreviation: Neb. Admin. R. & Regs.   (year).

Nebraska Constitution
    Abbreviation: Neb. Const. art.   , §   .

    Examples: Neb. Const. art. I, § 4. ——Cite provisions without date unless the cited provisions have been repealed or amended (Bluebook Rule 11).

                 Neb. Const. art. VII, § 11 (1875, amended 1976). ——Cite provisions which have been repealed or amended by giving the date of the adoption of the particular provision and the date of repeal or amendment (Bluebook Rule 11).

                 Neb. Const. of 1866, art. I, § I. ——Cite constitutions that have been totally superseded by year of adoption, giving parenthetically the year of adoption of the specific provision cited if different (Bluebook Rule 11).

Nebraska Law Review
    Abbreviation: Neb. L. Rev.

    Examples: Dworkin, Product Liability Reform and the Model Uniform Product Act, 60 Neb. L. Rev. 50 (1981). ——Article Cite.

                 Dworkin, Product Liability Reform and the Model Uniform Product Act, 60 Neb. L. Rev. 50, 60-65 (1981). ——Page Cite.

Nebraska Laws
    See   Laws of Nebraska

Nebraska, Report of the Attorney General
    See   Report of the Attorney General of the State of Nebraska

Nebraska Reports
    Abbreviation: Neb.

    Examples: Mader v. Kallos, 219 Neb. 579, 365 N.W.2d 408 (1985). ——Case Cite.

                 Mader v. Kallos, 219 Neb. 579, 582-83, 365 N.W.2d 408, 410-11 (1985). ——Page Cite.

Nebraska Revised Statutes
    See   Revised Statutes of Nebraska

Nebraska Session Laws
    See   Laws of Nebraska

Netherlands International Law Review
    Abbreviations: Neth. Int'l L. Rev.
                 NILR (publisher's abbreviation)

In law review footnotes, the titles of books and the names of cases are not underlined.

Examples: D'Oliveira, <u>Electoral Rights for Non-Nationals</u>, 31 Neth. Int'l L. Rev. 59 (1984). ——Article Cite.

D'Oliveira, <u>Electoral Rights for Non-Nationals</u>, 31 Neth. Int'l L. Rev. 59, 61-62 (1984). ——Page Cite.

Nevada Administrative Code
Abbreviation: Nev. Admin. Code ch. , § (year).

Nevada Constitution
Abbreviation: Nev. Const. art. , § .

Examples: Nev. Const. art. 5, § 5. ——Cite provisions without date unless the cited provisions have been repealed or amended (Bluebook Rule 11).

Nev. Const. art. 2, § 2 (1864, amended 1972). ——Cite provisions which have been repealed or amended by giving the date of the adoption of the particular provision and the date of repeal or amendment (Bluebook Rule 11).

Nevada Official Opinions of the Attorney General of Nevada
<u>See</u>   Official Opinions of the Attorney General of Nevada

Nevada Reports
Abbreviation: Nev.

Examples: <u>Stolz v. Grimm</u>, 100 Nev. 529, 689 P.2d 927 (1984). ——Case Cite.

<u>Stolz v. Grimm</u>, 100 Nev. 529, 533-35, 689 P.2d 927, 929-30 (1984). ——Page Cite.

Nevada Revised Statutes
Abbreviation: Nev. Rev. Stat. § (year).

Example: Nev. Rev. Stat. § 207.010 (1986).

Nevada Revised Statutes Annotated (Michie)
Abbreviation: Nev. Rev. Stat. Ann. § (Michie year).

Examples: Nev. Rev. Stat. Ann. § 282.170 (Michie 1986).

Nev. Rev. Stat. Ann. § 179A-210 (Michie Supp. 1987).

Nevada Session Laws
<u>See</u>   Statutes of Nevada

New England Law Review
Abbreviation: New Eng. L. Rev.

Examples: Weinberger, <u>Collateral Estoppel and the Mass Produced Product: A Proposal</u>, 15 New Eng. L. Rev. 1 (1979). ——Article Cite.

In law review footnotes, the following are in large and small capitals: periodicals, constitutions, codes, restatements, standards, authors of books, titles of books, and legislative materials except for bills and resolutions. Refer to Bluebook.

Weinberger, <u>Collateral Estoppel and the Mass Produced Product: A Proposal</u>, 15 New Eng. L. Rev. 1, 40-45 (1979). ——Page Cite.

New Hampshire Bar Journal
Abbreviation: N.H.B.J.

Examples: Reardon, <u>Some Current Thoughts on First Amendment Problems</u>, 23 N.H.B.J. 30 (1982). ——Article Cite.

Reardon, <u>Some Current Thoughts on First Amendment Problems</u>, 23 N.H.B.J. 30, 31-32 (1982). ——Page Cite.

New Hampshire Code of Administrative Rules
Abbreviation: N.H. Code Admin. R.   [department name] (year).

New Hampshire Constitution
Abbreviation: N.H. Const. pt.   , art.   .

Examples: N.H. Const. pt. 1, art. 16. ——Cite provisions without date unless the cited provisions have been repealed or amended (Bluebook Rule 11).

N.H. Const. pt. 2, art. 3 (1784, amended 1974). ——Cite provisions which have been repealed or amended by giving the date of the adoption of the particular provision and the date of repeal or amendment (Bluebook Rule 11).

New Hampshire Reports
Abbreviation: N.H.

Examples: <u>State v. Lamb</u>, 125 N.H. 495, 484 A.2d 1074 (1984). ——Case Cite.

<u>State v. Lamb</u>, 125 N.H. 495, 497, 484 A.2d 1074, 1075 (1984). ——Page Cite.

New Hampshire Revised Statutes Annotated
Abbreviation: N.H. Rev. Stat. Ann. §   (year).

Examples: N.H. Rev. Stat. Ann. § 101:2 (1978).

N.H. Rev. Stat. Ann. § 100-A:5 (Supp. 1987).

New Hampshire Rulemaking Register
Abbreviation: N.H. Rulemaking Reg.

New Hampshire Session Laws
<u>See</u>   Laws of the State of New Hampshire

New Jersey Administrative Code
Abbreviations: N.J. Admin. Code tit. , §   (year).

In law review footnotes, the titles of books and the names of cases are not underlined.

New Jersey Administrative Reports
     Abbreviation: N.J. Admin.

New Jersey Constitution
     Abbreviation: N.J. Const. art. , § , ¶ .

     Examples: N.J. Const. art. 4, § 1, ¶ 1. ——Cite provisions without date unless the cited provisions have been repealed or amended (Bluebook Rule 11).

                    N.J. Const. art. 6, § 6, ¶ 7 (1947, amended 1978). ——Cite provisions which have been repealed or amended by giving the date of the adoption of the particular provision and the date of repeal or amendment (Bluebook Rule 11).

                    N.J. Const. of 1844, art. 4, § 1, ¶ 1. ——Cite constitutions that have been totally superseded by year of adoption, giving parenthetically the year of adoption of the specific provision cited if different (Bluebook Rule 11).

New Jersey Equity Reports
     Abbreviation: N.J. Eq.

     Examples: McCarter v. Hudson County Water Co., 70 N.J. Eq. 695, 65 A. 489 (1906). ——Case Cite.

                    McCarter v. Hudson County Water Co., 70 N.J. Eq. 695, 720, 65 A. 489, 499 (1906). ——Page Cite.

New Jersey Law Reports
     Abbreviation: N.J.L.

     Examples: Trade Ins. Co. v. Barracliff, 45 N.J.L. 543 (1883). ——Case Cite.

                    Trade Ins. Co. v. Barracliff, 45 N.J.L. 543, 546 (1883). ——Page Cite.

New Jersey Lawyer
     Abbreviation: N.J. Law.

New Jersey Miscellaneous Reports
     Abbreviation: N.J. Misc.

     Examples: Cooper Lumber Co. v. Dammers, 2 N.J. Misc. 289, 125 A. 325 (Sup. Ct. 1924). ——Case Cite.

                    Cooper Lumber Co. v. Dammers, 2 N.J. Misc. 289, 292, 125 A. 325, 326-27 (Sup. Ct. 1924). ——Page Cite.

New Jersey Register
     Abbreviation: N.J. Reg.

New Jersey Reports
     Abbreviation: N.J.

In law review footnotes, the following are in large and small capitals: periodicals, constitutions, codes, restatements, standards, authors of books, titles of books, and legislative materials except for bills and resolutions. Refer to Bluebook.

Examples: <u>Kolitch v. Lindedahl</u>, 100 N.J. 485, 497 A.2d 183 (1985). ——Case
                 Cite.

                 <u>Kolitch v. Lindedahl</u>, 100 N.J. 485, 488, 497 A.2d 183, 185 (1985).
                 ——Page Cite.

New Jersey Revised Statutes
    Abbreviation: N.J. Rev. Stat. §   (year).

New Jersey Sessions Laws
    <u>See</u>   Laws of New Jersey and New Jersey Session Law Service (West)

New Jersey Session Law Service (West)
    Abbreviation: year N.J. Sess. Law Serv. (West).

New Jersey Statutes Annotated
    Abbreviation: N.J. Stat. Ann. §   (West year).

    Examples: N.J. Stat. Ann. § 2A:16-55 (West 1987).

                  N.J. Stat. Ann. § 2C:14-2 (West Supp. 1987).

New Jersey Superior Court Reports
    Abbreviation: N.J. Super.

    Examples: <u>Hart v. Fox</u>, 204 N.J. Super. 564, 499 A.2d 553 (Law Div. 1985).
                 ——Case Cite.

                 <u>Hart v. Fox</u>, 204 N.J. Super. 564, 568, 499 A.2d 553, 555 (Law Div.
                 1985). ——Page Cite.

New Jersey Tax Court Reports
    Abbreviation: N.J. Tax

New Law Journal
    Abbreviation: New L.J.

    Examples: Allen, <u>Complaints and the Lay Observer</u>, 130 New L.J. 818 (1980).
                 ——Article Cite.

                 Allen, <u>Complaints and the Lay Observer</u>, 130 New L.J. 818, 818
                 (1980). ——Page Cite.

New Mexico Constitution
    Abbreviation: N.M. Const. art.   , §   .

    Examples: N.M. Const. art. II, § 7. ——Cite provisions without date unless the
                 cited provisions have been repealed or amended (Bluebook Rule 11).

In law review footnotes, the titles of books and the names of cases are not underlined.

N.M. Const. art. IV, § 32 (1912, amended 1958). ——Cite provisions which have been repealed or amended by giving the date of the adoption of the particular provision and the date of repeal or amendment (Bluebook Rule 11).

New Mexico Court of Appeal
Abbreviation: N.M. Ct. App. ——Reported in New Mexico Reports.

Examples: Reynolds v. Swigert, 102 N.M. 504, 697 P.2d 504 (Ct. App. 1984). ——Case Cite.

Reynolds v. Swigert, 102 N.M. 504, 507, 697 P.2d 504, 507 (Ct. App. 1984). ——Page Cite.

New Mexico Law Review
Abbreviation: N.M.L. Rev.

Examples: Browde, Administrative Law, Survey of New Mexico Law, 11 N.M.L. Rev. 1 (1980). ——Article Cite.

Browde, Administrative Law, Survey of New Mexico Law, 11 N.M.L. Rev. 1, 5-7 (1980). ——Page Cite.

New Mexico Reports
Abbreviation: N.M.

Examples: Angle v. Slayton, 102 N.M. 521, 697 P.2d 940 (1985). ——Case Cite for New Mexico Supreme Court.

Angle v. Slayton, 102 N.M. 521, 522-23, 697 P.2d 940, 940-41 (1985). ——Page Cite for New Mexico Supreme Court.

New Mexico Session Laws
See   Laws of New Mexico

New Mexico Statutes Annotated
Abbreviation: N.M. Stat. Ann. §   (year).

Examples: N.M. Stat. Ann. § 59A-8-15 (1984).

N.M. Stat. Ann. § 59A-16-1 (Supp. 1985).

New York Appellate Division Reports
Abbreviation: A.D.

Examples: People ex rel. Higley v. Millspaw, 257 A.D. 40, 12 N.Y.S.2d 435 (1939). ——Case Cite.

People ex rel. Higley v. Millspaw, 257 A.D. 40, 41, 12 N.Y.S.2d 435, 437 (1939). ——Page Cite.

New York Appellate Division Reports, second series
Abbreviation: A.D.2d

In law review footnotes, the following are in large and small capitals: periodicals, constitutions, codes, restatements, standards, authors of books, titles of books, and legislative materials except for bills and resolutions. Refer to Bluebook.

Examples: McCasland v. McCasland, 110 A.D.2d 318, 494 N.Y.S.2d 534 (1985).
——Case Cite.

McCasland v. McCasland, 110 A.D.2d 318, 319-20, 494 N.Y.S.2d
534, 535-36 (1985). ——Page Cite.

New York Codes, Rules and Regulations
See   Official Compilation of Codes, Rules and Regulations of the State of New York

New York Consolidated Laws Service Annotated Statutes With Forms
Abbreviation: N.Y. subject Law §   (Consol. year).

——See Bluebook pages 200-202 for abbreviation of each subject.

Example: N.Y. Civ. Prac. L. & R. 3117 (Consol. 1978). ——Civil Practice Law
and Rules is an exception to the general citation form.

New York Constitution
Abbreviation: N.Y. Const. art.   , §   .

Examples: N.Y. Const. art. I, § 12. ——Cite provisions without date unless the
cited provisions have been repealed or amended (Bluebook Rule 11).

N.Y. Const. art. VII, § 1 (1938, amended 1977). ——Cite provisions
which have been repealed or amended by giving the date of the adoption
of the particular provision and the date of repeal or amendment
(Bluebook Rule 11).

N.Y. Const. of 1846, art. I, § 1. ——Cite constitutions that have been
totally superseded by year of adoption, giving parenthetically the year of
adoption of the specific provision cited if different (Bluebook Rule 11).

New York Law Journal
Abbreviation: N.Y.L.J.

Examples: Court of Appeals Uphold Brooklyn Primary Election, N.Y.L.J., Oct.
26, 1982, at 1, col. 2. ——news report.

Fox, Pins Proceedings Dismissed for Due Process Violation, N.Y.L.J.,
Oct. 26, 1982, at 1, col. 2. ——signed article.

New York Law School Journal of International and Comparative Law
Abbreviation: N.Y.L. Sch. J. Int'l & Comp. L.

Examples: Seeberg-Elverfeldt, The Limitation of Liability Statute and Its
Applicability to Oil Pollution Damage Resulting from Offshore Drilling,
2 N.Y.L. Sch. J. Int'l & Comp. L. 48 (1980). ——Article Cite.

Seeberg-Elverfeldt, The Limitation of Liability Statute and Its
Applicability to Oil Pollution Damage Resulting from Offshore Drilling,
2 N.Y.L. Sch. J. Int'l & Comp. L. 48, 51-54 (1980). ——Page Cite.

In law review footnotes, the titles of books and the names of cases are not underlined.

New York Law School Law Review
  Abbreviation: N.Y.L. Sch. L. Rev.

  Examples: George, <u>United States Supreme Court 1979-1980 Term: Criminal Law</u>
  <u>Decisions</u>, 26 N.Y.L. Sch. L. Rev. 99 (1981). ——Article Cite.

  George, <u>United States Supreme Court 1979-1980 Term: Criminal Law</u>
  <u>Decisions</u>, 26 N.Y.L. Sch. L. Rev. 99, 108-14 (1981). ——Page Cite.

New York, McKinney's Consolidated Laws Annotated
  <u>See</u>   McKinney's Consolidated Laws of New York Annotated

New York Miscellaneous Reports
  Abbreviation: Misc.

  Examples: <u>Vichnes v. Transcontinental & W. Air</u>, 173 Misc. 631, 18 N.Y.S.2d
  603 (Sup. Ct. 1940). ——Case Cite.

  <u>Vichnes v. Transcontinental & W. Air</u>, 173 Misc. 631, 632, 18
  N.Y.S.2d 603, 603 (Sup. Ct. 1940). ——Page Cite.

New York Miscellaneous Reports, second series
  Abbreviation: Misc. 2d

  Examples: <u>Pantaleoni v. City of Rome</u>, 126 Misc. 2d 809, 484 N.Y.S.2d 409 (Sup.
  Ct. 1984). ——Case Cite.

  <u>Pantaleoni v. City of Rome</u>, 126 Misc. 2d 809, 810-12, 484 N.Y.S.2d
  409, 411-14 (Sup. Ct. 1984). ——Page Cite.

New York Opinions of Attorney General
  <u>See</u>   Opinions of Attorney General of New York

New York Reports
  Abbreviation: N.Y.

  Examples: <u>Sinclair v. Purdy</u>, 235 N.Y. 245, 139 N.E. 255 (1923). ——Case Cite.

  <u>Sinclair v. Purdy</u>, 235 N.Y. 245, 254, 139 N.E. 255, 258 (1923).
  ——Page Cite.

New York Reports, second series
  Abbreviation: N.Y. 2d

  Examples: <u>Sorichetti v. City of New York</u>, 65 N.Y.2d 461, 482 N.E.2d 70, 492
  N.Y.S.2d 591 (1985). ——Case Cite.

  <u>Sorichetti v. City of New York</u>, 65 N.Y.2d 461, 464, 482 N.E.2d 70,
  72, 492 N.Y.S.2d 591, 594 (1985). ——Page Cite.

New York Session Laws
  <u>See</u>   Laws of New York

In law review footnotes, the following are in large and small capitals: periodicals, constitutions,
codes, restatements, standards, authors of books, titles of books, and legislative materials except
for bills and resolutions. Refer to Bluebook.

New York State Bar Journal
Abbreviation: N.Y. St. B.J.

Examples: Babiskin, <u>Sexual Harassment: How Can the Arbitrator Help?</u>, 54 N.Y.
St. B.J. 278 (1982). ——Article Cite.

Babiskin, <u>Sexual Harassment: How Can the Arbitrator Help?</u>, 54 N.Y.
St. B.J. 278, 280-81 (1982). ——Page Cite.

New York State Register
Abbreviation: N.Y. St. Reg.

New York Stock Exchange Guide (Commerce Clearing House)
Abbreviation: N.Y.S.E. Guide (CCH)

New York Supplement
See   West's New York Supplement

New York Supplement, second series
See   West's New York Supplement, second series

New York Times
Abbreviation: N.Y. Times

Examples: <u>Car Dealer Is Convicted of Faking Mileages</u>, N.Y. Times, Oct. 23,
1982, at 10, col. 6. ——news report.

Adams, <u>Canon Law Undergoing a New Look</u>, N.Y. Times, Oct. 23,
1982, at 10, col. 3. ——signed article.

New York University Institute on Federal Taxation
Abbreviation: Inst. on Fed. Tax'n

Example: Turlington, <u>The Long and Short of Straddles as a Tax Saving Device:
An Historical Update of Revenue Ruling 77-185</u>, 40 Inst. on Fed. Tax'n
§ 16.04 at 16-5 (1982).

New York University Journal of International Law and Politics
Abbreviation: N.Y.U. J. Int'l L. & Pol.

Examples: Feinrider, <u>America's Oil Pledges to Israel: Illegal but Binding Executive
Agreements</u>, 13 N.Y.U. J. Int'l L. & Pol. 525 (1981). ——Article Cite.

Feinrider, <u>America's Oil Pledges to Israel: Illegal but Binding Executive
Agreements</u>, 13 N.Y.U. J. Int'l L. & Pol. 525, 535-40 (1981).
——Page Cite.

New York University Law Review
Abbreviation: N.Y.U. L. Rev.

In law review footnotes, the titles of books and the names of cases are not underlined.

Examples: Garvey, <u>A Litigation Primer for Standing Dismissals</u>, 55 N.Y.U. L. Rev. 545 (1980). ——Article Cite.

Garvey, <u>A Litigation Primer for Standing Dismissals</u>, 55 N.Y.U. L. Rev. 545, 555-56 (1980). ——Page Cite.

New York University Review of Law and Social Change
Abbreviation: N.Y.U. Rev. L. & Soc. Change

Examples: Burnett, <u>Family Economic Integrity Under the Social Security System</u>, 7 N.Y.U. Rev. L. & Soc. Change 155 (1978). ——Article Cite.

Burnett, <u>Family Economic Integrity Under the Social Security System</u>, 7 N.Y.U. Rev. L. & Soc. Change 155, 156-58 (1978). ——Page Cite.

New Zealand Law Journal
Abbreviations: N.Z.L.J.
                  NZLJ (publisher's abbreviation)

Examples: Smith, <u>Ground Rents</u>, N.Z.L.J., Nov. 18, 1980, at 482. ——Article Cite.

Smith, <u>Ground Rents</u>, N.Z.L.J., Nov. 18, 1980, at 482, 482. ——Page Cite.

New Zealand Universities Law Review
Abbreviations: N.Z.U.L. Rev.
                  N.Z.U.L.R. (publisher's abbreviation)

Examples: Joseph, <u>The Apparent Futility of Constitutional Entrenchment in New Zealand</u>, 10 N.Z.U.L. Rev. 27 (1982). ——Article Cite.

Joseph, <u>The Apparent Futility of Constitutional Entrenchment in New Zealand</u>, 10 N.Z.U.L. Rev. 27, 33-34 (1982). ——Page Cite.

News Media and the Law
Abbreviation: News Media & L.

newsletter
Abbreviation: Newsl.

newspapers
Examples: <u>House Votes To Bar U.S. from Enforcing Busing of Students</u>, Wall St. J., June 10, 1981, at 4, col. 2. ——news report.

Adams, <u>Canon Law Undergoing a New Look</u>, N.Y. Times, Oct. 23, 1982, at 10, col. 3. ——signed article.

——This format also applies to weekly newspapers and magazines.

Nimmer on Copyright, by M. Nimmer
——Do not abbreviate the title.

In law review footnotes, the following are in large and small capitals: periodicals, constitutions, codes, restatements, standards, authors of books, titles of books, and legislative materials except for bills and resolutions. Refer to Bluebook.

Example: 1 M. Nimmer, Nimmer on Copyright § 1.01[B] (1987).

North Carolina Administrative Code
Abbreviation: N.C. Admin. Code tit. , r.   (month year).

North Carolina Advance Legislative Service
Abbreviation: year N.C. Adv. Legis. Serv.

North Carolina Attorney General Reports
Abbreviation: N.C. Att'y Gen. Rep.

Example: 45 N.C. Att'y Gen. Rep. 98 (1975-1976).

North Carolina Central Law Journal
Abbreviation: N.C. Cent. L.J.

Examples: Blumrosen, The Bottom Line Concept in Equal Employment
Opportunity Law, 12 N.C. Cent. L.J. 1 (1980). ——Article Cite.

Blumrosen, The Bottom Line Concept in Equal Employment
Opportunity Law, 12 N.C. Cent. L.J. 1, 15-17 (1980). ——Page Cite.

North Carolina Constitution
Abbreviation: N.C. Const. art.   , §   .

Examples: N.C. Const. art. I, § 20. ——Cite provisions without date unless the
cited provisions have been repealed or amended (Bluebook Rule 11).

N.C. Const. art. IV, § 12 (1970, amended 1982). ——Cite provisions
which have been repealed or amended by giving the date of the adoption
of the particular provision and the date of repeal or amendment
(Bluebook Rule 11).

N.C. Const. of 1868, art. I, § 15. ——Cite constitutions that have been
totally superseded by year of adoption, giving parenthetically the year of
adoption of the specific provision cited if different (Bluebook Rule 11).

North Carolina Court of Appeals Reports
Abbreviation: N.C. App.

Examples: Bearton v. Sisk, 70 N.C. App. 70, 318 S.E.2d 560 (1984). ——Case
Cite.

Bearton v. Sisk, 70 N.C. App. 70, 72-73, 318 S.E.2d 560, 562-63
(1984). ——Page Cite.

North Carolina General Statutes
See   General Statutes of North Carolina, The

North Carolina Journal of International Law and Commercial Regulation
Abbreviation: N.C.J. Int'l L. & Com. Reg.

In law review footnotes, the titles of books and the names of cases are not underlined.

Examples: Rodau, <u>Protection of Intellectual Property—Patent, Copyright, and</u>
                <u>Trade Secret Law in the United States and Abroad</u>, 10 N.C.J. Int'l L. &
                Com. Reg. 537 (1985). ——Article Cite.

                Rodau, <u>Protection of Intellectual Property—Patent, Copyright, and</u>
                <u>Trade Secret Law in the United States and Abroad</u>, 10 N.C.J. Int'l L. &
                Com. Reg. 537, 546-47 (1985). ——Page Cite.

North Carolina Law Review
Abbreviation: N.C.L. Rev.

Examples: Covington, <u>Arbitrators and the Board: A Revised Relationship</u>, 57
                N.C.L. Rev. 91 (1978). ——Article Cite.

                Covington, <u>Arbitrators and the Board: A Revised Relationship</u>, 57
                N.C.L. Rev. 91, 98-104 (1978). ——Page Cite.

North Carolina Reports
Abbreviation: N.C.

Examples: <u>Board of Trustees of Univ. of N.C. at Chapel Hill v. Heirs of Prince</u>,
                311 N.C. 644, 319 S.E.2d 239 (1984). ——Case Cite.

                <u>Board of Trustees of Univ. of N.C. at Chapel Hill v. Heirs of Prince</u>,
                311 N.C. 644, 646, 319 S.E.2d 239, 240 (1984). ——Page Cite.

North Carolina Session Laws
<u>See</u>   Session Laws of North Carolina and North Carolina Advance Legislative Service

North Dakota Administrative Code
Abbreviation: N.D. Admin. Code § (year).

Example: 1 N.D. Admin. Code § 4-01 (1982).

North Dakota Century Code Annotated
Abbreviation: N.D. Cent. Code §   (year).

Examples: N.D. Cent. Code § 23-13-11 (1978).

                N.D. Cent. Code § 54-12-04.1 (Supp. 1987).

North Dakota Constitution
Abbreviation: N.D. Const. art.   , §   .

Examples: N.D. Const. art. I, § 9. ——Cite provisions without date unless the
                cited provisions have been repealed or amended (Bluebook Rule 11).

                N.D. Const. art. IV, § 87 (1971, repealed 1978). ——Cite provisions
                which have been repealed or amended by giving the date of the adoption
                of the particular provision and the date of repeal or amendment
                (Bluebook Rule 11).

In law review footnotes, the following are in large and small capitals: periodicals, constitutions,
codes, restatements, standards, authors of books, titles of books, and legislative materials except
for bills and resolutions. Refer to Bluebook.

North Dakota Law Review
    Abbreviation: N.D.L. Rev.

    Examples: Lord, <u>Some Thoughts About Warranty Law: Express and Implied Warranties</u>, 56 N.D.L. Rev. 509 (1980). ——Article Cite.

                Lord, <u>Some Thoughts About Warranty Law: Express and Implied Warranties</u>, 56 N.D.L. Rev. 509, 610-15 (1980). ——Page Cite.

North Dakota, Opinions of the Attorney General
    <u>See</u>   Opinions of the Attorney General, State of North Dakota

North Dakota Reports
    Abbreviation: N.D.

    ——Discontinued after 79 N.D. 865 (1953). Thereafter cite only to N.W.2d.

    Examples: <u>Gunder v. Feeland</u>, 51 N.D. 784, 200 N.W. 909 (1924). ——Case Cite.

                <u>Gunder v. Feeland</u>, 51 N.D. 784, 787, 200 N.W. 909, 910 (1924). ——Page Cite.

    ——After 79 N.D. 865 (1953), cite as follows:

                <u>Cook v. Clark</u>, 375 N.W.2d 181 (N.D. 1985). ——Case Cite.

                <u>Cook v. Clark</u>, 375 N.W.2d 181, 183 (N.D. 1985). ——Page Cite.

North Dakota Session Laws
    <u>See</u>   Laws of North Dakota

North Eastern Reporter
    Abbreviation: N.E.

    Examples: <u>Town of Kankakee v. McGrew</u>, 178 Ill. 74, 52 N.E. 893 (1899). ——Case Cite.

                <u>Town of Kankakee v. McGrew</u>, 178 Ill. 74, 82, 52 N.E. 893, 895 (1899). ——Page Cite.

North Eastern Reporter, second series
    Abbreviation: N.E.2d

    Examples: <u>People v. McDowell</u>, 28 N.Y.2d 373, 270 N.E.2d 716, 321 N.Y.S.2d 894 (1971). ——Case Cite.

                <u>People v. McDowell</u>, 28 N.Y.2d 373, 375, 270 N.E.2d 716, 717, 321 N.Y.S.2d 894, 895 (1971). ——Page Cite.

    Indiana Court of Appeals Reports:

    ——After 396 N.E.2d 429 (1979), cite as follows:

                <u>City of Gary v. Belovich</u>, 504 N.E.2d 286 (Ind. Ct. App. 1987). ——Case Cite.

In law review footnotes, the titles of books and the names of cases are not underlined.

City of Gary v. Belovich, 504 N.E.2d 286, 289 (Ind. Ct. App. 1987).
——Page Cite.

Indiana Reports:

——After 419 N.E.2d 1286 (1981), cite as follows:

Blue v. State, 504 N.E.2d 583 (Ind. 1987). ——Case Cite.

Blue v. State, 504 N.E.2d 583, 584 (Ind. 1987). ——Page Cite.

North Western Reporter
Abbreviation: N.W.

Examples: Cohen v. Todd, 130 Minn. 227, 153 N.W. 531 (1915). ——Case Cite.

Cohen v. Todd, 130 Minn. 227, 228-29, 153 N.W. 531, 531 (1915).
——Page Cite.

North Western Reporter, second series
Abbreviation: N.W.2d

Examples: O'Neil v. A.F. Oys & Sons, Inc., 216 Minn. 391, 13 N.W.2d 8 (1944).
——Case Cite.

O'Neil v. A.F. Oys & Sons, Inc., 216 Minn. 391, 395, 13 N.W.2d 8,
10 (1944). ——Page Cite.

——Cite only to N.W.2d for the following state reports: Iowa Reports after 158 N.W.2d
147 (1968); Minnesota Reports after 253 N.W.2d 149 (1977); North Dakota
Reports after 60 N.W.2d 202 (1953); South Dakota Reports after 245 N.W.2d 481
(1976).

Iowa Reports:

——After 158 N.W.2d 147 (1968), cite as follows:

Beeck v. Kapalis, 302 N.W.2d 90 (Iowa 1981). ——Case Cite.

Beeck v. Kapalis, 302 N.W.2d 90, 91 (Iowa 1981). ——Page Cite.

Minnesota Reports:

——After 253 N.W.2d 149 (1977), cite as follows:

Gilmore v. Little Jack's Steak House, 292 N.W.2d 14 (Minn. 1980).
——Case Cite.

Gilmore v. Little Jack's Steak House, 292 N.W.2d 14, 16 (Minn.
1980). ——Page Cite.

North Dakota Reports:

——After 60 N.W.2d 202 (1953), cite as follows:

American Mut. Life Ins. Co. v. Jordan, 315 N.W.2d 290 (N.D. 1982).
——Case Cite.

American Mut. Life Ins. Co. v. Jordan, 315 N.W.2d 290, 292 (N.D.
1982). ——Page Cite.

South Dakota Reports:

——After 245 N.W.2d 481 (1976), cite as follows:

In law review footnotes, the following are in large and small capitals: periodicals, constitutions,
codes, restatements, standards, authors of books, titles of books, and legislative materials except
for bills and resolutions. Refer to Bluebook.

Van Zee v. Sioux Valley Hosp., 315 N.W.2d 489 (S.D. 1982).
——Case Cite.

Van Zee v. Sioux Valley Hosp., 315 N.W.2d 489, 490 (S.D. 1982).
——Page cite.

Northern Illinois University Law Review
Abbreviation: N. Ill. U.L. Rev.

Northern Ireland Legal Quarterly
Abbreviation: N. Ir. Legal Q.

Example: O'Malley, Book Review, 34 N. Ir. Legal Q. 262 (1983).

Northern Kentucky Law Review
Abbreviation: N. Ky. L. Rev.

Examples: Goldberg, Reflections on the Role of the Supreme Court in the Pursuit
                  of Equal Justice, 7 N. Ky. L. Rev. 1 (1980). ——Article Cite.

                  Goldberg, Reflections on the Role of the Supreme Court in the Pursuit
                  of Equal Justice, 7 N. Ky. L. Rev. 1, 3-5 (1980). ——Page Cite.

Northrop University Law Journal of Aerospace, Energy and the Environment
Abbreviation: Northrop U.L.J. Aero. Energy & Env't

Northwestern Journal of International Law and Business
Abbreviation: Nw. J. Int'l L. & Bus.

Examples: Allen, Problem Areas Concerning Foreign Investment in U.S. Real
                  Estate, 2 Nw. J. Int'l L. & Bus. 1 (1980). ——Article Cite.

                  Allen, Problem Areas Concerning Foreign Investment in U.S. Real
                  Estate, 2 Nw. J. Int'l L. & Bus. 1, 5-6 (1980). ——Page Cite.

Northwestern University Law Review
Abbreviation: Nw. U.L. Rev.

Examples: Boyle, International Law in Time of Crisis: From the Entebbe Raid to
                  the Hostages Convention, 75 Nw. U.L. Rev. 769 (1980). ——Article
                  Cite.

                  Boyle, International Law in Time of Crisis: From the Entebbe Raid to
                  the Hostages Convention, 75 Nw. U.L. Rev. 769, 840-45 (1980).
                  ——Page Cite.

Notre Dame Estate Planning Institute Proceedings
Abbreviation: Notre Dame Est. Plan. Inst. Proc.

Examples: Tucker, Estate and Income Tax Planning for Real Property Ownership,
                  4 Notre Dame Est. Plan. Inst. Proc. 159 (1979). ——Article Cite.

In law review footnotes, the titles of books and the names of cases are not underlined.

Tucker, Estate and Income Tax Planning for Real Property Ownership,
4 Notre Dame Est. Plan. Inst. Proc. 159, 197-98 (1979). ——Page
Cite.

Notre Dame Institute on Charitable Giving Foundations and Trusts
Abbreviation: Notre Dame Inst. on Char. Giving Found. & Tr.

Notre Dame Lawyer
Abbreviation: Notre Dame Law.

Examples: Karst, Equality and Community: Lessons from the Civil Rights Era, 56
Notre Dame Law. 183 (1980). ——Article Cite.

Karst, Equality and Community: Lessons from the Civil Rights Era, 56
Notre Dame Law. 183, 186-89 (1980). ——Page Cite.

Nova Law Journal
Abbreviation: Nova L.J.

Examples: Richmond, The Marriage Penalty: Restructuring Federal Law to
Remedy Tax Burdens on Married Couples, 5 Nova L.J. 31 (1980).
——Article Cite.

Richmond, The Marriage Penalty: Restructuring Federal Law to
Remedy Tax Burdens on Married Couples, 5 Nova L.J. 31, 34-48
(1980). ——Page Cite.

Nuclear Regulatory Commission Issuances
Abbreviation: N.R.C.

Examples: Metropolitan Edison Co. (Three Mile Island, Unit 2), 11 N.R.C. 519
(1980).

Pacific Gas and Electric Co. (Diablo Canyon Nuclear Power Plant, Unit
1), 14 N.R.C. 950 (1981). ——Citation to current unbound material.

Nuclear Regulation Reporter (Commerce Clearing House)
Abbreviation: Nuclear Reg. Rep. (CCH)

Examples: Illinois v. Kerr-McGee Chem. Corp., 2 Nuclear Reg. Rep. (CCH)
¶ 20,222 (7th Cir. May 4, 1982). ——Citation to looseleaf material.

Desrosiers v. Nuclear Regulatory Comm'n, [1964-1981 New
Developments Transfer Binder] Nuclear Reg. Rep. (CCH) ¶ 20,162
(E.D. Tenn. 1980). ——Citation to transfer binder.

Consumers Power Co. (Midland Plant, Units 1 and 2), 2 Nuclear Reg.
Rep. (CCH) ¶ 30,678 (Atomic Safety and Lic. App. Bd. May 5, 1982).
——Citation to looseleaf administrative material.

——The above examples are proper if the case is not yet available in an official or West
reporter, or is not reported in an official or West reporter.

In law review footnotes, the following are in large and small capitals: periodicals, constitutions,
codes, restatements, standards, authors of books, titles of books, and legislative materials except
for bills and resolutions. Refer to Bluebook.

——Citation to a transfer binder of this reporter is infrequent because most NRC administrative rulings appear promptly in the NRC's official reporter.

In law review footnotes, the titles of books and the names of cases are not underlined.

O

Occupational Safety and Health Reporter (Bureau of National Affairs)
    Abbreviation: O.S.H. Rep. (BNA)

    Examples: Rockford Drop Forge Co. v. Donovan, [Decisions] O.S.H. Rep. (BNA)
                 (10 O.S.H. Cas.) 1410 (7th Cir. Mar. 12, 1982). ——Citation to
                 looseleaf material.

                 Minnesota v. Federal Cartridge Corp., 6 O.S.H. Cas. (BNA) 1287 (D.
                 Minn. 1977). ——Citation to bound material.

——The above examples are proper if the case is not yet available in an official or West
reporter, or is not reported in an official or West reporter.

                 Kansas City Power & Light Co., [Decisions] O.S.H. Rep. (BNA) (10
                 O.S.H. Cas.) 1417 (O.S.H. Rev. Comm'n. Mar. 15, 1982).
                 ——Citation to looseleaf administrative material.

                 American Airlines, 6 O.S.H. Cas. (BNA) 1252 (O.S.H. Rev. Comm'n.
                 1977). ——Citation to bound administrative material.

Ocean Development and International Law Journal
    Abbreviation: Ocean Dev. & Int'l L.J.

    Examples: Richardson, The Politics of the Law of the Sea, 11 Ocean Dev. & Int'l
                 L.J. 9 (1982). ——Article Cite.

                 Richardson, The Politics of the Law of the Sea, 11 Ocean Dev. & Int'l
                 L.J. 9, 14-15 (1982). ——Page Cite.

Office of the Attorney General (State of Washington)—Opinions
    Abbreviation: Op. Wash. Att'y Gen.

    Example: 1979 Op. Wash. Att'y Gen. No. 6 (Mar. 28, 1979). ——The name of
                 the opinion may be included. See Bluebook Rule 14.4.

Official Code of Georgia Annotated (Michie Co.)
    Abbreviation: Ga. Code Ann. §   (year).

    Examples: Ga. Code Ann. § 27-4-2 (1986).

                 Ga. Code Ann. § 27-2-29 (Supp. 1987).

Official Compilation of Codes, Rules and Regulations of the State of New York
    Abbreviation: N.Y. Comp. Codes R. & Regs. tit. , § (year).

In law review footnotes, the following are in large and small capitals: periodicals, constitutions,
codes, restatements, standards, authors of books, titles of books, and legislative materials except
for bills and resolutions. Refer to Bluebook.

Official Compilation of the Rules and Regulations of the State of Georgia
 Abbreviation: Ga. Comp. R. & Regs. r.   (year).

Official Compilation Rules and Regulations of the State of Tennessee
 Abbreviations: Tenn. Comp. R. & Regs. tit.   , ch.   (year). ——Bluebook
  Abbreviation
  Tenn. Comp. R. & Regs. r.   (year).   ——Suggested abbreviation.

 Example: Tenn. Comp. R. & Regs. r. 0400-1-1-.01 (1982).   ——Suggested
  citation form.

——Bluebook guidelines do not conform with this publication's format.

Official Journal of the European Communities
 Abbreviation: O.J. Eur. Comm.

 Example: 28 O.J. Eur. Comm. (No. L 139) 1 (1985).

——As available before and after 1972. See Bluebook Rule 19.5.2.

Official Opinions of the Attorney General of Nevada
 Abbreviation: Op. Nev. Att'y Gen.

 Example: 1979 Op. Nev. Att'y Gen. 245.   ——The name of the opinion may be
  included. See Bluebook Rule 14.4.

Official Opinions of the Solicitor for the Post Office Department (U.S.) (1878-1951)
 Abbreviation: Op. Solic. P.O. Dep't

 Examples: 1. Op. Solic. P.O. Dept. 671 (1881).

  9. Op. Solic. P.O. Dept. 655 (1949).

Ohio Administrative Code (official compilation published by Banks-Baldwin)
 Abbreviations: Ohio Admin. Code §   (year).

Ohio Appellate Reports
 Abbreviation: Ohio App.

 Examples: Bruckman v. Bruckman Co., 60 Ohio App. 361, 21 N.E.2d 481 (1938).
  ——Case Cite.

  Bruckman v. Bruckman Co., 60 Ohio App. 361, 361-62, 21 N.E.2d
  481, 481 (1938). ——Page Cite.

Ohio Appellate Reports, second series
 Abbreviation: Ohio App. 2d

 Example: Alsop v. Heater, 45 Ohio App. 2d 201, 342 N.E.2d 698 (1975).
  ——Case Cite.

  Alsop v. Heater, 45 Ohio App. 2d 201, 202, 342 N.E.2d 698, 699
  (1975). ——Page Cite.

In law review footnotes, the titles of books and the names of cases are not underlined.

Ohio Appellate Reports, third series
    Abbreviation: Ohio App. 3d

    ——Beginning with 1 Ohio App. 3d (1980), bound with Ohio and Ohio Misc. in Ohio
    Official Reports.

    Examples: Finomore v. Epstein, 18 Ohio App. 3d 88, 481 N.E.2d 1193 (1984).
    ——Case Cite.

        Finomore v. Epstein, 18 Ohio App. 3d 88, 89, 481 N.E.2d 1193, 1195
    (1984). ——Page Cite.

Ohio Bar Reports
    Abbreviation: Ohio B.

Ohio Circuit Court Decisions
    Abbreviation: Ohio C.C. Dec.

    Examples: Ketterman v. Metzger, 13 Ohio C.C. Dec. 61 (1901). ——Case Cite.

        Ketterman v. Metzger, 13 Ohio C.C. Dec. 61, 62 (1901). ——Page
    Cite.

Ohio Circuit Court Reports
    Abbreviation: Ohio C.C.

    Examples: Bellaire Goblet Co. v. City of Findlay, 5 Ohio C.C. 418 (1891).
    ——Case Cite.

        Bellaire Goblet Co. v. City of Findlay, 5 Ohio C.C. 418, 430 (1891).
    ——Page Cite.

Ohio Circuit Court Reports, New Series
    Abbreviation: Ohio C.C. (n.s.)

    Examples: Strauss v. Village of Conneaut, 3 Ohio C.C. (n.s.) 445 (1902).
    ——Case Cite.

        Strauss v. Village of Conneaut, 3 Ohio C.C. (n.s.) 445, 447 (1902).
    ——Page Cite.

Ohio Circuit Decisions
    Abbreviation: Ohio Cir. Dec.

    Examples: Hickle v. Hickle, 3 Ohio Cir. Dec. 552 (1892). ——Case Cite.

        Hickle v. Hickle, 3 Ohio Cir. Dec. 552, 560 (1892). ——Page Cite.

Ohio Constitution
    Abbreviation: Ohio Const. art. , § .

    Examples: Ohio Const. art. I, § 7. ——Cite provisions without date unless the
    cited provisions have been repealed or amended (Bluebook Rule 11).

In law review footnotes, the following are in large and small capitals: periodicals, constitutions, codes, restatements, standards, authors of books, titles of books, and legislative materials except for bills and resolutions. Refer to Bluebook.

Ohio Const. art. VIII, § 12 (1851, repealed 1974). ——Cite provisions which have been repealed or amended by giving the date of the adoption of the particular provision and the date of repeal or amendment (Bluebook Rule 11).

Ohio Decisions
>   Abbreviation: Ohio Dec.
>
>   Examples: Anderson v. Joyce, 16 Ohio Dec. 320 (C.P. 1913). ——Case Cite.
>
>   Anderson v. Joyce, 16 Ohio Dec. 320, 325 (C.P. 1913). ——Page Cite.

Ohio Decisions, Reprint
>   Abbreviation: Ohio Dec. Reprint

Ohio Law Abstracts
>   Abbreviation: Ohio Law Abs.

——Cite to this reporter only if not found in a reporter listed in Bluebook pages 204-05.

Ohio Law Bulletin
>   Abbreviation: Ohio L. Bull.

Ohio Law Reporter
>   Abbreviation: Ohio L. Rep.

——Cite to this reporter only if not found in a reporter listed in Bluebook pages 204-05.

Ohio Legislative Bulletin (Anderson)
>   Abbreviation: year Ohio Legis. Bull. (Anderson)

Ohio Miscellaneous
>   Abbreviation: Ohio Misc.
>
>   Examples: In re Sergent, 49 Ohio Misc. 36, 360 N.E. 2d 761 (C.P. 1976). ——Case Cite.
>
>   In re Sergent, 49 Ohio Misc. 36, 40, 360, N.E. 2d 761, 764 (C.P. 1976). ——Page Cite.

——Parallel citation to N.E. 2d permissible but not required.

Ohio Miscellaneous, second series
>   Abbreviation: Ohio Misc. 2d

——Beginning with 1 Ohio Misc 2d 1 (1982), bound with Ohio and Ohio App. in Ohio Official Reports.

>   Examples: State v. Puthoff, 18 Ohio Misc. 2d 12, 482 N.E. 2d 348 (Sidney Mun. Ct. 1985). ——Case Cite.

In law review footnotes, the titles of books and the names of cases are not underlined.

<u>State v. Puthoff</u>, 18 Ohio Misc. 2d 12, 15, 482 N.E. 2d 348, 350 (Sidney Mun. Ct. 1985). ——Page Cite.

——Parallel citation to N.E. 2d permissible but not required.

Ohio Monthly Record
    Abbreviation: Ohio Monthly Rec.

Ohio Nisi Prius Reports
    Abbreviation: Ohio N.P.

    Examples: <u>Emery v. City of Elyria</u>, 8 Ohio N.P. 208 (C.P. 1899). ——Case Cite.

                <u>Emery v. City of Elyria</u>, 8 Ohio N.P. 208, 209 (C.P. 1899). ——Page Cite.

Ohio Nisi Prius Reports, new series
    Abbreviation: Ohio N.P. (n.s.)

    Examples: <u>City of Cincinnati v. Zeigler</u>, 16 Ohio N.P. (n.s.) 169 (C.P. 1914). ——Case Cite.

                <u>City of Cincinnati v. Zeigler</u>, 16 Ohio N.P. (n.s.) 169, 173 (C.P. 1914). ——Page Cite.

Ohio Northern University Law Review
    Abbreviation: Ohio N.U.L. Rev.

    Examples: Brown & Truitt, <u>Euthanasia and the Right to Die</u>, 3 Ohio N.U.L. Rev. 615 (1976). ——Article Cite.

                Brown & Truitt, <u>Euthanasia and the Right to Die</u>, 3 Ohio N.U.L. Rev. 615, 616-24 (1976). ——Page Cite.

Ohio Opinions, first series
    Abbreviation: Ohio Op.

    Examples: <u>Ohio Edison Co. v. McElrath</u>, 60 Ohio Op. 462 (C.P. 1955). ——Case Cite.

                <u>Ohio Edison Co. v. McElrath</u>, 60 Ohio Op. 462, 464 (C.P. 1955). ——Page Cite.

Ohio Opinions, second series
    Abbreviation: Ohio Op. 2d

    Examples: <u>Whiting v. Roxy Ltd.</u>, 66 Ohio Op. 2d 369 (C.P. 1973). ——Case Cite.

                <u>Whiting v. Roxy Ltd.</u>, 66 Ohio Op. 2d 369, 371 (C.P. 1973). ——Page Cite.

Ohio Opinions, third series
    Abbreviation: Ohio Op. 3d

In law review footnotes, the following are in large and small capitals: periodicals, constitutions, codes, restatements, standards, authors of books, titles of books, and legislative materials except for bills and resolutions. Refer to Bluebook.

Examples: State v. Ackerman, 19 Ohio Op. 3d 347 (C.P. 1979). ——Case Cite.

State v. Ackerman, 19 Ohio Op ed 347, 348 (C.P. 1979). ——Page Cite.

——Ohio Op. 3d was discontinued in 1982.

Ohio, Opinions of the Attorney General
See   Opinions of the Attorney General of Ohio

Ohio Revised Code Annotated, Baldwin's
See   Baldwin's Ohio Revised Code Annotated

Ohio Revised Code Annotated (Anderson), Page's
See   Page's Ohio Revised Code Annotated.

Ohio Session Laws
See   State of Ohio: Legislative Acts Passed and Joint Resolutions Adopted

Ohio State Law Journal
Abbreviation: Ohio St. L.J.

Examples: Gerety, Doing Without Privacy, 42 Ohio St. L.J. 143 (1981).
——Article Cite.

Gerety, Doing Without Privacy, 42 Ohio St. L.J. 143, 150-55 (1981).
——Page Cite.

Ohio State Reports
Abbreviation: Ohio St.

Examples: In re Thatcher, 80 Ohio St. 492, 89 N.E. 39 (1909). ——Case Cite.

In re Thatcher, 80 Ohio St. 492, 668, 89 N.E. 39, 88 (1909). ——Page Cite.

Ohio State Reports, second series
Abbreviation: Ohio St. 2d

Examples: United Air Lines v. Porterfield, 28 Ohio St. 2d 97, 276 N.E.2d 629 (1971). ——Case Cite.

United Air Lines v. Porterfield, 28 Ohio St. 2d 97, 105, 276 N.E.2d 629, 635 (1971). ——Page Cite.

Ohio State Reports, third series
Abbreviation: Ohio St. 3d

——Beginning with 1 Ohio St. 3d 1 (1982), bound with Ohio App. and Ohio Misc. in Ohio Official Reports.

In law review footnotes, the titles of books and the names of cases are not underlined.

Examples: Celebrezze v. Hughes, 18 Ohio St. 3d 71, 479 N.E.2d 886 (1985).
——Case Cite.

Celebrezze v. Hughes, 18 Ohio St. 3d 71, 74, 479 N.E.2d 886, 888
(1985). ——Page Cite.

Oil and Gas Tax Quarterly
Abbreviation: Oil & Gas Tax Q.

Examples: Munro, Oil and Gas Tax Partnerships: Do They Truly Exist?, 28 Oil &
Gas Tax Q. 275 (1980). ——Article Cite.

Munro, Oil and Gas Tax Partnerships: Do They Truly Exist?, 28 Oil &
Gas Tax Q. 275, 276-78 (1980). ——Page Cite.

Oklahoma Bar Journal
Abbreviation: Okla. B.J.

Examples: Richardson, Should We Allow the Hinckley Backlash to Cause Bad
Law? The Insanity Defense, 53 Okla. B.J. 2180 (1982). ——Article
Cite.

Richardson, Should We Allow the Hinckley Backlash to Cause Bad
Law? The Insanity Defense, 53 Okla. B.J. 2180, 2182-83 (1982).
——Page Cite.

Oklahoma City University Law Review
Abbreviation: Okla. City U.L. Rev.

Examples: Kenderdine, Contributions to Spouse's Education: The Search for
Compensation When the Marriage Ends, 5 Okla. City U.L. Rev. 409
(1980). ——Article Cite.

Kenderdine, Contributions to Spouse's Education: The Search for
Compensation When the Marriage Ends, 5 Okla. City U.L. Rev. 409,
413-18 (1980). ——Page Cite.

Oklahoma Constitution
Abbreviation: Okla. Const. art. , § .

Examples: Okla. Const. art. 1, § 2. ——Cite provisions without date unless the
cited provisions have been repealed or amended (Bluebook Rule 11).

Okla. Const. art. 1, § 5 (1907, repealed 1959). ——Cite provisions
which have been repealed or amended by giving the date of the adoption
of the particular provision and the date of repeal or amendment
(Bluebook Rule 11).

Oklahoma Criminal Reports
Abbreviation: Okla. Crim.

——Discontinued after 97 Okla. Crim. 415 (1953). Thereafter cite only to P.2d.

In law review footnotes, the following are in large and small capitals: periodicals, constitutions,
codes, restatements, standards, authors of books, titles of books, and legislative materials except
for bills and resolutions. Refer to Bluebook.

Examples: <u>Simmons v. State</u>, 68 Okla. Crim. 337, 98 P.2d 623 (1940). ——Case
               Cite.

               <u>Simmons v. State</u>, 68 Okla. Crim. 337, 340, 98 P.2d 623, 624 (1940).
               ——Page Cite.

——After 97 Okla. Crim. 415 (1954), cite as follows:

               <u>Roubideaux v. State</u>, 707 P.2d 35 (Okla. Crim. App. 1985). ——Case
               Cite.

               <u>Roubideaux v. State</u>, 707 P.2d 35, 36 (Okla. Crim. App. 1985).
               ——Page Cite.

Oklahoma Gazette
      Abbreviation: Okla. Gaz.

      Example: 19 Okla. Gaz. 1199 (1981).

Oklahoma Law Review
      Abbreviation: Okla. L. Rev.

      Examples: Kutner, <u>Judicial Identification of "Penal Laws" in the Conflict of Laws</u>,
                       31 Okla. L. Rev. 590 (1978). ——Article Cite.

                       Kutner, <u>Judicial Identification of "Penal Laws" in the Conflict of Laws</u>,
                       31 Okla. L. Rev. 590, 594-600 (1978). ——Page Cite.

Oklahoma Register
      Abbreviation: Okla. Reg.

Oklahoma Reports
      Abbreviation: Okla.

      ——Discontinued after 208 Okla. 695 (1953). Thereafter cite only to P.2d.

      Examples: <u>Powell v. Moore</u>, 204 Okla. 505, 231 P.2d 695 (1951). ——Case Cite.

                       <u>Powell v. Moore</u>, 204 Okla. 505, 514, 231 P.2d 695, 704 (1951).
                       ——Page Cite.

      ——After 208 Okla. 695 (1953), cite as follows:

                       <u>Butcher v. McGinn</u>, 706 P.2d 878 (Okla. 1985). ——Case Cite.

                       <u>Butcher v. McGinn</u>, 706 P.2d 878, 879 (Okla. 1985). ——Page Cite.

Oklahoma Session Laws
      Abbreviations: year Okla. Sess. Laws

Oklahoma Session Law Service (West)
      Abbreviation: year Okla. Sess. Law Serv.   (West)

In law review footnotes, the titles of books and the names of cases are not underlined.

Oklahoma Statutes
>   Abbreviation: Okla. Stat. tit.   , §   (year).
>
>   Example: Okla. Stat. tit. 42, § 141 (1979).

Oklahoma Statutes Annotated
>   Abbreviation: Okla. Stat. Ann. tit.   , §   (West year).
>
>   Examples: Okla. Stat. Ann. tit. 70, § 5-134 (West 1972).
>
>   Okla. Stat. Ann. tit. 70, § 1210.271 (West Supp. 1988).

O'Neal on Close Corporations
>   See   O'Neal's Close Corporations, by F. O'Neal & R. Thompson

O'Neal's Close Corporations, by F. O'Neal & R. Thompson
>   ——Do not abbreviate the title.
>
>   Examples: 2 F. O'Neal & R. Thompson, O'Neal'sClose Corporations § 7.40 (3d
>   ed. 1987).
>
>   2 F. O'Neal & R. Thompson, O'Neal's Close Corporations § 7.40, at
>   195-96 (3d ed. 1987).
>
>   2 F. O'Neal & R. Thompson, O'Neal's Close Corporations § 10.45 (3d
>   ed. Supp. 1987). ——Cite to pocket part

Opinions of the Attorney General (U.S.) (1789-date)
>   Abbreviation: Op. Att'y Gen.
>
>   Examples: Carriage in United States Vessels of Exports Financed by a Government
>   Agency, 42 Op. Att'y Gen. 301 (1965).
>
>   42 Op. Att'y Gen. 327 (1966). ——Citation to bound material.
>
>   43 Op. Att'y Gen. No. 13 (Jan. 26, 1978). ——Citation to current
>   unbound material.
>
>   Disposition by Treaty of Territory or Property Belonging to the United
>   States, 43 Op. Att'y Gen. No. 18 (Aug. 11, 1977). ——Citation to
>   current unbound material when a title is to be given.

Opinions of the Attorney General and Report to the Governor of Virginia
>   Abbreviation: Op. Va. Att'y Gen.
>
>   Example: 1980-1981 Op. Va. Att'y Gen. 468. ——The name of the opinion may
>   be included. See Bluebook Rule 14.4.

Opinions of the Attorney General of California
>   Abbreviation: Op. Cal. Att'y Gen.
>
>   Example: 64 Op. Cal. Att'y Gen. 676 (1981). ——The name of the opinion may
>   be included. See Bluebook Rule 14.4.

In law review footnotes, the following are in large and small capitals: periodicals, constitutions, codes, restatements, standards, authors of books, titles of books, and legislative materials except for bills and resolutions. Refer to Bluebook.

Opinions of the Attorney General of New York
          Abbreviation: Op. N.Y. Att'y Gen.

Examples: 1979 Op. N.Y. Att'y Gen. 31. ——Citation to formal opinions.

                   1979 Op. N.Y. Att'y Gen. 209 (informal). ——Citation to informal
                   opinions even though both the formal and informal opinions are bound
                   in one volume.

——The name of the opinion may be included. See Bluebook Rule 14.4.

Opinions of the Attorney General of Ohio
          Abbreviation: Op. Ohio Att'y Gen.

Example: 1982 Op. Ohio Att'y Gen. pt. 2 at 2. ——The name of the opinion may
                   be included. See Bluebook Rule 14.4.

Opinions of the Attorney General of Oklahoma
          Abbreviation: Op. Okla. Att'y Gen.

Example: 12 Op. Okla. Att'y Gen. 136 (1980). ——The name of the opinion may
                   be included. See Bluebook Rule 14.4.

Opinions of the Attorney General of Oregon
          Abbreviation: Op. Or. Att'y Gen.

Example: 41 Op. Or. Att'y Gen. 351 (1980-1981). ——The name of the opinion
                   may be included. See Bluebook Rule 14.4.

Opinions of the Attorney General of Pennsylvania
          Abbreviation: Op. Pa. Att'y Gen.

Example: 1978 Op. Pa. Att'y Gen. 117. ——The name of the opinion may be
                   included. See Bluebook Rule 14.4.

Opinions of the Attorney General of Tennessee
          Abbreviation: Op. Tenn. Att'y Gen.

Examples: 11 Op. Tenn. Att'y Gen. No. 173 (June 23, 1982). ——Citation for
                   opinions that appear in unpaginated advance sheets.

                   9 Op. Tenn. Att'y Gen. 144 (1979). ——Citation for opinions that
                   appear in the paginated volume or binder.

——The name of the opinion may be included. See Bluebook Rule 14.4.

Opinions of the Attorney General of Texas
          Abbreviation: Op. Tex. Att'y Gen.

Example: 1979 Op. Tex. Att'y Gen. No. n.w. — 107 (December 20, 1979).
                   ——Citation to unpaginated slip opinion. The name of the opinion may
                   be included. See Bluebook Rule 14.4.

In law review footnotes, the titles of books and the names of cases are not underlined.

Opinions of the Attorney General of the State of Louisiana
    Abbreviation: Op. La. Att'y Gen.

    Example: 1976-1978 Op. La. Att'y Gen. 15. ——The name of the opinion may be
                   included. See Bluebook Rule 14.4.

Opinions of the Attorney General of the State of Wisconsin
    Abbreviation: Op. Wis. Att'y Gen.

    Example: 68 Op. Wis. Att'y Gen. 140 (1979). ——The name of the opinion may
                   be included. See Bluebook Rule 14.4.

Opinions of the Attorney General, State of Georgia
    Abbreviation: Op. Ga. Att'y Gen.

    Example: 1981 Op. Ga. Att'y Gen. No. 81-105. ——The name of the opinion
                   may be included. See Bluebook Rule 14.4.

Opinions of the Attorney General, State of Kansas
    Abbreviation: Op. Kan. Att'y Gen.

    Example: 8 Op. Kan. Att'y Gen. 12 (1974). ——The name of the opinion may be
                   included. See Bluebook Rule 14.4.

Opinions of the Attorney General State of Minnesota
    Abbreviation: Op. Minn. Att'y Gen.

    Example: 13 Op. Minn. Att'y Gen. 36 (1980). ——The name of the opinion may
                   be included. See Bluebook Rule 14.4.

Opinions of the Attorney General, State of North Dakota
    Abbreviation: Op. N.D. Att'y Gen.

    Example: 1979 Op. N.D. Att'y Gen. 26. ——The name of the opinion may be
                   included. See Bluebook Rule 14.4.

Oppenheim on International Law
    <u>See</u>   International Law, by L. Oppenheim

Order of authorities within each signal
    ——See Bluebook Rule 2.4.

Order of signals
    ——See Bluebook Rule 2.3.

ordinances
    ——Do not abbreviate

    Examples: Knoxville, Tenn., Ordinance 0-155-78 (Sept. 8, 1978). ——uncodified.

                  Memphis, Tenn., Code § 2-295 (1979). ——codified.

In law review footnotes, the following are in large and small capitals: periodicals, constitutions, codes, restatements, standards, authors of books, titles of books, and legislative materials except for bills and resolutions. Refer to Bluebook.

Nashville and Davidson County, Tenn., Metropolitan Code § 30A-1-24 (1967). ——A unified county/city government.

Oregon Administrative Rules
Abbreviations: Or. Admin. R.   (year).

Oregon Administrative Rules Bulletin
Abbreviation: Or. Admin. R. Bull.

Example: Or. Admin. R. 461-26-030 (1982).

Oregon Attorney General Opinions
See   Opinions of the Attorney General of Oregon

Oregon Constitution
Abbreviation: Or. Const. art.   , §   .

Examples: Or. Const. art. I, § 9. ——Cite provisions without date unless the cited provisions have been repealed or amended (Bluebook Rule 11).

Or. Const. art. IX, § 1 (1859, amended 1917). ——Cite provisions which have been repealed or amended by giving the date of the adoption of the particular provision and the date of repeal or amendment (Bluebook Rule 11).

Oregon Law Review
Abbreviation: Or. L. Rev.

Examples: Lacy, Chief Justice O'Connell's Contributions to the Law of Civil Procedure, 56 Or. L. Rev. 191 (1977). ——Article Cite.

Lacy, Chief Justice O'Connell's Contributions to the Law of Civil Procedure, 56 Or. L. Rev. 191, 202-06 (1977). ——Page Cite.

Oregon Laws and Resolutions
Abbreviations: year Or. Laws.
                  year Or. Laws Spec. Sess.
                  year Or. Laws Adv. Sh. No.

Oregon Reports
Abbreviation: Or.

Examples: Illingworth v. Bushong, 297 Or. 675, 688 P.2d 379 (1984). ——Case Cite.

Illingworth v. Bushong, 297 Or. 675, 677, 688 P.2d 379, 380 (1984). ——Page Cite.

Oregon Reports, Court of Appeal
Abbreviation: Or. App.

In law review footnotes, the titles of books and the names of cases are not underlined.

Examples: <u>Paprock v. Defenbaugh</u>, 71 Or. App. 624, 693 P.2d 654 (1985).
——Case Cite.

<u>Paprock v. Defenbaugh</u>, 71 Or. App. 624, 626, 693 P.2d 654, 655 (1985). ——Page Cite.

Oregon Revised Statutes
Abbreviation: Or. Rev. Stat. §   (year).

Example: Or. Rev. Stat. § 687.115 (1985).

Oregon Revised Statutes Annotated
Abbreviation: Oreg. Rev. Stat. Ann. §   (Butterworths year).

Example: Oreg. Rev. Stat. Ann. § 261.005 (Butterworths 1986).

——Not listed in Bluebook.

Oregon Session Laws
<u>See</u>   Oregon Laws and Resolutions

Oregon State Bar Bulletin
Abbreviation: Or. St. B. Bull.

Examples: Hingson, <u>'Just a DUII'?</u>, 43 Or. St. B. Bull. 15 (1982). ——Article Cite.

Hingson, <u>'Just a DUII'?</u>, 43 Or. St. B. Bull. 15, 16-17 (1982). ——Page Cite.

Oregon Tax Reports
Abbreviation: Or. Tax

Example: <u>Rogers v. Department of Revenue</u>, 6 Or. Tax. 139, 142 (1975).

Orphans' Court
Abbreviation: Orphans' Ct.

Osgoode Hall Law Journal
Abbreviation: Osgoode Hall L.J.

Examples: Magnet, <u>The Presumption of Constitutionality</u>, 18 Osgoode Hall L.J. 87 (1980). ——Article Cite.

Magnet, <u>The Presumption of Constitutionality</u>, 18 Osgoode Hall L.J. 87, 87-89 (1980). ——Page Cite.

Otago Law Review
Abbreviations: Otago L. Rev.
Otago L.R. (publisher's abbreviation)

In law review footnotes, the following are in large and small capitals: periodicals, constitutions, codes, restatements, standards, authors of books, titles of books, and legislative materials except for bills and resolutions. Refer to Bluebook.

Ottawa Law Review
     Abbreviation: Ottawa L. Rev.

     Examples: Magnet, <u>Neonatal Intensive Care: The Dilemma for Medical Law</u>, 13
                      Ottawa L. Rev. 345 (1981). ——Article Cite.

                      Magnet, <u>Neonatal Intensive Care: The Dilemma for Medical Law</u>, 13
                      Ottawa L. Rev. 345, 351-52 (1981). ——Page Cite.

Oxford Journal of Legal Studies
     Abbreviation: Oxford J. Legal Stud.

     Examples: Reuben, <u>Subrogation in Insurance Law—A Critical Evaluation</u>, 5
                      Oxford J. Legal Stud. 416 (1985). ——Article Cite.

                      Reuben, <u>Subrogation in Insurance Law—A Critical Evaluation</u>, 5
                      Oxford J. Legal Stud. 416, 420-21 (1985). ——Page Cite.

In law review footnotes, the titles of books and the names of cases are not underlined.

P

Pace Law Review

    Abbreviation: Pace L. Rev.

    Examples: Adede, <u>Streamlining the System for Settlement of Disputes Under the Law of the Sea Convention</u>, 1 Pace L. Rev. 15 (1980). ——Article Cite.

                Adede, <u>Streamlining the System for Settlement of Disputes Under the Law of the Sea Convention</u>, 1 Pace L. Rev. 15, 19-26 (1980). ——Page Cite.

Pacific Law Journal

    Abbreviation: Pac. L.J.

    Examples: Kelso & Pawluc, <u>Focus on Cameras in the Courtroom: The Florida Experience, the California Experiment, and the Pending Decision in Chandler v. Florida</u>, 12 Pac. L.J. 1 (1980). ——Article Cite.

                Kelso & Pawluc, <u>Focus on Cameras in the Courtroom: The Florida Experience, the California Experiment, and the Pending Decision in Chandler v. Florida</u>, 12 Pac. L.J. 1, 3-9 (1980). ——Page Cite.

Pacific Reporter

    Abbreviation: P.

    Examples: <u>West v. Kern</u>, 88 Or. 247, 171 P. 413 (1918). ——Case Cite.

                <u>West v. Kern</u>, 88 Or. 247, 253, 171 P. 413, 415 (1918). ——Page Cite.

Pacific Reporter, second series

    Abbreviation: P.2d

    Examples: <u>Bloss v. Rahilly</u>, 16 Cal. 2d 70, 104 P.2d 1049 (1940). ——Case Cite.

                <u>Bloss v. Rahilly</u>, 16 Cal. 2d 70, 79-80, 104 P.2d 1049, 1053 (1940). ——Page Cite.

——Cite only to P.2d for the following state reporters: Alaska Reports after 348 P.2d 587 (1960); Colorado Reports after 619 P.2d 38 (1980); Colorado Appeals Reports after 620 P.2d 52 (1980); Oklahoma Reports after 258 P.2d 1184 (1953); Oklahoma Criminal Reports after 266 P.2d 992 (1953); Utah Reports after 519 P.2d 1344 (1974); Wyoming Reports after 345 P.2d 234 (1959).

Alaska Reports:

——After 348 P.2d 587 (1960), cite as follows:

                <u>Newell v. National Bank</u>, 646 P.2d 224 (Alaska 1982). ——Case Cite.

In law review footnotes, the following are in large and small capitals: periodicals, constitutions, codes, restatements, standards, authors of books, titles of books, and legislative materials except for bills and resolutions. Refer to Bluebook.

> Newell v. National Bank, 646 P.2d 224, 226 (Alaska 1982). ——Page Cite.

Arizona Appeals Reports:

——Discontinued after 558 P.2d 992 (1976). Thereafter cite to Arizona Reports and P.2d as follows:

> Rhodes v. International Harvester Co., 141 Ariz. 418, 641 P.2d 906 (Ct. App. 1982). ——Case Cite.
>
> Rhodes v. International Harvester Co., 141 Ariz. 418, 421, 641 P.2d 906, 908 (Ct. App. 1982). ——Page Cite.

Colorado Appeals Reports:

——After 620 P.2d 52 (1980), cite as follows:

> Zertuche v. Montgomery Ward & Co., 706 P.2d 424 (Colo. Ct. App. 1985). ——Case Cite.
>
> Zertuche v. Montgomery Ward & Co., 706 P.2d 424, 425-26 (Colo. Ct. App. 1985). ——Page Cite.

Colorado Reports:

——After 619 P.2d 38 (1980), cite as follows:

> People v. Bertine, 706 P.2d 411 (Colo. 1985). ——Case Cite.
>
> People v. Bertine, 706 P.2d 411, 412-13 (Colo. 1985). ——Page Cite.

Oklahoma Criminal Reports:

——After 266 P.2d 992 (1953), cite as follows:

> Stratton v. State, 643 P.2d 645 (Okla. Crim. App. 1982). ——Case Cite.
>
> Stratton v. State, 643 P.2d 645, 647 (Okla. Crim. App. 1982). ——Page Cite.

Oklahoma Reports:

——After 258 P.2d 1184 (1953), cite as follows:

> Drummond v. Johnson, 643 P.2d 634 (Okla. 1982). ——Case Cite.
>
> Drummond v. Johnson, 643 P.2d 634, 635 (Okla. 1982). ——Page Cite.

Utah Reports:

——After 519 P.2d 1344 (1974), cite as follows:

> Taylor Nat'l, Inc. v. Jensen Bros. Constr. Co., 641 P.2d 150 (Utah 1982). ——Case Cite.
>
> Taylor Nat'l, Inc. v. Jensen Bros. Constr. Co., 641 P.2d 150, 152 (Utah 1982). ——Page Cite.

Wyoming Reports:

——After 345 P.2d 234 (1959), cite as follows:

In law review footnotes, the titles of books and the names of cases are not underlined.

Moewes v. Farmer's Ins. Group, 641 P.2d 740 (Wyo. 1982). ——Case
Cite.

Moewes v. Farmer's Ins. Group, 641 P.2d 740, 742 (Wyo. 1982).
——Page Cite.

page

Examples: Trautman, The Income Taxation of Estate Distributions—A Need for
Reform, 44 Ind. L.J. 397 (1968).

Trautman, The Income Taxation of Estate Distributions—A Need for
Reform, 44 Ind. L.J. 397, 397 (1968). ——Repeat page number when
citing to material on the first page of an article or case.

——See generally supra p. 18.

——p. is used only for cross-reference

546 F.2d at 917-18.

Id. at 918-19.

79 Dep't State Bull. No. 2023, at 14 (1979).

——"at _____." Used in subsequent citations and to avoid confusion with other kinds of
numbers.

Page on the Law of Wills, by W. Bowe & D. Parker
——Do not abbreviate the title.

Examples: 7 (part 3) W. Bowe & D. Parker, Page on the Law of Wills § 65.35
(rev. 1982).

7 (part 3) W. Bowe & D. Parker, Page on the Law of Wills § 65.35, at
326 (rev. 1982).

3 W. Bowe & D. Parker, Page on the Law of Wills § 29.24 (Supp.
1987).

Page's Ohio Revised Code Annotated
Abbreviation: Ohio Rev. Code Ann. § (Anderson year).

Examples: Ohio Rev. Code Ann. § 1901.09 (Anderson 1983).

Ohio Rev. Code Ann. § 1923.02 (Anderson Supp. 1987).

Paine on Tennessee Law of Evidence
See Tennessee Law of Evidence, by D. Paine

Pan-American Treaty Series
Abbreviation: Pan-Am T.S.

paragraph(s)
Abbreviations: ¶, ¶¶ if so in source. Otherwise para., paras.

In law review footnotes, the following are in large and small capitals: periodicals, constitutions,
codes, restatements, standards, authors of books, titles of books, and legislative materials except
for bills and resolutions. Refer to Bluebook.

Examples: 2A R. Powell & P. Rohan, <u>Powell on Real Property</u> ¶ 269 (1986).

                2A R. Powell & P. Rohan, <u>Powell on Real Property</u> ¶¶ 269-273 (1986).

——See generally Bluebook Rule 3.4.

parenthetical information and explanatory parenthetical phrases
——See Bluebook Rules 2.5, 2.6, 10.6, and 12.7.

part(s)
Abbreviation: pt., pts.

Partnership, by A. Bromberg
<u>See</u>   Crane and Bromberg on Partnership, by A. Bromberg

Partnership Taxation, by A. Willis, J. Pennell & P. Postlewaite
——Do not abbreviate the title.

Example: 1 A. Willis, J. Pennel & P. Postlewaite, <u>Partnership Taxation</u> § 6.02 (1987).

Patent Law Annual
Abbreviation: Pat. L. Ann.

Patent, Trademark and Copyright Infringement, by R. Nordhaus
——Do not abbreviate the title.

Examples: R. Nordhaus, <u>Patent, Trademark and Copyright Infringement</u> § 6 (1971).

                R. Nordhaus, <u>Patent, Trademark and Copyright Infringement</u> § 6, at 12 (1971).

Patents, Decisions of the Commissioner and of U.S. Courts (1869-date)
——Cite administrative decisions appearing herein to the Official Gazette of the United States Patent Office (Off. Gaz. Pat. Office).

Patents, Trademark & Copyright Journal (Bureau of National Affiars)
Abbreviation: Pat. Trademark & Copyright J. (BNA)

pending and unreported cases
Examples: <u>Slotkin v. Citizens Casualty Co.</u>, No. 78-7167 (2d Cir. argued Jan. 17, 1979). ——Pending case.

                <u>Gray v. Hutto</u>, No. 80-6679 (4th Cir. Apr. 1, 1981). ——Cite to unreported decision.

                <u>Gray v. Hutto</u>, No. 80-6679, slip. op. at 4 (4th Cir. Apr. 1, 1981). ——Cite to page in unreported decisions.

In law review footnotes, the titles of books and the names of cases are not underlined.

Fled v. Cooper, No. 85-2255-S (D. Kan. Dec. 23, 1985) (LEXIS, Genfed Library, Dist file).

Pennsylvania Bar Association Quarterly
Abbreviation: Pa. B.A.Q.

Examples: Rosenstein & Pitt, Practicing Under the New Pennsylvania Condominium Law, 51 Pa. B.A.Q. 244 (1980). ——Article Cite.

Rosenstein & Pitt, Practicing Under the New Pennsylvania Condominium Law, 51 Pa. B.A.Q. 244, 252-53 (1980). ——Page Cite.

Pennsylvania Bulletin
Abbreviation: Pa. Bull.

Pennsylvania Code
Abbreviation: Pa. Code § (year).

Pennsylvania Commonwealth Court Reports
Abbreviation: Pa. Commw.

Examples: Lyles v. City of Philadelphia, 88 Pa. Commw. 509, 490 A.2d 936 (1985). ——Case Cite.

Lyles v. City of Philadelphia, 88 Pa. Commw. 509, 511, 490 A.2d 936, 938 (1985). ——Page Cite.

Pennsylvania Consolidated Statutes
Abbreviation: title Pa. Cons. Stat. § (year).

Pennsylvania Consolidated Statutes Annotated
Abbreviation: title Pa. Cons. Stat. Ann. § (Purdon year).

Examples: 18 Pa. Cons. Stat. Ann. § 912 (Purdon 1983).

18 Pa. Cons. Stat. Ann. § 908 (Purdon Supp. 1987).

Pennsylvania Constitution
Abbreviation: Pa. Const. art. , § .

Examples: Pa. Const. art. I, § 3. ——Cite provisions without date unless the cited provisions have been repealed or amended (Bluebook Rule 11).

Pa. Const. art. IV, § 17 (1968, amended 1978). ——Cite provisions which have been repealed or amended by giving the date of the adoption of the particular provision and the date of repeal or amendment (Bluebook Rule 11).

Pa. Const. of 1776, art. I, § 9. ——Cite constitutions that have been totally superseded by year of adoption, giving parenthetically the year of adoption of the specific provision cited if different (Bluebook Rule 11).

In law review footnotes, the following are in large and small capitals: periodicals, constitutions, codes, restatements, standards, authors of books, titles of books, and legislative materials except for bills and resolutions. Refer to Bluebook.

Pennsylvania District and County Reports
    Abbreviation: Pa. D. & C.

    Examples: Grady's Estate, 34 Pa. D. & C. 143 (Orphan's Ct. 1938). ——Case Cite.

                     Grady's Estate, 34 Pa. D. & C. 143, 149 (Orphan's Ct. 1938). ——Page Cite.

Pennsylvania District and County Reports, second series
    Abbreviation: Pa. D. & C.2d

    Examples: Academy of Natural Sciences v. Philadelphia, 6 D. & C.2d 145 (C.P. 1955). ——Case Cite.

                     Academy of Natural Sciences v. Philadelphia, 6 D. & C.2d 145, 149 (C.P. 1955). ——Page Cite.

Pennsylvania District and County Reports, third series
    Abbreviation: Pa. D. & C.3d

    Examples: Hurley v. Inland Fin. Co., 34 Pa. D. & C.3d 336 (C.P. 1984). ——Case Cite.

                     Hurley v. Inland Fin. Co., 34 Pa. D. & C.3d 336, 337 C.P. 1984). ——Page Cite.

Pennsylvania Fiduciary Reporter
    Abbreviation: Pa. Fiduc.

    Examples: Zappardino Estate, 14 Pa. Fiduc. 212 (Orphan's Ct. 1964). ——Case Cite.

                     Zappardino Estate, 14 Pa. Fiduc. 212, 216 (Orphan's Ct. 1964). ——Page Cite.

   ——Above examples are correct if case not reported in Pa. D. & C., Pa. D. & C.2d, or Pa. D. & C.3d.

Pennsylvania Fiduciary Reporter, second series
    Abbreviation: Pa. Fiduc. 2d

    Examples: Dolinger Estate, 4 Pa. Fiduc. 2d 327 (Orphan's Ct. 1984). ——Case Cite.

                     Dolinger Estate, 4 Pa. Fiduc. 2d 327, 330 (Orphan's Ct. 1984). ——Page Cite.

   ——Above examples are correct if case not reporter in Pa. D. & C.3d.

Pennsylvania Legislative Service (Purdon)
    Abbreviation: year Pa. Legis. Serv. (Purdon).

In law review footnotes, the titles of books and the names of cases are not underlined.

Pennsylvania Session Laws
    See   Laws of Pennsylvania

Pennsylvania State Reports
    Abbreviation: Pa.

    Examples: Leonard v. Thornburgh, 507 Pa. 317, 489 A.2d 1349 (1985). ——Case
    Cite.

    Leonard v. Thornburgh, 507 Pa. 317, 319, 489 A.2d 1349, 1350
    (1985). ——Page Cite.

Pennsylvania Statutes Annotated, Purdon's
    See   Purdon's Pennsylvania Statutes Annotated

Pennsylvania Superior Court Reports
    Abbreviation: Pa. Super.

    Examples: Lichtenfels v. Bridgeview Coal Co., 344 Pa. Super. 257, 496 A.2d 782
    (1985). ——Case Cite.

    Lichtenfels v. Bridgeview Coal Co., 344 Pa. Super. 257, 260-62, 496
    A.2d 782, 784 (1985). ——Page Cite.

Pension and Profit Sharing (Prentice-Hall)
    Abbreviation: Pens. & Profit Sharing (P-H)

Pension Plan Guide (Commerce Clearing House)
    Abbreviation: Pens. Plan Guide (CCH)

Pension Reporter (Bureau of National Affairs)
    Abbreviation: Pens. Rep. (BNA)

Pepperdine Law Review
    Abbreviation: Pepperdine L. Rev.

    Examples: Breed & Voss, Procedural Due Process in the Discipline of Incarcerated
    Juveniles, 5 Pepperdine L. Rev. 641 (1978). ——Article Cite.

    Breed & Voss, Procedural Due Process in the Discipline of Incarcerated
    Juveniles, 5 Pepperdine L. Rev. 641, 652-59 (1978). ——Page Cite.

per curiam
    ——Do not abbreviate.

    Examples: Gibbons v. United States Dist. Court , 416 F.2d 14 (9th Cir. 1969) (per
    curiam).

    Anderson v. Gladden, 303 F. Supp. 1134 (D. Or. 1967), aff'd per
    curiam, 416 F.2d 447 (9th Cir. 1969).

    Kent v. Prasse, 385 F.2d 406 (3d Cir. 1967) (per curiam).

In law review footnotes, the following are in large and small capitals: periodicals, constitutions, codes, restatements, standards, authors of books, titles of books, and legislative materials except for bills and resolutions. Refer to Bluebook.

——See Bluebook Rules 10.6 and 10.7.1.

periodicals
Examples:

law review article, single:

> McCoy, <u>Current State Action Theories, the Jackson Nexus
> Requirement, and Employee Discharges by Semi-Public and State-Aided
> Institutions</u>, 31 Vand. L. Rev. 785 (1978). ——Article Cite.

> McCoy, <u>Current State Action Theories, the Jackson Nexus
> Requirement, and Employee Discharges by Semi-Public and State-Aided
> Institutions</u>, 31 Vand. L. Rev. 785, 809-13 (1978). ——Page Cite.

articles, multiple:

> Costas & Harris, <u>Patents, Trademarks and Copyrights—The Legal
> Monopolies</u> (pts. 1-2) 36 Conn. B.J. 569, 37 Conn. B.J. 420 (1962-
> 1963). ——For the series.

> Costas & Harris, <u>Patents, Trademarks and Copyrights— The Legal
> Monopolies</u> (pt. 2) 37 Conn. B.J. 420 (1963). ——For a single part of
> the series.

comment:

> Case Comment, <u>FSLIC Discretion in Insuring State Chartered
> Institutions: West Helena Savings & Loan Association v. Federal Home
> Loan Bank Board</u>, 91 Harv. L. Rev. 1090 (1978). ——Case comment.

> Comment, <u>The State Action Exemption in Antitrust from Parker v.
> Brown to Cantor v. Detroit Edison Co.</u>, 1977 Duke L.J. 871.
> ——Comment.

> Comment, <u>Sunbathers Versus Property Owners: Public Access to North
> Carolina Beaches</u>, 64 N.C.L. Rev. 159 (1985) (authored by Alice
> Gibbon Carmichael). ——The student author's name may be indicated
> parenthetically.

> Washington, <u>Comment: History and Role of Black Law Schools</u>, 18
> How. L.J. 385 (1974). ——Comment by non-student.

note:

> Note, <u>Fairness and Unfairness in Television Product Advertising</u>, 76
> Mich. L. Rev. 498 (1978).

> Note, <u>Dronenburg v. Zech: The Wrong Case for Asserting a Right of
> Privacy for Homosexuals</u>, 63 N.C.L. Rev. 749 (1985) (authored by
> Katherine M. Allen). ——The student author's name may be indicated
> parenthetically.

special project:

> Special Project, <u>Admission to the Bar: A Constitutional Analysis</u>, 34
> Vand. L. Rev. 655 (1981).

symposium:

In law review footnotes, the titles of books and the names of cases are not underlined.

Transnational Technology Transfer: Current Problems and Solutions for the Corporate Practitioner, 14 Vand. J. Transnat'l L. 249 (1981). ——Symposium as a whole.

Wilner, The Transfer of Technology to Latin America, 14 Vand. J. Transnat'l L. 269 (1981). ——Article within the symposium.

Market Oriented Approaches to Achieving Health Policy Goals, 34 Vand. L. Rev. 849 (1981). ——Symposium as a whole.

book review:

Black, Book Review, 90 Yale L.J. 232 (1980).

Black, Book Review, 90 Yale L.J. 232 (1980) (reviewing D. Konig, Law and Society in Puritan Massachusetts (1979)). ——Citation which includes the title of the book reviewed.

Black, Community and Law in Seventeenth Century Massachusetts (Book Review), 90 Yale L.J. 232 (1980). ——Alternative citation to a book review with a title other than the title of the book reviewed.

book note:

Book Note, 95 Harv. L. Rev. 735 (1982).

article in separately paginated issue:

Creedon, Lifetime Gifts of Life Insurance, Prac. Law. Oct. 1974, at 27. ——Article Cite.

Creedon, Lifetime Gifts of Life Insurance, Prac. Law. Oct. 1974, at 27, 31-33. ——Page Cite.

——When a periodical is paginated only within each issue, the date or period of the issue must be included in the citation (Bluebook Rule 16).

year used as the volume number:

Bloch, Cooperative Federalism and the Role of Litigation in the Development of Federal AFDC Eligibility Policy, 1979 Wis. L. Rev. 1. ——Article Cite.

Student-Written Materials:

Note, Broadcasters' First Amendment Rights: A New Approach?, 39 Vand. L. Rev. 323 (1986) (authored by L. Allyn Dixon, Jr.). ——Optional inclusion of student author's name.

Case Comment, 37 U. Fla. L. Rev. 889 (1985). ——Citation by designation alone for short commentary.

——See generally Bluebook Rule 16.1.2.

permanent
   Abbreviation: perm.

In law review footnotes, the following are in large and small capitals: periodicals, constitutions, codes, restatements, standards, authors of books, titles of books, and legislative materials except for bills and resolutions. Refer to Bluebook.

Permanent Court of International Justice Advisory Opinions, Cases, Judgments, Pronouncements
    Abbreviation: P.C.I.J.

    Examples: Legal Status of Eastern Greenland, [1933] P.C.I.J., ser. C, No. 64.
        ——Case Cite.

        Legal Status of Eastern Greenland, [1933] P.C.I.J., ser. C, No. 64, at
        1708-09. ——Page Cite.

Permanent Court of International Justice Annual Reports
    Abbreviation: P.C.I.J. Ann. R.

    Example: 6 P.C.I.J. Ann. R. (ser. E) No. 6 (1930).

Peters (United States Reports)
    See   United States Reports

photoduplicated reprint
    Abbreviation: photo. reprint

Pike & Fischer
    Abbreviation: (P & F)

Police Justice's Court
    Abbreviation: Police J. Ct.

Poverty Law Reporter (Commerce Clearing House)
    Abbreviation: Pov. L. Rep. (CCH)

Powell on Real Property (multivolume edition)
    See   The Law of Real Property, by R. Powell and P. Rohan

Practical Lawyer
    Abbreviation: Prac. Law.

    Examples: Creedon, Lifetime Gifts of Life Insurance, Prac. Law., Oct. 1974, at
        27. ——Article Cite.

        Creedon, Lifetime Gifts of Life Insurance, Prac. Law., Oct. 1974, at
        27, 31-33. ——Page Cite.

    ——When a periodical is paginated only within each issue, the date or period of the
    issue must be included in the citation (Bluebook Rule 16a).

prefaces and forewords (to books)
    Examples: J. Thomas, The Institutes of Justinian at v (1975). ——Preface or
        foreword by the author.

In law review footnotes, the titles of books and the names of cases are not underlined.

McGuire, Introduction to J. Beck, May It Please the Court at xiii
(1930). ——Preface or foreword by another person.

Preface to Estates in Land and Future Interests, by Thomas F. Bergin and Paul. G. Haskell
——Do not abbreviate the title.

Example: T. Bergin & P. Haskell, Preface to Estates in Land and Future Interests
97 (1966).

Prentice-Hall, Inc.
Abbreviation: P-H

Presidential Papers
Executive Orders

Abbreviation: Exec. Order No.

Examples: Exec. Order No. 12,375, 47 Fed. Reg. 34,105 (1982). ——Citation to
material not yet available in the Code of Federal Regulations.

Exec. Order No. 12,261, 3 C.F.R. 83 (1982).

Exec. Order No. 11,574, 3 C.F.R. 188 (1970), reprinted in 33 U.S.C.
§ 407 app. at 115 (1976). ——Citation if the order is reprinted in
U.S.C., U.S.C.A., or U.S.C.S.

Proclamations

Abbreviation: Proclamation No.

Examples: Proclamation No. 4957, 47 Fed. Reg. 34,105 (1982). ——Citation to
material not yet available in the Code of Federal Regulations.

Proclamation No. 4871, 3 C.F.R. 56 (1982).

Proclamation No. 4420, 3 C.F.R. 11 (1976), reprinted in 90 Stat. 3081
(1976). ——Citation with optional parallel reference to a printing in
Statutes at Large.

Private Acts of the State of Tennessee
Abbreviation: year Tenn. Priv. Acts.

Examples: Act of Apr. 24, 1981, ch. 93, 1981 Tenn. Priv. Acts 207.

Act of Apr. 24, 1981, ch. 93, § 3, 1981 Tenn. Priv. Acts 207, 207.
——Citation to a section of a session law.

Private Foundations Reporter (Commerce Clearing House)
Abbreviation: Priv. Found. Rep. (CCH)

Private Laws (U.S. Statutes at Large)
Abbreviation: Priv. L. No.   , Stat.   (year).

Example: Priv. L. No. 92-23, 85 Stat. 842 (1971).

In law review footnotes, the following are in large and small capitals: periodicals, constitutions,
codes, restatements, standards, authors of books, titles of books, and legislative materials except
for bills and resolutions. Refer to Bluebook.

Pritchard on the Law of Wills and Administration of Estates, by H. Phillips & J. Robinson
——Do not abbreviate the title.

Examples: 2 H. Phillips & J. Robinson, Pritchard on the Law of Wills and
                Administration of Estates § 549 (4th ed. 1983).

                2 H. Phillips & J. Robinson, Pritchard on the Law of Wills and
                Administration of Estates § 549, at 58 (4th ed. 1983).

Probate Court
Abbreviation: P. Ct.

Product Safety & Liability Reporter (Bureau of National Affairs)
Abbreviation: Prod. Safety & Liab. Rep (BNA)

Products Liability Reporter (Commerce Clearing House)
Abbreviation: Prod. Liab. Rep. (CCH)

Examples: Oldham's Farm Sausage Co. v. Salco, Inc., 2 Prod. Liab. Rep. (CCH)
                ¶ 9270 (Mo. Ct. App. Mar. 30, 1982). ——Citation to looseleaf
                material.

                Franklin v. Westinghouse Airbrake Co., [Jan. 1980 - Dec. 1981
                Transfer Binder] Prod. Liab. Rep. (CCH) ¶ 8651 (Tenn. Ct. App.
                1980). ——Citation to transfer binder.

——The above examples are proper if the case is not yet available in an official or West
    reporter, or is not reported in an official or West reporter.

Professional Corporation Guide (Prentice-Hall)
Abbreviation: Prof. Corp. Guide (P-H)

Prosser and Keeton on the Law of Torts, by W. Keeton
——Do not abbreviate the title.

Examples: W. Keeton, Prosser and Keeton on the Law of Torts § 19 (5th ed.
                1984).

                W. Keeton, Prosser and Keeton on the Law of Torts § 19, at 124 (5th
                ed. 1984).

Public Acts of the State of Tennessee
Abbreviation: year Tenn. Pub. Acts

Examples: Act of June 5, 1979, ch. 437, 1979 Tenn. Pub. Acts 1223.

                Act of Apr. 1, 1981, ch. 158, § 1, 1981 Tenn. Pub. Acts 193, 193.
                ——Citation to a section of a session law.

                The Uniform Standards Code for Factory Manufactured Structures and
                Recreational Vehicles Act, ch. 310, 1979 Tenn. Pub. Acts 668.
                ——Citation to a session law with a popular name.

In law review footnotes, the titles of books and the names of cases are not underlined.

Act of Apr. 23, 1979, ch. 254, 1979 Tenn. Pub. Acts 496 (codified at Tenn. Code Ann. § 51-415 (Supp. 1981)). ——Citation to a session law when that law will be or is codified and the code location is known.

Public and Local Acts of the Legislature of the State of Michigan
    Abbreviation: year Mich. Pub. Acts

Public Bargaining Cases (¶)
    Abbreviation: Pub. Bargaining Cas. (CCH)

Public Contract Law Journal
    Abbreviation: Pub. Cont. L.J.

Public Employee Bargaining (¶)
    Abbreviation: Pub. Employee Bargaining (CCH)

Public Land Law Review
    Abbreviation: Pub. Land L. Rev.

Public Law
    Abbreviation: Pub. L.

Public Law Forum
    Abbreviation: Pub. L.F.

    Examples: Goldman, The Supreme Court and the Law of School Desegregation, 2 Pub. L.F. 17 (1982). ——Article Cite.

                 Goldman, The Supreme Court and the Law of School Desegregation, 2 Pub. L.F. 17, 24 (1982). ——Page Cite.

Public Laws (U.S.)
    Abbreviation: Pub. L.

    Examples: Act of June 13, 1978, Pub. L. No. 95-292, 92 Stat. 307. ——Act Cite.

                 Act of June 13, 1978, Pub. L. No. 95-292, § 2, 92 Stat. 307, 308-15. ——Section Cite.

Public Laws of Rhode Island
    Abbreviation: year R.I. Pub. Laws

Public Utilities Fortnightly
    Abbreviation: Pub. Util. Fort.

    Examples: Johnson & Thomas, Deregulation and Divestiture in a Changing Telecommunications Industry, 110 Pub. Util. Fort. 17 (1982). ——Article Cite.

In law review footnotes, the following are in large and small capitals: periodicals, constitutions, codes, restatements, standards, authors of books, titles of books, and legislative materials except for bills and resolutions. Refer to Bluebook.

Johnson & Thomas, <u>Deregulation and Divestiture in a Changing Telecommunications Industry</u>, 110 Pub. Util. Fort. 17, 20-21 (1982). ——Page Cite.

Puerto Rico Laws
     <u>See</u>   Laws of Puerto Rico

Puerto Rico Laws Annotated
     Abbreviation: P.R. Laws Ann. tit.   , §   (year).

     Examples: P.R. Laws Ann. tit. 30, § 1770e (1985).

                     P.R. Laws Ann. tit. 32, § 1678 (Supp. 1987).

Puerto Rico Reports (1899-1972)
     Abbreviation: P.R.R.

     Examples: <u>People v. Martinez Rivera</u>, 99 P.R.R. 551 (1971). ——Case Cite.

                     <u>People v. Martinez Rivera</u>, 99 P.R.R. 551, 557 (1971). ——Page Cite.

Purdon's Pennsylvania Statutes Annotated
     Abbreviation: Pa. Stat. Ann. tit.   , §   (Purdon year).

     Examples: Pa. Stat. Ann. tit. 71, § 765 (Purdon 1962).

                     Pa. Stat. Ann. tit. 71, § 755-1 (Purdon Supp. 1987).

In law review footnotes, the titles of books and the names of cases are not underlined.

Q

Queensland Law Society Journal
Abbreviation: Queensl. L. Soc'y J.

Queen's Law Journal
Abbreviation: Queen's L.J.

quotations
——Details for quotations are well explained and illustrated in Rule 5 of the Bluebook.

quoted in
Examples: TSC Indus., Inc. v. Northway, Inc., 426 U.S. 438, 449 (1976), quoted in Fiflis, Soft Information: The SEC's Former Exogenous Zone, 26 UCLA L. Rev. 95, 116 n.71 (1978). ——Where the quoted work is the primary authority.

"As Wigmore notes sequestration 'already had in English practice an independent and continuous existence, even in the time of those earlier modes of trial which preceded the jury and were a part of our inheritance of the common Germanic law.' VI Wigmore on Evidence § 1837 at 348 (3rd 1940), quoted in Geders v. United States, 425 U.S. 80, 87, 96 S. Ct. 1330, 1334, 47 L. Ed. 2d 592 (1976). The rule serves two salutary purposes: (1) it prevents witnesses from tailoring testimony ..." ——Taken from 675 F.2d 825, 835 (1982).

quoting
Examples: Fiflis, Soft Information: The SEC's Former Exogeneous Zone, 26 UCLA L. Rev. 95, 116 n.71 (1978) ("A fact is material if there is a substantial likelihood that a reasonable shareholder would consider it important in deciding how to vote.") (quoting TSC Indus. Inc. v. Northway, Inc., 426 U.S. 438, 449 (1976)). ——Where the quoting work is the primary authority.

Hollywood Baseball Ass'n v. Commissioner, 423 F.2d 494 (9th Cir. 1970) (quoting Corn Products Refining Co. v. Commissioner 350 U.S. 46, 51 (1955)).

In law review footnotes, the following are in large and small capitals: periodicals, constitutions, codes, restatements, standards, authors of books, titles of books, and legislative materials except for bills and resolutions. Refer to Bluebook.

In law review footnotes, the titles of books and the names of cases are not underlined.

R

Rabkin & Johnson's Current Legal Forms with Tax Analysis
See   Current Legal Forms with Tax Analysis, by J. Rabkin & M. Johnson

Radio Regulation Second Series (Pike and Fischer)
Abbreviation: Rad. Reg. 2d (P & F)

Examples: Democratic Nat'l Comm., 51 Rad. Reg. 2d (P & F) 905 (F.C.C. May 27, 1982). ——Citation to looseleaf administrative material. Such a citation is proper if the material is not yet available in or is not reported in an official reporter.

Midcontinent Broadcasting Co., 50 Rad. Reg. 2d (P & F) 17 (F.C.C. 1981). ——Citation to bound administrative material. Such a citation is proper only if the material is not currently available in an official reporter.

Real Estate Commission
Abbreviation: Real Est. Comm'n

Real Estate Law Journal
Abbreviation: Real Est. L.J.

Real Property Probate and Trust Journal
Abbreviation: Real Prop. Prob. & Tr. J.

Examples: Taub, Rights and Remedies Under a Title Policy, 15 Real Prop. Prob. & Tr. J. 422 (1980).

Best, Transfers of Bodies and Body Parts Under the Uniform Anatomical Gift Act, 15 Real Prop. Prob. & Tr. J. 806 (1980).

record (court), citation to
——See Bluebook Rule 10.8.3.

Regulations of Connecticut State Agencies
Abbreviation: Conn. Agencies Regs. §   (year).

In law review footnotes, the following are in large and small capitals: periodicals, constitutions, codes, restatements, standards, authors of books, titles of books, and legislative materials except for bills and resolutions. Refer to Bluebook.

related authority
    <u>See</u>   cited in
           construed in
           quoted in
           quoting
           reprinted in

Reorganization Plans (U.S.)
    Abbreviation: Reorg. Plan No. of year

    Examples: Reorg. Plan No. 1 of 1978, 43 Fed. Reg. 19,807. ——Citation to
                 material not yet available in the Code of Federal Regulations.

                 Reorg. Plan No. 3 of 1970, 3 C.F.R. 199 (1970).

                 Reorg. Plan No. 1 of 1967, 3 C.F.R. 220 (1969), <u>reprinted in</u> 5 U.S.C.
                 app. at 822 (1976) (repealed 1978). ——Citation if the plan is reprinted
                 in U.S.C., U.S.C.A., or U.S.C.S. In this example, the repeal of the
                 plan is noted parenthetically.

                 Reorg., Plan No. 4 of 1978, 3 C.F.R. 332 (1979), <u>reprinted in</u> 5 U.S.C.
                 app. at 412 (Supp. IV 1980) <u>and in</u> 92 Stat. 3790 (1978). ——Citation
                 with optional parallel reference to a printing in Statutes at Large.

replacement
    Abbreviation: repl.

Report of the Attorney General of the State of Nebraska
    Abbreviation: Neb. Att'y Gen. Rep.

    Example: 1977-1978 Neb. Att'y Gen. Rep. 212.

Report of the Attorney General, State of Massachusetts
    Abbreviation: Mass. Att'y Gen. Rep.

    Example: 1973 Mass. Att'y Gen. Rep. 39.

Reports, Congressional
    <u>See</u>   Congressional Reports

Reports of Family Law
    Abbreviation: Rep. Fam. L.

Reports of the United States Board of Tax Appeals
    Abbreviation: B.T.A.

    Example: <u>Tennessee Egg Co. v. Commissioner</u>, 47 B.T.A. 558 (1942).

reprint
    Example: W. Blackstone, <u>Commentaries</u> 35 (1765-1769 & photo reprint 1979).

In law review footnotes, the titles of books and the names of cases are not underlined.

reprinted in
    Example: United States Policy on Nonrecognition of Communist China, 39 Dep't
         St. Bull. 385 (1958), reprinted in W. Bishop, International Law Cases
         and Materials 351-54 (3d ed. 1962).

Res Gestae
    Abbreviation: Res Gestae

    Examples: Harvey, Rules, Rulings for the Trial Lawyer, 29 Res Gestae 456 (1986).
         ——Article Cite.

         Harvey, Rules, Rulings for the Trial Lawyer, 29 Res Gestae 456, 459-
         60 (1986). ——Page Cite.

Research in Law and Economics
    Abbreviation: Res. L. & Econ.

    Examples: Armitage, Economic Efficiency as a Legal Norm, 7 Res. L. & Econ. 1
         (1985). ——Article Cite.

         Armitage, Economic Efficiency as a Legal Norm, 7 Res. L. & Econ. 1,
         18-19 (1985). ——Page Cite.

Resolutions, Congressional
    See   Congressional Resolutions

Restatement (Second) of Agency (A.L.I.)
    Abbreviation: Restatement (Second) of Agency § (year).

    Examples: Restatement (Second) of Agency § 307A, comments a & c (1957).

         Restatement (Second) of Agency § 275 app. (1957). ——Cite for
         Agency Appendix.

Restatement (Second) of Conflict of Laws (A.L.I.)
    Abbreviation: Restatement (Second) of Conflict of Laws § (year).

    Examples: Restatement (Second) of Conflict of Laws § 288 reporter's note (1971).

         Restatement (Second) of Conflict of Laws § 103 (1969).

         Restatement (Second) of Conflict of Laws § 115 comment e, illustration
         4 (1969).

Restatement of Contracts (A.L.I.)
    Abbreviation: Restatement of Contracts § (year).

    Example: Restatement of Contracts § 405(1) (1932). ——Citation to section as
         well as to comment.

Restatement (Second) of Contracts (A.L.I.)
    Abbreviation: Restatement (Second) of Contracts § (year).

In law review footnotes, the following are in large and small capitals: periodicals, constitutions,
codes, restatements, standards, authors of books, titles of books, and legislative materials except
for bills and resolutions. Refer to Bluebook.

Example: Restatement (Second) of Contracts § 367 & comment a (1979).

Restatement of Foreign Relations Law of the United States (A.L.I.)
Abbreviation: Restatement (Second) of Foreign Relations Law of the United States §
                  (year).

Examples: Restatement (Second) of Foreign Relations Law of the United States
                  § 17 (1965).

                  Restatement (Second) of Foreign Relations Law of the United States
                  § 621 app. (1969). ——Cite for Foreign Relations Appendix.

Restatement (Second) of Foreign Relations Law of the United States (revised) (A.L.I., Tentative Draft).
Abbreviation: Restatement of Foreign Relations Law of the United States (revised) §
                  (Tent. Draft No.   , year).

Examples: Restatement of Foreign Relations Law of the United States (revised)
                  § 206 (Tent. Draft No. 6, 1985).

                  Restatement of Foreign Relations Law of the United States (revised)
                  § 403 (Tent. Draft No. 7, 1986).

Restatement (Third) of Foreign Relations Law of the United States (A.L.I.)
Abbreviation: Restatement (Third) of Foreign Relations Law of the United States §
                  (year).

Examples: Restatement (Third) of Foreign Relations Law of the United States
                  § 415 (1987).

                  Restatement (Third) of Foreign Relations Law of the United States
                  § 415 reporter's note 1 (1987).

Restatement of Judgments (A.L.I.)
Abbreviation: Restatement of Judgments §   (year).

Example: Restatement of Judgments ch. 3 introductory note (1942).

Restatement (Second) of Judgments (A.L.I.)
Abbreviation: Restatement (Second) of Judgments §   (year).

Example: Restatement (Second) of Judgments § 4 (1980).

Restatement (Second) of Property (A.L.I.)
Abbreviation: Restatement (Second) of Property, subdivision, §   (status if
                  necessary, year).

Example: Restatement (Second) of Property, Donative Transfers, § 8.1 (1981).

Restatement (Second) of Property (A.L.I., Tentative Draft)
Abbreviation: Restatement (Second) of Property, subdivision, §   (Tent. Draft
                  No.   , year).

In law review footnotes, the titles of books and the names of cases are not underlined.

Example: Restatement (Second) of Property, Donative Transfers, § 26.1 (Tent. Draft No. 9, 1986).

Restatement of Restitution (A.L.I.)
Abbreviation: Restatement of Restitution §   (year).

Example: Restatement of Restitution § 189 comment a (1936).

Restatement (Second) of Restitution (A.L.I., Tentative Draft)
Abbreviation: Restatement (Second) of Restitution §   (Tent. Draft No. , year).

Example: Restatement (Second) of Restitution § 31 (Tent. Draft No. 2, 1984).

Restatement (Second) of Torts (A.L.I.)
Abbreviation: Restatement (Second) of Torts §   (year).

Examples: Restatement (Second) of Torts § 520 (1976).

Restatement (Second) of Torts § 520 comment k (1976).

Restatement (Second) of Torts § 47 app. (1963). ——Cite for Torts Appendix.

Restatement (Second) of Trusts (A.L.I.)
Abbreviation: Restatement (Second) of Trusts §   (year).

Examples: Restatement (Second) of Trusts § 158 (1957).

Restatement (Second) of Trusts § 126 app. (1957). ——Cite for Trusts Appendix.

Revenue Procedures
Abbreviation: Rev. Proc.

Examples: Rev. Proc. 86-43, 1986-46 I.R.B. 15. ——Citation to a Revenue Procedure not yet available in bound form.

Rev. Proc. 85-39, 1985-2 C.B. 443. ——Bound.

Revenue Rulings
Abbreviation: Rev. Rul.

Examples: Rev. Rul. 82-9, 1982-2 I.R.B. 5. ——Citation to a Revenue Ruling not yet available in bound form.

Rev. Rul. 81-17, 1981-1 C.B. 75. ——Bound. For examples of citations to earlier Cumulative Bulletins, see Cumulative Bulletin.

reversed
Abbreviation: rev'd

Examples: Young v. Edgcomb Steel Co., 363 F. Supp. 961 (M.D.N.C. 1973), rev'd, 499 F.2d 97 (4th Cir. 1974).

In law review footnotes, the following are in large and small capitals: periodicals, constitutions, codes, restatements, standards, authors of books, titles of books, and legislative materials except for bills and resolutions. Refer to Bluebook.

Griggs v. Duke Power Co., 420 F.2d 1225 (4th Cir. 1970), rev'd in part, 401 U.S. 424 (1971).

Karlen v. Harris, 590 F.2d 39 (2d Cir. 1978), rev'd sub nom. Stryker's Bay Neighborhood Council v. Karlen, 444 U.S. 223 (1980).
——Citation if the case has a different name on appeal.

Review of Taxation of Individuals
    Abbreviation: Rev. Tax'n Indiv.

revised
    Abbreviation: rev.

Revised Code of Washington
    Abbreviation: Wash. Rev. Code §   (year).

Revised Code of Washington Annotated
    Abbreviation: Wash. Rev. Code Ann. §   (year).

    Examples: Wash. Rev. Code Ann. § 11.28.120 (1987).

                Wash. Rev. Code Ann. § 80.50.010 (Supp. 1988).

Revised Statutes of Nebraska
    Abbreviation: Neb. Rev. Stat. §   (year).

    Examples: Neb. Rev. Stat. § 7-103 (1983).

                Neb. Rev. Stat. § 9-203 (Supp. 1986).

Revista de Derecho Puertorriqueño
    Abbreviation: Rev. D.P.

    Examples: Morales, La resolución integral de disputas redefinición de la tarea judicial, 23 Revista de Derecho Puertorriqueño [Rev. D.P.] 77 (1983-1984).

                Vargas, El error como vicio del consentimeinto, 22 Rev. D.P. 57 (1982).

——When using foreign language titles, the first citation should indicate in brackets any abbreviation to be used subsequently. (See Bluebook Rule 20.6)

Revista del Colegio de Abogados de Puerto Rico
    Abbreviation: Rev. Col. Ab. P.R.

    Example: Fuster, La misión de la Universidad Católica de Puerto Rico y la situación actual del pais, 21 Revista de Derecho del Colegio de Abogados de Puerto Rico [Rev. Col. Ab. P.R.] 147 (1981).

——When using foreign language titles, the first citation should indicate in brackets any abbreviation to be used subsequently. (See Bluebook Rule 20.6)

In law review footnotes, the titles of books and the names of cases are not underlined.

Revista Juridica de la Universidad de Puerto Rico
Abbreviation: Rev. Jur. U.P.R.

Example: Reed, International Humanitarian Law: An Introduction to Its Concepts,
Historical Background and Recent Developments, 49 Revista Juridica de
la Universidad de Puerto Rico [Rev. Jur. U.P.R.] 279 (1980).

——When using foreign language titles, the first citation should indicate in brackets any
abbreviation to be used subsequently. (See Bluebook Rule 20.6)

Revista Juridica de la Universidad Interamericana
Abbreviation: Rev. Jur. U.I.

See   Bluebook Rule 20.6.

Revue Critique de Droit International Prive
Abbreviation: R.C.D.I.P.

See   Bluebook Rule 20.6.

Revue de Droit (Université de Sherbrooke)
Abbreviation: R.D.U.S.

Examples: Cote, The Operation in Time of the Statute of Frauds and of the Statute
of Limitations, 16 Revue de Droit (Université de Sherbrooke)
[R.D.U.S.] 315 (1985).

Grandbois, Le droit fédéral et quebecois de la conservation de la faune,
16 R.D.U.S. 261 (1985).

——When using foreign language titles, the first citation should indicate in brackets any
abbreviation to be used subsequently. (See Bluebook Rule 20.6)

Revue de Droit International et de Droit Compare
Abbreviation: R. Dr. Int. Dr. Comp.

See   Bluebook Rule 20.6.

Revue Générale De Droit
Abbreviation: Rev. Gén.

Examples: Magnet, Administrative Delicts: A Case Study in Unlawful Municipal
Administration, 16 Revue Générale De Droit [Rev. Gén.] 153 (1985).
——Article Cite.

Archambault, Les sources juridiques de la responsabilité extra-
contractuelle municipale, 16 Rev. Gén. 101 (1985).

——When using foreign language titles, the first citation should indicate in brackets any
abbreviation to be used subsequently. (See Bluebook Rule 20.6)

Revue Internationale de Droit Compare
Abbreviation: R.I.D.C.

In law review footnotes, the following are in large and small capitals: periodicals, constitutions,
codes, restatements, standards, authors of books, titles of books, and legislative materials except
for bills and resolutions. Refer to Bluebook.

See   Bluebook Rule 20.6.

Revue Juridique Thémis
Abbreviation: R.J.T.

Examples: Jobin, L'échec à la prolongation du bail residentiel, 17 Revue Juridique Thémis [R.J.T.] 79 (1982-1983).

Lippel, Droit des travailleurs québecois en matière de santé, 16 R.J.T. 329 (1981-1982).

——When using foreign language titles, the first citation should indicate in brackets any abbreviation to be used subsequently. (See Bluebook Rule 20.6)

Rhode Island Bar Journal
Abbreviation: R.I.B.J.

Examples: Holden, Representing the Potential Defendant in a Criminal Tax Investigation, 30 R.I.B.J. 10 (1982). ——Article Cite.

Holden, Representing the Potential Defendant in a Criminal Tax Investigation, 30 R.I.B.J. 10, 10-11 (1982). ——Page Cite.

Rhode Island Constitution
Abbreviation: R.I. Const. art.   , §   .

Examples: R.I. Const. art. I, § 8. ——Cite provisions without date unless the cited provisions have been repealed or amended. Bluebook Rule 11.

R.I. Const. art. I, § 17 (1843, amended 1970). ——Cite provisions which have been repealed or amended by giving the date of the adoption of the particular provision and the date of repeal or amendment. Bluebook Rule 11.

Rhode Island General Laws
See   General Laws of Rhode Island

Rhode Island Reports
Abbreviation: R.I.

——Discontinued after 122 R.I. 923 (1980). Thereafter cite only to A.2d

Examples: Morgan v. Thomas, 98 R.I. 204, 200 A.2d 696 (1964). ——Case Cite.

Morgan v. Thomas, 98 R.I. 204, 210, 200 A.2d 696, 699 (1964). ——Page Cite.

——After 122 R.I. 923 (1980), cite as follows:

Panciera v. Panciera, 500 A.2d 221 (R.I. 1985). ——Case Cite.

Panciera v. Panciera, 500 A.2d 221, 223 (R.I. 1985). ——Page Cite.

Rhode Island Session Laws
See   Public Laws of Rhode Island

In law review footnotes, the titles of books and the names of cases are not underlined.

Rocky Mountain Law Review
    Abbreviation: Rocky Mtn. L. Rev.

    Examples: Rostow, <u>American Legal Realism and the Sense of the Profession</u>, 34
                  Rocky Mtn. L. Rev. 123 (1962). ——Article Cite.

                  Rostow, <u>American Legal Realism and the Sense of the Profession</u>, 34
                  Rocky Mtn. L. Rev. 123, 134-35 (1962). ——Page Cite.

Rocky Mountain Mineral Law Institute
    Abbreviation: Rocky Mtn. Min. L. Inst.

    Examples: Short, <u>Wilderness Policies and Mineral Potential on the Public Lands</u>,
                  26 Rocky Mtn. Min. L. Inst. 39 (1980). ——Article Cite.

                  Short, <u>Wilderness Policies and Mineral Potential on the Public Lands</u>,
                  26 Rocky Mtn. Min. L. Inst. 39, 40-41 (1980). ——Page Cite.

Rules of the Court of Claims of the United States
    <u>See</u>   Court of Claims Rules

Rules of the Supreme Court of the United States
    <u>See</u>   Supreme Court Rules

Rules of the United States Customs Court
    <u>See</u>   Customs Court Rules

Rutgers-Camden Law Journal
    Abbreviation: Rut.-Cam. L.J.

    Examples: Hughes, <u>Judicial Independence</u>, 11 Rut.-Cam. L.J. 13 (1979).
                  ——Article Cite.

                  Hughes, <u>Judicial Independence</u>, 11 Rut.-Cam. L.J. 13, 20-25 (1979).
                  ——Page Cite.

Rutgers Law Journal
    Abbreviation: Rutgers L.J.

Rutgers Law Review
    Abbreviation: Rutgers L. Rev.

    Examples: Hyman, <u>Bargaining and Criminal Justice</u>, 33 Rutgers L. Rev. 3 (1980).
                  ——Article Cite.

                  Hyman, <u>Bargaining and Criminal Justice</u>, 33 Rutgers L. Rev. 3, 40-45
                  (1980). ——Page Cite.

In law review footnotes, the following are in large and small capitals: periodicals, constitutions, codes, restatements, standards, authors of books, titles of books, and legislative materials except for bills and resolutions. Refer to Bluebook.

In law review footnotes, the titles of books and the names of cases are not underlined.

S

St. John's Law Review

Abbreviation: St. John's L. Rev.

Examples: Rosen, Media Lament—The Rise and Fall of Involuntary Public Figures, 54 St. John's L. Rev. 487 (1980). ——Article Cite.

Rosen, Media Lament—The Rise and Fall of Involuntary Public Figures, 54 St. John's L. Rev. 487, 488-93 (1980). ——Page Cite.

Saint Louis University Law Journal

Abbreviation: St. Louis U.L.J.

Examples: Belton, Title VII of the Civil Rights Act of 1964: A Decade of Private Enforcement and Judicial Developments, 20 St. Louis U.L.J. 225 (1976). ——Article Cite.

Belton, Title VII of the Civil Rights Act of 1964: A Decade of Private Enforcement and Judicial Developments, 20 St. Louis U.L.J. 225, 254-57 (1976). ——Page Cite.

St. Mary's Law Journal

Abbreviation: St. Mary's L.J.

Examples: Edgar, Procedural Aspects of Settlement: An Overview of Texas Law, 12 St. Mary's L.J. 279 (1980). ——Article Cite.

Edgar, Procedural Aspects of Settlement: An Overview of Texas Law, 12 St. Mary's L.J. 279, 315-20 (1980). ——Page Cite.

Samford University (Cumberland School of Law) Law Review

See   Cumberland Law Review

San Diego Law Review

Abbreviation: San Diego L. Rev.

Examples: Daniels, The Supreme Court and Obscenity: An Exercise in Empirical Constitutional Policy-Making, 17 San Diego L. Rev. 757 (1980). ——Article Cite.

Daniels, The Supreme Court and Obscenity: An Exercise in Empirical Constitutional Policy-Making, 17 San Diego L. Rev. 757, 762-69 (1980). ——Page Cite.

San Fernando Valley Law Review

Abbreviation: San Fern. V.L. Rev.

In law review footnotes, the following are in large and small capitals: periodicals, constitutions, codes, restatements, standards, authors of books, titles of books, and legislative materials except for bills and resolutions. Refer to Bluebook.

Examples: Gould, <u>Human Rights for Labor—An International Perspective</u>, 8 San
                   Fern. V.L. Rev. 45 (1980). ——Article Cite.

                   Gould, <u>Human Rights for Labor—An International Perspective</u>, 8 San
                   Fern. V.L. Rev. 45, 49-52 (1980). ——Page Cite.

Santa Clara Law Review
Abbreviation: Santa Clara L. Rev.

Examples: Marsh, <u>Betamax and Fair Use: A Shotgun Marriage</u>, 21 Santa Clara L.
                   Rev. 49 (1981). ——Article Cite.

                   Marsh, <u>Betamax and Fair Use: A Shotgun Marriage</u>, 21 Santa Clara L.
                   Rev. 49, 50-55 (1981). ——Page Cite.

Saskatchewan Law Review
Abbreviation: Sask. L. Rev.

Examples: Craig, Book Review, 49 Sask. L. Rev. 133 (1984-1985). ——Article
                   Cite.

                   Craig, Book Review, 49 Sask. L. Rev. 133, 133 (1984-1985). ——Page
                   Cite.

Scott on Trusts
<u>See</u>   Law of Trusts, by A. Scott

Search and Seizure, by W. LaFave
——Do not abbreviate the title.

Examples: 3 W. LaFave, <u>Search and Seizure</u> § 7.3(c) (2d ed. 1987).

                   3 W. LaFave, <u>Search and Seizure</u> § 7.3(c), at 91 (2d ed. 1987).

Search & Seizure Bulletin (Quinlan)
Abbreviation: Search & Seizure Bull. (Quinlan)

SEC Docket (CCH)
Abbreviation: SEC Docket

Example: <u>Boston Stock Exchange, Inc.</u>, 19 SEC Docket 1099 (1980).

section(s)
Abbreviations: § , ¶

Examples: G. Bogert & G. Bogert, <u>Handbook of the the Law of Trusts</u> § 36 (5th
                   ed. 1973).

                   G. Bogert & G. Bogert, <u>Handbook of the the Law of Trusts</u> §§ 106-108
                   (5th ed. 1973).

——See generally Bluebook Rule 3.4.

In law review footnotes, the titles of books and the names of cases are not underlined.

sections and paragraphs
──See various title entries in this work. See also Bluebook Rule 3.4.

Secured Transactions Guide (Commerce Clearing House)
Abbreviation: Secured Transactions Guide (CCH)

Securities and Exchange Commission Compliance (Prentice-Hall)
Abbreviation: SEC Compl. (P-H)

Securities and Exchange Commission Decisions and Reports (1934-date)
Abbreviation: S.E.C.

Examples: Thomas Lee Jarvis, 40 S.E.C. 692 (1961).

              Commonwealth Bond Corp., 1 S.E.C. 13 (FTC 1934). ──Citation to
              an early decision rendered by the FTC.

              Lewis Airways, Inc., 1 S.E.C. 330 (1936).

──See Bluebook Rule 14.6 for citations to SEC releases or SEC no-action letters.

Securities and Exchange Commission No-Action Letters
Abbreviation: SEC No-Action Letter

Example: McDonald's Corp., SEC No-Action Letter, [1985-1986 Transfer
              Binder] Fed. Sec. L. Rep. (CCH) È 78,134 (Aug. 13, 1985).

Securities and Exchange Commission Releases
Abbreviation: (act) Release No.

Examples: Adoption of Form D Amendments, Exchange Act Release No. 6663,
              [1986-1987 Transfer Binder] Fed. Sec. L. Rep. (CCH) ¶ 84,032 (Oct.
              2, 1986).

              Lester Kuznets, Exchange Act Release No. 23,525, [1986-1987
              Transfer Binder] Fed. Sec. L. Rep. (CCH) ¶ 84,021 (Aug. 12, 1986).
              ──Cite to a release that is an adjudication.

──See Bluebook Rule 14.6(b).

Securities and Federal Corporate Law Report (Clark Boardman)
Abbreviation: Sec. & Fed. Corp. L. Rep. (Clark Boardman)

Securities Fraud & Commodities Fraud, by A. Bromberg and L. Lowenfels
──Do not abbreviate the title.

Examples: 3 A. Bromberg & L. Lowenfels, Securities Fraud and Commodities
              Fraud § 8.4(210) (1986).

              3 A. Bromberg & L. Lowenfels, Securities Fraud and Commodities
              Fraud § 8.4(210), at 204.2 (1986).

In law review footnotes, the following are in large and small capitals: periodicals, constitutions,
codes, restatements, standards, authors of books, titles of books, and legislative materials except
for bills and resolutions. Refer to Bluebook.

Securities Law Review
    Abbreviation: Sec. L. Rev.

Securities Regulation, by L. Loss
    ——Do not abbreviate the title.

    Examples: 2 L. Loss, Securities Regulation 1123 (2d ed. 1961).

                     5 L. Loss, Securities Regulation 3089 (2d ed. Supp. 1969). ——The
citation form in parenthesis is different from the guideline of the
Bluebook because this set of books is arranged unusually. The last three
volumes supplement the first three volumes of the set. In this instance,
volume 5 supplements volume 2.

Securities Regulation and Law Report (Bureau of National Affairs)
    Abbreviation: Sec. Reg. & L. Rep. (BNA)

    Example: Grossman v. Johnson, [Jan.-June] Sec. Reg. & L. Rep. (BNA) (14 Sec.
Reg. & L. Rep.) 631 (1st Cir. Mar. 29, 1982). ——Citation to looseleaf
material. Such a citation is proper if the case is not yet available in an
official or West reporter, or is not reported in an official or West
reporter.

Securities Regulation Guide (Prentice-Hall)
    Abbreviation: Sec. Reg. Guide (P-H)

Securities Regulation Law Journal
    Abbreviation: Sec. Reg. L.J.

    Examples: Janvey, SEC Investigation of Insider Trading, 13 Sec. Reg. L.J. 299
(1986). ——Article Cite.

                     Janvey, SEC Investigation of Insider Trading, 13 Sec. Reg. L.J. 299,
309-10 (1986). ——Page Cite.

See
    Examples: "We find that the additional allegation was related to the same series of
allegedly unfair labor practices designed to keep R.M. Tanaka
nonunion. See NLRB v. Jack La Lanne Management Corp., 539 F.2d
at 295." ——Taken from 675 F.2d 1029, 1036 (1982).

                     "[3] Unless a federal statute requires a government tax lien to be
recorded, the unrecorded lien may be enforced against subsequent
transferees. United States v. Curry, 201 F. 371, 374 (D. Md. 1912).
See Detroit Bank v. United States, 317 U.S. at 334, 63 S. Ct. at 299
(priority of estate tax liens over subsequent mortgagees)."

In law review footnotes, the titles of books and the names of cases are not underlined.

See also
      Examples: "Circulation of even a deficient draft EIS may be sufficient so long as it does not frustrate the goal of obtaining informed agency and public comment. National Wildlife Federation v. Adams, 629 F.2d 587 (9th Cir. 1980); Lathan II, 506 F.2d at 693. See also Warm Springs Dam Task Force v. Gribble, 621 F.2d 1017, 1022-1023 (9th Cir. 1980)."
——Taken from 675 F.2d 1085, 1096 (1982).

                      "Similar deference is evident in Ulster County..., cert. denied, 450 U.S. 933, 101 S. Ct. 1395, 67 L.Ed.2d 367(1981); ...See also Cannon v. Alabama, 558 F.2d 1211, 1216 n.12 (5th Cir. 1977), cert. denied, 434 U.S. 1087, 98 S. Ct. 1281, 55 L. Ed. 2d 792 (1978)." ——Taken from 675 F.2d 1007, 1009 (1982).

See, e.g.
      Examples: "Most conflict of interest issues in criminal cases are raised at the post-conviction stage, where the inquiry focuses on whether the defendant has made a showing of harm sufficient to require reversal of his conviction. See, e.g. Cuyler v. Sullivan, supra, 446 U.S. at 350, 100 S. Ct. at 1719 [no objection made at trial; the Supreme Court held the defendant must demonstrate that 'an actual conflict adversely affected his lawyer's performance']." ——Taken from 675 F.2d 965, 970 (1982).

                      "Nor did the district court abuse its discretion in refusing to order pretrial disclosure of testimony before the grand jury, for Cronic had shown no particularized need for such disclosure. See, e.g. United States v. Parker, 469 F.2d 884, 889 (10th Cir. 1972)." ——Taken from 675 F.2d 1126, 1130 (1982).

See generally
      Example: "A brief outline of the history of FDA regulation will provide a background and perspective to our discussion. See Weinberger v. Hynson, Westcott & Dunning, Inc., 412 U.S. 609, 93 S. Ct. 2469, 37 L. Ed. 2d 207 (1973); USV Pharmaceutical Corp. v. Weinberger, 412 U.S. 655, 93 S. Ct. 2498, 37 L. Ed. 2d 244 (1973); see generally Note, Drug Efficacy and the 1962 Drug Amendments, 60 Geo. L.J. 185 (1971)." ——Taken from 675 F.2d 994, 997 (1982).

Selections from Williston's Treatise on the Law of Contracts, by S. Williston & G. Thompson
    ——Do not abbreviate the title.

      Examples: S. Williston & G. Thompson, Selections from Williston's Treatise on the Law of Contracts § 422 (rev. ed. 1938).

                      S. Williston & G. Thompson, Selections from Williston's Treatise on the Law of Contracts § 422, at 399 (rev. ed. 1938).

Sell on Agency
    See   Agency, by W. Sell

In law review footnotes, the following are in large and small capitals: periodicals, constitutions, codes, restatements, standards, authors of books, titles of books, and legislative materials except for bills and resolutions. Refer to Bluebook.

Senate bill (U.S. Congress)
      See   Congressional Bills

Senate Concurrent Resolution
      See   Congressional Resolutions

Senate Conference Report
      Example: S. Conf. Rep. No. 302, 99th Cong., 2d Sess. 97 (1986).

Senate Joint Resolution
      See   Congressional Resolutions

Senate Resolution
      See   Congressional Resolutions

Senator
      Abbreviation: Sen.

Separation Agreements and Ante-Nuptial Contracts, by A. Lindey
      ——Do not abbreviate the title.

      Examples: 2 A. Lindey, <u>Separation Agreements and Ante-Nuptial Contracts</u>
                     § 36.04 (1987).

                     2 A. Lindey, <u>Separation Agreements and Ante-Nuptial Contracts</u>
                     § 36.04, at 36-8 (1987).

                     2 A. Lindey, <u>Separation Agreements and Ante-Nuptial Contracts</u> § 82
                     (Supp. Oct. 1987).

series, serial(s)
      Abbreviation: ser.

Services
      See   Looseleaf

Session Laws, Arizona
      See   Arizona Session Laws and Arizona Legislative Service

Session Laws of Colorado
      Abbreviation: year Colo. Sess. Laws

Session Laws of Hawaii
      Abbreviation: year Hawaii Sess. Laws

Session Laws (of) Idaho
      Abbreviation: year Idaho Sess. Laws

In law review footnotes, the titles of books and the names of cases are not underlined.

Session Laws of Kansas
Abbreviation: year Kan. Sess. Laws

Session Laws of North Carolina
Abbreviations: year N.C. Sess. Laws

Session Laws of Wyoming
Abbreviation: year Wyo. Sess. Laws

Seton Hall Law Review
Abbreviation: Seton Hall L. Rev.

Examples: Brennan & Burdick, Does the Guarantor Guarantee? Lender, Beware!,
11 Seton Hall L. Rev. 353 (1981). ——Article Cite.

Brennan & Burdick, Does the Guarantor Guarantee? Lender, Beware!,
11 Seton Hall L. Rev. 353, 360-65 (1981). ——Page Cite.

short form of case citations
See   subsequent citation to cases, statutes, and prior citations

short forms
See   subsequent citation to cases, statutes, and prior citations.

signals
See   E.g., Accord, See, See also, Cf., Compare, But see, But cf., See Generally.

——See also Bluebook Rules 2.2 and 2.3.

signals, order of
——See Bluebook Rule 2.3.

slip opinions
Abbreviation: slip op.

Examples: United States v. Cutler, No. 86-3058, slip op. at 3 (9th Cir. Dec. 19,
1986). ——Separately paginated.

Freeman v. Rideout, No. 86-2153, slip op. 6801, 6812 (2d Cir. Dec.
20, 1986). ——Not separately paginated.

Smith-Hurd Illinois Annotated Statutes
Abbreviation: Ill. Ann. Stat. ch.   , para.   (Smith-Hurd year).

Examples: Ill. Ann. Stat. ch. 15½, para. 22.43 (Smith-Hurd 1963).

Ill. Ann. Stat. ch. 10, para. 101 (Smith-Hurd Supp. 1987).

Social Security Claims and Procedures, by H. McCormick
——Do not abbreviate the title.

In law review footnotes, the following are in large and small capitals: periodicals, constitutions,
codes, restatements, standards, authors of books, titles of books, and legislative materials except
for bills and resolutions. Refer to Bluebook.

Examples: 2 H. McCormick, <u>Social Security Claims and Procedures</u> § 504 (3d ed.
                 1983).

                 2 H. McCormick, <u>Social Security Claims and Procedures</u> § 504, at 23
                 (3d ed. 1983).

Social Security Rulings, Cumulative Edition
Abbreviation: S.S.R. (Cum. Ed. year).

Example: <u>Rahman v. Harris</u> 58 S.S.R. (Cum. Ed. 1982).

South Carolina, administrative compilation
<u>See</u>   Code of Laws of South Carolina 1976 Annotated (Law. Co-op.), Code of
      Regulations

South Carolina, Annual Report of the Attorney General
<u>See</u>   Annual Report of the Attorney General for the State of South Carolina to the
      General Assembly

South Carolina Code Annotated
<u>See</u>   Code of Laws of South Carolina Annotated

South Carolina Constitution
Abbreviation: S.C. Const. art.   , §   .

Examples: S.C. Const. art. III, § 27. ——Cite provisions without date unless the
                 cited provisions have been repealed or amended (Bluebook Rule 11).

                 S.C. Const. art. X, § 16 (1895, amended 1979). ——Cite provisions
                 which have been repealed or amended by giving the date of the adoption
                 of the particular provision and the date of repeal or amendment
                 (Bluebook Rule 11).

                 S.C. Const. of 1868, art. I, § 4. ——Cite constitutions that have been
                 totally superseded by year of adoption, giving parenthetically the year of
                 adoption of the specific provision cited if different (Bluebook Rule 11).

South Carolina Law Review
Abbreviation: S.C.L. Rev.

Examples: Ely, <u>Charleston's Court of Wardens, 1783-1800: A Post-Revolutionary</u>
                 <u>Experiment in Municipal Justice</u>, 27 S.C.L. Rev. 645 (1976).
                 ——Article Cite.

                 Ely, <u>Charleston's Court of Wardens, 1783-1800: A Post-Revolutionary</u>
                 <u>Experiment in Municipal Justice</u>, 27 S.C.L. Rev. 645, 653-57 (1976).
                 ——Page Cite.

South Carolina Reports
Abbreviation: S.C.

In law review footnotes, the titles of books and the names of cases are not underlined.

Examples: Smoak v. Liebherr-America, Inc., 281 S.C. 420, 315 S.E.2d 116
(1984). ——Case Cite.

Smoak v. Liebherr-America, Inc., 281 S.C. 420, 424, 315 S.E.2d 116,
119 (1984). ——Page Cite.

South Carolina Session Laws
See   Acts and Joint Resolutions, South Carolina

South Carolina State Register
Abbreviation: S.C. Reg.

South Dakota Administrative Rules
See   Administrative Rules of South Dakota

South Dakota, Biennial Report of the Attorney General
See   Biennial Report of the Attorney General of the State of South Dakota

South Dakota Codified Laws Annotated
Abbreviation: S.D. Codified Laws Ann. §   (year).

Examples: S.D. Codified Laws Ann. § 15-6-3 (1984).

S.D. Codified Laws Ann. § 15-6-23(a) (Supp. 1987).

South Dakota Constitution
Abbreviation: S.D. Const. art.   , §   .

Examples: S.D. Const. art. VI, § 6. ——Cite provisions without date unless the
cited provisions have been repealed or amended (Bluebook Rule 11).

S.D. Const. art. VII, § 2 (1889, amended 1974)——Cite provisions
which have been repealed or amended by giving the date of the adoption
of the particular provision and the date of repeal or amendment
(Bluebook Rule 11).

South Dakota Law Review
Abbreviation: S.D.L. Rev.

Examples: Groseclose, Hospital Privilege Cases: Braving the Dismal Swamp, 26
S.D.L. Rev. 1 (1981). ——Article Cite.

Groseclose, Hospital Privilege Cases: Braving the Dismal Swamp, 26
S.D.L. Rev. 1, 6-10 (1981). ——Page Cite.

South Dakota Register
Abbreviation: S.D. Reg.

South Dakota Reports
Abbreviation: S.D.

In law review footnotes, the following are in large and small capitals: periodicals, constitutions,
codes, restatements, standards, authors of books, titles of books, and legislative materials except
for bills and resolutions. Refer to Bluebook.

——Discontinued after 90 S.D. 692 (1976). Thereafter cite only to to N.W.2d.

Examples: <u>Dunham v. First Nat'l Bank</u>, 86 S.D. 727, 201 N.W.2d 227 (1972). ——Case Cite.

<u>Dunham v. First Nat'l Bank</u>, 86 S.D. 727, 733, 201 N.W.2d 227, 230 (1972). ——Page Cite.

——After 90 S.D. 692 (1976), cite as follows:

<u>State v. Chief Eagle</u>, 377 N.W.2d 141 (S.D. 1985). ——Case Cite.

<u>State v. Chief Eagle</u>, 377 N.W.2d 141, 144 (S.D. 1985). ——Page Cite.

South Dakota Session Laws
<u>See</u> Laws of South Dakota

South Eastern Reporter
Abbreviation: S.E.

Examples: <u>Jackson v. Crutchfield</u>, 184 Ga. 412, 191 S.E. 468 (1937). ——Case Cite.

<u>Jackson v. Crutchfield</u>, 184 Ga. 412, 417, 191 S.E. 468, 471 (1937). ——Page Cite.

South Eastern Reporter, second series
Abbreviation: S.E.2d

Examples: <u>Jefferson Standard Life Ins. Co. v. Bridges</u>, 147 Ga. App. 5, 248 S.E.2d 5 (1978). ——Case Cite.

<u>Jefferson Standard Life Ins. Co. v. Bridges</u>, 147 Ga. App. 5, 7, 248 S.E.2d 5, 7 (1978). ——Page Cite.

South Texas Law Journal
Abbreviation: S. Tex. L.J.

Examples: Calvert & Perin, <u>Is the Castle Crumbling?—Harmless Error Revisited</u>, 20 S. Tex. L.J. 1 (1979). ——Article Cite.

Calvert & Perin, <u>Is the Castle Crumbling?—Harmless Error Revisited</u>, 20 S. Tex. L.J. 1, 3-6 (1979). ——Page Cite.

South Western Reporter
Abbreviation: S.W.

——Cite only to S.W. (and S.W.2d) for Texas Civil Appeals Reports after 135 S.W. 209 (1911).

Examples: <u>Fidelity Phenix Fire Ins. Co. v. Roth</u>, 164 Ark. 608, 262 S.W. 643 (1924). ——Case Cite.

<u>Fidelity Phenix Fire Ins. Co. v. Roth</u>, 164 Ark. 608, 610, 262 S.W. 643, 643-44 (1924). ——Page Cite.

In law review footnotes, the titles of books and the names of cases are not underlined.

Texas Civil Appeals Reports:

——After 135 S.W. 209 (1911), cite as follows:

> McDaniel v. Henderson, 148 S.W. 332 (Tex. Civ. App. 1912).
> ——Case Cite.
>
> McDaniel v. Henderson, 148 S.W. 332, 333 (Tex. Civ. App. 1912).
> ——Page Cite.

South Western Reporter, second series
Abbreviation: S.W.2d

Examples: Ex parte Herring, 438 S.W.2d 801 (Tex. 1969). ——Case Cite.

Ex parte Herring, 438 S.W.2d 801, 803 (Tex. 1969). ——Page Cite.

——Citation suitable for case that does not appear in a state reporter.

——Cite only to S.W.2d for the following state reports: Kentucky Reports after 236
S.W.2d 901 (1951); Missouri Reports after 295 S.W.2d 388 (1956); Missouri
Appeals Reports after 252 S.W.2d 88 (1952); Tennessee Reports after 476 S.W.2d
636 (1972); Tennessee Appeals Reports after 480 S.W.2d 152 (1972); Tennessee
Criminal Appeals Reports after 475 S.W.2d 228 (1971); Texas Criminal Reports
after 363 S.W.2d 459 (1963); Texas Reports after 358 S.W.2d 547 (1962).

——Cite only to S.W. (and S.W.2d) for Texas Civil Appeals Reports after 135 S.W.
209 (1911).

Kentucky Reports:

——After 236 S.W.2d 901 (1951), cite as follows:

> Genex/London, Inc. v. Kentucky Bd. of Tax Appeals, 622 S.W.2d 499
> (Ky. 1981). ——Case Cite.
>
> Genex/London, Inc. v. Kentucky Bd. of Tax Appeals, 622 S.W.2d 499,
> 501 (Ky. 1981). ——Page Cite.

Missouri Appeals Reports:

——After 252 S.W.2d 88 (1952), cite as follows:

> Tobler's Flowers, Inc. v. Southwestern Bell Tel. Co., 632 S.W.2d 15
> (Mo. Ct. App. 1982). ——Case Cite.
>
> Tobler's Flowers, Inc. v. Southwestern Bell Tel. Co., 632 S.W.2d 15,
> 17 (Mo. Ct. App. 1982). ——Page Cite.

Missouri Reports

——After 295 S.W.2d 388 (1956), cite as follows:

> Aronson's Men's Stores, Inc. v. Potter Elec. Signal Co., 632 S.W.2d
> 472 (Mo. 1982). ——Case Cite.
>
> Aronson's Men's Stores, Inc. v. Potter Elec. Signal Co., 632 S.W.2d
> 472, 474 (Mo. 1982). ——Page Cite.

Tennessee Appeals Reports:

——After 480 S.W.2d 152 (1972), cite as follows:

In law review footnotes, the following are in large and small capitals: periodicals, constitutions,
codes, restatements, standards, authors of books, titles of books, and legislative materials except
for bills and resolutions. Refer to Bluebook.

Craig v. Turner, 628 S.W.2d 33 (Tenn. Ct. App. 1981). ——Case
Cite.

Craig v. Turner, 628 S.W.2d 33, 34 (Tenn. Ct. App. 1981). ——Page
Cite.

Tennessee Criminal Appeals Reports:

——After 475 S.W.2d 228 (1971), cite as follows:

Ferguson v. State, 628 S.W.2d 37 (Tenn. Crim. App. 1981). ——Case
Cite.

Ferguson v. State, 628 S.W.2d 37, 39 (Tenn. Crim. App. 1981).
——Page Cite.

Tennessee Reports:

——After 476 S.W.2d 636 (1972), cite as follows:

State v. Gorman, 628 S.W.2d 739 (Tenn. 1982). ——Case Cite.

State v. Gorman, 628 S.W.2d 739, 740 (Tenn. 1982). ——Page Cite.

Texas Civil Appeals Reports:

——After 135 S.W. 209 (1911), cite as follows:

Cassity v. Gulf States Utils. Co., 628 S.W.2d 86 (Tex. Civ. App.
1981). ——Case Cite.

Cassity v. Gulf States Utils. Co., 628 S.W.2d 86, 88 (Tex. Civ. App.
1981). ——Page Cite.

Butler v. Wright Way Spraying Serv., 743 S.W.2d 304 (Tex. Ct. App.
1987). ——Case Cite.

Butler v. Wright Way Spraying Serv., 743 S.W.2d 304, 307 (Tex. Ct.
App. 1987). ——Page Cite.

——Texas Court of Civil Appeals became Texas Court of Appeals in 1981.

Texas Criminal Reports:

——After 363 S.W.2d 459 (1962), cite as follows:

Bowden v. State, 628 S.W.2d 782 (Tex. Crim. App. 1982). ——Case
Cite.

Bowden v. State, 628 S.W.2d 782, 784 (Tex. Crim. App. 1982).
——Page Cite.

Texas Reports:

——After 358 S.W.2d 547 (1962), cite as follows:

Bryan v. Citizens Nat'l Bank, 628 S.W.2d 761 (Tex 1982). ——Case
Cite.

Bryan v. Citizens Nat'l Bank, 628 S.W.2d 761, 763 (Tex 1982).
——Page Cite.

In law review footnotes, the titles of books and the names of cases are not underlined.

Southern California Law Review
  Abbreviation: S. Cal. L. Rev.

  Examples: Musewicz, The Failure of Foster Care: Federal Statutory Reform and the Child's Right to Permanence, 54 S. Cal. L. Rev. 633 (1981). ——Article Cite.

       Musewicz, The Failure of Foster Care: Federal Statutory Reform and the Child's Right to Permanence, 54 S. Cal. L. Rev. 633, 640-45 (1981). ——Page Cite.

Southern California Tax Institute
  Abbreviation: S. Cal. Tax Inst.

  Examples: Scheifly, Partnership Recapitalization: Achieving a Capital Freeze, 32 S. Cal. Tax Inst. ¶ 500 (1980). ——Article Cite.

       Scheifly, Partnership Recapitalization: Achieving a Capital Freeze, 32 S. Cal. Tax Inst. ¶ 500, ¶ 511.6 at 5-25 (1980). ——Page Cite.

Southern Illinois University Law Journal
  Abbreviation: S. Ill. U.L.J.

  Examples: Weinberg, From Contract to Conveyance: The Law of Landlord and Tenant, 1800-1920 (Part I), 1980 S. Ill. U.L.J. 29. ——Article Cite.

       Weinberg, From Contract to Conveyance: The Law of Landlord and Tenant, 1800-1920 (Part I), 1980 S. Ill. U.L.J. 29, 32-38. ——Page Cite.

Southern Methodist University Law Journal
  See Southwestern Law Journal

Southern Reporter
  Abbreviation: So.

  Examples: Rochelle v. Rochelle, 235 Ala. 526, 179 So. 825 (1938). ——Case Cite.

       Rochelle v. Rochelle, 235 Ala. 526, 529, 179 So. 825, 828 (1938). ——Page Cite.

  Louisiana Appeals Reports:

  ——After 141 So. 809 (1932), cite as follows:

       Rapides Constr., Inc. v. Gaspard, 411 So. 2d 81 (La. Ct. App. 1982). ——Case Cite.

       Rapides Constr., Inc. v. Gaspard, 411 So. 2d 81, 84 (La. Ct. App. 1982). ——Page Cite.

Southern Reporter, Second Series
  Abbreviation: So. 2d

In law review footnotes, the following are in large and small capitals: periodicals, constitutions, codes, restatements, standards, authors of books, titles of books, and legislative materials except for bills and resolutions. Refer to Bluebook.

Examples: <u>Guterrez v. Murdocke</u>, 300 So. 2d 689 (Fla. Dist. Ct. App. 1974).
                   ——Case Cite.

                   <u>Guterrez v. Murdocke</u>, 300 So. 2d 689, 691 (Fla. Dist. Ct. App. 1974).
                   ——Page Cite.

——Citation suitable for case that does not appear in a state reporter.

——Cite only to So. 2d for the following state reports: Alabama Reports after 330 So.
2d 614 (1976); Alabama Appellate Reports after 296 So. 2d 796 (1974); Florida
Reports after 38 So. 2d 224 (1948); Louisiana Reports after 270 So. 2d 526 (1972);
Mississippi Reports after 183 So. 2d 525 (1966).

——Cite only to So. (and So. 2d) for Louisiana Appeals Reports after 141 So. 809
(1932).

Alabama Appellate Court Reports:

——After 296 So. 2d 796 (1974), cite as follows:

                   <u>Sansom v. Sansom</u>, 409 So. 2d 430 (Ala. Civ. App. 1981). ——Case
                   Cite.

                   <u>Sansom v. Sansom</u>, 409 So. 2d 430, 431 (Ala. Civ. App. 1981).
                   ——Page Cite.

                   <u>Hams v. State</u>, 409 So. 2d 1006 (Ala. Crim. App. 1982). ——Case
                   Cite.

                   <u>Hams v. State</u>, 409 So. 2d 1006, 1008 (Ala. Crim. App. 1982).
                   ——Page Cite.

Alabama Reports:

——After 330 So. 2d 614 (1976), cite as follows:

                   <u>Baird v. Spradlin</u>, 409 So. 2d 820 (Ala. 1982). ——Case Cite.

                   <u>Baird v. Spradlin</u>, 409 So. 2d 820, 821 (Ala. 1982). ——Page Cite.

Florida Reports:

——After 38 So. 2d 224 (1948), cite as follows:

                   <u>Rosenberg v. Levin</u>, 409 So. 2d 1016 (Fla. 1982). ——Case Cite.

                   <u>Rosenberg v. Levin</u>, 409 So. 2d 1016, 1017 (Fla. 1982). ——Page
                   Cite.

Louisiana Reports:

——After 270 So. 2d 526 (1972), cite as follows:

                   <u>Chauvin v. Bohn</u>, 411 So. 2d 442 (La. 1982). ——Case Cite.

                   <u>Chauvin v. Bohn</u>, 411 So. 2d 442, 444 (La. 1982). ——Page Cite.

Mississippi Reports:

——After 183 So. 2d 525 (1966), cite as follows:

                   <u>Buntyn v. Smallwood</u>, 412 So. 2d 236 (Miss. 1982). ——Case Cite.

In law review footnotes, the titles of books and the names of cases are not underlined.

Buntyn v. Smallwood, 412 So. 2d 236, 237 (Miss. 1982). ——Page
Cite.

Southern University Law Review
Abbreviation: S.U.L. Rev.

Examples: De Bessonet, Hintze & Waller, Automated Retrieval of Information:
Toward the Development of a Formal Language for Expressing
Statutes, 6 S.U.L. Rev. 1 (1979). ——Article Cite.

De Bessonet, Hintze & Waller, Automated Retrieval of Information:
Toward the Development of a Formal Language for Expressing
Statutes, 6 S.U.L. Rev. 1, 10-12 (1979). ——Page Cite.

Southwestern Law Journal
Abbreviation: Sw. L.J.

Examples: Blunk, Analyzing Texas Articles of Incorporation: Is the Statutory
Close Corporation Format Viable?, 34 Sw. L.J. 941 (1980).
——Article Cite.

Blunk, Analyzing Texas Articles of Incorporation: Is the Statutory
Close Corporation Format Viable?, 34 Sw. L.J. 941, 947-50 (1980).
——Page Cite.

Southwestern Legal Foundation Institute on Oil and Gas Law and Taxation
See   Institute on Oil and Gas Law and Taxation

Southwestern University Law Review
Abbreviation: Sw. U.L. Rev.

Examples: Fernandez, Custom and the Common Law: Judicial Restraint and
Lawmaking by the Courts, 11 Sw. U.L. Rev. 1237 (1979).

Fernandez, Custom and the Common Law: Judicial Restraint and
Lawmaking by the Courts, 11 Sw. U.L. Rev. 1237, 1240-45 (1979).

special
Abbreviation: spec.

Special Court Regional Rail Reorganization Act
Abbreviation: Regional Rail Reorg. Ct.

Standard Excess Profits Tax Reporter (Commerce Clearing House)
Abbreviation: Stand. Ex. Prof. Tax. Rep. (CCH)

Standard Federal Tax Reporter (Commerce Clearing House)
Abbreviation: Stand. Fed. Tax Rep. (CCH)

In law review footnotes, the following are in large and small capitals: periodicals, constitutions,
codes, restatements, standards, authors of books, titles of books, and legislative materials except
for bills and resolutions. Refer to Bluebook.

Examples: Field v. Commissioner, [U.S. Tax Cases Advance Sheets] Stand. Fed.
Tax Rep. (CCH) (82-1 U.S. Tax Cas.) ¶ 9418 (7th Cir. June 11, 1982).
——Citation to looseleaf material.

National Ass'n of Mfrs. v. Blumenthal, 79-1 U.S. Tax Cas. (CCH)
¶ 9239 (D.D.C. 1979). ——Citation to bound material.

——The above examples are proper if the case is not yet available in an official or West
reporter, or is not reported in an official or West reporter.

Standards for Inmates Legal Rights
Abbreviation: Standards for Inmates Legal Rights Right   (National Sheriffs' Ass'n
year).

Standards for Traffic Justice
Abbreviation: Standards for Traffic Justice §   (year).

Examples: Standards for Traffic Justice § 1.2 (1975).

Standards for Traffic Justice § 3.1 commentary at 5 (1975).

Standards Relating to Appellate Courts
Abbreviation: Standards Relating to Appellate Courts §   (year).

Example: Standards Relating to Appellate Courts § 3.20 (1977).

Standards Relating to Court Organization
Abbreviation: Standards Relating to Court Org. §   (year).

Example: Standards Relating to Court Org. § 1.52 (1974).

Standards Relating to the Function of the Trial Judge
Abbreviation: Standards Relating to the Function of the Trial Judge § (status if
necessary year).

Example: Standards Relating to the Function of the Trial Judge § 2.4 (Tent. Draft
1972).

Stanford Environmental Annual
Abbreviation: Stan. Envtl. Ann.

Stanford Journal of International Law
Abbreviation: Stan. J. Int'l L.

Examples: Archer, The Role of Administrative Agencies Regulating Joint Ventures
in China, 21 Stan. J. Int'l L. 195 (1985). ——Article Cite.

Archer, The Role of Administrative Agencies Regulating Joint Ventures
in China, 21 Stan. J. Int'l L. 195, 198 (1985). ——Page Cite.

Stanford Journal of International Studies
Abbreviation: Stan. J. Int'l Stud.

In law review footnotes, the titles of books and the names of cases are not underlined.

Examples: Barton, <u>Tacit Political Restraints as a Way to Control Conventional</u>
<u>Arms</u>, 14 Stan. J. Int'l Stud. 29 (1979). ——Article Cite.

Barton, <u>Tacit Political Restraints as a Way to Control Conventional</u>
<u>Arms</u>, 14 Stan. J. Int'l Stud. 29, 40-45 (1979). ——Page Cite.

Stanford Law Review
Abbreviation: Stan. L. Rev.

Examples: Rose, <u>Preservation and Community: New Directions in the Law of</u>
<u>Historic Preservation</u>, 33 Stan. L. Rev. 473 (1981). ——Article Cite.

Rose, <u>Preservation and Community: New Directions in the Law of</u>
<u>Historic Preservation</u>, 33 Stan. L. Rev. 473, 480-85 (1981). ——Page
Cite.

State and Local Taxes (Bureau of National Affairs)
Abbreviation: St. & Loc. Taxes (BNA)

State and Local Tax Service (Prentice-Hall)
Abbreviation: St. & Loc. Tax Serv. (P-H)

State Court Journal
Abbreviation: State Ct. J.

State Motor Carrier Guide (Commerce Clearing House)
Abbreviation: St. Mot. Carr. Guide (CCH)

State of Louisiana: Acts of the Legislature
Abbreviation: year La. Acts

State of Ohio: Legislative Acts Passed and Joint Resolutions Adopted
Abbreviation: year Ohio Laws

State of Utah Bulletin
Abbreviation: Utah Bull.

State Tax Cases Reports (Commerce Clearing House)
(formerly Reporter)

Abbreviation: St. Tax Cas. Rep. (CCH)

State Tax Guide (Commerce Clearing House)
Abbreviation: State Tax Guide (CCH)

State Tax Guide (Prentice-Hall)
Abbreviation: State Tax Guide (P-H)

In law review footnotes, the following are in large and small capitals: periodicals, constitutions,
codes, restatements, standards, authors of books, titles of books, and legislative materials except
for bills and resolutions. Refer to Bluebook.

State Tax Reports (Commerce Clearing House)
    Abbreviation: [number state] St. Tax Rep. (CCH)

    Example: Coca-Cola Bottling Co. United v. Woods, [Tennessee] St. Tax Rep.
                (CCH) ¶ 200-463 (Tenn. Aug. 3, 1981). ——Since State Tax Reports
                for Tennessee is contained in one volume; there is no volume number.

State University of New York at Buffalo Law Review
    See   Buffalo Law Review

Statute of the International Court of Justice
    Abbreviation: Stat. I.C.J.

    Example: Stat. I.C.J. art. 36, para. 2(a).

Statutes of California
    Abbreviation: year Cal. Stat.

    Examples: Act of July 12, 1979, ch. 333, 1979 Cal. Stat. 1191.

                Act of Sept. 19, 1979, ch. 729, § 2, 1979 Cal. Stat. 2458, 2460-61.
                ——Citation to a section of a session law.

                Budget Act of 1979, ch. 259, 1979 Cal. Stat. 576. ——Citation to a
                session law with a popular name.

                Act of Sept. 30, 1980, ch. 1312, 1980 Cal. Stat. 4442 (codified at Cal.
                Welf. & Inst. Code ¶¶ 11450.5, 15060 (Supp. 1982)). ——Citation to
                a session law when that law will be or is codified, and the code location
                is known.

statutes and legislative materials
    ——See specific entries for examples. See also Bluebook Rules 12.2 to 12.8 and 13.2 to
       13.6.

Statutes at Large
    Abbreviation: Stat.   (year).

    Examples: Act of June 15, 1933, ch. 86, 48 Stat. 152. ——Citation to pre-1957
                session law. The citation is to a chapter in Statutes at Large.

                Act of May 24, 1982, Pub. L. No. 97-179, 96 Stat. 90. ——Citation to
                a post-1956 session law.

                National Monument Act, ch. 3060, 34 Stat. 225 (1906) (codified at 16
                U.S.C. §§ 431-433). ——Citation to a pre-1957 session law with a
                popular name. The citation is to a chapter in Statutes at Large.

                Northern Pacific Halibut Act of 1982, Pub. L. No. 97-176, 97 Stat. 78
                (to be codified at 16 U.S.C. §§ 773-773k). ——Citation to a post 1956
                session law with a popular name.

In law review footnotes, the titles of books and the names of cases are not underlined.

Economic Recovery Tax Act of 1981, Pub. L. No. 97-34, § 403, 95 Stat. 172, 301-05 (codified in scattered sections in the I.R.C.). ——Citation to a section within a session law.

Tennessee Valley Authority Act, ch. 32, 48 Stat. 58 (1933) (codified as amended at 16 U.S.C. §§ 83la-83ldd (1982)). ——Illustration of a citation when a session law has been codified and the code location is known. Some of the examples above also illustrate this situation.

The Bankruptcy Act, ch. 541, 30 Stat. 544 (1898) (repealed 1978). ——Citation to a repealed statute.

National Industrial Recovery Act, ch. 90, § 3, 48 Stat. 195, 196-97 (1933), repealed by Act of June 14, 1935, ch. 246, 49 Stat. 375. ——Citation to a repealed statute with a complete citation to the repealing statute.

Securities Act of 1933, ch. 38, § 2, 48 Stat. 74, 74 (current version at 15 U.S.C. § 77(b) (1976 & Supp. IV 1980)). ——Citation to a version of a statute no longer in force. The current version is indicated parenthetically.

Securities Act of 1933, 15 U.S.C. § 77(b) (1976 & Supp. IV 1980) (original version at ch. 38, § 2, 48 Stat. 74, 74 (1933)). ——Citation to a code provision's prior history.

Treaty of Alliance, Feb. 6, 1778, United States—France, 8 Stat. 6, T.S. No. 82. ——Citation to treaties dated prior to 1945 to which the U.S. is a party. See Bluebook Rule 19.2.5.

Agreement Respecting Mutual Aid, Apr. 17, 1945, United States—South Africa, 60 Stat. 1576, T.I.A.S. No. 15ll. ——Citation to treaties from 1945 to the present to which the U.S. is a party. See Bluebook Rule 19.2.5.

Statutes of Nevada
Abbreviation: year Nev. Stat.

statutes, subsequent citation to
——See subsequent citation to cases, statutes, and prior citations

Stetson Law Review
Abbreviation: Stetson L. Rev.

Examples: Thurman, Contempt for Nonsupport in Florida—Civil or Criminal Proceeding?, 9 Stetson L. Rev. 333 (1980). ——Article Cite.

Thurman, Contempt for Nonsupport in Florida—Civil or Criminal Proceeding?, 9 Stetson L. Rev. 333, 337-43 (1980). ——Page Cite.

student material in law reviews
Examples:

Long student material (Project, special project, note)

In law review footnotes, the following are in large and small capitals: periodicals, constitutions, codes, restatements, standards, authors of books, titles of books, and legislative materials except for bills and resolutions. Refer to Bluebook.

Special Project, <u>Drugs and Criminal Responsibility</u>, 33 Vand. L. Rev. 1145 (1980).

Note, <u>Dronenburg v. Zech: The Wrong Case for Asserting a Right of Privacy for Homosexuals</u>, 63 N.C.L. Rev. 749 (1985) (authored by Katherine M. Allen). ——The student author's name may be indicated. Bluebook Rule 16.1.2.

Case Comment, 65 Minn. L. Rev. 488 (1981). ——Citation by designation alone for short commentary.

——For more examples, see the entry for periodicals.

——See generally Bluebook Rule 16.1.2.

sub nom.
Examples: <u>United Jewish Org. v. Wilson</u>, 510 F.2d 512 (2d Cir. 1975), <u>cert. granted sub nom.</u> <u>United Jewish Org. v. Carey</u>, 430 U.S. 144 (1977).

<u>Graves v. Barnes</u>, 378 F. Supp. 640 (W.D. Tex. 1974), <u>vacated as moot sub nom.</u> <u>White v. Regester</u>, 422 U.S. 935 (1975). ——Bluebook Rule 10.7.2.

subsequent citation to cases, statutes, and prior citations
Examples: <u>DeFunis</u>, 416 U.S. at 334. ——subsequent cite for <u>DeFunis v. Odegaard</u>, 416 U.S. 312 (1974).

§ 1983. ——subsequent cite for 42 U.S.C. § 1983 (1976).

<u>Id.</u> ——Cite for material in preceding footnote.

<u>Id.</u> at 470. ——Cite for page 470 of material in preceding footnote.

——See generally Bluebook Rule 4.3 and the rules for the particular authority.

Suffolk Transnational Law Journal
Abbreviation: Suffolk Transnat'l L.J.

Examples: Salimbene, <u>National Sovereignty: Britain Against the European Court</u>, 3 Suffolk Transnat'l L.J. 185 (1979). ——Article Cite.

Salimbene, <u>National Sovereignty: Britain Against the European Court</u>, 3 Suffolk Transnat'l L.J. 185, 190-95 (1979). ——Page Cite.

Suffolk University Law Review
Abbreviation: Suffolk U.L. Rev.

Examples: Reid, <u>In the Taught Tradition—The Meaning of Law in Massachusetts Bay Two-Hundred Years Ago</u>, 14 Suffolk U.L. Rev. 931 (1980). ——Article Cite.

Reid, <u>In the Taught Tradition—The Meaning of Law in Massachusetts Bay Two-Hundred Years Ago</u>, 14 Suffolk U.L. Rev. 931, 950-55 (1980). ——Page Cite.

In law review footnotes, the titles of books and the names of cases are not underlined.

Sullivan on Antitrust
>   See   Handbook of the Law of Antitrust, by L. Sullivan

Superior Court
>   Abbreviation: Super. Ct.

supplement
>   ——See the various title entries in this work and Bluebook Rule 3.2(c).

supra
>   ——Should not be used in referring to cases, statutes, or similar material except in extraordinary circumstances. Bluebook Rule 4.2.

Supreme Court (federal)
>   Abbreviation: U.S.

Supreme Court (other)
>   Abbreviation: Sup. Ct.

Supreme Court, Appellate Division
>   Abbreviation: App. Div.

Supreme Court, Appellate Term
>   Abbreviation: App. Term

Supreme Court Historical Society Yearbook
>   Abbreviation: Sup. Ct. Hist. Soc'y Y.B.

Supreme Court Practice, by R. Stern & E. Gressman
>   ——Do not abbreviate the title.

>   Example: R. Stern & E. Gressman, Supreme Court Practice 433 (6th ed. 1986).

Supreme Court Reporter
>   Abbreviation: S. Ct.

>   Examples: New York v. Ferber, 102 S. Ct. 3348 (1982). ——Case Cite.

>   New York v. Ferber, 102 S. Ct. 3348, 3354 (1982). ——Page Cite.

>   ——Cite only proper if not in United States Reports.

Supreme Court Review
>   Abbreviation: Sup. Ct. Rev.

>   Examples: Garvey, Freedom and Equality in the Religion Clauses, 1981 Sup. Ct. Rev. 193. ——Article Cite.

In law review footnotes, the following are in large and small capitals: periodicals, constitutions, codes, restatements, standards, authors of books, titles of books, and legislative materials except for bills and resolutions. Refer to Bluebook.

Garvey, <u>Freedom and Equality in the Religion Clauses</u>, 1981 Sup. Ct.
Rev. 193, 212-13. ——Page Cite.

Supreme Court Rules (Rules of the Supreme Court of the United States).
Abbreviation: Sup. Ct. R.

Example: Sup. Ct. R. 5.

Supreme Judicial Court
Abbreviation: Sup. Jud. Ct.

Surrogate's Court
Abbreviation: Sur. Ct.

survey
Examples: Hart, <u>Commercial Law, Survey of New Mexico Law</u>, 11 N.M.L. Rev.
                  69 (1980-1981). ——Article Cite.

                  Hart, <u>Commercial Law, Survey of New Mexico Law</u>, 11 N.M.L. Rev.
                  69, 70-74 (1980-1981). ——Page Cite.

Survey of the Law of Property, by R. Boyer
——Do not abbreviate the title.

Example: R. Boyer, <u>Survey of the Law of Property</u> 43 (3d ed. 1981).

Sydney Law Review
Abbreviation: Sydney L. Rev.

Examples: Hetherington, <u>Inherent Powers and the Mareva Jurisdiction</u>, 10 Sydney
                  L. Rev. 76 (1983). ——Article Cite.

                  Hetherington, <u>Inherent Powers and the Mareva Jurisdiction</u>, 10 Sydney
                  L. Rev. 76, 79-80 (1983). ——Page Cite.

symposium
Examples: <u>Recent Developments in Securities Regulation: The Special Study of
                  Securities Markets</u>, 62 Mich. L. Rev. 557 (1964). ——Cite for the
                  whole symposium.

                  Knauss, <u>A Reappraisal of the Role of Disclosure</u>, 62 Mich. L. Rev. 607
                  (1962). ——Cite for article within the symposium.

Syracuse Journal of International Law and Commerce
Abbreviations: Syracuse J. Int'l L. & Com.
                  Syr. J. Int'l L. & Com. (publisher's abbreviation)

Syracuse Law Review
Abbreviation: Syracuse L. Rev.

In law review footnotes, the titles of books and the names of cases are not underlined.

Examples: Nordenberg, <u>The Supreme Court and Discovery Reform: The Continuing Need for an Umpire</u>, 31 Syracuse L. Rev. 543 (1980). ——Article Cite.

Nordenberg, <u>The Supreme Court and Discovery Reform: The Continuing Need for an Umpire</u>, 31 Syracuse L. Rev. 543, 545-53 (1980). ——Page Cite.

In law review footnotes, the following are in large and small capitals: periodicals, constitutions, codes, restatements, standards, authors of books, titles of books, and legislative materials except for bills and resolutions. Refer to Bluebook.

In law review footnotes, the titles of books and the names of cases are not underlined.

T

Tax Adviser
    Abbreviation: Tax Adviser

Tax Court
    Abbreviation: T.C.

Tax Court Memorandum Decisions (CCH)
    Abbreviations: Tax Ct. Mem. Dec. (CCH) ——for looseleaf service
                     T.C.M. (CCH) ——for bound material

    Examples: Allison v. Commissioner, 52 Tax Ct. Mem. Dec. (CCH) 42 (Aug. 4,
                     1986). ——Looseleaf.

                     Porter v. Commissioner, 51 T.C.M. (CCH) 477 (1986). ——Bound.

    ——The above examples are proper if the case is not yet available in Tax Court of the
        United States Reports (T.C.).

Tax Court Memorandum Decisions (Prentice-Hall)
    Abbreviations: Tax Court Mem. Dec. (P-H) ——for looseleaf service
                     T.C.M. ——for bound material

    Examples: Egan v. Commissioner., Tax Ct. Mem. Dec. (P-H) ¶ 82,574 (Sept. 30,
                     1982). ——Citation to looseleaf material.

                     Brownlee v. Commissioner, 50 T.C.M. (P-H) ¶ 81,416 (1981).
                     ——Citation to bound material.

    ——The above examples are proper if the case is not yet available in Tax Court of the
        United States Reports (T.C.).

Tax Court of the United States Reports
    Abbreviation: T.C.

    Example: Hager v. Commissioner, 76 T.C. 66 (1981).

Tax Court Reported Decisions (Prentice-Hall)
    Abbreviation: Tax Ct. Rep. Dec. (P-H)

    Example: Drucker v. Commissioner, Tax Ct. Rep. Dec. (P-H) (79 Tax Ct. Rep.
                     Dec.) ¶ 79.38 (Sept. 30, 1982). ——Citation to looseleaf material.

    ——The above example is proper if the case is not yet available in an official or West
        reporter, or is not reported in an official or West reporter.

In law review footnotes, the following are in large and small capitals: periodicals, constitutions,
codes, restatements, standards, authors of books, titles of books, and legislative materials except
for bills and resolutions. Refer to Bluebook.

Tax Court Reports (Commerce Clearing House)
    (formerly Reporter)

    Abbreviation: Tax Ct. Rep. (CCH)

    Examples: Hager v. Commissioner, 76 T.C. No. 66, [1981 Transfer Binder] Tax
    Ct. Rep. (CCH) No. 37,905 (1981). ――Tax Court Reports is not a
    preferred source. When case becomes available in Reports of the
    United States Tax Court (T.C.), the citation to the Tax Court Reporter
    should be dropped. See Bluebook Rule 14.3.2.

    Service Bolt & Nut Co. Profit Sharing Trust v. Commissioner, [Current
    Regular Decisions] Tax Ct. Rep. (CCH) No. 39,036 (May 20, 1982).
    ――Citation to looseleaf material.

    Neil v. Commissioner, [Current Memo Decisions] Tax Ct. Rep. (CCH)
    No. 39,379 (Sept. 23, 1982). ――Citation to looseleaf material.

――The above examples are proper if the case is not yet available in an official or West
reporter, or is not reported in an official or West reporter.

Tax Executive
    Abbreviation: Tax Executive

    Examples: Thiewes, The Normalization Requirements of Public Utility Tax
    Accounting and its Ratemaking, 35 Tax Executive 217 (1983).
    ――Article Cite.

    Thiewes, The Normalization Requirements of Public Utility Tax
    Accounting and its Ratemaking, 35 Tax Executive 217, 217 (1983).
    ――Page Cite.

Tax-Exempt Organizations (Prentice-Hall)
    Abbreviation: Tax-Exempt Org. (P-H)

Tax Law Review
    Abbreviation: Tax L. Rev.

    Examples: Faber, The Use and Misuse of the Plan of Reorganization Concept, 38
    Tax L. Rev. 515 (1983). ――Article Cite.

    Faber, The Use and Misuse of the Plan of Reorganization Concept, 38
    Tax L. Rev. 515, 528-29 (1983). ――Page Cite.

Tax Lawyer
    Abbreviation: Tax Law.

Tax Management (Bureau of National Affairs)
    Abbreviation: Tax Mgmt. (BNA)

Tax Management International Journal
    Abbreviations: Tax Mgmt. Int'l J.
                TMIJ (publisher's abbreviation)

In law review footnotes, the titles of books and the names of cases are not underlined.

Examples: Ruchelman, <u>The Service Proposes New Regulations Under Section 897</u>, 13 Tax Mgmt. Int'l J. 3 (1984). ——Article Cite.

Ruchelman, <u>The Service Proposes New Regulations Under Section 897</u>, 13 Tax Mgmt. Int'l J. 3, 9-10 (1984). ——Page Cite.

Tax Management Memo (Bureau of National Affairs)
Abbreviation: Tax Mgmt. Memo

Tax Notes
Abbreviation: Tax Notes

Examples: Galvin, <u>The Commissioner's Statistics of Income: Required Reading for Tax Reformers</u>, 27 Tax Notes 945 (1985). ——Article Cite.

Galvin, <u>The Commissioner's Statistics of Income: Required Reading for Tax Reformers</u>, 27 Tax Notes 945, 948 (1985). ——Page Cite.

Tax Treaties (Commerce Clearing House)
Abbreviation: Tax Treaties (CCH)

Taxation for Lawyers
Abbreviation: Tax'n for Law.

Examples: Greenblatt & Banoff, <u>Corporations Can Reduce the After-Tax Cost of Fringe Benefits Through VEBAs</u>, 11 Tax'n for Law. 24 (1982). ——Article Cite.

Greenblatt & Banoff, <u>Corporations Can Reduce the After-Tax Cost of Fringe Benefits Through VEBAs</u>, 11 Tax'n for Law. 24, 26-27 (1982). ——Page Cite.

Taxation of the Closely Held Corporation, by T. Ness & E. Vogel
——Do not abbreviate the title.

Examples: T. Ness & E. Vogel, <u>Taxation of the Closely Held Corporation</u> ¶ 4.01[1] (4th ed. 1986).

T. Ness & E. Vogel, <u>Taxation of the Closely Held Corporation</u> ¶ 4.01[1], at 4-5 (4th ed. 1986).

Taxes—The Tax Magazine
Abbreviation: Taxes

Examples: Karzon, <u>No Smooth Sailing for Fiduciaries Waiving Attribution in Stock Redemptions</u>, 59 Taxes 3 (1981). ——Article Cite.

Karzon, <u>No Smooth Sailing for Fiduciaries Waiving Attribution in Stock Redemptions</u>, 59 Taxes 3, 6-9 (1981). ——Page Cite.

Temple Law Quarterly
Abbreviation: Temp. L.Q.

In law review footnotes, the following are in large and small capitals: periodicals, constitutions, codes, restatements, standards, authors of books, titles of books, and legislative materials except for bills and resolutions. Refer to Bluebook.

Examples: Weissenberger, The Landlord's Duty to Mitigate Damages on the Tenant's Abandonment: A Survey of Old Law and New Trends, 53 Temp. L.Q. 1 (1980). ——Article Cite.

Weissenberger, The Landlord's Duty to Mitigate Damages on the Tenant's Abandonment: A Survey of Old Law and New Trends, 53 Temp. L.Q. 1, 30-35 (1980). ——Page Cite.

temporary
Abbreviation: temp.

Tennessee Administrative Code
See Official Compilation Rules and Regulations of the State of Tennessee

Tennessee Administrative Register
Abbreviation: Tenn. Admin. Reg. (month year).

Example: 8 Tenn. Admin. Reg. 25 (Oct. 1982).

Tennessee Appeals Reports
Abbreviation: Tenn. App.

——Discontinued after 63 Tenn. App. 732 (1972). Thereafter cite only to S.W.2d.

Examples: Stevens v. Moore, 24 Tenn. App. 61, 139 S.W.2d 710 (1940). ——Case Cite.

Stevens v. Moore, 24 Tenn. App. 61, 72, 139 S.W.2d 710, 717 (1940). ——Page Cite.

——After 63 Tenn. App. 732 (1972), cite as follows:

Panter v. Miller, 698 S.W.2d 634 (Tenn. Ct. App. 1985). ——Case Cite.

Panter v. Miller, 698 S.W.2d 634, 635 (Tenn. Ct. App. 1985). ——Page Cite.

Tennessee Bar Journal
Abbreviation: Tenn. B.J.

Examples: Gilman, The Holographic Codicil, 18 Tenn. B.J. 60 (1982). ——Article Cite.

Gilman, The Holographic Codicil, 18 Tenn. B.J. 60, 61-62 (1982). ——Page Cite.

Tennessee Code Annotated
Abbreviation: Tenn. Code Ann. § (year).

Examples: Tenn. Code Ann. § 11-4-301 (1980).

Tenn. Code Ann. § 49-6-3401 (Supp. 1987).

In law review footnotes, the titles of books and the names of cases are not underlined.

Tennessee Constitution

Abbreviation: Tenn. Const. art. , §   .

Examples: Tenn. Const. art. 1, § 4. ——Cite provisions without date unless the cited provisions have been repealed or amended (Bluebook Rule 11).

Tenn. Const. art. 4, § 1 (1870, amended 1978). ——Cite provisions which have been repealed or amended by giving the date of the adoption of the particular provision and the date of repeal or amendment (Bluebook Rule 11).

Tenn. Const. of 1796, art. I, § IV. ——Cite constitutions that have been totally superseded by year of adoption, giving parenthetically the year of adoption of the specific provision cited if different (Bluebook Rule 11).

Tennessee Corporations, by R. Gilman

——Do not abbreviate the title.

Examples: R. Gilman, <u>Tennessee Corporations</u> § 5.1 (1985).

R. Gilman, <u>Tennessee Corporations</u> § 5.1, at 43 (1985).

Tennessee Criminal Appeals Reports

Abbreviation: Tenn. Crim. App.

——Discontinued after 4 Tenn. Crim. App. 723 (1971). Thereafter cite only to S.W.2d.

Examples: <u>Stokely v. State</u>, 4 Tenn. Crim. App. 241, 470 S.W.2d 37 (1971). ——Case Cite.

<u>Stokely v. State</u>, 4 Tenn. Crim. App. 241, 245, 470 S.W.2d 37, 39 (1971). ——Page Cite.

——After 4 Tenn. Crim. App. 723 (1971), cite as follows:

<u>State v. Grimes</u>, 698 S.W.2d 358 (Tenn. Crim. App. 1985). ——Case Cite.

<u>State v. Grimes</u>, 698 S.W.2d 358, 360 (Tenn. Crim. App. 1985). ——Page Cite.

Tennessee Jurisprudence

Abbreviations: Tenn. Jur. <u>article's name</u> § (year).
                 Tenn. Juris. (publisher's abbreviation)

Example: 26 Tenn. Jur. <u>Working Contracts</u> § 5 (1985).

Tennessee Law of Evidence, by Donald F. Paine

——Do not abbreviate the title.

Examples: D. Paine, <u>Tennessee Law of Evidence</u> § 137 (1974).

D. Paine, <u>Tennessee Law of Evidence</u> § 137, at 153 (1974).

In law review footnotes, the following are in large and small capitals: periodicals, constitutions, codes, restatements, standards, authors of books, titles of books, and legislative materials except for bills and resolutions. Refer to Bluebook.

Tennessee Law Review
   Abbreviation: Tenn. L. Rev.

   Examples: Daughtrey, <u>Cross Sectionalism in Jury-Selection Procedures After</u>
                  <u>Taylor v. Louisiana</u>, 43 Tenn. L. Rev. 1 (1975). ——Article Cite.

                  Daughtrey, <u>Cross Sectionalism in Jury-Selection Procedures After</u>
                  <u>Taylor v. Louisiana</u>, 43 Tenn. L. Rev. 1, 7-13 (1975). ——Page Cite.

Tennessee Lawyer
   Abbreviation: Tenn. Law.

   Examples: <u>Five County Bars Launch Pro Bono Project</u>, Tenn. Law., Mar. 1985, at
                  1. ——Article Cite.

                  <u>Five County Bars Launch Pro Bono Project</u>, Tenn. Law., Mar. 1985, at
                  1, 5. ——Page Cite.

Tennessee Practice, by W. Bigham et. al.
   ——Do not abbreviate the title.

   Examples: 6 N. MacLean & B. MacLean, <u>Tennessee Practice</u> § 70.33 (2d ed.
                  1987).

                  6 N. MacLean & B. MacLean, <u>Tennessee Practice</u> § 70.33 comment
                  (2d ed. 1987).

   ——Volumes in this series are written by a variety of authors. Therefore cite the author
      of the particular volume.

Tennessee Private Acts
   <u>See</u>   Private Acts of the State of Tennessee

Tennessee Public Acts
   <u>See</u>   Public Acts of the State of Tennessee

Tennessee Reports
   Abbreviation: Tenn.

   ——Discontinued after 225 Tenn. 727 (1972). Thereafter cite only to S.W.2d.

   Examples: <u>Cultra v. Cultra</u>, 188 Tenn. 506, 221 S.W.2d 533 (1959). ——Case
                  Cite.

                  <u>Cultra v. Cultra</u>, 188 Tenn. 506, 509, 221 S.W.2d 533, 5 (1959).
                  ——Page Cite.

   ——After 225 Tenn. 727 (1972), cite as follows:

                  <u>Pate v. City of Martin</u>, 614 S.W.2d 46 (Tenn. 1979). ——Case Cite.

                  <u>Pate v. City of Martin</u>, 614 S.W.2d 46, 48 (Tenn. 1979). ——Page
                  Cite.

In law review footnotes, the titles of books and the names of cases are not underlined.

Tennessee Rules and Regulations
    See   Official Compilation Rules and Regulations of the State of Tennessee

Tennessee Session Laws
    See   Public Acts of the State of Tennessee and Private Acts of the State of Tennessee

Texas Administrative Code
    Abbreviations: Tex. Admin. Code tit., § (year).

    Example: Tex. Admin. Code tit. 1 § 79 (1982).

Texas Revised Civil Statutes Annotated
    See   Vernon's Annotated Revised Civil Statutes of the State of Texas

Texas Bar Journal
    Abbreviation: Tex. B.J.

    Examples: Joe, The Judicial Recommendation Against Deportation, 45 Tex. B.J. 712 (1982). ——Article Cite.

                Joe, The Judicial Recommendation Against Deportation, 45 Tex. B.J. 712, 714-15 (1982). ——Page Cite.

Texas Civil Appeals Reports
    Abbreviation: Tex. Civ. App.

——Discontinued after 63 Tex. Civ. App. 590 (1911). Thereafter cite only to S.W. and S.W.2d.

    Examples: Guiderian v. Clark, 59 Tex. Civ. App. 248, 127 S.W. 564 (1910). ——Case Cite.

                Guiderian v. Clark, 59 Tex. Civ. App. 248, 250, 127 S.W. 564, 506 (1910). ——Page Cite.

——After 63 Tex. Civ. App. 590 (1911), cite as follows:

                Carreon v. Morales, 698 S.W.2d 241 (Tex. Ct. App. 1985). ——Case Cite.

                Carreon v. Morales, 698 S.W.2d 241, 244 (Tex. Ct. App. 1985). ——Page Cite.

——The Texas Court of Civil Appeals (Tex. Civ. App.) became the Texas Court of Appeals in 1981.

Texas Codes Annotated (Vernon)
    See   Vernon's Texas Codes Annotated

Texas Constitution
    Abbreviation: Tex. Const. art. , § .

In law review footnotes, the following are in large and small capitals: periodicals, constitutions, codes, restatements, standards, authors of books, titles of books, and legislative materials except for bills and resolutions. Refer to Bluebook.

Examples: Tex. Const. art. 1, § 12. ——Cite provisions without date unless the
                 cited provisions have been repealed or amended (Bluebook Rule 11).

                 Tex. Const. art. 3, § 51a (1945, amended 1954). ——Cite provisions
                 which have been repealed or amended by giving the date of the adoption
                 of the particular provision and the date of repeal or amendment
                 (Bluebook Rule 11).

                 Tex. Const. of 1845, art. V., § 12. ——Cite constitutions that have
                 been totally superseded by year of adoption, giving parenthetically the
                 year of adoption of the specific provision cited if different (Bluebook
                 Rule 11).

Texas Criminal Reports (Texas Court of Appeals Reports)
Abbreviation: Tex. Crim.

——Discontinued after 172 Tex. Crim. 655 (1962). Thereafter cite only to S.W.2d.

Examples: Ex parte Burnett, 85 Tex. Crim. 315, 211 S.W. 934 (1919). ——Case
                 Cite.

                 Ex parte Burnett, 85 Tex. Crim. 315, 319, 211 S.W. 934, 935 (1919).
                 ——Page Cite.

——After 172 Tex. Crim. 655 (1962), cite the following:

                 Streetman v. State, 698 S.W.2d 132 (Tex. Crim. App. 1985). ——Case
                 Cite.

                 Streetman v. State, 698 S.W.2d 132, 133 (Tex. Crim. App. 1985).
                 ——Page Cite.

Texas Digest of Opinions of the Attorney General
See   Digest of Opinions of the Attorney General of Texas

Texas International Law Forum
Abbreviation: Tex. Int'l L.F.

Examples: Butte, "Act of the Thing" in French Law Today, 6 Tex Int'l L.F. 50
                 (1970). ——Article Cite.

                 Butte, "Act of the Thing" in French Law Today, 6 Tex Int'l L.F. 50,
                 58-59 (1970). ——Page Cite.

Texas International Law Journal
Abbreviation: Tex. Int'l L.J.

Examples: Folsom, The Resurrection of Machiavelli: International Law and the
                 United Nations, 17 Tex. Int'l L.J. 1 (1982). ——Article Cite.

                 Folsom, The Resurrection of Machiavelli: International Law and the
                 United Nations, 17 Tex. Int'l L.J. 1, 12-13 (1982). ——Page Cite.

Texas Law Review
Abbreviation: Tex. L. Rev.

In law review footnotes, the titles of books and the names of cases are not underlined.

Examples: Deutsch, <u>Politics, Economics, and Corporate Power: The Challenge of Bureaucracy</u>, 58 Tex. L. Rev. 777 (1980). ——Article Cite.

Deutsch, <u>Politics, Economics, and Corporate Power: The Challenge of Bureaucracy</u>, 58 Tex. L. Rev. 777, 780-85 (1980). ——Page Cite.

Texas Register
Abbreviation: Tex. Reg.

Texas Reports
Abbreviation: Tex.

——Discontinued after 163 Tex. 638 (1962). Thereafter cite only to S.W.2d.

Examples: <u>Gleich v. Bongio</u>, 128 Tex. 606, 99 S.W.2d 881 (1937). ——Case Cite.

<u>Gleich v. Bongio</u>, 128 Tex. 606, 611-12, 99 S.W.2d 881, 884 (1937). ——Page Cite.

——After 163 Tex. 638 (1962), cite as follows:

<u>Cherokee Water Co. v. Ross</u>, 698 S.W.2d 363 (Tex. 1985). ——Case Cite.

<u>Cherokee Water Co. v. Ross</u>, 698 S.W.2d 363, 365 (Tex. 1985). ——Page Cite.

Texas Session Laws
<u>See</u> General and Special Laws of the State of Texas and Texas Session Law Service

Texas Session Law Service
Abbreviation: year Tex. Sess. Law Serv. (Vernon).

Texas Southern University Law Review
Abbreviation: Tex. S.U.L. Rev.

Examples: Owens, <u>The Establishment of a Doctrine: Executive Privilege After United States v. Nixon</u>, 4 Tex. S.U.L. Rev. 22 (1976). ——Article Cite.

Owens, <u>The Establishment of a Doctrine: Executive Privilege After United States v. Nixon</u>, 4 Tex. S.U.L. Rev. 22, 28-33 (1976). ——Page Cite.

Texas Tech Law Review
Abbreviation: Tex. Tech L. Rev.

Examples: Bubany, <u>The Texas Confession Statute: Some New Wine in the Same Old Bottle</u>, 10 Tex. Tech L. Rev. 67 (1978). ——Article Cite.

Bubany, <u>The Texas Confession Statute: Some New Wine in the Same Old Bottle</u>, 10 Tex. Tech L. Rev. 67, 70-75 (1978). ——Page Cite.

In law review footnotes, the following are in large and small capitals: periodicals, constitutions, codes, restatements, standards, authors of books, titles of books, and legislative materials except for bills and resolutions. Refer to Bluebook.

Thurgood Marshall Law Journal
    Abbreviation: T. Marshall L.J.

title(s)
    Abbreviations: tit., tits.

Title News
    Abbreviation: Title News

Trade Regulation Reporter (Commerce Clearing House)
    Abbreviation: Trade Reg. Rep. (CCH)

    Examples: Hyde v. Jefferson Parish Hosp. Dist. No. 2, 5 Trade Reg. Rep. (CCH) (1982-2 Trade Cas.) ¶ 64,945 (Former 5th Cir. Sept. 20, 1982). ——Citation to looseleaf material.

                Vanco Beverage, Inc. v. Falls City Indus., 1980-2 Trade Cas. (CCH) ¶ 63,357 (S.D. Ind. 1980). ——Citation to bound material.

——The above examples are proper if the case is not yet available in an official or West reporter, or is not reported in an official or West reporter.

Trademark Reporter
    Abbreviation: Trademark Rep.

    Examples: Cullen, Using Computers for Trademark Management, 72 Trademark Rep. 162 (1982). ——Article Cite.

                Cullen, Using Computers for Trademark Management, 72 Trademark Rep. 162, 168 (1982). ——Page Cite.

translation
    Abbreviation: trans.

translator
    Abbreviation: trans.

Transportation Law Journal
    Abbreviation: Transp. L.J.

    Examples: Freeman, The Ties That Bind: Railroads, Coal, Utilities, the ICC, and the Public Interest, 14 Transp. L.J. 1 (1985). ——Article Cite.

                Freeman, The Ties That Bind: Railroads, Coal, Utilities, the ICC, and the Public Interest, 14 Transp. L.J. 1, 18-19 (1985). ——Page Cite.

Transportation Practitioners Journal
    Abbreviation: Transp. Prac. J.

    Examples: Mewhinney, Motor Carrier Ratings, Fairness and the Public Safety, 53 Transp. Prac. J. 393 (1986). ——Article Cite.

In law review footnotes, the titles of books and the names of cases are not underlined.

Mewhinney, <u>Motor Carrier Ratings, Fairness, and the Public Safety</u>, 53 Transp. Prac. J. 393, 398 (1986). ——Page Cite.

Treasury Decisions Under Customs and Other Laws (1898-1965)
Abbreviation: Treas. Dec.

Examples: T.D. 20,472, 1 Treas. Dec. 16 (1899).

              T.D. 56,416, 100 Treas. Dec. 249 (1965).

Treasury Decisions Under Internal Revenue Laws (1898-1942)
Abbreviation: Treas. Dec. Int. Rev.

Examples: T.D. 5072, 36 Treas. Dec. Int. Rev. 265 (1941).

              T.D. 20,459, 1 Treas. Dec. Int. Rev. 7 (1898).

Treasury Delegation Orders
Abbreviation: Deleg. Order

Examples: Deleg Order No. 213, 1985-46 I.R.B. 35. ——Unbound.

              Deleg. Order No. 11 (Rev. 15), 1985-1 C.B. 423. ——Bound.

Treasury Department Orders
Abbreviation: Treas. Dep't Order

Examples: Treas. Dep't Order 150-02, 1986-19 I.R.B. 12. ——Unbound.

              Treas. Dep't Order 150-106, 1985-2 C.B. 758. ——Bound.

Treasury Regulations (U.S.)
Abbreviation: Treas. Reg.

Examples: Treas. Reg. § 1.466-1(a)(1)(1960). ——Unamended.

              Treas. Reg. § 1.466-1(a)(1)(as amended in 1986). ——Amended. See Bluebook Rule 14.5.1.

treaties (specific treaties)
Examples: Definitive Treaty of Peace, Sept. 3, 1783, United States—Great Britain, 8 Stat. 80, T.S. No. 104.

              Treaty of Ghent, Dec. 24, 1814, United States—Great Britain, 8 Stat. 218, T.S. No. 109. ——Citation to a treaty with a widely known popular name.

              Treaty of Ghent, Dec. 24, 1814, United States—Great Britain, art. 10, 8 Stat. 218, 223, T.S. No. 109, at 7. ——Citation to a subdivision of a treaty.

              Moscow Agreement, 1945, United States—United Kingdom—U.S.S.R., 60 Stat. 1899, T.I.A.S. No. 1555. ——Citation to a treaty with three parties.

In law review footnotes, the following are in large and small capitals: periodicals, constitutions, codes, restatements, standards, authors of books, titles of books, and legislative materials except for bills and resolutions. Refer to Bluebook.

Charter of the United Nations, June 26, 1945, 59 Stat. 1031, T.S. No. 993. ——Citation to a treaty with four or more parties.

Convention Respecting Sanitary Aerial Navigation, opened for signature Dec. 15, 1944, 59 Stat. 991, T.S. No. 992. ——Citation to multilateral treaty which is not signed on a single date.

Instrument for the Amendment of the Constitution of the International Labor Organization, April 20, 1948, 62 Stat. 3485, T.I.A.S. No. 1868, 15 U.N.T.S. 35. ——Agreement among four or more parties to which the United States is a party.

Constitution of the United Nations Educational, Scientific and Cultural Organization, Nov. 16, 1945, 4 U.N.T.S. 275. ——Agreement among four or more parties to which the United States is not a party.

——See generally Bluebook Rule 19.2.

Treaties and Other International Acts Series (U.S.)
    Abbreviation: T.I.A.S. No.

    Examples: Agreement Respecting Mutual Aid, Apr. 17, 1945, United States—South Africa, 60 Stat. 1576, T.I.A.S. No. 15ll. ——Proper citation from 1945 to 1949.

                  Treaty on the Limitation of Anti Ballistic Missile Systems, May 26, 1972, United States—U.S.S.R., 23 U.S.T. 3435, T.I.A.S. No. 7503. ——Proper citation from 1950 onward.

Treatise on the Law of Contracts, by S. Williston
    ——Do not abbreviate the title.

    Examples: 4 S. Williston, A Treatise on the Law of Contracts § 613 (3d ed. 1961).

                  4 S. Williston, A Treatise on the Law of Contracts § 613, at 578-79 (3d ed. 1961).

                  10 S. Williston, A Treatise on the Law of Contracts § 1181 (3d ed. Supp. 1982).

treatises
    Examples: 5A A. Corbin, Corbin on Contracts § 1157 (1964).

                  A. Casner, Estate Planning § 6.8.10 (5th ed. Supp. 1987).

    ——See also authors

Treaty Series (U.S.)
    Abbreviation: T.S. No.

    Example: Definitive Treaty of Peace, Sept. 3, 1783, United States—Great Britain, 8 Stat. 80, T.S. No. 104.

Trent Law Journal
    Abbreviation: Trent L.J.

In law review footnotes, the titles of books and the names of cases are not underlined.

Trial

    Abbreviation: Trial

Trial Lawyer's Guide

    Abbreviations: Trial Law. Guide
                     Tr. Law Guide (publisher's abbreviation)

    Examples: Soiret, The Freedom of Information Act: A Viable Alternative to the Federal Rules?, 29 Trial Law. Guide 484 (1986). ——Article Cite.

                    Soiret, The Freedom of Information Act: A Viable Alternative to the Federal Rules?, 29 Trial Law. Guide 484, 489-90 (1986). ——Page Cite.

Trial Lawyers Quarterly

    Abbreviation: Trial Law. Q.

Tribe on American Constitutional Law

    See   American Constitutional Law, by L. Tribe

Trusts and Estates

    Abbreviation: Tr. & Est.

    Examples: Teitell, Rev. Rul. 82-128: New Requirements for Charitable Remainder Trusts, 1982 Tr. & Est. 19. ——Article Cite.

                    Teitell, Rev. Rul. 82-128: New Requirements for Charitable Remainder Trusts, 1982 Tr. & Est. 19, 20-21. ——Page Cite.

Tulane Law Review

    Abbreviation: Tul. L. Rev.

    Examples: Yiannopoulos, Louisiana Civil Law: A Lost Cause?, 54 Tul. L. Rev. 830 (1980). ——Article Cite.

                    Yiannopoulos, Louisiana Civil Law: A Lost Cause?, 54 Tul. L. Rev. 830, 840-45 (1980). ——Page Cite.

Tulsa Law Journal

    Abbreviation: Tulsa L.J.

    Examples: Clark, Witchcraft and Legal Pluralism: The Case of Celimo Mirquirucama, 15 Tulsa L.J. 679 (1980). ——Article Cite.

                    Clark, Witchcraft and Legal Pluralism: The Case of Celimo Mirquirucama, 15 Tulsa L.J. 679, 680-85 (1980). ——Page Cite.

typeface conventions for briefs

    ——See Bluebook Rules 1.1 and 7.

In law review footnotes, the following are in large and small capitals: periodicals, constitutions, codes, restatements, standards, authors of books, titles of books, and legislative materials except for bills and resolutions. Refer to Bluebook.

typeface conventions for law review footnotes
——See Bluebook Rules 1.2.2 and 7. See also the excellent examples on the facing page next to the inside cover of the Bluebook.

typeface conventions for law review texts
——See Bluebook Rules 1.2.1 and 7.

typeface conventions for legal memoranda
——See Bluebook Rules 1.1 and 7.

In law review footnotes, the titles of books and the names of cases are not underlined.

U

U.C. Davis Law Review
  Abbreviation: U.C. Davis L. Rev.

  Examples: Barrett, "The Uncharted Area" —Commercial Speech and the First Amendment, 13 U.C. Davis L. Rev. 175 (1980). ——Article Cite.

    Barrett, "The Uncharted Area" —Commercial Speech and the First Amendment, 13 U.C. Davis L. Rev. 175, 180-85 (1980). ——Page Cite.

U.C.L.A.—Alaska Law Review
  Abbreviation: UCLA —Alaska L. Rev.

  Examples: Feldman, Criminal Procedure in Alaska, 9 UCLA—Alaska L. Rev. 109 (1980). ——Article Cite.

    Feldman, Criminal Procedure in Alaska, 9 UCLA—Alaska L. Rev. 109, 135-40 (1980). ——Page Cite.

U.C.L.A. Intramural Law Review
  Abbreviation: UCLA Intramural L. Rev.

U.C.L.A.—Journal of Environmental Law and Policy
  Abbreviation: UCLA J. Envtl. L. & Pol'y

UCLA Law Review
  Abbreviation: UCLA L. Rev.

  Examples: Lawrence & Minan, Solar Energy and Public Utility Rate Regulation, 26 UCLA L. Rev. 550 (1979). ——Article Cite.

    Lawrence & Minan, Solar Energy and Public Utility Rate Regulation, 26 UCLA L. Rev. 550, 559-64 (1979). ——Page Cite.

U.C.L.A.—Pacific Basin Law Journal
  Abbreviation: UCLA Pac. Basin L.J.

  Examples: Harlow, The Law of Neutrality at Sea for the 80's and Beyond, 3 UCLA Pac. Basin L.J. 42 (1984). ——Article Cite.

    Harlow, The Law of Neutrality at Sea for the 80's and Beyond, 3 UCLA Pac. Basin L.J. 42, 50-51 (1984). ——Page Cite.

In law review footnotes, the following are in large and small capitals: periodicals, constitutions, codes, restatements, standards, authors of books, titles of books, and legislative materials except for bills and resolutions. Refer to Bluebook.

UMKC Law Review
    Abbreviation: UMKC L. Rev.

    Examples: Stern & Sellers, <u>Property Settlements upon Divorce: Yours, Mine and the Commissioner's</u>, 48 UMKC L. Rev. 293 (1980). ——Article Cite.

                    Stern & Sellers, <u>Property Settlements upon Divorce: Yours, Mine and the Commissioner's</u>, 48 UMKC L. Rev. 293, 294-97 (1980). ——Page Cite.

UN Chronicle
    Abbreviation: UN Chron.

    Examples: <u>Disarmament Commission Chairman Says 'Excessive Time' Spent on Procedure</u>, UN Chron., May 1985, at 37. ——Article Cite.

                    <u>Disarmament Commission Chairman Says 'Excessive Time' Spent on Procedure</u>, UN Chron., May 1985, at 37, 37. ——Page Cite.

Unemployment Insurance Reports (Commerce Clearing House)
    Abbreviation: Unempl. Ins. Rep. (CCH)

Uniform Commercial Code
    Abbreviation: U.C.C. §   (year U.C.C. last amended).

    Example: U.C.C. § 9-312(5)(c) (1977).

Uniform Commercial Code Law Journal
    Abbreviation: U.C.C. L.J.

    Examples: Buchanan, <u>Mobile Home Sales Under the UCC</u>, 18 U.C.C. L.J. 216 (1986). ——Article Cite.

                    Buchanan, <u>Mobile Home Sales Under the UCC</u>, 18 U.C.C. L.J. 216, 233-34 (1986). ——Page Cite.

Uniform Commercial Code Reporting Service (Callaghan)
    Abbreviation: U.C.C. Rep. Serv. (Callaghan)

    Examples: <u>Rush v. Farmers & Merchants Bank</u>, [2 Current Materials] U.C.C. Rep. Serv. (Callaghan) (33 U.C.C. Rep. Serv.) 1823 (Ga. Ct. App. Apr. 7, 1982). ——Citation to looseleaf material.

                    <u>In re Utah Argicorp, Inc.</u>, 31 U.C.C. Rep. Serv. (Callaghan) 1712 (Bankr. D. Utah 1981). ——Citation to bound material.

——The above examples are proper only if the case is not yet available in an official or West reporter, or is not reported in an official or West reporter.

uniform laws
    ——See Bluebook Rule 12.8.4.

    Examples: U.C.C. § 9-312(5)(c) (1977).

In law review footnotes, the titles of books and the names of cases are not underlined.

Unif. Partnership Act § 22 (1914).

Unif. Consumer Credit Code § 4.109 (1974).

Unif. Probate Code § 6-107 (1975).

Unif. R. of Crim. P. 432 (1987).

Uniform Laws Annotated
Abbreviation: U.L.A.

Example: Unif. Child Custody Jurisdiction Act § 6, 9 U.L.A. 134 (1968).

Uniform System of Citation
Abbreviation: Unif. Sys. Citation (14th ed.) or Bluebook

United Nations Charter
See   Charter of the United Nations

United Nations Documents
Abbreviation: U.N. Doc.

——See generally Bluebook Rule 19.4

United Nations Juridical Yearbook
Abbreviation: U.N. Jurid. Y.B.

Example: 1981 U.N. Jurid. Y.B. 142, U.N. Doc. ST/LEG/SER.C/19.

United Nations Official Records:
Economic and Social Council Official Records

Abbreviation: U.N. ESCOR

——See generally Bluebook Rule 19.4.1.2(c).

General Assembly Official Records

Abbreviation: U.N. GAOR

——See generally Bluebook Rule 19.4.1.2(a).

Security Council Official Records

Abbreviation: U.N. SCOR

——See generally Bluebook Rule 19.4.1.2(b).

Trusteeship Council Official Records

Abbreviation: U.N. TCOR

——See generally Bluebook Rule 19.4.1.2(b)

United Nations Resolutions in GAOR
Examples:

In law review footnotes, the following are in large and small capitals: periodicals, constitutions, codes, restatements, standards, authors of books, titles of books, and legislative materials except for bills and resolutions. Refer to Bluebook.

——First four sessions (before 1950):

G.A. Res. 133, U.N. Doc. A/519, at 43 (1947).

——Fifth session to present (1950-present)

G.A. Res. 77, 38 U.N GAOR Supp. (No. 47) at 69, U.N. Doc. A/38/646 (1983).

G.A. Res. 152, 39 U.N. GAOR Supp. (No 51) at 94, U.N. Doc. A/29/756 (1984).

United Nations Treaty Series
Abbreviation: U.N.T.S.

Example: International Labor Organization (No. 100) concerning equal remuneration for men and women workers for work of equal value, Aug. 2, 1951, 165 U.N.T.S. 303.

United Nations Yearbook
Abbreviation: U.N.Y.B.

Example: 1965 U.N.Y.B. 26.

United States Agricultural Decisions
See   Agricultural Decisions (U.S)

United States Atomic Energy Commission Reports
See   Atomic Energy Commission Reports (U.S.)

United States Civil Aeronautics Board Reports (vol. 1 by C.A.A.)
See   Civil Aeronautics Board Reports (U.S.)

United States Claims Court Rules (Rules of the United States Claims Court)
Abbreviation: Cl. Ct. R.

Example: Cl. Ct. R. 43(b).

United States Code
Abbreviation: U.S.C.

Examples: 42 U.S.C. § 2000(e) (1982).

37 U.S.C. § 411f (Supp. III 1985). ——Supplemental volume to U.S.C.

36 U.S.C. § 1401 (1982 & Supp. III 1985).

Sherman Act § 2, 15 U.S.C. § 2 (1982). ——Citation to a section which is part of an act known by a popular name.

50 U.S.C. app. § 2093 (1982 & Supp. III 1985). ——Citation to an appendix which is divided into sections.

In law review footnotes, the titles of books and the names of cases are not underlined.

37 U.S.C. § 312 (1982), amended by 37 U.S.C. § 312 (Supp. III 1985). ——Citation to a non-current version of a code section with a complete citation to the amending statute.

37 U.S.C. § 312 (Supp. III 1985) (amending 37 U.S.C. 312 (1982)). ——Citation to a statute giving prior history parenthetically.

1 U.S.C. § 108 (1982) (originally enacted as Act of July 30, 1947, ch. 388, § 108, 61 Stat. 634, 635). ——Citation to a statute giving prior history parenthetically.

2 U.S.C. § 25 (1982) (corresponds to Act of June 1, 1789, ch. 1, § 2, 1 Stat. 23, 23). ——Citation to a statute giving prior history parenthetically.

United States Code Annotated
Abbreviation: U.S.C.A. §   (West year).

Examples: 35 U.S.C.A. § 104 (West 1984).

22 U.S.C.A. § 5011 (West Supp. 1980-1987). ——Citation to a statute found in a supplement volume.

35 U.S.C.A. § 103 (West Supp. 1988). ——Citation to a statute found in a pocket part.

United States Code Congressional and Administrative News
Abbreviation: U.S. Code Cong. & Ad. News

Example: H.R. Rep. No. 518, 94th Cong., 2d Sess. 4, reprinted in 1976 U.S. Code Cong. & Admin. News 4312, 4314-15.

United States Code Service (Lawyers Co-op)
Abbreviation: U.S.C.S. §   (Law. Co-op. year).

Examples: 21 U.S.C.S. § 331(e) (Law. Co-op. 1984).

21 U.S.C.S. § 331 (Law. Co-op. 1984 & Supp. 1988). ——Citation to a statute found in both the main body and supplement of a code.

United States Comptroller General's Opinion
See   Comptroller General's Opinion (U.S. Treasury Department)

United States Comptroller Treasury Decisions
See   Comptroller Treasury Decisions (U.S.)

United States Constitution
Abbreviation: U.S. Const.

Examples: U.S. Const. art. II, § 2.

U.S. Const. amend. XIV, § 1.

In law review footnotes, the following are in large and small capitals: periodicals, constitutions, codes, restatements, standards, authors of books, titles of books, and legislative materials except for bills and resolutions. Refer to Bluebook.

United States Copyright Decisions
    See   Copyright Decisions (U.S)

United States Court-Martial Reports
    See   Court-Martial Reports

United States Court of Appeals for the First Circuit
    Cases:

    Abbreviation: (1st Cir. year)

    Example: Montilla Records, Inc. v. Morales, 575 F.2d 324 (1st Cir. 1978).

    Court Rules:

    Abbreviation: 1st Cir. R.

    Example: 1st Cir. R. 3(a).

United States Court of Appeals for the Second Circuit
    Cases:

    Abbreviation: (2d Cir. year)

    Example: Central Hanover Bank & Trust Co. v. Herbst, 93 F.2d 510 (2d Cir. 1937).

    Court Rules:

    Abbreviation: 2d Cir. R.

    Example: 2d Cir. R. 0.22.

United States Court of Appeals for the Third Circuit
    Cases:

    Abbreviation: (3d Cir. year)

    Example: Hart v. J.T. Baker Chem. Corp., 589 F.2d 829 (3d Cir. 1979).

    Court Rules:

    Abbreviation: 3d Cir. R.

    Example: 3d Cir. R. 7(1).

United States Court of Appeals for the Fourth Circuit
    Cases:

    Abbreviation: (4th Cir. year)

    Example: Fennell v. Monongahela Power Co., 350 F.2d 867 (4th Cir. 1965).

    Court Rules:

    Abbreviation: 4th Cir. R.

    Example: 4th Cir. R. 14.

In law review footnotes, the titles of books and the names of cases are not underlined.

United States Court of Appeals for the Fifth Circuit
Cases:

Abbreviation: (5th Cir. year)

Example: John P. McGuire Co. v. Herzog, 421 F.2d 419 (5th Cir. 1970).

Court Rules:

Abbreviation: 5th Cir. R.

Example: 5th Cir. R. 7.1.

United States Court of Appeals for Fifth Circuit, (Decisions rendered in 1981)
——Decisions rendered in 1981, labeled as "5th Cir.":

Example: Lewis v. Reagan, 660 F.2d 124 (5th Cir. Oct. 1981).

——Decisions with unit information:

Example: U.S. v. Wright, 661 F.2d 60 (5th Cir. Unit A 1981).

——Decisions rendered after September 30, 1981, labeled as Former Fifth Circuit
    judgment:

Example: Helms v. Jones, 660 F.2d 120 (Former 5th Cir. 1981).

United States Court of Appeals for the Sixth Circuit
Cases:

Abbreviation: (6th Cir. year)

Example: Leake v. University of Cincinnati, 605 F.2d 255 (6th Cir. 1979).

Court Rules:

Abbreviation: 6th Cir. R.

Example: 6th Cir. R. 6.

United States Court of Appeals for the Seventh Circuit
Cases:

Abbreviation: (7th Cir. year)

Example: Pleatmaster, Inc. v. J.L. Golding Mfg. Co., 240 F.2d 894 (7th Cir.
                  1957).

Court Rules:

Abbreviation: 7th Cir. R.

Example: 7th Cir. R. 5(b).

United States Court of Appeals for the Eighth Circuit
Cases:

Abbreviation: (8th Cir. year)

Example: NLRB v. Skelly Oil Co., 473 F.2d 1079 (8th Cir. 1973).

In law review footnotes, the following are in large and small capitals: periodicals, constitutions, codes, restatements, standards, authors of books, titles of books, and legislative materials except for bills and resolutions. Refer to Bluebook.

Court Rules:

Abbreviation: 8th Cir. R.

Example: 8th Cir. R. 21(3).

United States Court of Appeals for the Ninth Circuit
Cases:

Abbreviation: (9th Cir. year)

Example: United States v. Neff, 615 F.2d 1235 (9th Cir. 1980).

Court Rules:

Abbreviation: 9th Cir. R.

Example: 9th Cir. R. 7.

United States Court of Appeals for the Tenth Circuit
Cases:

Abbreviation: (10th Cir. year).

Example: United States Fidelity & Guar. Co. v. Sidwell, 525 F.2d 472 (10th Cir. 1975).

Court Rules:

Abbreviation: 10th Cir. R.

Example: 10th Cir. R. 2(b).

United States Court of Appeals for the Eleventh Circuit
Cases:

Abbreviation: (11th Cir. year).

Example: Profitt v. Wainwright, 685 F.2d 1227 (11th Cir. 1982).

Court Rules:

Abbreviation: 11th Cir. R.

Example: 11th Cir. R. 6(b).

United States Court of Appeals for the District of Columbia Circuit
Cases:

Abbreviation: (D.C. Cir. year).

Example: Vaughn v. Rosen, 484 F.2d 820 (D.C. Cir. 1973).

Court Rules:

Abbreviation: D.C. Cir. R.

Example: D.C. Cir. R. 5(b).

In law review footnotes, the titles of books and the names of cases are not underlined.

United States Court of Appeals for the Federal Circuit
    Cases:

    Abbreviation: (Fed. Cir. year)

    Example: Medtronic Inc. v. Intermedics, Inc., 799 F.2d 734 (Fed. Cir. 1986).

    Court Rules:

    Abbreviation: Fed. Cir. R.

    Example: Fed. Cir. R. 9(h).

    ——Succeeded United States Court of Customs and Patent Appeals and the appellate
       jurisdiction of the Court of Claims.

    ——If not in F.2d, cite to the official reporter (Court of Claims Reports or Court of
       Customs and Patent Appeals Reports).

United States Court of Appeals Reports (1941-date)
    Abbreviation: U.S. App. D.C.

    Examples: United States v. Battle, 166 U.S. App. D.C. 396 (1975). ——Case
                 Cite.

                 United States v. Battle, 166 U.S. App. D.C. 396, 398 (1975). ——Page
                 Cite.

    ——Correct only if case not reported in the Federal Reporter.

United States Court of Claims Reports
    See   Court of Claims Reports

United States Court of Customs and Patent Appeals Reports
    See   Court of Customs and Patent Appeals Reports

United States Court of Military Appeals
    See   Court of Military Appeals

United States Cumulative Bulletin
    See   Cumulative Bulletin (U.S.)

United States Customs Bulletin and Decisions
    See   Customs Bulletin and Decisions (U.S.)

United States Decisions of the Comptroller General
    See   Decisions of the Comptroller General (U.S.)

United States Decisions of the Department of the Interior
    See   Decisions of the Department of the Interior (U.S.)

In law review footnotes, the following are in large and small capitals: periodicals, constitutions,
codes, restatements, standards, authors of books, titles of books, and legislative materials except
for bills and resolutions. Refer to Bluebook.

United States Decisions of the Employees' Compensation Appeals Board
    See   Decisions of the Employees' Compensation Appeals Board (U.S.)

United States Decisions of the Federal Maritime Commission
    See   Decisions of the Federal Maritime Commission (U.S)

United States Decisions of the United States Maritime Commission
    See   Decisions of the United States Maritime Commission

United States Department of Justice
    Abbreviation: U.S. Dep't of Justice

    Example: Bureau of Justice Statistics, U.S. Dep't of Justice, Tracking Offenders:
              The Child Victim 1-2 (1984).

    ——For citations to works by institutional authors, see Bluebook Rule 15.1(b).

United States Department of State
    Abbrevation: U.S. Dep't of State

    Example: U.S. Dep't of State, Documents on Germany 1944-1985, at 348 (1985).

    ——For citations to works by institutional authors, see Bluebook Rule 15.1(b).

United States Department of State Bulletin
    See   Department of State Bulletin (U.S.)

United States District Court for the Middle District of Alabama
    Abbreviation: (M.D. Ala. year)

United States District Court for the Northern District of Alabama
    Abbreviation: (N.D. Ala. year)

United States District Court for the Southern District of Alabama
    Abbreviation: (S.D. Ala. year)

United States District Court for the District of Alaska
    Abbreviation: (D. Alaska year)

United States District Court for the District of Arizona
    Abbreviation: (D. Ariz. year)

United States District Court for the Eastern District of Arkansas
    Abbreviations: (E.D. Ark. year)

United States District Court for the Western District of Arkansas
    Abbreviations: (W.D. Ark. year)

In law review footnotes, the titles of books and the names of cases are not underlined.

United States District Court for the Central District of California
    Abbreviation: (C.D. Cal. year)

United States District Court for the Eastern District of California
    Abbreviation: (E.D. Cal. year)

United States District Court for the Northern District of California
    Abbreviation: (N.D. Cal. year)

United States District Court for the Southern District of California
    Abbreviation: (S.D. Cal. year)

United States District Court for the District of Colorado
    Abbreviation: (D. Colo. year)

United States District Court for the District of Connecticut
    Abbreviation: (D. Conn. year)

United States District Court for the District of Delaware
    Abbreviation: (D. Del. year)

United States District Court for the District of Columbia
    Abbreviation: (D.D.C. year)

United States District Court for the Middle District of Florida
    Abbreviation: (M.D. Fla. year)

United States District Court for the Northern District of Florida
    Abbreviation: (N.D. Fla. year)

United States District Court for the Southern District of Florida
    Abbreviation: (S.D. Fla. year)

United States District Court for the Middle District of Georgia
    Abbreviation: (M.D. Ga. year)

United States District Court for the Northern District of Georgia
    Abbreviation: (N.D. Ga. year)

United States District Court for the Southern District of Georgia
    Abbreviation: (S.D. Ga. year)

United States District Court for the District of Guam
    Abbreviation: (D. Guam year)

In law review footnotes, the following are in large and small capitals: periodicals, constitutions, codes, restatements, standards, authors of books, titles of books, and legislative materials except for bills and resolutions. Refer to Bluebook.

United States District Court for the District of Hawaii
    Abbreviation: (D. Hawaii year)

United States District Court for the District of Idaho
    Abbreviation: (D. Idaho year)

United States District Court for the Central District of Illinois
    Abbreviation: (C.D. Ill. year)

United States District Court for the Northern District of Illinois
    Abbreviation: (N.D. Ill. year)

United States District Court for the Southern District of Illinois
    Abbreviation: (S.D. Ill. year)

United States District Court for the Northern District of Indiana
    Abbreviation: (N.D. Ind. year)

United States District Court for the Southern District of Indiana
    Abbreviation: (S.D. Ind. year)

United States District Court for the Northern District of Iowa
    Abbreviation: (N.D. Iowa year)

United States District Court for the Southern District of Iowa
    Abbreviation: (S.D. Iowa year)

United States District Court for the District of Kansas
    Abbreviation: (D. Kan. year)

United States District Court for the Eastern District of Kentucky
    Abbreviation: (E.D. Ky. year)

United States District Court for the Western District of Kentucky
    Abbreviation: (W.D. Ky. year)

United States District Court for the Eastern District of Louisiana
    Abbreviation: (E.D. La. year)

United States District Court for the Middle District of Louisiana
    Abbreviation: (M.D. La. year)

United States District Court for the Western District of Louisiana
    Abbreviation: (W.D. La. year)

In law review footnotes, the titles of books and the names of cases are not underlined.

United States District Court for the District of Maine
    Abbreviation: (D. Me. year)

United States District Court for the District of Maryland
    Abbreviation: (D. Md. year)

United States District Court for the District of Massachusetts
    Abbreviation: (D. Mass. year)

United States District Court for the Eastern District of Michigan
    Abbreviation: (E.D. Mich. year)

United States District Court for the Western District of Michigan
    Abbreviation: (W.D. Mich. year)

United States District Court for the District of Minnesota
    Abbreviation: (D. Minn. year)

United States District Court for the Northern District of Mississippi
    Abbreviation: (N.D. Miss. year)

United States District Court for the Southern District of Mississippi
    Abbreviation: (S.D. Miss. year)

United States District Court for the Eastern District of Missouri
    Abbreviation: (E.D. Mo. year)

United States District Court for the Western District of Missouri
    Abbreviation: (W.D. Mo. year)

United States District Court for the District of Montana
    Abbreviation: (D. Mont. year)

United States District Court for the District of Nebraska
    Abbreviation: (D. Neb. year)

United States District Court for the District of Nevada
    Abbreviation: (D. Nev. year)

United States District Court for the District of New Hampshire
    Abbreviation: (D.N.H. year)

United States District Court for the District of New Jersey
    Abbreviation: (D.N.J. year)

In law review footnotes, the following are in large and small capitals: periodicals, constitutions, codes, restatements, standards, authors of books, titles of books, and legislative materials except for bills and resolutions. Refer to Bluebook.

United States District Court for the District of New Mexico
    Abbreviation: (D.N.M. year)

United States District Court for the Eastern District of New York
    Abbreviation: (E.D.N.Y. year)

United States District Court for the Northern District of New York
    Abbreviation: (N.D.N.Y. year)

United States District Court for the Southern District of New York
    Abbreviation: (S.D.N.Y. year)

United States District Court for the Western District of New York
    Abbreviation: (W.D.N.Y. year)

United States District Court for the Eastern District of North Carolina
    Abbreviation: (E.D.N.C. year)

United States District Court for the Middle District of North Carolina
    Abbreviation: (M.D.N.C. year)

United States District Court for the Western District of North Carolina
    Abbreviation: (W.D.N.C. year)

United States District Court for the District of North Dakota
    Abbreviation: (D.N.D. year)

United States District Court for the Northern District of Ohio
    Abbreviation: (N.D. Ohio year)

United States District Court for the Southern District of Ohio
    Abbreviation: (S.D. Ohio year)

United States District Court for the Eastern District of Oklahoma
    Abbreviation: (E.D. Okla. year)

United States District Court for the Northern District of Oklahoma
    Abbreviation: (N.D. Okla. year)

United States District Court for the Western District of Oklahoma
    Abbreviation: (W.D. Okla. year)

United States District Court for the District of Oregon
    Abbreviation: (D. Or. year)

In law review footnotes, the titles of books and the names of cases are not underlined.

United States District Court for the Eastern District of Pennsylvania
    Abbreviation: (E.D. Pa. year)

United States District Court for the Middle District of Pennsylvania
    Abbreviation: (M.D. Pa. year)

United States District Court for the Western District of Pennsylvania
    Abbreviation: (W.D. Pa. year)

United States District Court for the District of Puerto Rico
    Abbreviation: (D.P.R. year)

United States District Court for the District of Rhode Island
    Abbreviation: (D.R.I. year)

United States District Court for the District of South Carolina
    Abbreviation: (D.S.C. year)

United States District Court for the District of South Dakota
    Abbreviation: (D.S.D. year)

United States District Court for the Eastern District of Tennessee
    Abbreviation: (E.D. Tenn. year)

United States District Court for the Middle District of Tennessee
    Abbreviation: (M.D. Tenn. year)

United States District Court for the Western District of Tennessee
    Abbreviation: (W.D. Tenn. year)

United States District Court for the Eastern District of Texas
    Abbreviation: (E.D. Tex. year)

United States District Court for the Northern District of Texas
    Abbreviation: (N.D. Tex. year)

United States District Court for the Southern District of Texas
    Abbreviation: (S.D. Tex. year)

United States District Court for the Western District of Texas
    Abbreviation: (W.D. Tex. year)

United States District Court for the District of Utah
    Abbreviation: (D. Utah year)

In law review footnotes, the following are in large and small capitals: periodicals, constitutions, codes, restatements, standards, authors of books, titles of books, and legislative materials except for bills and resolutions. Refer to Bluebook.

United States District Court for the District of Vermont
        Abbreviation: (D. Vt. year)

United States District Court for the District of the Virgin Islands
        Abbreviation: (D.V.I. year)

United States District Court for the Eastern District of Virginia
        Abbreviation: (E.D. Va. year)

United States District Court for the Western District of Virginia
        Abbreviation: (W.D. Va. year)

United States District Court for the Eastern District of Washington
        Abbreviation: (E.D. Wash. year)

United States District Court for the Western District of Washington
        Abbreviation: (W.D. Wash. year)

United States District Court for the Northern District of West Virginia
        Abbreviation: (N.D.W. Va. year)

United States District Court for the Southern District of West Virginia
        Abbreviation: (S.D.W. Va. year)

United States District Court for the Eastern District of Wisconsin
        Abbreviation: (E.D. Wis. year)

United States District Court for the Western District of Wisconsin
        Abbreviation: (W.D. Wis. year)

United States District Court for the District of Wyoming
        Abbreviation: (D. Wyo. year)

United States Federal Communications Commission Reports
        See   Federal Communications Commission Reports

United States Federal Power Commission Reports
        See   Federal Power Commission Reports

United States Federal Reserve Bulletin
        See   Federal Reserve Bulletin

United States Federal Trade Commission Decisions
        See   Federal Trade Commission Decisions

In law review footnotes, the titles of books and the names of cases are not underlined.

United States Interstate Commerce Commission, Motor Carrier Cases
    See   Interstate Commerce Commission, Motor Carrier Cases

United States Interstate Commerce Commission Reports
    See   Interstate Commerce Commission Reports

United States Interstate Commerce Commission, Valuation Reports
    See   Interstate Commerce Commission, Valuation Reports

United States Law Week (Bureau of National Affairs)
    Abbreviation: U.S.L.W.

    Examples: Rowan Co., v. United States, 49 U.S.L.W. 4646 (U.S. June 8, 1981).
    ——Cite to looseleaf only until case is available in United States Reports
    or Supreme Court Reporter.

    National Football League v. North American Soccer League, 670 F.2d
    1249 (2d Cir. 1982), petition for cert. filed, 50 U.S.L.W. 3998.04
    (U.S. June 15, 1982) (No. 81-2296).

    Schweiker, v. Campbell, 665 F.2d 48 (2d Cir. 1981), cert. granted, 50
    U.S.L.W. 3998.01 (U.S. June 21, 1982) (No. 81-1983).

    United States v. Sharpe, 50 U.S.L.W. 3998 (U.S. June 21, 1982),
    vacating 660 F.2d 967 (4th Cir. 1981).

    United States v. Goodwin, 50 U.S.L.W. 4696 (U.S. June 18, 1982).

United States Motor Carrier Cases
    See   Interstate Commerce Commission (U.S.), Motor Carrier Cases (U.S.)

United States National Labor Relations Board Decisions and Orders
    See   National Labor Relations Board Decisions and Orders (U.S.)

United States National Railroad Adjustment Board, 1st-4th Div.
    See   National Railroad Adjustment Board, 1st-4th Div. (U.S.) (1934-date)

United States National Transportation Safety Board Decisions
    See   National Transportation Safety Board Decisions (U.S.) (1967-date)

United States Official Opinions of the Solicitor for the Post Office Department
    See   Official Opinions of the Solicitor for the Post Office Department (1878-1951)

United States Opinions of the Attorney General
    See   Opinions of the Attorney General (U.S.) (1789-date)

United States Patents, Decisions of the Commissioner and of United States Courts
    See   Patents, Decisions of the Commissioner and of U.S. Courts (1869-date)

In law review footnotes, the following are in large and small capitals: periodicals, constitutions,
codes, restatements, standards, authors of books, titles of books, and legislative materials except
for bills and resolutions. Refer to Bluebook.

United States Patents Quarterly (Bureau of National Affairs)
    Abbreviation: U.S.P.Q. (BNA)

    Examples: In re Phillips and Crick, [Advance Sheets] U.S.P.Q. (BNA) (213
                 U.S.P.Q.) 353 (C.C.P.A. Mar. 25, 1982). ——Citation to looseleaf
                 material.

                 Miller v. Universal City Studios, Inc., 200 U.S.P.Q. (BNA) 232 (S.D.
                 Fla. 1978). ——Citation to bound material.

——The above examples are proper if the case is not yet available in an official or West
reporter, or is not reported in an official or West reporter.

United States Public Laws
    See Public Laws (U.S.)

United States Reports
    (91 U.S., 1875 to date)

    Abbreviation: U.S.

    Examples: Monroe v. Pape, 365 U.S. 167 (1961). ——Case Cite.

                 Monroe v. Pape, 365 U.S. 167, 181-82 (1961). ——Page Cite.

United States Reports
    (1 U.S. -90 U.S., pre-1875)

    Dallas (1790-1800):

    Abbreviation: Dall.

    Examples: The Eliza, 4 U.S. (4 Dall.) 32 (1800). ——Case Cite.

                 The Eliza, 4 U.S. (4 Dall.) 32, 38-39 (1800). ——Page Cite.

    Cranch (1801-1815):

    Abbreviation: Cranch

    Examples: Finley v. Williams, 13 U.S. (9 Cranch) 164 (1815). ——Case Cite.

                 Finley v. Williams, 13 U.S. (9 Cranch) 164, 167 (1815). ——Page
                 Cite.

    Wheaton (1816-1827):

    Abbreviation: Wheat.

    Examples: Janney v. Columbian Ins. Co., 23 U.S. (10 Wheat.) 409 (1825).
                 ——Case Cite.

                 Janney v. Columbian Ins. Co., 23 U.S. (10 Wheat.) 409, 416 (1825).
                 ——Page Cite.

    Peters (1828-1842):

    Abbreviation: Pet.

In law review footnotes, the titles of books and the names of cases are not underlined.

Examples: United States v. One Hundred and Twelve Casks of Sugar, 33 U.S. (8 Pet.) 275 (1834). ——Case Cite.

                United States v. One Hundred and Twelve Casks of Sugar, 33 U.S. (8 Pet.) 275, 279-80 (1834). ——Page Cite.

Howard (1843-1860):

Abbreviation: How.

Examples: Taylor v. Doe, 54 U.S. (13 How.) 287 (1851). ——Case Cite.

                Taylor v. Doe, 54 U.S. (13 How.) 287, 291 (1851). ——Page Cite.

Black (1861-1862):

Abbreviation: Black

Examples: Chicago City v. Robbins, 67 U.S. (2 Black) 418 (1862). ——Case Cite.

                Chicago City v. Robbins, 67 U.S. (2 Black) 418, 423 (1862). ——Page Cite.

Wallace (1863-1874):

Abbreviation: Wall.

Examples: Gaines v. Thompson, 74 U.S. (7 Wall.) 347 (1868). ——Case Cite.

                Gaines v. Thompson, 74 U.S. (7 Wall.) 347, 353 (1868). ——Page Cite.

United States Securities and Exchange Commission Decisions and Reports
    See   Securities and Exchange Commission Decisions and Reports

United States Statutes at Large
    See   Statutes at Large

United States Supreme Court Bulletin (Commerce Clearing House)
    Abbreviation: S. Ct. Bull. (CCH)

    Example: Ford Motor Credit Co. v. Gronce, 41 S. Ct. Bull. (CCH) B3008 (June 1, 1981).

    ——This is not a preferred source. Preferred sources are the United States Reports, Supreme Court Reporter, and United States Law Week. See Bluebook 173.

United States Supreme Court Reports
    See   Supreme Court Reporter

United States Supreme Court Reports, Lawyer's Edition
    ——According to Bluebook, this is not a preferred source. Preferred sources are the United States Reports, Supreme Court Reporter, and United States Law Week. See Bluebook 173.

    Abbreviation: L. Ed.

In law review footnotes, the following are in large and small capitals: periodicals, constitutions, codes, restatements, standards, authors of books, titles of books, and legislative materials except for bills and resolutions. Refer to Bluebook.

Examples: United States v. Di Re, 332 U.S. 581, 68 S. Ct. 222, 92 L. Ed. 210
                 (1948). ——Case Cite.

                 United States v. Di Re, 332 U.S. 581, 592, 68 S. Ct. 222, 227, 92 L.
                 Ed. 210, 219 (1948). ——Page Cite.

United States Supreme Court Reports, Lawyers' Edition, second series
     ——According to Bluebook, this is not a preferred source. Preferred sources are the
        United States Reports, Supreme Court Reporter, and United States Law Week. See
        Bluebook 173.

Abbreviation: L. Ed. 2d

Examples: International Brotherhood of Teamsters v. United States, 431 U.S. 324,
                 97 S. Ct. 1843, 52 L. Ed. 2d 396 (1977). ——Case Cite.

                 International Brotherhood of Teamsters v. United States, 431 U.S. 334,
                 336-37, 97 S. Ct. 1843, 1854-55, 52 L. Ed. 2d 396, 416 (1977).
                 ——Page Cite.

United States Supreme Court Rule
     Abbreviation: Sup. Ct. R.

Example: Sup. Ct. R. 6.

                 Sup. Ct. R. 8, 266 U.S. 658 (1925). ——Citation to a rule no longer in
                 force.

United States Treasury Decisions Under Internal Revenue Laws (1942)
     See   Treasury Decisions Under Internal Revenue Laws (1942) (U.S.)

United States Treasury Decisions Under Customs & Other Laws (1943-date)
     See   Treasury Decisions Under Customs & Other Laws (1943-date) (U.S.)

United States Treasury Department, Comptroller General's Opinion
     See   Comptroller General's Opinion (U.S. Treasury Department)

United States Treasury Regulations
     See   Treasury Regulations (U.S.)

United States Treaties and Other International Acts Series
     See   Treaties and Other International Acts Series (U.S.)

United States Treaties and Other International Agreements (1950-date)
     Abbreviation: U.S.T.

Examples: Convention on the High Seas, opened for signature April 29, 1958, 13
                 U.S.T. 2313, T.I.A.S. No. 5200, 450 U.N.T.S. 82.

                 Proclamation on Extradition, Feb. 12, 1970, United States-France, 22
                 U.S.T. 407, T.I.A.S. No. 7075.

In law review footnotes, the titles of books and the names of cases are not underlined.

Interim Agreement on the Limitation of Strategic Offensive Arms, May 26, 1972, United States—U.S.S.R., 23 U.S.T. 3462, T.I.A.S. No. 7504.

United States Treaty Series
See   Treaty Series (U.S.)

University of Akron Law Review
See   Akron Law Review

University of Alabama Law Review
See   Alabama Law Review

University of Arizona Law Review
See   Arizona Law Review

University of Arkansas Law Review
See   Arkansas Law Review

University of Arkansas at Little Rock Law Journal
Abbreviations: U. Ark. Little Rock L.J.
UALR L.J. (publisher's abbreviation)

Examples: Younger, The Facts of a Case, 3 U. Ark. Little Rock L.J. 345 (1980). ——Article Cite.

Younger, The Facts of a Case, 3 U. Ark. Little Rock L.J. 345, 349-52 (1980). ——Page Cite.

University of Baltimore Law Review
Abbreviation: U. Balt. L. Rev.

Examples: Lasson, Homosexual Rights: The Law in Flux and Conflict, 9 U. Balt. L. Rev. 47 (1979). ——Article Cite.

Lasson, Homosexual Rights: The Law in Flux and Conflict, 9 U. Balt. L. Rev. 47, 60-65 (1979). ——Page Cite.

University of Bridgeport Law Review
Abbreviation: U. Bridgeport L. Rev.

University of British Columbia Law Review
Abbreviation: U.B.C. L. Rev.

University of California Law Review
See   California Law Review

In law review footnotes, the following are in large and small capitals: periodicals, constitutions, codes, restatements, standards, authors of books, titles of books, and legislative materials except for bills and resolutions. Refer to Bluebook.

University of Chicago Law Review
    Abbreviation: U. Chi. L. Rev.

    Examples: Wright, Color-Blind Theories and Color-Conscious Remedies, 47 U.
    Chi. L. Rev. 213 (1980). ——Article Cite.

    Wright, Color-Blind Theories and Color-Conscious Remedies, 47 U.
    Chi. L. Rev. 213, 216-19 (1980). ——Page Cite.

University of Cincinnati Law Review
    Abbreviation: U. Cin. L. Rev.

    Examples: Van Geel, Racial Discrimination from Little Rock to Harvard, 49 U.
    Cin. L. Rev. 49 (1980). ——Article Cite.

    Van Geel, Racial Discrimination from Little Rock to Harvard, 49 U.
    Cin. L. Rev. 49, 60-65 (1980). ——Page Cite.

University of Colorado Law Review
    Abbreviation: U. Colo. L. Rev.

    Examples: Wesson, Mens Rea and the Colorado Criminal Code, 52 U. Colo. L.
    Rev. 167 (1981). ——Article Cite.

    Wesson, Mens Rea and the Colorado Criminal Code, 52 U. Colo. L.
    Rev. 167, 210-15 (1981). ——Page Cite.

University of Connecticut Law Review
    See   Connecticut Law Review

University of Dayton Law Review
    Abbreviation: U. Dayton L. Rev.

    Examples: Richardson, Lawyers, Law and Civilization, 5 U. Dayton L. Rev. 1
    (1980). ——Article Cite.

    Richardson, Lawyers, Law and Civilization, 5 U. Dayton L. Rev. 1, 3-
    5 (1980). ——Page Cite.

University of Denver Law Journal
    See   Denver Law Journal

University of Detroit Journal of Urban Law
    Abbreviation: U. Det. J. Urb. L.

    Examples: Millspaugh, Eminent Domain: The Emerging Government/Business
    Interface, 59 U. Det. J. Urb. L. 167 (1982). ——Article Cite.

    Millspaugh, Eminent Domain: The Emerging Government/Business
    Interface, 59 U. Det. J. Urb. L. 167, 174-75 (1982). ——Page Cite.

University of Detroit Law Journal
    Abbreviation: U. Det. L.J.

In law review footnotes, the titles of books and the names of cases are not underlined.

University of Florida Law Review
    Abbreviation: U. Fla. L. Rev.

    Examples: Bostick, The Revocable Trust: A Means of Avoiding Probate in the Small Estate, 21 U. Fla. L. Rev. 44 (1968). ——Article Cite.

                     Bostick, The Revocable Trust: A Means of Avoiding Probate in the Small Estate, 21 U. Fla. L. Rev. 44, 51-56 (1968). ——Page Cite.

University of Georgia Law Review
    See   Georgia Law Review

University of Hawaii Law Review
    Abbreviation: U. Haw. L. Rev.

    Examples: Miller, The Scope of Liability for Negligent Infliction of Emotional Distress: Making "the Punishment Fit the Crime", 1 U. Haw. L. Rev. 1 (1979). ——Article Cite.

                     Miller, The Scope of Liability for Negligent Infliction of Emotional Distress: Making "the Punishment Fit the Crime", 1 U. Haw. L. Rev. 1, 3-9 (1979). ——Page Cite.

University of Houston Law Review
    See   Houston Law Review

University of Idaho Law Review
    See   Idaho Law Review

University of Illinois Law Forum
    Abbreviation: U. Ill. L.F.

    Examples: Sullivan, New Perspectives in Antitrust Litigation: Towards a Right of Comparative Contribution, 1980 U. Ill. L.F. 389. ——Article Cite.

                     Sullivan, New Perspectives in Antitrust Litigation: Towards a Right of Comparative Contribution, 1980 U. Ill. L.F. 389, 392-96. ——Page Cite.

University of Illinois Law Review
    Abbreviation: U. Ill. L. Rev.

University of Iowa Law Review
    See   Iowa Law Review

University of Kansas Law Review
    Abbreviation: U. Kan. L. Rev.

    Examples: Menninger, The Right to the Least Restrictive Sentence, 28 U. Kan. L. Rev. 553 (1980). ——Article Cite.

In law review footnotes, the following are in large and small capitals: periodicals, constitutions, codes, restatements, standards, authors of books, titles of books, and legislative materials except for bills and resolutions. Refer to Bluebook.

Menninger, <u>The Right to the Least Restrictive Sentence</u>, 28 U. Kan. L. Rev. 553, 554-58 (1980). ——Page Cite.

University of Kentucky Law Review
 <u>See</u>   Kentucky Law Journal

University of Louisville Journal of Family Law
 <u>See</u>   Journal of Family Law

University of Maine Law Review
 <u>See</u>   Maine Law Review

University of Maryland Law Review
 <u>See</u>   Maryland Law Review

University of Miami Law Review
 Abbreviation: U. Miami L. Rev.

 Examples: Younger, <u>In Search of Premises</u>, 34 U. Miami L. Rev. 807 (1980). ——Article Cite.

 Younger, <u>In Search of Premises</u>, 34 U. Miami L. Rev. 807, 814-17 (1980). ——Page Cite.

University of Michigan Journal of Law Reform
 Abbreviation: U. Mich. J.L. Ref.

 Examples: Smith, <u>The Monopoly Component of Inflation in Food Prices</u>, 14 U. Mich. J.L. Ref. 149 (1981). ——Article Cite.

 Smith, <u>The Monopoly Component of Inflation in Food Prices</u>, 14 U. Mich. J.L. Ref. 149, 151-53 (1981). ——Page Cite.

University of Michigan Law Review
 <u>See</u>   Michigan Law Review

University of Minnesota Law Review
 <u>See</u>   Minnesota Law Review

University of Mississippi Law Journal
 <u>See</u>   Mississippi Law Journal

University of Missouri-Kansas City Law Review
 <u>See</u>   UMKC Law Review

University of Missouri Law Review
 <u>See</u>   Missouri Law Review

In law review footnotes, the titles of books and the names of cases are not underlined.

University of Montana Law Review
    See   Montana Law Review

University of Nebraska Law Review
    See   Nebraska Law Review

University of New Brunswick Law Journal
    Abbreviation: U.N.B.L.J.

University of New Mexico Law Review
    See   New Mexico Law Review

University of New South Wales Law Journal
    Abbreviation: U.N.S.W.L.J.

    Examples: Lansdowne, Domestic Violence and the New South Wales Legislation, 8 U.N.S.W.L.J. 80 (1985). ——Article Cite.

                       Lansdowne, Domestic Violence and the New South Wales Legislation, 8 U.N.S.W.L.J. 80, 94-95 (1985). ——Page Cite.

University of North Carolina Law Review
    See   North Carolina Law Review

University of North Dakota Law Review
    See   North Dakota Law Review

University of Queensland Law Journal
    Abbreviation: U. Queensl. L.J.

    Examples: Gibbs, Developments in the Jurisdiction of Federal Courts, U. Queensl. L.J., Dec. 1981, at 3. ——Article Cite.

                       Gibbs, Developments in the Jurisdiction of Federal Courts, U. Queensl. L.J., Dec. 1981, at 3, 9-11. ——Page Cite.

University of Oklahoma Law Review
    See   Oklahoma Law Review

University of Oregon Law Review
    See   Oregon Law Review

University of Pennsylvania Journal of International Business Law
    Abbreviation: U. Pa. J. Int'l Bus. L.

University of Pennsylvania Law Review
    Abbreviation: U. Pa. L. Rev.

In law review footnotes, the following are in large and small capitals: periodicals, constitutions, codes, restatements, standards, authors of books, titles of books, and legislative materials except for bills and resolutions. Refer to Bluebook.

Examples: Schulhofer, <u>Due Process of Sentencing</u>, 128 U. Pa. L. Rev. 733 (1980).
——Article Cite.

Schulhofer, <u>Due Process of Sentencing</u>, 128 U. Pa. L. Rev. 733, 743-48
(1980). ——Page Cite.

University of Pittsburgh Law Review
Abbreviation: U. Pitt. L. Rev.

Examples: Milhollin, <u>Long-Term Liability for Environmental Harm</u>, 41 U. Pitt. L.
Rev. 1 (1979). ——Article Cite.

Milhollin, <u>Long-Term Liability for Environmental Harm</u>, 41 U. Pitt. L.
Rev. 1, 12-16 (1979). ——Page Cite.

University of Puget Sound Law Review
Abbreviation: U. Puget Sound L. Rev.

Examples: Jackson, <u>The Pacific Northwest Electric Power Planning and
Conservation Act—Solution for a Regional Dilemma</u>, 4 U. Puget Sound
L. Rev. 7 (1980). ——Article Cite.

Jackson, <u>The Pacific Northwest Electric Power Planning and
Conservation Act—Solution for a Regional Dilemma</u>, 4 U. Puget Sound
L. Rev. 7, 10-13 (1980). ——Page Cite.

University of Richmond Law Review
Abbreviation: U. Rich. L. Rev.

Examples: Austin, <u>The Legality of Ticket Tie-Ins in Intercollegiate Athletics</u>, 15
U. Rich. L. Rev. 1 (1980). ——Article Cite.

Austin, <u>The Legality of Ticket Tie-Ins in Intercollegiate Athletics</u>, 15
U. Rich. L. Rev. 1, 13-17 (1980). ——Page Cite.

University of San Diego Law Review
<u>See</u>   San Diego Law Review

University of San Francisco Law Review
Abbreviation: U.S.F. L. Rev.

Examples: Kessenick & Peer, <u>Physicians' Access to the Hospital: An Overview</u>, 14
U.S.F. L. Rev. 43 (1980). ——Article Cite.

Kessenick & Peer, <u>Physicians' Access to the Hospital: An Overview</u>, 14
U.S.F. L. Rev. 43, 47-52 (1980). ——Page Cite.

University of Santa Clara Law Review
<u>See</u>   Santa Clara Law Review

University of South Carolina Law Review
<u>See</u>   South Carolina Law Review

In law review footnotes, the titles of books and the names of cases are not underlined.

University of South Dakota Law Review
    See   South Dakota Law Review

University of Southern California Tax Institute
    See   Southern California Tax Institute

University of Tasmania Law Review
    Abbreviation: U. Tas. L. Rev.

University of Tennessee Law Review
    See   Tennessee Law Review

University of Texas Law Review
    See   Texas Law Review

University of the Pacific Law Journal
    See   Pacific Law Journal

University of Toledo Law Review
    Abbreviation: U. Tol. L. Rev.

    Examples: Kawalski, Penal Transfer Treaties and the Application of
        "Unconstitutional Conditions" Analysis, 12 U. Tol. L. Rev. 1 (1980).
        ——Article Cite.

        Kawalski, Penal Transfer Treaties and the Application of
        "Unconstitutional Conditions" Analysis, 12 U. Tol. L. Rev. 1, 3-8
        (1980). ——Page Cite.

University of Toronto Faculty of Law Review
    Abbreviations: U. Toronto Fac. L. Rev.
                   U.T. Fac. L. Rev. (publisher's abbreviation)

University of Toronto Law Journal
    Abbreviation: U. Toronto L.J.

University of Tulsa Law Journal
    See   Tulsa Law Journal

University of Utah Law Review
    See   Utah Law Review

University of Virginia Law Review
    See   Virginia Law Review

In law review footnotes, the following are in large and small capitals: periodicals, constitutions, codes, restatements, standards, authors of books, titles of books, and legislative materials except for bills and resolutions. Refer to Bluebook.

University of Washington Law Quarterly
  <u>See</u> Washington University Law Quarterly

University of West Los Angeles Law Review
  Abbreviation: U. West L.A. L. Rev.

  Examples: Douglas, <u>The First Amendment and the Electronic Press</u>, 10 U. West
       L.A. L. Rev. 123 (1978). ——Article Cite.

       Douglas, <u>The First Amendment and the Electronic Press</u>, 10 U. West
       L.A. L. Rev. 123, 125-30 (1978). ——Page Cite.

University of Western Australia Law Review
  Abbreviations: U. W. Austl. L. Rev.
        U.W.A. L. Rev. (publisher's abbreviation)

  Examples: Flick, <u>Error of Law or Error of Fact?</u>, 15 U. W. Austl. L. Rev. 193
       (1983). ——Article Cite.

       Flick, <u>Error of Law or Error of Fact?</u>, 15 U. W. Austl. L. Rev. 193,
       201 (1983). ——Page Cite.

University of Wisconsin Law Review
  <u>See</u> Wisconsin Law Review

University of Wyoming Law Review
  <u>See</u> Land and Water Law Review

unpublished materials
  ——Well explained and illustrated in Bluebook Rule 15.5.2.

unreported cases
  <u>See</u> pending and unreported cases

Urban Affairs Reporter (Commerce Clearing House)
  Abbreviation: Urb. Aff. Rep. (CCH)

Urban Law and Policy
  Abbreviation: Urb. L. & Pol'y

Urban Law Review
  Abbreviation: Urb. L. Rev.

  Examples: Kennedy & Graffeo, <u>A National Energy Plan—Or What?</u>, 2 Urb. L.
       Rev. 17 (1977-1978). ——Article Cite.

       Kennedy & Graffeo, <u>A National Energy Plan—Or What?</u>, 2 Urb. L.
       Rev. 17, 22-23 (1977-1978). ——Page Cite.

In law review footnotes, the titles of books and the names of cases are not underlined.

Urban Lawyer

    Abbreviation: Urb. Law.

    Examples: Howe, <u>Code Enforcement in Three Cities: An Organizational Analysis</u>, 13 Urb. Law. 65 (1981). ——Article Cite.

        Howe, <u>Code Enforcement in Three Cities: An Organizational Analysis</u>, 13 Urb. Law. 65, 68 (1981). ——Page Cite.

Utah Administrative Rules

    <u>See</u>   Administrative Rules of the State of Utah and State of Utah Bulletin

Utah Bar Journal

    Abbreviation: Utah B.J.

Utah Bulletin

    Abbreviation: Utah Bull.

Utah Code Annotated

    Abbreviation: Utah Code Ann. §   (year).

    Examples: Utah Code Ann. § 31A-18-105 (1986).

        Utah Code Ann. § 40-8-9 (Supp. 1987).

Utah Constitution

    Abbreviation: Utah Const. art. , §   .

    Examples: Utah Const. art. I, § 7. ——Cite provisions without date unless the cited provisions have been repealed or amended (Bluebook Rule 11).

        Utah Const. art. VI, § 9 (1896, amended 1969). ——Cite provisions which have been repealed or amended by giving the date of the adoption of the particular provision and the date of repeal or amendment (Bluebook Rule 11).

Utah Law Review

    Abbreviation: Utah L. Rev.

    Examples: Davis, <u>Administrative Common Law and the Vermont Yankee Opinion</u>, 1980 Utah L. Rev. 3. ——Article Cite.

        Davis, <u>Administrative Common Law and the Vermont Yankee Opinion</u>, 1980 Utah L. Rev. 3, 7-12. ——Page Cite.

Utah Reports

    Abbreviation: Utah

    Examples: <u>Holt v. Bayles</u>, 85 Utah 364, 39 P.2d 715 (1934). ——Case Cite.

        <u>Holt v. Bayles</u>, 85 Utah 364, 370, 39 P.2d 715, 717 (1934). ——Page Cite.

In law review footnotes, the following are in large and small capitals: periodicals, constitutions, codes, restatements, standards, authors of books, titles of books, and legislative materials except for bills and resolutions. Refer to Bluebook.

Utah Reports, second series
    Abbreviation: Utah 2d

——Discontinued after 30 Utah 2d 462 (1974). Therafter cite only to P.2d.

    Examples: Hobbs v. Fenton, 25 Utah 2d 206, 479 P.2d 472 (1971). ——Case Cite.

                  Hobbs v. Fenton, 25 Utah 2d 206, 209, 479 P.2d 472, 473-74 (1971). ——Page Cite.

——After 30 Utah 2d 462 (1974), cite as follows:

                  Haddon v. Haddon, 707 P.2d 669 (Utah 1985). ——Case Cite.

                  Haddon v. Haddon, 707 P.2d 669, 670 (Utah 1985). ——Page Cite.

Utah Session Laws
    See   Laws of Utah

Utilities Law Reports (Commerce Clearing House)
    Abbreviation: Util. Ł. Rep. (CCH)

In law review footnotes, the titles of books and the names of cases are not underlined.

V

Valparaiso University Law Review
Abbreviation: Val. U.L. Rev.

Examples: Ahrens & Hauserman, <u>Fundamental Election Rights: Association,</u> <u>Voting and Candidacy</u>, 14 Val. U.L. Rev. 465 (1980). ——Article Cite.

Ahrens & Hauserman, <u>Fundamental Election Rights: Association,</u> <u>Voting and Candidacy</u>, 14 Val. U.L. Rev. 465, 466-73 (1980). ——Page Cite.

Vanderbilt Journal of Transnational Law
Abbreviation: Vand. J. Transnat'l L.

Examples: Kavass & Christian, <u>The 1977 Soviet Constitution: A Historical</u> <u>Comparison</u>, 12 Vand. J. Transnat'l L. 533 (1979). ——Article Cite.

Kavass & Christian, <u>The 1977 Soviet Constitution: A Historical</u> <u>Comparison</u>, 12 Vand. J. Transnat'l L. 533, 592-96 (1979). ——Page Cite.

Vanderbilt Law Review
Abbreviation: Vand. L. Rev.

Examples: McCoy, <u>Current State Action Theories, the Jackson Nexus</u> <u>Requirement, and Employee Discharges by Semi-Public and State-Aided</u> <u>Institutions</u>, 31 Vand. L. Rev. 785 (1978). ——Article Cite.

McCoy, <u>Current State Action Theories, the Jackson Nexus</u> <u>Requirement, and Employee Discharges by Semi-Public and State-Aided</u> <u>Institutions</u>, 31 Vand. L. Rev. 785, 809-13 (1978). ——Page Cite.

Vermont Administrative Procedures Compilation
Abbreviation: Vt. Admin. Proc. Comp. [agency name] r. [or §] (year).

Vermont Administrative Procedures Bulletin
Abbreviation: Vt. Admin. Proc. Bull.

Vermont, Biennial Report of the Attorney General
<u>See</u> Biennial Report of the Attorney General of the State of Vermont

Vermont Constitution
Abbreviation: Vt. Const. ch. , § .

In law review footnotes, the following are in large and small capitals: periodicals, constitutions, codes, restatements, standards, authors of books, titles of books, and legislative materials except for bills and resolutions. Refer to Bluebook.

Examples: Vt. Const. ch. II, § 1. ——Cite provisions without date unless the cited
                   provisions have been repealed or amended (Bluebook Rule 11).

                   Vt. Const. ch. II, § 53 (1973, amended 1870). ——Cite provisions
                   which have been repealed or amended by giving the date of the adoption
                   of the particular provision and the date of repeal or amendment
                   (Bluebook Rule 11).

                   Vt. Const. of 1777, ch. I. ——Cite Constitutions that have been totally
                   superseded by year of adoption, giving parenthetically the year of
                   adoption of the specific provision cited if different (Bluebook Rule 11).

Vermont Law Review
        Abbreviation: Vt. L. Rev.

        Examples: Freeman, The Negotiating Impasse in Labor Relations for Teachers, 5
                           Vt. L. Rev. 39 (1980). ——Article Cite.

                           Freeman, The Negotiating Impasse in Labor Relations for Teachers, 5
                           Vt. L. Rev. 39, 45-50 (1980). ——Page Cite.

Vermont Reports
        Abbreviation: Vt.

        Examples: Whipple v. Lambert, 145 Vt. 339, 488 A.2d 439 (1985). ——Case
                           Cite.

                           Whipple v. Lambert, 145 Vt. 339, 343, 488 A.2d 439, 441 (1985).
                           ——Page Cite.

Vermont Session Laws
        See   Laws of Vermont

Vermont Statutes Annotated
        Abbreviation: Vt. Stat. Ann. tit.   , §   (year).

        Examples: Vt. Stat. Ann. tit. 32, § 3803 (1981).

                           Vt. Stat. Ann. tit. 32, § 5079 (Supp. 1987).

Vernon's Annotated Missouri Statutes
        Abbreviation: Mo. Ann. Stat. §   (Vernon year)

        Examples: Mo. Ann. Stat. § 569.160 (Vernon (1979).

                           Mo. Ann. Stat. § 193.145 (Vernon Supp. 1988).

Vernon's Annotated Revised Civil Statutes of the State of Texas
        Abbreviation: Tex. Rev. Civ. Stat. Ann. art. (Vernon year).

        Example: Tex. Rev. Civ. Stat. Ann. art. 5206 (Vernon 1987).

In law review footnotes, the titles of books and the names of cases are not underlined.

Vernon's Kansas Statutes Annotated
  Abbreviation: Kan. subject Ann. § (Vernon year).

——See Bluebook page 188 for the abbreviation of each subject.

  Examples: Kan. U.C.C. Ann. § 84-6-102 (Vernon 1968).

  Kan. U.C.C. Ann. § 84-6-106 (Vernon Supp. 1986).

Vernon's Texas Codes Annotated
  ——See pages 212-13 of the Bluebook for the abbreviation of each subject

  Abbreviation: Tex. subject Code Ann. § (Vernon year).

  Examples: Tex. Educ. Code Ann. § 17.01 (Vernon 1972).

  Tex. Fam. Code Ann. § 4.031 (Vernon Supp. 1988).

Vice Chancellor
  Abbreviation: V.C.

Victoria University of Wellington Law Review
  Abbreviation: Vict. U. Wellington L. Rev.

  Examples: Keith, The Courts and the Constitution, 15 Vict. U. Wellington L. Rev. 29 (1985). ——Article Cite.

  Keith, The Courts and the Constitution, 15 Vict. U. Wellington L. Rev. 29, 37-38 (1985). ——Page Cite.

Villanova Law Review
  Abbreviation: Vill. L. Rev.

  Examples: Cirace, Five Conflicts over Income Distribution in the Motion Picture-Television Industry, 25 Vill. L. Rev. 417 (1980). ——Article Cite.

  Cirace, Five Conflicts over Income Distribution in the Motion Picture-Television Industry, 25 Vill. L. Rev. 417, 421-27 (1980). ——Page Cite.

Virgin Islands Code Annotated
  Abbreviation: V.I. Code Ann. tit. , §   (year).

  Examples: V.I. Code Ann. tit. 22, § 563 (1970).

  V.I. Code Ann. tit. 23, § 1128 (Supp. 1985).

Virgin Islands Reports
  Abbreviation: V.I.

  Examples: Vidal v. Virgin Islands Housing Auth., 20 V.I. 3 (Terr. Ct. 1983). ——Case Cite.

  Vidal v. Virgin Islands Housing Auth., 20 V.I. 3, 5 (Terr. Ct. 1983). ——Page Cite.

In law review footnotes, the following are in large and small capitals: periodicals, constitutions, codes, restatements, standards, authors of books, titles of books, and legislative materials except for bills and resolutions. Refer to Bluebook.

Virginia Bar Association Journal
    Abbreviation: Va. B.A.J.

Virginia Circuit Court Opinions
    Abbreviation: Va. Cir.

    Examples: Todd v. Todd, 1 Va. Cir. 350 (Cir. Ct. 1983). ——Case Cite.

                  Todd v. Todd, 1 Va. Cir. 350, 352 (Cir. Ct. 1983). ——Page Cite.

Virginia Code
    See   Code of Virginia

Virginia Constitution
    Abbreviation: Va. Const. art. , § .

    Examples: Va. Const. art. I, § 9. ——Cite provisions without date unless the cited provisions have been repealed or amended (Bluebook Rule 11).

                  Va. Const. art. X, § 6 (1971, amended 1978). ——Cite provisions which have been repealed or amended by giving the date of the adoption of the particular provision and the date of repeal or amendment (Bluebook Rule 11).

Virginia Court of Appeals Reports
    Abbreviation: Va. App.

    Examples: Goodwin v. Commonwelath, 3 Va. App. 249, 349 S.E.2d 161 (1986). ——Case Cite.

                  Goodwin v. Commonwelath, 3 Va. App. 249, 257, 349 S.E.2d 161, 166 (1986). ——Page Cite.

Virginia Journal of International Law
    Abbreviation: Va. J. Int'l L.

    Examples: Reese, The Hague Convention on Celebration and Recognition of the Validity of Marriages, 20 Va. J. Int'l L. 25 (1979). ——Article Cite.

                  Reese, The Hague Convention on Celebration and Recognition of the Validity of Marriages, 20 Va. J. Int'l L. 25, 31-34 (1979). ——Page Cite.

Virginia Journal of Natural Resources Law
    Abbreviation: Va. J. Nat. Resources L.

    Examples: Watkiss, Utility Diversification and Federal Rate Regulation of Inter-Affiliate Transactions, 2 Va. J. Nat. Resources L. 1 (1982). ——Article Cite.

                  Watkiss, Utility Diversification and Federal Rate Regulation of Inter-Affiliate Transactions, 2 Va. J. Nat. Resources L. 1, 22-23 (1982). ——Page Cite.

In law review footnotes, the titles of books and the names of cases are not underlined.

Virginia Law Register, new series
     Abbreviation: Va. L. Reg. (n.s.)

Virginia Law Review
     Abbreviation: Va. L. Rev.

     Examples: Schwartz, Options in Constructing a Sentencing System: Sentencing Guidelines Under Legislative or Judicial Hegemony, 67 Va. L. Rev. 637 (1981). ——Article Cite.

                Schwartz, Options in Constructing a Sentencing System: Sentencing Guidelines Under Legislative or Judicial Hegemony, 67 Va. L. Rev. 637, 648-55 (1981). ——Page Cite.

Virginia Opinions of the Attorney General and Report to the Governor
     See   Opinions of the Attorney General and Report to the Governor of Virginia

Virginia Register of Regulations
     Abbreviation: Va. Regs. Reg.

Virginia Reports
     Abbreviation: Va.

     Examples: White v. Pleasants, 227 Va. 508, 317 S.E.2d 489 (1984). ——Case Cite.

                White v. Pleasants, 227 Va. 508, 511, 317 S.E.2d 489, 491 (1984). ——Page Cite.

Virginia Session Laws
     See   Acts of the General Assembly of the Commonwealth of Virginia

Virginia Tax Review
     Abbreviation: Va. Tax Rev.

volume(s)
     Abbreviations: vol., vols.

In law review footnotes, the following are in large and small capitals: periodicals, constitutions, codes, restatements, standards, authors of books, titles of books, and legislative materials except for bills and resolutions. Refer to Bluebook.

In law review footnotes, the titles of books and the names of cases are not underlined.

W

Wage and Hour Cases (Bureau of National Affairs)
    Abbreviation: Wage and Hour Cas. (BNA)

Wage-Price Law and Economics Review
    Abbreviation: Wage-Price L. & Econ. Rev.

Wake Forest Law Review
    Abbreviation: Wake Forest L. Rev.

    Examples: Divine, Parole Release and Due Process, 11 Wake Forest L. Rev. 641
    (1975). ——Article Cite.

        Divine, Parole Release and Due Process, 11 Wake Forest L. Rev. 641,
        645-50 (1975). ——Page Cite.

Wallace (United States Reports)
    See   United States Reports

Washburn Law Journal
    Abbreviation: Washburn L.J.

    Examples: Smoot & Clothier, Open Meetings Profile: The Prosecutor's View, 20
    Washburn L.J. 241 (1981). ——Article Cite.

        Smoot & Clothier, Open Meetings Profile: The Prosecutor's View, 20
        Washburn L.J. 241, 243-49 (1981). ——Page Cite.

Washington Administrative Code
    Abbreviations: Wash. Admin. Code §   (year).

Washington and Lee Law Review
    Abbreviation: Wash. & Lee L. Rev.

    Examples: Sherrard, Federal Judicial and Regulatory Responses to Sante Fe
    Industries, Inc. v. Green, 35 Wash. & Lee L. Rev. 695 (1978).
    ——Article Cite.

        Sherrard, Federal Judicial and Regulatory Responses to Sante Fe
        Industries, Inc. v. Green, 35 Wash. & Lee L. Rev. 695, 698-703
        (1978). ——Page Cite.

Washington Appellate Reports
    Abbreviation: Wash. App.

In law review footnotes, the following are in large and small capitals: periodicals, constitutions, codes, restatements, standards, authors of books, titles of books, and legislative materials except for bills and resolutions. Refer to Bluebook.

Examples: Heim v. Longview Fibre Co., 41 Wash. App. 745, 707 P.2d 689
                 (1985). ——Case Cite.

                 Heim v. Longview Fibre Co., 41 Wash. App. 745, 749, 707 P.2d 689,
                 692 (1985). ——Page Cite.

Washington Bar News
Abbreviation: Wash. B. News

Examples: Schwartz, Federal Grand Jury Practice for the Business Practitioner,
                 Wash. B. News, Mar. 1986, at 27. ——Article Cite.

                 Schwartz, Federal Grand Jury Practice for the Business Practitioner,
                 Wash. B. News, Mar. 1986, at 27, 28. ——Page Cite.

Washington Constitution
Abbreviation: Wash. Const. art. , §   .

Examples: Wash. Const. art. I, § 9. ——Cite provisions without date unless the
                 cited provisions have been repealed or amended (Bluebook Rule 11).

                 Wash. Const. art. III, § 20 (1889, repealed 1948). ——Cite provisions
                 which have been repealed or amended by giving the date of the adoption
                 of the particular provision and the date of repeal or amendment
                 (Bluebook Rule 11).

Washington Law Review
Abbreviation: Wash. L. Rev.

Examples: Loh, The Impact of Common Law and Reform Rape Statutes on
                 Prosecution: An Empirical Study, 55 Wash. L. Rev. 543 (1980).
                 ——Article Cite.

                 Loh, The Impact of Common Law and Reform Rape Statutes on
                 Prosecution: An Empirical Study, 55 Wash. L. Rev. 543, 547-54
                 (1980). ——Page Cite.

Washington Legislative Service (West)
Abbreviation: year Wash. Legis. Serv.   (West)

Washington, Opinions of the Office of the Attorney General
See   Office of the Attorney General (State of Washington)--Opinions

Washington Reports
Abbreviation: Wash.

Examples: State ex rel. Murphy v. Taylor, 101 Wash. 148, 172 P. 217 (1918).
                 ——Case Cite.

                 State ex rel. Murphy v. Taylor, 101 Wash. 148, 156, 172 P. 217, 219
                 (1918). ——Page Cite.

In law review footnotes, the titles of books and the names of cases are not underlined.

Washington Reports, second series
    Abbreviation: Wash. 2d

    Examples: Gammon v. Clark Equip. Co., 104 Wash. 2d 613, 707 P.2d 685 (1985).
                ——Case Cite.

                Gammon v. Clark Equip. Co., 104 Wash. 2d 613, 616, 707 P.2d 685,
                687 (1985). ——Page Cite.

Washington Revised Code
    See   Revised Code of Washington

Washington Revised Code Annotated
    See   Revised Code of Washington Annotated

Washington Session Laws
    See   Laws of Washington and Washington Legislative Service

Washington State Register
    Abbreviation: Wash. St. Reg.

Washington Territory Reports
    Abbreviation: Wash. Terr.

Washington University Journal of Urban and Contemporary Law
    Abbreviation: Wash. U.J. Urb. & Contemp. L.

    Examples: Berger, Anarchy Reigns Supreme, 29 Wash. U.J. Urb. & Contemp. L.
                39 (1985). ——Article Cite.

                Berger, Anarchy Reigns Supreme, 29 Wash. U.J. Urb. & Contemp. L.
                39, 45-46 (1985). ——Page Cite.

Washington University Law Quarterly
    Abbreviation: Wash. U.L.Q.

    Examples: Stewart & Roberts, Viability of the Antitrust Per Se Illegality Rule:
                Schwinn Down, How Many to Go?, 58 Wash. U.L.Q. 727 (1980).
                ——Article Cite.

                Stewart & Roberts, Viability of the Antitrust Per Se Illegality Rule:
                Schwinn Down, How Many to Go?, 58 Wash. U.L.Q. 727, 733-38
                (1980). ——Page Cite.

Wayne Law Review
    Abbreviation: Wayne L. Rev.

    Examples: Bridgesmith, Representing the Title VII Class Action: A Question of
                Degree, 26 Wayne L. Rev. 1413 (1980). ——Article Cite.

In law review footnotes, the following are in large and small capitals: periodicals, constitutions, codes, restatements, standards, authors of books, titles of books, and legislative materials except for bills and resolutions. Refer to Bluebook.

Bridgesmith, <u>Representing the Title VII Class Action: A Question of Degree</u>, 26 Wayne L. Rev. 1413, 1415-19 (1980). ——Page Cite.

Weekly Compilation of Presidential Documents
    Abbreviation: Weekly Comp. Pres. Doc.

    Example: <u>Remarks at the 53rd Annual Academy Awards Presentation Ceremonies</u>, 17 Weekly Comp. Pres. Doc. 377 (Mar. 31, 1981).

Weinstein's Evidence, by Jack B. Weinstein and Margaret A. Berger
    ——Do not abbreviate the title.

    Examples: 3 J. Weinstein & M. Berger, <u>Weinstein's Evidence</u> ¶ 607[04] (1987).

                 1 J. Weinstein & M. Berger, <u>Weinstein's Evidence</u> ¶ 607[04], at 607-61 (1987).

West Virginia, Biennial Report & Official Opinions of the Attorney General
    <u>See</u>   Biennial Report & Official Opinions of the Attorney General of the State of West Virginia

West Virginia Code
    Abbreviation: W. Va. Code §   (year).

    Examples: W. Va. Code § 20-5C-2 (1985).

                 W. Va. Code § 24-2-4a (Supp. 1987).

West Virginia Constitution
    Abbreviation: W. Va. Const. art.   , §   .

    Examples: W. Va. Const. art. III, § 5. ——Cite provisions without date unless the cited provisions have been repealed or amended (Bluebook Rule 11).

                 W. Va. Const. art. X, § 1 (1872, amended 1932). ——Cite provisions which have been repealed or amended by giving the date of the adoption of the particular provision and the date of repeal or amendment (Bluebook Rule 11).

West Virginia Criminal Justice Review
    Abbreviation: W. Va. Crim. Just. Rev.

West Virginia Law Review
    Abbreviation: W. Va. L. Rev.

    Examples: Elkins, <u>Legal Representation of the Mentally Ill</u>, 82 W. Va. L. Rev. 157 (1979). ——Article Cite.

                 Elkins, <u>Legal Representation of the Mentally Ill</u>, 82 W. Va. L. Rev. 157, 170-75 (1979). ——Page Cite.

In law review footnotes, the titles of books and the names of cases are not underlined.

West Virginia Reports
    Abbreviation: W. Va.

    Examples: Peremba v. Peremba, 163 W. Va. 741, 206 S.E.2d 289 (1979).
               ——Case Cite.

               Peremba v. Peremba, 163 W. Va. 741, 742, 206 S.E.2d 289, 290
               (1979). ——Page Cite.

West Virginia Session Laws
    See   Acts of the Legislature of West Virginia

West Virginia State Bar Journal
    Abbreviation: W. Va. St. B.J.

    Examples: Herndon, Systemizing the Simple Will, 9 W. Va. St. B.J. 28 (1984).
               ——Article Cite.

               Herndon, Systemizing the Simple Will, 9 W. Va. St. B.J. 28, 35-36
               (1984). ——Page Cite.

West's Annotated California Codes
    Abbreviation: Cal. subject Code §   (West year).

    ——See pages 180 of the Bluebook for the abbreviations of each subject.

    Examples: Cal. Civ. Proc. Code § 1879 (West 1983).

               Cal. Evid. Code § 605 (West Supp. 1988).

West's Annotated Indiana Code
    Abbreviation: Ind. Code Ann. §   (West year).

West's California Reporter
    Abbreviation: Cal. Rptr.

    Examples: People v. Memro, 38 Cal. 3d 658, 700 P.2d 446, 214 Cal. Rptr. 832
               (1985). ——Case Cite.

               People v. Memro, 38 Cal. 3d 658, 661-62, 700 P.2d 446, 448-49, 214
               Cal. Rptr. 832, 834-35 (1985). ——Page Cite.

West's Louisiana Civil Code Annotated
    Abbreviation: La. Civ. Code Ann. art.   (West year).

    Example: La. Civ. Code Ann. art. 2043 (West 1987).

West's Louisiana Code of Civil Procedure Annotated
    Abbreviation: La. Code Civ. Proc. Ann. art.   (West year).

    Example: La. Code Civ. Proc. Ann. art. 2122 (West 1961).

In law review footnotes, the following are in large and small capitals: periodicals, constitutions, codes, restatements, standards, authors of books, titles of books, and legislative materials except for bills and resolutions. Refer to Bluebook.

West's Louisiana Code of Criminal Procedure Annotated
    Abbreviation: La. Code Crim. Proc. Ann. art. (West year).
    Example: La. Code Crim. Proc. Ann. art. 798 (West 1981).

West's Louisiana Code of Juvenile Procedure Annotated
    Abbreviation: La. Code Juv. Proc. Ann. art. (West year).
    Example: La. Code Juv. Proc. Ann. art. 67 (West 1988).

West's Louisiana Revised Statutes Annotated
    Abbreviation: La. Rev. Stat. Ann. § (West year).
    Examples: La. Rev. Stat. Ann. § 47:678 (West 1970).

                     La. Rev. Stat. Ann. § 47:462 (West Supp. 1988).

West's New York Supplement
    Abbreviation: N.Y.S.
    Examples: O'Hara v. Harman, 14 A.D. 167, 43 N.Y.S. 556 (1897). ——Case Cite.

                     O'Hara v. Harman, 14 A.D. 167, 172, 43 N.Y.S. 556, 559 (1897). ——Page Cite.

West's New York Supplement, second series
    Abbreviation: N.Y.S.2d
    Examples: Freihofer v. Hearst Corp., 65 N.Y.2d 135, 480 N.E.2d 349, 490 N.Y.S.2d 735 (1985). ——Case Cite.

                     Freihofer v. Hearst Corp., 65 N.Y.2d 135, 139, 480 N.E.2d 349, 352, 490 N.Y.S.2d 735, 738 (1985). ——Page Cite.

West's Wisconsin Statutes Annotated
    Abbreviation: Wis. Stat. Ann. § (West year).
    Examples: Wis. Stat. Ann. § 939.72 (West 1982).

                     Wis. Stat. Ann. § 940.22 (West Supp. 1987).

Western New England Law Review
    Abbreviation: W. New Eng. L. Rev.
    Examples: Note, Poirier v. Town of Plymouth, The Hidden Defect Rule, and New Patterns of Tort Law Reform in Massachusetts, 1 W. New Eng. L. Rev. 537 (1979). ——Article Cite.

                     Note, Poirier v. Town of Plymouth, The Hidden Defect Rule, and New Patterns of Tort Law Reform in Massachusetts, 1 W. New Eng. L. Rev. 537, 540-45 (1979). ——Page Cite.

In law review footnotes, the titles of books and the names of cases are not underlined.

Western State University Law Review
Abbreviation: W. St. U.L. Rev.

Examples: Gassel, Levy-Warren & Weiss, <u>Representing the Helpless: Toward an Ethical Guide for the Perplexed Attorney</u>, 5 W. St. U.L. Rev. 173 (1978). ——Article Cite.

Gassel, Levy-Warren & Weiss, <u>Representing the Helpless: Toward an Ethical Guide for the Perplexed Attorney</u>, 5 W. St. U.L. Rev. 173, 175-80 (1978). ——Page Cite.

Wharton's Criminal Procedure, by C. Torcia
——Do not abbreviate the title.

Examples: 3 C. Torcia, <u>Wharton's Criminal Procedure</u> § 410 (12th ed. 1975).

3 C. Torcia, <u>Wharton's Criminal Procedure</u> § 410, at 99 (12th ed. 1975).

Wheaton (United States Reports)
See   United States Reports

White and Summers on the UCC
See   Handbook of the Law Under the Uniform Commercial Code, by J. White & R. Summers

Whittier Law Review
Abbreviation: Whittier L. Rev.

Examples: Dizenfeld, <u>Advertising and the California Medical Professional</u>, 2 Whittier L. Rev. 61 (1979). ——Article Cite.

Dizenfeld, <u>Advertising and the California Medical Professional</u>, 2 Whittier L. Rev. 61, 70-74 (1979). ——Page Cite.

Wigmore on Evidence
See   Evidence in Trials at Common Law, by J. Wigmore

Willamette Law Journal
Abbreviation: Willamette L.J.

Examples: Cannon, <u>Double Jeopardy in Oregon</u>, 14 Willamette L.J. 21 (1977). ——Article Cite.

Cannon, <u>Double Jeopardy in Oregon</u>, 14 Willamette L.J. 21, 22-25 (1977). ——Page Cite.

Willamette Law Review
Abbreviation: Willamette L. Rev.

Examples: Bailey, <u>Deterrence and the Death Penalty for Murder in Oregon</u>, 16 Willamette L. Rev. 67 (1979). ——Article Cite.

In law review footnotes, the following are in large and small capitals: periodicals, constitutions, codes, restatements, standards, authors of books, titles of books, and legislative materials except for bills and resolutions. Refer to Bluebook.

Bailey, <u>Deterrence and the Death Penalty for Murder in Oregon</u>, 16 Willamette L. Rev. 67, 70-75 (1979). ——Page Cite.

William and Mary Review of Virginia Law
    Abbreviation: Wm. & Mary Rev. Va. L.

William & Mary Law Review
    Abbreviation: Wm. & Mary L. Rev.

    Examples: Richards, <u>Constitutional Privacy, the Right to Die and the Meaning of Life: A Moral Analysis</u>, 22 Wm. & Mary L. Rev. 327 (1981). ——Article Cite.

        Richards, <u>Constitutional Privacy, the Right to Die and the Meaning of Life: A Moral Analysis</u>, 22 Wm. & Mary L. Rev. 327, 337-43 (1981). ——Page Cite.

William Mitchell Law Review
    Abbreviation: Wm. Mitchell L. Rev.

    Examples: Kirwin, <u>Compensation for Disease Under the Minnesota Workers' Compensation Law</u>, 6 Wm. Mitchell L. Rev. 619 (1980). ——Article Cite.

        Kirwin, <u>Compensation for Disease Under the Minnesota Workers' Compensation Law</u>, 6 Wm. Mitchell L. Rev. 619, 623-30 (1980). ——Page Cite.

Williston on Contracts Multivolume Treatise
    <u>See</u>   A Treatise on the Law of Contracts, by S. Williston

Williston on Contracts Student Edition
    <u>See</u>   Selections from Williston's Treatise on the Law of Contracts, by S. Williston and G. Thompson

Wills, Estates and Trust Service (Prentice-Hall)
    Abbreviation: Wills Est. & Tr. Serv. (P-H)

Wisconsin Administrative Code
    Abbreviation: Wis. Admin. Code § [agency name as abbreviated in code] (month year).

Wisconsin Bar Bulletin
    Abbreviation: Wis. B. Bull.

    Examples: Grove, <u>Successor Products Liability: Wisconsin's Approach in Tift v. Forage King Industries, Inc.</u>, 55 Wis. B. Bull. 17 (1982). ——Article Cite.

In law review footnotes, the titles of books and the names of cases are not underlined.

Grove, <u>Successor Products Liability: Wisconsin's Approach in Tift v. Forage King Industries, Inc.</u>, 55 Wis. B. Bull. 17, 18-19 (1982). ——Page Cite.

Wisconsin Board of Tax Appeals Reports
    Abbreviation: Wis. B.T.A.

Wisconsin Constitution
    Abbreviation: Wis. Const. art. , § .

    Examples: Wis. Const. art. 1, § 6. ——Cite provisions without date unless the cited provisions have been repealed or amended (Bluebook Rule 11).

                     Wis. Const. art. 4, § 26 (1848, amended 1965). ——Cite provisions which have been repealed or amended by giving the date of the adoption of the particular provision and the date of repeal or amendment (Bluebook Rule 11).

Wisconsin Court of Appeals
    Abbreviation: Wis. Ct. App.

    Examples: <u>McMahon v. Brown</u>, 125 Wis. 2d 351, 371 N.W.2d 414 (Ct. App. 1985). ——Case Cite.

                     <u>McMahon v. Brown</u>, 125 Wis. 2d 351, 352, 371 N.W.2d 414, 415 (Ct. App. 1985). ——Page Cite.

Wisconsin International Law Journal
    Abbreviation: Wis. Int'l L.J.

Wisconsin Law Review
    Abbreviation: Wis. L. Rev.

    Examples: Bloch, <u>Cooperative Federalism and the Role of Litigation in the Development of Federal AFDC Eligibility Policy</u>, 1979 Wis. L. Rev. 1. ——Article Cite.

                     Bloch, <u>Cooperative Federalism and the Role of Litigation in the Development of Federal AFDC Eligibility Policy</u>, 1979 Wis. L. Rev. 1, 28-34. ——Page Cite.

Wisconsin Legislative Service (West)
    Abbreviation: year Wis. Legis. Serv. (West)

Wisconsin, Opinions of the Attorney General
    <u>See</u>   Opinions of the Attorney General of the State of Wisconsin

Wisconsin Reports
    Abbreviation: Wis.

    Examples: <u>Francken v. State</u>, 190 Wis. 424, 209 N.W. 766 (1926). ——Case Cite.

In law review footnotes, the following are in large and small capitals: periodicals, constitutions, codes, restatements, standards, authors of books, titles of books, and legislative materials except for bills and resolutions. Refer to Bluebook.

Francken v. State, 190 Wis. 424, 429, 209 N.W. 766, 767-68 (1926).
——Page Cite.

Wisconsin Reports, second series
    Abbreviation: Wis. 2d

    Examples: Brown v. Maxey, 124 Wis. 2d 426, 369 N.W.2d 677 (1985). ——Case
    Cite.

    Brown v. Maxey, 124 Wis. 2d 426, 430, 369 N.W.2d 677, 680 (1985).
    ——Page Cite.

Wisconsin Session Laws
    See   Laws of Wisconsin and Wisconsin Legislative Service

Wisconsin Statutes
    Abbreviation: Wis. Stat. §   (year).

    Examples: Wis. Stat. § 757.295 (1977).

    Wis. Stat. § 939.62 (Supp. 1980).

Wisconsin Statutes Annotated, West's
    See   West's Wisconsin Statutes Annotated

Women Lawyers Journal
    Abbreviation: Women Law. J.

Women's Rights Law Reporter
    Abbreviation: Women's Rts. L. Rep.

    Examples: Shoemaker, The Scope of Judicial and Derivative Immunities Under 42
    U.S.C. 1983, 6 Women's Rts. L. Rep. 107 (1979-1980). ——Article
    Cite.

    Shoemaker, The Scope of Judicial and Derivative Immunities Under 42
    U.S.C. 1983, 6 Women's Rts. L. Rep. 107, 121-22 (1979-1980).
    ——Page Cite.

workmen's compensation
    Abbreviation: workmen's comp.

Workmen's Compensation Law Reports (Commerce Clearing House)
    Abbreviation: Workmen's Comp. L. Rep. (CCH)

Workmen's Compensation Law Review
    Abbreviation: Workmen's Comp. L. Rev.

    Examples: Feldman & Smith, Workmen's Compensation Immunity: In Search of a
    Defendant, 5 Workmen's Comp. L. Rev. 235 (1979). ——Article Cite.

In law review footnotes, the titles of books and the names of cases are not underlined.

Feldman & Smith, Workmen's Compensation Immunity: In Search of a Defendant, 5 Workmen's Comp. L. Rev. 235, 237-39 (1979). ——Page Cite.

Wright & Miller on Federal Practice and Procedure
See   Federal Practice and Procedure, by C. Wright & A. Miller

Wright on the Federal Courts
See   Handbook of the Law of Federal Courts, by C. Wright

Wyoming, Attorney General Opinions
See   Attorney General of the State of Wyoming Opinions

Wyoming Constitution
Abbreviation: Wyo. Const. art.   , §   .

Examples: Wyo. Const. art. 3, § 36. ——Cite provisions without date unless the cited provisions have been repealed or amended (Bluebook Rule 11).

Wyo. Const. art. 5, § 5 (1890, amended 1972). ——Cite provisions which have been repealed or amended by giving the date of the adoption of the particular provision and the date of repeal or amendment (Bluebook Rule 11).

Wyoming Reports
Abbreviation: Wyo.

——Discontinued after 80 Wyo. 492 (1959). Thereafter cite only to P.2d.

Examples: Lucksinger v. Salisbury, 72 Wyo. 164, 262 P.2d 396 (1953). ——Case Cite.

Lucksinger v. Salisbury, 72 Wyo. 164, 173, 262 P.2d 396, 398-99 (1953). ——Page Cite.

——After 80 Wyo. 492 (1959), cite as follows:

Kinderknecht v. Poulos, 707 P.2d 184 (Wyo. 1985). ——Case Cite.

Kinderknecht v. Poulos, 707 P.2d 184, 185 (Wyo. 1985). ——Page Cite.

Wyoming Session Laws
See   Session Laws of Wyoming

Wyoming Statutes
Abbreviation: Wyo. Stat. §   (year).

Examples: Wyo. Stat. § 7-13-409 (1987).

Wyo. Stat. § 10-5-201 (Supp. 1987).

In law review footnotes, the following are in large and small capitals: periodicals, constitutions, codes, restatements, standards, authors of books, titles of books, and legislative materials except for bills and resolutions. Refer to Bluebook.

Y

Yale Journal of International Law

Abbreviation: Yale J. Int'l L.

Examples: McCrudden, <u>Comparative Worth: A Common Dilemma</u>, 11 Yale J. Int'l L. 396 (1986). ——Article Cite.

McCrudden, <u>Comparative Worth: A Common Dilemma</u>, 11 Yale J. Int'l L. 396, 397 (1986). ——Page Cite.

Yale Journal of World Public Order

Abbreviation: Yale J. World Pub. Ord.

Examples: Bozeman, <u>Human Rights and National Security</u>, 9 Yale J. World Pub. Ord. 40 (1982). ——Article Cite.

Bozeman, <u>Human Rights and National Security</u>, 9 Yale J. World Pub. Ord. 40, 62-63 (1982). ——Page Cite.

Yale Journal on Regulation

Abbreviation: Yale J. on Reg.

Examples: DeMuth, <u>The Case Against Credit Card Interest Rate Regulation</u>, 3 Yale J. on Reg. 201 (1986). ——Article Cite.

DeMuth, <u>The Case Against Credit Card Interest Rate Regulation</u>, 3 Yale J. on Reg. 201, 209 (1986). ——Page Cite.

Yale Law and Policy Review

Abbreviation: Yale L. & Pol'y Rev.

Examples: Comment, <u>Apple v. Franklin: An Essay on Technology and Judicial Competence</u>, 2 Yale L. & Pol'y Rev. 62 (1983). ——Article Cite.

Comment, <u>Apple v. Franklin: An Essay on Technology and Judicial Competence</u>, 2 Yale L. & Pol'y Rev. 62, 67 (1983). ——Page Cite.

Yale Law Journal

Abbreviation: Yale L.J.

Examples: Weinreb, <u>Manifest Criminality, Criminal Intent, and the "Metamorphosis of Larceny"</u>, 90 Yale L.J. 294 (1980). ——Article Cite.

Weinreb, <u>Manifest Criminality, Criminal Intent, and the "Metamorphosis of Larceny"</u>, 90 Yale L.J. 294, 296-99 (1980). ——Page Cite.

In law review footnotes, the following are in large and small capitals: periodicals, constitutions, codes, restatements, standards, authors of books, titles of books, and legislative materials except for bills and resolutions. Refer to Bluebook.

Yearbook of the European Convention on Human Rights
    Abbreviation: ⸱ Y.B. Eur. Conv. on Hum. Rts.

    Example: Farrell v. United Kingdom, 1982 Y.B. Eur. Conv. on Hum. Rts. (Eur.
                Comm'n on Hum. Rts.) 124.

Yearbook of the International Law Commission
    See   International Law Commission Yearbook

Yearbook of the United Nations
    Abbreviation: U.N.Y.B.

    Example: 1982 U.N.Y.B. 194, U.N. Sales No. E.85.1.1.

Youth Court
    Abbreviation: Youth Ct.

In law review footnotes, the titles of books and the names of cases are not underlined.

Z

Zoning and Planning Law Report
  Abbreviation: Zoning & Plan. L. Rep.

  Examples: Costonis, <u>Of Breadboxes, Presumptions and Per Se Rules: Making Sense of the Taking Issue</u>, 7 Zoning & Plan. L. Rep. 33 (1984).
      ——Article Cite.

      Costonis, <u>Of Breadboxes, Presumptions and Per Se Rules: Making Sense of the Taking Issue</u>, 7 Zoning & Plan. L. Rep. 33, 34-35 (1984).
      ——Page Cite.

In law review footnotes, the following are in large and small capitals: periodicals, constitutions, codes, restatements, standards, authors of books, titles of books, and legislative materials except for bills and resolutions. Refer to Bluebook.

In law review footnotes, the titles of books and the names of cases are not underlined.